"Combining his immense learning in anthr
concern for the Christian faith Arbuckle aga
leaders in his debt with this splendid volum
prose and thought-provoking insights our
entirely the relation between faith and cultu.~ ... ~~. ~~~~.~~~.. ~~~. .... .~ ~
landmark book and the future of Christianity and Christian mission may well
depend on how its proposals are taken seriously and put into practice."

> —Dr. Peter C. Phan
> The Ignacio Ellacuria Chair of Catholic Social Thought
> Theology Department, Georgetown University

"Gerald Arbuckle has done theologians a great service by bringing together a
comprehensive picture of where the discussion now is on understandings of
culture and cultural processes. This will greatly aid the theological task of
inculturation that still lies ahead of us as efforts continue to engage theology
and cultures in a world church."

> —Robert Schreiter, CPPS
> Author of *Constructing Local Theologies*

"Only a master could write a book like this. Gerald Arbuckle brings together his
vast pastoral experience, expertise as an anthropologist, and theological savvy
in a way that is an absolute MUST read for pastors, theologians, and ministerial
students. This book could bring efforts of inculturation to a new level."

> —Steve Bevans, SVD
> Louis J. Luzbetak, SVD Professor of Mission and Culture
> Catholic Theological Union, Chicago

Culture, Inculturation, and Theologians

A Postmodern Critique

Gerald A. Arbuckle, SM

Foreword by Anthony Gittins, CSSp

A Michael Glazier Book

LITURGICAL PRESS

Collegeville, Minnesota

www.litpress.org

A Michael Glazier Book published by Liturgical Press

Excerpts from documents of the Second Vatican Council are from *Vatican Council II: Volume 1, The Conciliar and Post Conciliar Documents*, by Austin Flannery, OP © 1996 (Costello Publishing Company, Inc.). Used with permission.

Scripture texts in this work are taken from the *New Revised Standard Version Bible* © 1989, Division of Christian Education of the National Council of the Churches of Christ in the United States of America. Used by permission. All rights reserved.

Cover design by Ann Blattner. Cover illustration courtesy of Photos.com.

2   3   4   5   6   7   8   9

Library of Congress Cataloging-in-Publication Data

Arbuckle, Gerald A.
    Culture, inculturation, and theologians : a postmodern critique / Gerald A. Arbuckle ; foreword by Anthony Gittins.
        p. cm.
    "A Michael Glazier Book."
    Includes bibliographical references and index.
    ISBN 978-0-8146-5458-3 — ISBN 978-0-8146-5732-4 (e-book)
    1. Christianity and culture.   2. Theology.   3. Modernism (Christian theology)   I. Title.
BR115.C8A66   2010
261—dc22   2009050569

In memory of Hermann Janssen, MSC, and Joe Knoebel, SVD,
two creative and faith-inspired anthropologists.

By the same author

The Chatham Islands in Perspective: A Socio-Economic Review
(Wellington: Hicks Smith, 1971)

Strategies for Growth in Religious Life
(Alba House / St. Pauls Publications, 1987)

Out of Chaos: Refounding Religious Congregations
(Paulist Press / Geoffrey Chapman, 1988) (Catholic Press Award)

Earthing the Gospel: An Inculturation Handbook for Pastoral Workers
(Geoffrey Chapman / Orbis Books / St. Pauls Publications, 1990)
(Catholic Press Award)

Grieving for Change: A Spirituality for Refounding Gospel Communities
(Geoffrey Chapman / St. Pauls Publications, 1991)

Refounding the Church: Dissent for Leadership
(Geoffrey Chapman / Orbis Books / St Pauls Publications, 1993)
(Catholic Press Award)

From Chaos to Mission: Refounding Religious Life Formation
(Geoffrey Chapman / Liturgical Press, 1996)

Healthcare Ministry: Refounding the Mission in Tumultuous Times
(Liturgical Press, 2000) (Catholic Press Award)

Dealing with Bullies: A Gospel Response to the Social Disease of Adult Bullying
(St Pauls Publications, 2003)

Confronting the Demon: A Gospel Response to Adult Bullying
(Liturgical Press, 2003)

Violence, Society and the Church: A Cultural Approach
(Liturgical Press, 2004)

Crafting Catholic Identity in Postmodern Australia
(Catholic Health Australia, 2007)

A 'Preferential Option for the Poor':
Application to Catholic Health and Aged Care Ministries in Australia
(Catholic Health Australia, 2008)

Laughing with God: Humor, Culture, and Transformation
(Liturgical Press, 2008)

Acknowledgments

My particular thanks to Hans Christoffersen, editorial director at Liturgical Press, for his invitation to write this book; to the community of Campion Hall, Oxford University, for providing me with a hospitable research atmosphere to prepare the book; to Margaret Zucker for her patient and detailed reading and commenting on the text; and to Professor Anthony Gittins, CSSp, for his support throughout the writing of the text.

Contents

Foreword

It is a pleasure to introduce this book by Gerald Arbuckle, a friend and respected colleague. Having discussed with him some of the ideas behind and within the following pages, and particularly now since having read it, it is quite apparent to me not only how difficult this enterprise has been for the author but that it has indeed been a labor of love. Writing from within one's primary discipline (here, social anthropology), but addressing readers from a different primary discipline (here, theology) runs the risk that what one writes can be interpreted as condescending or frankly incomprehensible. Significantly different disciplines develop their own jargon or *patois* independently until they hardly share a common language any longer, however much the practitioners of each may fail to realize it. For that reason, this book may be no less difficult a read for the scholar or student than writing it has been for the author. After all, readers need to understand more than the constituent words: some unfamiliar ideas or concepts must also be assimilated, familiar usages or phrases must be reevaluated, and relationships among all of these must be grasped if the reader is to receive what the writer wishes to offer.

The serious reader of *Culture, Inculturation, and Theologians* will surely be rewarded for attentive perseverance, and the book's final chapters will clarify many ideas adumbrated in the earlier part of the book. However, to skip the earlier chapters and move directly to the final ones would be quite ill advised: the book builds systematically, so that the last four chapters require the understanding accumulated from the assimilation of earlier ideas and themes.

The structure and rationale underlying the book can perhaps be identified here. The opening chapter characterizes *culture* as one of the most intractable concepts in the language. A plethora of definitions have contested the field, none of which has won universal approval. Nevertheless, these definitions can be systematized by placing them in one of three categories: classicist, modern, and postmodern. Simply put, classicist definitions understand culture as a single entity, best and most clearly seen perhaps—ancient Egypt, Greece, or Rome notwithstanding—in what was deemed the very finest of (Victorian) European achievement in the arts and sciences, expressed in terms of civilized behavior or refinement (though there could be and was disagreement about where and what those achievements might actually include and what "refinement" might entail).

By contrast, modern definitions acknowledge that a plurality, indeed, a multiplicity of cultures can be found diachronically (historically) and synchronically (across the globe at any given time). These definitions, moreover, assume that such particular or discrete cultures are homogeneous, stable, enduring, and bounded by or clearly delimited from adjacent cultures. More recently, postmodernity has introduced or encountered rather different views: now cultures are seen to be much more frangible or fluid, inconsistent and flawed as previously admitted, as well as mutually interactive, internally contested, and indeed always prone to entropy, viral diseases, and even breakdown, as history attests.

When commenting on human culture, much contemporary theological language still adopts an uncritical and even naïve classicist view despite the fact that social and cultural anthropologists and sociologists, whose subject of inquiry is human culture, have seriously reworked earlier inadequate understandings of the subject, based on their increased and cumulative empirical research. Therefore if the church and Christian ministers are to encounter, communicate with, and prove in any way relevant to the people of myriad different cultures today they must adjust their understanding of cultural dynamics lest their best efforts prove ineffective and unworkable.

If the basic question is "how can the Good News of Jesus Christ engage with humanity?" then, given the multiplicity of human cultures and the fact that to be human is to have and to participate in culture, social and cultural contexts must be carefully identified and studied so that people can be approached and encountered appropriately. Otherwise the consequences may be dire, if indeed there are any significant consequences. We are all familiar with the observation—currently most loudly voiced by Pentecostals in Latin America—that over the past half millennium millions of people have been baptized Catholic, yet many have never been or are not yet truly Christian. In contemporary theological language, the faith has not been truly inculturated because it has not truly encountered people in their everyday cultural reality and become embedded in their lives and experience.

This book represents a timely attempt to equip theologians and pastoral workers with an appropriate understanding of the dynamics of culture and inculturation and to provide them with some well-designed and effective analytical tools. The bulk of the book looks at culture under different lenses or from different perspectives. After the opening chapter, which explicates *classicist,* *modern,* and *postmodern* understandings, we are taken for a walk through the forest of postmodern anthropology and invited to look in turn at cultures as webs of symbolic and mythical meaning (Chapter 2), as systems of order and classification (Chapter 3) and boundary-maintaining (Chapter 4), as matrices for identity formation (Chapter 5), as orchestrations of human life (Chapter 6), and as systems for negotiating differences (Chapter 7). These chapters establish the theoretical foundations on which the concrete understanding and practical action of theologians and pastoral agents in specific contexts can build. They embody a wide range of concepts, all of which are helpful hints and some of which are essential learning for anyone committed to the engagement of the Good News of Jesus Christ (Gospel) with actual groups of people (societies) in their enormous organizational diversity (cultures).

The field of theoretical linguistics has also developed a number of ideas that fit very well with anthropological and, indeed, theological attempts to understand culture. One is "rule-governed creativity," which sounds at first like an oxymoron. Noam Chomsky (b. 1927) famously "reduced" the English language to a base of some 150 rules. Familiarity with this very finite number of rules and with the creative ways in which they can be applied within the legitimate linguistic parameters allows anyone to generate a virtually infinite number of utterances (spoken or written sequences), including many that had never been formulated before in exactly the same way (like any of the sentences on this page). Other people, hearing or reading such utterances or sentences for the first time, can actually—by virtue of their own knowledge of English grammar and syntax—understand them quite easily and routinely. This is truly amazing. People do not operate like automata but—in theory at least, aware of the "rules" of their own culture and the consequences of breaking them—are able to be creative, innovative, disobedient, or destructive. A grasp of the principles of "rule-governed creativity" provides an interpretive tool for outsiders, whether anthropologists, theologians, or other interested parties.

Applied to culture generally, the principle of "rule-governed creativity" might illustrate how those who share a common culture can communicate not only in traditional or conventional (familiar), but also in groundbreaking and creative (new) modes. Yet not every communication is or needs to be perfect in order to be effective, and cultures too can survive reasonably well in a less than perfect world. Linguists contrast three modes or levels of intelligibility: the grammatical, the acceptable, and the meaningful. *Grammaticality* is the most standard and widely applied test, but not everything grammatical is meaningful or comprehensible. Again, Chomsky's famous (and grammatically perfect!) utterance, "colorless green ideas sleep furiously," is quite meaningless! A cautionary tale, this, for theological propositions or theses that might be perfectly orthodox doctrinally ("grammatical") and yet meaningless, incomprehensible, or irrelevant to "the (non-theologically-adept) faithful."

A second measure of communicability is *acceptability*. "I don't have no money" is ungrammatical by the criteria of Standard English, but it makes perfect sense to most English speakers (those with an intuitive understanding of the language). It is *acceptable*, and to deny that would be pedantic. Likewise, a three-year-old's "my foots are hurting," while not syntactically correct, can be both understandable and very *acceptable* to a proud mother's ears. *Meaningfulness* is the third criterion of intelligibility. If someone explains, "I put the thingummajig inside the big square whatsit, next to the—you know what I mean," there may be absolutely no need for further clarification because context and native understanding simply supply what is grammatically lacking. In short, a culture need not function perfectly—by virtue of people keeping all the laws or conventions at all times—in order to qualify as a working or functioning culture.

Notions of grammaticality, acceptability, and meaningfulness can be helpfully applied as interpretive keys. The language of theoretical linguistics can illustrate the fact that cultures can tolerate a certain number of less-than-perfect "grammatical" forms so long as they generate behaviors that are *acceptable* or *meaningful*, and so long as the members of a given social group are able to discriminate between what is minimally acceptable and what is simply intolerable. Theologically, this would be to acknowledge that cultures (all cultures) rather like people (all people) are a mixture, an amalgam, of sin and grace. But to compare the grace in one's own culture with the sin in another is simply unfair and unjust; we must understand cultures by comparing and contrasting beliefs, attitudes, or behaviors that are comparable, acknowledging that there may be some elements that are strictly incommensurable and therefore must be understood on their own terms and not as a degraded form of something with which we are familiar and of which we approve (or disapprove) in our own culture. Before attempting to judge another culture and its people, therefore, any and every student needs to appropriate the criteria of cultural grammaticality, acceptability, and meaningfulness.

Another way of understanding a culture is to see it as a meaning-making system. Despite initial appearances to outsiders, no surviving culture (society) acts irrationally and meaninglessly for long; to do so would be to sow the seeds of its own demise. Therefore, however imperfect and inconsistent any given culture may be, as a social organism it is always struggling to make and maintain meaning. Meaning is socially (and not simply individually) created: mental institutions are filled with isolated individuals, many of whom think they live in a meaningful world, but because they are alone in that world they are unable to live in society ("the real world"). When encountering another culture, any outsider should attempt—and not by guesswork—to understand, if not to enter, the prevailing world of meaning, and *then* to look at the world through the lenses discovered there. At least this shows some respect for the culture of others; at best it provides a platform for continuing dialogue.

Two other points impinge on the topic of cultural analysis or interpretation: the nature of *muted groups* and the matter of *representation*. Every culture, by virtue of its being a human development or creation, is imperfect. Social equality at many levels may or may not be espoused by the whole society but is virtually impossible to achieve, due to vested interests, whether of individuals or groups and whether consciously or unconsciously pursued. One consequence is that not everyone in a society has a social voice, or not everyone's voice is equally acknowledged or listened to. "Muted groups" are those classes or categories of people whose voices are not heard, either because they are effectively silenced or because they are not allowed to be raised. Theologians must look for the muted groups in any society and identify why they are muted and by whom: the reign or realm of God does not tolerate muted groups, though every society does in fact create or tolerate some.

"Representation" refers simply to the question of who speaks for whom, and how effectively it is done. If women represent themselves and articulate their insights and interests, their "representation" will be rather different from what is articulated when certain designated men "speak for" women and "represent" their voices and interests. And so on. Questions for theologians include: who, in the church, represents whom; who speaks on behalf of whom; who is effectively muted; how well various constituencies are actually represented by their representatives, however designated; and whether actual or intentional *mis*representation occurs. The institutional church is always limited, as well as positively served, by the culture in which it is incarnated. But failure to acknowledge this can contribute negatively to the coming of God's reign. Sensitivity to and respect for cultural facts such as muted groups and representation is something Gerald Arbuckle's book is designed to foster.

This book stimulates many more thoughts, but it may be helpful at this juncture simply to emphasize a number of Gerald Arbuckle's many insights, lest some of them slip by, their significance unnoticed. I will take one from each of the last four chapters—the chapters that bring theory into an encounter with pastoral and anthropological practice and present insights and concrete challenges for theology and theologians.

Chapter 7 explores aspects of multiculturalism, a polysemic and confusing term. But, after describing its sometimes inconsistent applications, Arbuckle helps us look at some of its most important features as far as theologians are concerned: multiethnic groups within a single country or nation, and subcultures within a single identifiable culture. The treatment is highly nuanced and informative, and the author alerts us to the (ab)use of power in multicultural contexts. He then poses a number of pertinent questions that theologians would need to address in any attempt to foster inculturation in practice.

Chapter 8, perhaps the most immediately relevant chapter in the whole book, is an exposition of the thesis that all religions are necessarily embodied and expressed culturally, and an effort to tease out some of the theological and ecclesial implications of this. The examples are particularly telling, as is the conclusion: "This is a time rich in potentiality for refounding the church through the passionate collaborative efforts of people in touch with the hopes and anxieties of [others] who possess boundless faith, imagination, and creativity to bring the Gospel alive within this postmodern world. Conditions could not be better."

Chapter 9 scrutinizes ecclesial documents and other theological writings, exposing the manifest or latent understandings of the word "culture" therein. A quotation from Bernard Lonergan is very much to the point: "When the classicist notion of culture prevails, theology is conceived as a permanent achievement, and then one discourses on its nature," rather than on how it is to relate to a changing world.

There are trenchant comments on some of the assumptions and demands of *Sacrosanctum Concilium*, the Vatican II document on the liturgy, especially in regard to the much-quoted "noble simplicity of the Roman Rite" that, rather like democracy, may be quite inappropriate for many cultures in the contemporary world that struggle mightily under the weight of this universal liturgical requirement. The author also contests the phrase "liturgical inculturation," judging it inadequate to describe what is in principle (in sociological terminology) acculturation. Karl Rahner's respect for the integrity of cultures led him to make the following telling prediction: "There will no longer be any one single and universal basic formula of the Christian faith applicable to the whole Church and, indeed, prescribed for her as authoritatively binding." And here is an oft-quoted and devastating criticism from Paul Tillich: "The tragedy of the Roman Catholic Church [is] its way of dealing with culture [which is] the result of its unwillingness to subject itself to the judgment of this event [i. e., the life, death, and resurrection of Jesus Christ]."

Chapter 10 explores the notion that inculturation is a "dialectical interaction between Christian faith and cultures." Having argued that the world of Jesus fits far better within a postmodern than a modern understanding of culture, the author provides very telling examples of the pastoral (and cultural) strategy of Jesus. This chapter is vintage Arbuckle—excellent anthropology and fine pastoral and practical theology. Finally, Chapter 11 concludes the book with a friendly but serious challenge to theologians to engage seriously with the anthropological aspects of inculturation. Gerald Arbuckle examines some of the most significant recent theological works, offers some interpretation and constructive criticism, and identifies the significance—and limitations—of syncretism as a component of authentic inculturation.

In offering this foreword, I very much hope that this thoughtful, insightful, timely and wise book will help to further the dialogue between theologians and interested anthropologists, for the glory of God and the good of God's people.

Anthony J. Gittins, CSSp
Professor of Theology and Culture
Catholic Theological Union
Chicago, Illinois

Introduction

> The split between the Gospel and culture is without doubt the drama
> of our time. . . . [Every] effort must be made to ensure a full evange-
> lization . . . of cultures.
>
> — Paul VI, *Evangelii Nuntiandi*[1]

> Demonising postmodernism is not the appropriate response from a
> mature Christianity.
>
> — Daniel O'Leary, *Begin With the Heart*[2]

The most powerful challenge to the church in recent decades is the
above no-nonsense statement of Paul VI in 1975. John Paul II repeated
the challenge in 1982 with even sharper urgency: "I have considered the
church's dialogue with the cultures of our time to be a vital area, one in
which the destiny of the world at the end of this twentieth century is at
stake."[3] Inculturation is the term that describes this dialogue. But how
a challenge is defined and then explained inevitably affects what is actually done about it. Inaccurate perceptions of and defective attitudes to
cultures and dialogue invariably result in bad theology as well as defective pastoral policies and practices. This book particularly focuses on

---

1. Paul VI, Apostolic Exhortation *Evangelii Nuntiandi* (On Evangelization) (Sydney:
St Paul Publications, 1982), 25.
2. Daniel O'Leary, *Begin With the Heart: Recovering a Sacrament of Vision* (Dublin:
Columba, 2008), 148.
3. John Paul II, Letter to Agostino Cardinal Casaroli, *Osservatore Romano* (English
ed.) (28 June 1982), 7.

clarifying the meaning of culture because an accurate understanding of the concept is crucial to effective inculturation.[4]

In 1989 missiologist Father Robert Schreiter, CPPS, complained that the challenge of bridging the gap between faith and cultures had remained largely unmet and in fact the process was going backwards in some areas.[5] Twenty years later, despite the frequent references to inculturation and its importance by ecclesiastical authorities and theologians, the situation has become worse. Few are seriously taking up the challenge to enter into realistic dialogue with the cultures of our time, and there are deliberate movements to reject inculturation entirely.[6]

Schreiter suggests two reasons for this impasse. There are no adequate methodologies among theologians "to break through the conceptual logjams, and [there is a] lack of tools that can be used readily and easily" by practitioners. Second, there is the official unwillingness at the international and local levels of the church "to permit legitimate experiments in inculturation and to sanction successful experiments for ongoing use."[7] I detect a third reason, namely a revitalized fundamentalist view that the study of culture(s) is unimportant for evangelization, that it is even a waste of time, and that all we need to do is preach the Good News just as Jesus Christ did in his time! Yet inculturation is a fundamental imperative of the Gospel itself. In fact, Jesus Christ was extremely sensitive in his preaching to the cultures of his day. As the master of inculturation, he knew that his message had to penetrate to the "very roots"[8] of cultures.

As a cultural anthropologist, I believe the thorniest methodological problem in inculturation is the confusion surrounding the meaning of culture. The concept of culture is contentious and complex. Anyone who writes today on culture is confronted with a disheartening task, because the word is applied indiscriminately to vastly different situations. So we read about "global culture," "youth culture," "pop culture," "postmodern

---

4. The meaning of "inculturation" is fully defined in chaps. 10 and 11.

5. See Robert J. Schreiter, "Faith and Cultures: Challenges to a World Church," *Theological Studies* 50 (1989): 758.

6. Neil Ormerod, "A Dialectic Engagement with the Social Sciences in an Ecclesiological Context," *Theological Studies* 66 (2005): 816, concludes his review of theological views on social sciences: "In general, the engagement with social sciences by ecclesiologists has been eclectic, sporadic, intermittent, and secondary to what they view as their primary task."

7. Ibid.

8. Paul VI, *Evangelii Nuntiandi*, 25.

culture," "cafe culture," "gun culture," "corporate culture," "print culture," "transnational culture," "culture of violence," "culture of poverty," "culture wars." Rarely is any serious thought given to what these expressions mean. Politicians employ the word to rationalize their anti-immigrant policies and indigenous activists use it to legitimate their rights to particular expressions of identity and property. Management texts commonly define it simplistically as "what we do around here," yet culture is far more complex than this. Given this widespread and arbitrary use of the term culture, Raymond Williams, the well-known British cultural historian, once expressed the frustration of many people when he wrote: "I don't know how many times I've wished that I'd never heard the damned word."[9]

Culture: Seismic Shifts in Meaning

This frustrating confusion and lack of precision about how to define the term is not surprising because even cultural anthropologists, whose specialist task is the study of cultures, are questioning their traditional use of the word. Until the 1980s most anthropologists accepted the modern description of cultures as discrete entities, frozen in time, homogeneous and without internal dissent, unreceptive to outside influences. Yet now in these postmodern times it is clear that cultures simply do not fit this description. Every culture is fragmented to some degree or other, internally contested, its borders permeable. There is no such thing as a "pure" culture: never has been, never will be. Cultures are hybrid, constantly interacting, mixing, and changing.[10] With globalization this process is intensifying so that happenings in one part of the world are being shaped by events developing many miles away and vice versa.[11] At the same time, in reaction to the uncertainties evoked by globalization, new nationalist and fundamentalist movements are appearing everywhere. People confronted with chaos feel the need to belong behind clearly defined identifying borders.

9. Raymond Williams, *Politics and Letters: Interviews with New Left Review* (London: New Left Books, 1979), 125.

10. See Sheila G. Daveney, "Theology and the Turn to Cultural Analysis," in *Converging on Culture: Theologians in Dialogue with Cultural Analysis and Criticism*, eds. Delwin Brown, Sheila G. Davaney, Kathryn Tanner (Oxford: Oxford University Press, 2001), 5.

11. See Anthony Giddens, *The Consequences of Modernity* (Stanford: Stanford University Press, 1990), 64.

Theological Reactions

The wide confusion about the meaning of culture is mirrored in ecclesial documents and the writings of theologians. Sometimes it is applied in a classicist sense to stand for the intellectual, artistic, and spiritual achievements of a people. More commonly in recent decades it is used according to its modern meaning, namely, that a culture is a homogeneous and integrated whole. The crucial postmodern insights into cultures such as their polyphonic, fragmentary, and hybrid qualities, and their internal struggles for power, are not being recognized. Sadly, if we continue to accept the modern definition of culture we are trying to dialogue with something that does not exist!

In ecclesial texts there is also no awareness of the major problem that the culture of the institutional church is itself Eurocentric, a grave barrier to the development of a vibrant multicultural church as envisioned by Vatican II. The church in fact is today a multilingual and multicultural community, with its center of vitality and growth in Latin America, Africa and Asia, not in Europe and North America.

The third obstacle to inculturation, namely, a fundamentalist denial of the importance of culture in evangelization, is a return to the pre-Vatican II rejection of the world, which holds that cultures have nothing to teach us and get in the way of evangelization. Since fundamentalism is an emotion-driven, simplistic solution to complex issues, this dogmatism is difficult, if not impossible, to dialogue with.[12] I first met this type of fundamentalism among theologians and practitioners shortly after the end of the Vatican Council. Using supportive arguments from the council's documents, I approached a superior general of a congregation about the need to train his men for ministry in foreign countries. He sharply responded: "No, I have finished with theories. All we need are more men and more money!" Later, with an internationally known economist, I had to review sociodevelopment projects that had been started by members of the superior general's congregation in several Third World countries. Wherever we went we met failures, leaving local people angry and most missionaries despondent or broken men. All this was the result of a devastating lack of anthropological knowledge of cultures. I asked one zealous missionary if he had received any formal training in the local culture. He paused and then broke into tears: "When I first came to this remote island I asked the bishop, 'How can I best know the local

---

12. See Gerald A. Arbuckle, *Violence, Society, and the Church: A Cultural Approach* (Collegeville, MN: Liturgical Press, 2004), 195–201.

culture?' The bishop replied, 'Kneel down, and I will bless you. No further preparation is needed. Just trust in Providence!'"

This fundamentalism has reasserted itself in the church. For example, faced with declining congregational membership and chaos in the church, superiors attempt quick-fix responses and a dramatic sign that their congregations are still alive. They are prepared to send their religious with no adequate cultural formation into vastly complex cultures like those found in Asia. Theologically and humanly speaking this is unjust. Respect for people of different cultures, which will show itself in a willingness to learn about the local culture in the most professional manner possible, is the first requirement of dialogue.

Overview

The primary purpose of this book is to describe the multifaceted character of culture in this postmodern and globalizing world. Secondary aims are to explain the meaning of inculturation and why it is an imperative of the Gospel, to analyze the views of some theologians regarding inculturation, and to clarify why ecclesiastical authorities are reluctant to encourage it despite their supportive rhetoric.

Chapter 1 summarizes the changing meanings of culture over time by cultural anthropologists. As culture cannot be reduced any longer to one or two neat definitions, the titles of the next seven chapters will be different definitions of culture, to be followed by explanations and examples. These chapters will illustrate that cultures are complex realities and that glib analyses can be offensive, even unjust. Chapter 9 reviews the way culture is used in ecclesial documents and by some theologians. Chapter 10 highlights the various ways Jesus Christ approaches the cultures of his time. Chapter 11 explains the meaning of inculturation and particular obstacles to its implementation. Each chapter concludes with a short theological reflection.

The book is written for people with little or no knowledge of cultural anthropology and is thus designed for a wide range of readers, such as bishops, theologians, formators, seminary staffs, pastoral workers, college students, and others who are committed to understanding and dialoguing with contemporary cultures. Readers who wish to go more deeply into issues raised in the chapters will be helped by the many relevant references to contemporary authors in the social sciences. The book is also a reminder to psychologists that mental processes such as perception, memory, social interaction, and individual thinking are culturally influenced. A culture structures life experiences into thinking processes, provides names for important feelings and significant environmental features, and permits communication with other persons of the same culture.

I have previously written about culture and inculturation in *Earthing the Gospel: An Inculturation Handbook for Pastoral Workers* (Orbis Books, 1990), in *Refounding the Church: Dissent for Leadership* (Orbis Books, 1993), in *Violence, Society, and the Church: A Cultural Approach* (Liturgical Press, 2004), and in *Laughing with God: Humor, Culture, and Transformation* (Liturgical Press, 2008), but this book builds on anthropologists' dramatic rethinking of the nature of culture in significantly new ways.

Chapter 1

Cultures as Anthropologists See Them: An Overview

> Culture is one of the two or three most complicated words in the English language . . . mainly because it has now come to be used for important concepts in several . . . disciplines, and in several distinct and incompatible systems of thought.
>
> —Raymond Williams, *Keywords*[1]

For centuries the concept of culture has remained the subject of vigorous controversy; in fact, anthropologists have never been able to agree on a single definition of culture. Back in 1952 researchers estimated that there were at least two hundred rival definitions of culture,[2] and over subsequent decades the number of definitions has increased by still more hundreds. Despite this confusion, definitions belong to one of three broad categories, namely, classicist, modern, and postmodern.[3] The purpose of this chapter is to explain the historical origin of, and differences between these categories. Particular emphasis will be given to clarifying the distinction between modern and postmodern definitions; this will require reviewing the historical development of cultural anthropology over the last hundred years. This introductory chapter will indicate something of the contentious nature and complexity of cultures; subsequent chapters will expand on the key themes that emerge.

1. Raymond Williams, *Keywords: A Vocabulary of Culture and Society* (New York: Oxford University Press, 1985), 87.
2. See Alfred Kroeber and Clyde Kluckhohn, "Culture: A Critical Review of Concepts and Definitions," in *Papers of the Peabody Museum of American Archaeology and Ethnology* 47 (Cambridge: Harvard University Press, 1952): 5.
3. See Anna Green, *Cultural History: Theory and History* (New York: Palgrave, 2009), 1–10.

Classicist Definitions

A definition popular in the nineteenth century with anthropologists and still widely held by nonspecialists views a culture as a visible, comprehensible entity, the conscious creation of rational minds. It is the sum total of the spiritual, intellectual, and aesthetic aspects of human society. The definition stresses the need to detail the observable phenomena: for example, foods, literature, dances. Cultures are then graded aesthetically, with European civilization as the normative culture at the top of the list. Non-European peoples are definitely inferior, but it is possible for them to acquire the normative civilization with its elite values and lifestyles as gifts from above.

The definition has many deficiencies in addition to its assumption of Eurocentric superiority. It overstresses historical lifestyles or customs of ethnic groups and downplays their struggles to adapt to the world in which they live. It freezes a culture in a time period and encourages romantic or fossilized views of a people's way of living in the past. A culture is likened to a machine—something with visible, rationally constructed and interconnecting parts; each part, such as a custom or institution, can be readily replaced by another component without people experiencing any sense of hurt or loss. The definition simply ignores how people feel about what they do.

Modern Definitions

Edward Tylor first used the term "culture" in 1871 to mean that "complex whole which includes knowledge, belief, art, morals, law, custom, and any other capabilities and habits acquired by man as a member of society."[4] There are two key aspects to his definition. First, culture comprises those human attributes that are learned and learnable and are therefore passed on socially and mentally rather than biologically. Second, culture is in some sense a "complex whole"; unity and harmony are key assumptions. These insights profoundly influence the development of cultural anthropology for decades to come.

Constraining Quality

Cultural anthropology began to develop as a scholarly discipline in the early decades of the last century, particularly under the influence of

---

4. Edward Tylor, *Primitive Culture*, vol. 1 (New York: Harper, 1871), 1.

several important figures such as Emile Durkheim (1885–1917), Max Weber (1864–1920), and later, more specifically, Franz Boas (1858–1942) and Bronislaw Malinowski (1884–1942). Durkheim believed that cultures are like the body of an animal. The purpose of each organ is to contribute to the unity and order of the whole body. So also in cultures: institutions or social structures exist to maintain order and the survival of cultures. Individuals are so constrained, even coerced, by these structures that their behavior has a certain social and cultural regularity. Weber did not emphasize this coercive role of culture, but rather focused on the role of ideas and individuals in evoking change. Anthropologists continue to struggle with this tension between the power of culture to restrain individual behavior and the role of the individual in resisting cultural constraints.

Under the strong influence of Malinowski and Boas in the years following World War I, anthropology emerged as a quite distinctive academic discipline. Boas's definition of culture shows the influence of Durkheim: "Culture embraces all the manifestations of social habits of a community, the reactions of the individual as affected by the habits of the group in which he [*sic*] lives, and the products of human activities as determined by these habits."[5] People are bound together by at least an unconscious feeling of unity; as emotions are the result of cultural influences, the emotional reactions of people will differ from culture to culture.[6] The power of culture to constrain and unify human activity is also evident in later definitions of culture by American anthropologists. For example, Clyde Kluckhohn and William Kelly: "A culture is an historically derived system of explicit and implicit designs for living, which tends to be *shared by all* or specially designated members of a group."[7] For the influential Talcott Parsons a culture is a unitary set of attributes that distinguish a social group. Roger Keesing could claim that cultures

---

5. Franz Boas, "Anthropology," in *Encyclopedia of the Social Sciences,* vol. 2, ed. E. R. A. Seligman (New York: Macmillan, 1930), 79.

6. Encouraged by this notion, Margaret Mead (1901–1978) in her study of adolescent behavior in Samoa claims that gendered patterns of behavior are culturally, not biologically, determined (see her *Coming of Age in Samoa* [New York: William Morrow, 1928]). The objectivity of her research is now questioned. See Derek Freeman, *Margaret Mead and Samoa* (Cambridge: Harvard University Press, 1983).

7. Clyde Kluckhohn and William H. Kelly, "The Concept of Culture," in *The Science of Man in the World Crisis,* ed. Ralph Linton (New York: Columbia University Press, 1945), 98. Italics not in original.

"comprise systems of shared ideas, systems of concepts and rules and meanings that underlie and are expressed in ways that humans live."[8]

Functionalism

The notion of the static, discrete, and homogeneous nature of cultures was further reinforced by Malinowski's principle of *functionalism*. He argued that culture "consists in . . . satisfying the innate biological desires of man [*sic*]."[9] Following Durkheim, he views all social actions and institutions as functional in the sense that they collectively fit together to maintain the unity of the whole. Malinowski believed the biological and psychological needs of individuals to be the fundamental force for social stability. Another influential functionalist, Alfred Radcliffe-Brown (1881–1955), however, shifted the primary emphasis in defining culture from the satisfying of individual needs to the importance of maintaining social structures or institutions. Cultures are held together in a fixed manner by structures of juridical rules, status, and moral norms; actual people, their feelings and their relationships, ceased to be important to Radcliffe-Brown and his followers.

In brief, modern definitions of culture emphasize a type of "billiard ball" model of cultures as separate, impenetrable units, passing with little or no change from one generation to the next in a quasi-automatic way, self-integrating to maintain the status quo, resistant to external influences, homogeneous, and devoid of internal dissent.[10] Since this homogeneity is believed to define the unchanging, essential uniqueness of each culture in relation to other cultures, the modern approach to culture is especially favored by nationalists. Hence in threatening times nationalists emphasize the need to identify and maintain an all-embracing "Englishness," "Americanness," "Australianness," and so forth (see Figure 1.1).[11]

---

8. Roger M. Keesing, *Cultural Anthropology: A Contemporary Perspective* (New York: Holt, Rinehart and Winston, 1976), 68–69.

9. Bronislaw Malinowski, *Freedom and Civilization* (London: Unwin, 1947), 33.

10. See Alan Barnard, *History and Theory in Anthropology* (Cambridge: Cambridge University Press, 2000), 158–84; Kathryn Tanner, *Theories of Culture: A New Agenda for Theology* (Cambridge: Cambridge University Press, 1997), 3–58.

11. See Jan Nederveen Pieterse, *Globalization and Culture* (Lanham, MD: Rowman & Littlefield, 2004), 46–47.

Cultures: Typology		
Modern		**Postmodern**
Internal	homogeneous	fragmented
Borders	closed	porous
Identity	essentialist	multiple
Metaphor	order	chaos
Place	territorial	translocal
Dissenters	marginalized	integrated
Other cultures	inferior	interdependent
Power	hegemonic	contested

Figure 1.1

Postmodern Definitions

While postmodernity is a highly controversial term, nonetheless authors generally agree it has the following characteristics:[12] the rejection of rational criteria as the exclusive source of knowledge; the dismissal of overarching or universal myths or narratives and the acceptance of individual stories; the celebration of differences, spontaneity, superficiality, and humor; chaos, not order, at the center of cultures as people struggle for identities and power. The impact of postmodernity on cultural anthropology continues to be profound; reactions can be summarized under two broad headings: antifunctionalism and poststructuralism (Figure 1.2).

12. See James A. Beckford, *New Religious Movements and Rapid Social Change* (London: Sage, 1992), 19.

Postmodern Anthropology

Anti-functionalism:
types

Symbolic interpretive:
Geertz/Ricoeur/Douglas/
Turner

Structuralism
Levi-Strauss

Postmodern
Anthropology:

Poststructuralism:
emphases

Culture is becoming
Turner/Derrida

Individual action
Bourdieu/Sahlins/Giddens

Discourse/power
Foucault/Barthes/Williams

Feminist critique
Moore/Ortner

Individual narratives
Lyotard

Chaos
Mosko/Damon

Reflexivity
Clifford/Marcus/Fischer/Ong

Figure 1.2

A. Anti-Functionalism

Symbolic Interpretative

The most influential anthropologist questioning the assumptions of modern anthropology is the American Clifford Geertz. Anthropology is not "an experimental science in search of law but an interpretive one in search of meaning."[13] Culture is a system of shared symbols and meanings; symbolic action needs to be interpreted, read, or deciphered in order to be understood. Contrary to functionalists, however, Geertz insists not just on the role of the anthropologist in interpreting symbols, but also on the importance of people themselves in deciphering their symbols. Real-life social action of individuals, including their feelings, must never be ignored in the study of cultures; that is, symbols cannot be studied in the abstract and without the collaboration of people— observers *and* actors—themselves. For Geertz, therefore, culture itself is a system of symbols, of which religion is a particularly important one. We are suspended in webs of significance we ourselves have spun, and culture is these webs. No longer can we say that people "have a culture," because we exist in the midst of, respond to, use, and create cultural symbols (see chap. 2).

In interpreting symbols Geertz insists on rigorous field work that must involve in his own terms "thick layers" of description of many kinds such as ethnographic details, different informants' interpretations, and the ethnographer's interpretations. Under the influence of Paul Ricoeur, Geertz sees that understanding another culture is like reading, and interpreting, a text. Ricoeur writes that culture can be interpreted as a text by applying the interpretive methods of hermeneutics. That is, a text is at the same time a collection of individual parts and a flawless whole; this means that those who interpret a text must be able to move easily as though on a continuum between these two points. The interpreter must seek access to the fleeting subjective intentions of those being observed, as we do with any written text.[14]

Victor Turner (1920–1983) and Mary Douglas (1921–2007) also follow the symbolic interpretive trend in anthropology and develop theories applicable to all kinds of cultures. While both owe much to Durkheim's

13. Clifford Geertz, *The Interpretation of Cultures* (New York: Basic Books, 1973), 4–6.

14. See Paul Ricoeur, "The Model of the Text: Meaningful Action Considered as a Text," in *Interpretive Social Science: A Reader* (Berkeley: University of California Press, 1979), 73–101.

emphasis on the constraining nature of culture they, nonetheless, allow for the individual freedom of people in challenging the cultural status quo and effecting change. Douglas focuses on apparently ordinary things of life and finds extraordinary insights in them. She investigates rituals of purity and impurity, analyzes the importance of dirt and cleanliness in everyday life, shows that the selections people make about what they eat and the ways they prepare it mirror the way they organize their social life. Among Turner's lasting insights is a clear statement that culture is not a frozen entity, but a process whereby people are constantly interacting with one another, sometimes harmoniously and at other times in conflicting ways (see chaps. 3 and 6).

Structuralism

Ferdinand de Saussure (1857–1913) aimed to discover the underlying rules of language, those deep structures that must be present for language to achieve its purpose of communication. These structures are autonomous, that is, independent of the people using a language, something like a genetic program that predetermines human behavior. It is this dislodging of language from people that is one of the startling qualities of the movement that became known as *structuralism*. Claude Levi-Strauss (1908–2009), a French anthropologist, applies structuralist insights to anthropological studies. After examining the complex norms governing kinship relationships and the myths of peoples in traditional cultures, he highlights the importance of binary oppositions such as pure/polluted, order/chaos, parent/child in the way people think and act. Our minds are programmed to categorize things in binary ways and myths are able to reconcile these oppositions.[15]

The complex insights of Levi-Strauss have had a profound, but controversial, impact on anthropology as well as on other disciplines, including scriptural studies. On the positive side, he refocused academic attention on the power of myths and the emotions they evoke. Symbols are extremely complex realities and the understanding of their meanings demands significant expertise that not all analysts and social actors may possess. On the negative side, Levi-Strauss seems to deny the role of the acting subject; culture operates in a rather deterministic way to guide

---

15. See Claude Levi-Strauss, *The Raw and the Cooked: Introduction to a Science of Mythology* (London: Cape, 1970); for an overview of his theories see Edmund R. Leach, *Levi-Strauss* (London: Fontana, 1970).

behavior. At one point he writes: "We claim . . . to show not how men [*sic*] think in myths, but rather how myths think themselves through men [*sic*], without their knowing."[16] As two critics comment: "The cultural system, it seems, dances to its own peculiar, mathematical logic."[17] Finally, lacking any analysis of power, he ignores the fact that people can manipulate mythologies to oppress others and enhance their own dominance. His thinking is almost a return to the orderly cultural assumptions of functionalism.

B. Poststructuralism

Poststructuralist anthropologists freely draw on multidisciplinary sources in their criticism of structuralism. They rebel against its oppressive determinism in which individuals are depicted as simple vehicles of deep predetermined structures, with no room for chance in human events. By contrast to this orderly view of cultures, poststructuralists offer a far more chaotic or disordered picture. The emphasis is on difference rather than likeness as the central quality; there are many gaps and paradoxes in the operation of systems that lack the predictability so enthusiastically proclaimed by structuralists. The philosopher Jacques Derrida (1930–2004) is reacting against structuralists when he insists on what he terms the "innocence of becoming"[18] that characterizes human behavior. This is in contrast to the structuralist view that actions are derived from some predetermined subterranean-like design. Under his influence and that of others the focus in the study of cultures shifted from linearity and causality to discontinuity. The future is never predictable, but is always open to chance. Derrida also deconstructs a text not to oppose or subvert it, but to uncover what it seeks to excuse and suppress, and to examine its conceptual and ideological schemata. Deconstruction is not a matter of opposing modern discourse, "but of unceasingly analyzing the whole conceptual machinery and its disinterestedness,"[19] that is, showing how it is used or manipulated for political power, for example the maintenance of patriarchal power, and

16. Claude Levi-Strauss, *Mythologiques* (Paris: Plon, 1964), 20.

17. Philip Smith and Alexander Riley, *Cultural Theory: An Introduction* (Oxford: Blackwell, 2009), 100.

18. Jacques Derrida, quoted in *The Routledge Companion to Postmodernism,* ed. Stuart Sim (London: Routledge, 2005), 291.

19. Jacques Derrida, "This Strange Institution called Literature: An Interview with Jacques," in *Acts of Literature*, ed. Derek Attridge (New York: Routledge, 1992), 109.

for ideological purposes. The postmodern view of the self as a storyteller, based on the assumption that the self cannot get in touch with any deeper reality within, is challenged by the deconstructionists. They aim to peel back the layers of stories and expose reality; out of this process people will then be able freely to construct a reality-based sense of self.

Summary: Implications for Anthropology

- culture is not an entity, but a process of becoming;

- definitions of culture must be examined to uncover hidden assumptions of political, gender, or ideological power by authors;

- no observer is able to achieve a totally objective view of a culture;

- no one definition of culture can capture the complexity of a culture;

- globalization means that borders between cultures are softening;

- because people belong to particular cultures does not mean that they must act in predictable ways.

The following are key themes found emerging in poststructural anthropology, and they illustrate the inadequacy of the modern understanding of culture as a conceptual instrument in the study of individual cultures. Particular themes will be more fully treated in subsequent chapters.

"Acting Subject" Returns

"Practice theory" evolved in the late 1970s and early 1980s, deeply influencing the anthropological understanding of culture. Its major representatives are Pierre Bourdieu (1930–2002), Marshall Sahlins (1930–), and Anthony Giddens (1938–). Practice theory emphasizes individual action over the deterministic influences of culture so popular with structuralists. It reinstates the individual's ability to act freely without ignoring the larger structures in cultures that constrain social action. For example, Bourdieu's study highlights the relationship between collective norms, social power, and individual action, as these are expressed through and by the human body. Instead of a structuralist binary distinction between consciousness and the unconscious, Bourdieu insists on a continuum between these two poles. Most human activity occurs in the space between these two poles that is termed "the domain of habit"; it is here that culture becomes encoded on the individual body. External social structures produce in individuals what he calls the *"habitus,"* that is, a system of lasting dispositions and practices; *habitus* is culturally defined, but its location is the mind of the individual. He is rejecting any assumption that structures or cultures are static or rule-dominated, and therefore he strongly emphasizes the role of individuals in intuitively choosing what aspect of the *habitus* they wish to follow at a particular time (see chaps. 3 and 6).[20]

Centrality of Power

The term "discourse" is a central focus for many poststructuralists such as Michel Foucault (1926–1984), who continues to have significant influence on anthropological studies. For Foucault, discourse is the pattern of texts, the specialized languages and networks of power relations operating in and defining a particular field. For him power and knowledge are really the same thing and he is a master of revealing vested power interests (see chap. 3). For example, he examines the discourses of madness and sexuality, both of which he concludes are socially constructed. There is no such thing as madness or sexuality except ideas about them that are formed through discourse. The disciplines of medicine, psychiatry, biology, economics, and linguistics have through history inflexibly defined their "proper" subjects, dividing the world into ordered, controllable entities. Thus, once people are socially defined as mad, they must be controlled accordingly. People who control specialized disciplines hold extraordinary power in society, power that can rarely be challenged by outsiders. Power insidiously permeates every aspect of a culture and is psychologically invasive and oppressive. Both agents and subjects of power are rarely aware of this.[21] Functionalists among anthropologists, for example, are criticized for unknowingly misusing their power in

20. See Smith and Riley, *Cultural Theory*, 128–36, and Pierre Bourdieu, *Outline of a Theory of Practice* (Cambridge: Cambridge University Press, 1977), 72.
21. See Michel Foucault, *The Order of Things: An Archaeology of the Human Sciences* (New York: Vintage Books, 1974).

research to ignore the negative consequences of colonial domination and its support for traditional elites and oppression of women.[22]

Another French academic, Roland Barthes (1915–1980), focuses on the immense power of symbols and myths within popular culture to coerce people. He shows how racism, sexism, and colonialism loiter behind seemingly innocent advertisements. The power of myth is to be found, he argues, in its potential to make an arbitrary system of values appear as a system of facts. Use this or that soap and you will be "pure."[23]

Feminist Critique

Partly influenced by the writings of Derrida and Foucault, feminist anthropologists such as Henrietta Moore and Sherry Ortner began to concentrate on deconstructing evidence of male bias in the writings of anthropologists.[24] Women are too frequently portrayed as of little consequence in traditional societies; their often central role in social life has been neglected.

Negotiating Relationships

An academic discipline generally termed "cultural studies" is also affecting the way anthropologists view culture. Its multidisciplinary roots are to be found particularly in the works of the British academics Raymond Williams and Richard Hoggart.[25] Culture is what people do to negotiate their relationship to natural, social, and economic realities in the midst of a rapidly changing, chaotic globalizing world. Theorists avoid the simplistic reductionist, determinist, doctrinaire, and antihumanist focus of classical Marxism by stressing instead the idea that culture is a product of shifting power struggles between different social groups based on age, gender, race, ethnicity, and economic class divisions. Because these struggles evoke powerful emotions, Williams defines culture as "structure

---

22. Edward Said's highly controversial book, *Orientalism* (London: Routledge, 1978), is an example. In his view anthropologists have either ignored colonialism's influence or have been only halfhearted in resisting it.

23. See Roland Barthes, *Mythologies* (St Albans: Paladin, 1973).

24. See Henrietta L. Moore, *Feminism and Anthropology* (Cambridge: Polity, 1988).

25. See Raymond Williams, *Culture and Society* (London: Penguin, 1971).

of feeling."[26] Like Foucault, researchers in cultural studies are especially concerned about the relations between culture and power, particularly focusing on the ways in which various marginal and subcultural groups negotiate for political power. For example, ethnographers conclude that the fads and often outlandish fashions of some working class groups of youth, with their use of obscene and fetishistic symbols, are political protests against the ruling elites (see chap. 7).[27]

Multiplicity of Narratives

Jean-François Lyotard describes the postmodern as "incredulity toward metanarratives."[28] A metanarative is an overarching story or theory that supposedly accounts for, explains, or interprets the truth of all other stories. Following Michel Foucault, Lyotard claims that scientists, philosophers, and other intellectuals just happen to be good storytellers, but there is no objective foundation to what they say. Foucault speaks of the "Other" to refer to those people who are excluded from positions of power by political or academic elites controlling the *metanarratives*. Excluded people have the right to tell their own stories or narratives to claim their identity. (See chaps. 2 and 6.)

This has significant consequences for cultures in a globalizing world. Nationalistic metanarratives insist that cultures must be related to a definite territorial place, so they speak of "the fatherland" or "the motherland." Cultures in this sense are "inward-looking" and discourage individual storytelling beyond national borders of place. But the postmodern emphasis on individual narratives involves an outward-looking or porous sense of place. People are freed to tell and listen to stories across the boundaries of place; the more they do this, the more interdependence grows. Cultures are then called "translocal."[29]

---

26. Raymond Williams, *The Long Revolution* (London: Chatto and Windus, 1961), 41.

27. See Dick Hebdige, *Subculture: The Meaning of Style* (London: Methuen, 1979), 18.

28. Jean-François Lyotard, *The Postmodern Condition: A Report on Knowledge* (Manchester: Manchester University Press, 1984), xxiv.

29. See Pieterse, *Globalization*, 78–79.

Embracing Chaos

For Peter Berger, culture protects people from the awesome insecurities and meaninglessness of chaos (*anomy*). Culture (*nomos*) is "an area of meaning carved out of a vast mass of meaninglessness, a small clearing of lucidity in a formless, dark, almost ominous jungle."[30] Disruptive experiences of chaos can be catalysts for radical cultural changes (see chap. 6). Anthropologists are now turning to the chaos theory of physics and applying its basic assumptions to the study of cultures. Broadly defined, the theory is "the science of process rather than state, of becoming rather than being . . . [resulting in] a science of the global nature of systems."[31] It means that chaos and order interact and are always on the borders of the other. The movement of change is not smooth, but lurching, and its necessary impetus is stress. At certain points, changes may amplify into disturbances so profound and deep that a culture breaks apart, but it may eventually reconfigure itself into a much more complex system.[32]

Reflexivity

A new school of anthropology in the United States, "reflexive anthropology," developed in the 1980s and continues to have a deep impact on ethnographical studies. In their book *Anthropology as Cultural Critique*[33] George Marcus and James Fischer argue that anthropologists must now move their critical focus from the Third World to cultures of Western societies. They write: "The challenge of serious cultural criticism is to bring the insights gained on the periphery back to the center [i.e., the Eurocentric world] to raise havoc with our settled ways of thinking and conceptualization."[34] Another book, *Writing Culture: The Poetics and Politics of Ethnography*,[35] edited by James Clifford and George Marcus, especially caused controversy among anthropologists. As with any poetic

30. Peter Berger, *The Sacred Canopy: Elements of a Sociological Theory of Religion* (New York: Doubleday, 1969), 23.

31. James Glieck, *Chaos: Making a New Science* (New York: Penguin, 1987), 5.

32. See Mark S. Mosko and Frederick H. Damon, eds., *On the Order of Chaos: Social Anthropology and the Science of Chaos* (New York: Berghahn, 2005).

33. See George E. Marcus and James Clifford, *Anthropology as Cultural Critique: An Experimental Moment in the Human Sciences* (Chicago: University of Chicago Press, 1986).

34. Ibid., 138.

35. See James Clifford and George E. Marcus, eds., *Writing Culture: The Poetics and Politics of Ethnography* (Berkeley: University of California Press, 1986).

and narrative manuscript, the writings of Western anthropologists on Third World cultures cannot be considered objective and scientifically neutral; the hidden assumptions of superiority must be uncovered and critiqued. As described by these anthropologists, cultures were self-contained, with neat boundaries, internally consistent and unified entities of beliefs and values simply passed on from generation to generation. If hypothetically such self-contained cultures did exist in the past, they certainly are not to be found today in this globalizing world. Clifford in his critique compliments Walter Ong, SJ, (1912–2003) for pointing out significant weaknesses in anthropological texts written by Westerners. Ong rejected what he called "visualism," that is, the overconcentration in anthropological research on visual observation to the neglect of the feelings of touch, smell, and taste that are so important in non-literate cultures.[36]

In a later book, *The Predicament of Culture*,[37] Clifford forcefully reiterates the theme of *Writing Culture*. Anthropological writings are literary fictions of their authors, who are insensitive to the fact that their own biases determine how they see reality. Taken to its logical postmodern conclusion, therefore, this means that an anthropologist can never claim that he or she is speaking about reality as it is. The only reality ultimately is the text of the book as a literary device and it needs to be critiqued accordingly; ultimately the real object of anthropology must be the study by the anthropologist of himself or herself.[38] In short, reflexive anthropologists conclude "that the old anthropology had been rendered obsolete."[39] If anthropology is to survive, there has to be a methodological renewal that must take place within the context of "global movements of difference and power."[40]

Critiquing Poststructuralists

While many conclusions of postmodern anthropologists are timely, some insights from reflexive anthropology must be rejected. Ernest

36. See Clifford, "Introduction: Partial Truths," *Writing Culture*, 11.

37. See James Clifford, *The Predicament of Culture: Twentieth-Century Ethnography, Literature, and Art* (Cambridge, MA: Harvard University Press, 1988).

38. See Robert Layton, *An Introduction to Theory in Anthropology* (Cambridge: Cambridge University Press, 197), 202.

39. Adam Kuper, *Culture: The Anthropologist's Account* (Cambridge, MA: Harvard University Press, 1999), 209.

40. James Clifford, as cited by Kuper, *Culture*, 209.

Gellner, Professor of Social Anthropology at Cambridge University, argued that anthropologists who accept this conclusion become purely narcissistic as they "agonize so much about their inability to know themselves and the Other, at any level of regress, that they no longer need to trouble too much about the Other."[41] Marshall Sahlins correctly complains that some anthropologists have exaggerated the breakdown of boundaries and unities within cultures because in reaction to the disruptive forces of globalization "conscious and conspicuous boundary-making has been increasing."[42] People increasingly identify themselves as members of national, ethnic, or tribal groups. To hold back total disintegration, every culture must at a minimum maintain a level of unity by arousing a collective sense of transcendence and significance among its people (see chap. 5). It is interesting to note that by 2007 George Marcus, who earlier had rejected the possibility of saying anything universal about culture, writes that: "now is the time when there is once again a strong desire or appetite for macro narratives or explanatory frames in the human sciences."[43]

Working Definition

Some postmodern anthropologists are so dissatisfied with the modern understanding of culture that they desire to drop the word "culture" entirely in their research and writings. For them the word carries too much negative academic baggage. Today, however, most contemporary anthropologists accept the concept of culture, but with reservations. As Geertz writes: "Whatever the infirmities of the concept of 'culture' there is nothing for it but to persist in spite of them."[44] Even Clifford, a trenchant critic of the term culture, admits that though it is "a deeply compromised idea," he "cannot yet do without"[45] it. There is simply no other word to take its place. Sherry Ortner accepts this conclusion, but then suggests the way to proceed: "[The] issue is . . . one of reconfiguring

41. Ernest Gellner, *Postmodernism, Reason and Religion* (London: Routledge, 1992), 45.

42. Marshall Sahlins, "Two or Three Things that I Know About Culture," *Journal of the Royal Anthropological Institute* 5 (1999): 414.

43. George Marcus, "The Passion of Anthropology," *Anthropological Yearbook of European Cultures* 16 (2007): 36.

44. Clifford Geertz, *After the Fact* (Cambridge, MA: Harvard University Press, 1995), 43.

45. Clifford, *Predicament of Culture*, 10.

this enormously productive concept for a changing world, a changing relationship between politics and academic life, and a changing landscape of theoretical possibilities." She concludes that "the fate of 'culture' will depend on its uses."[46]

I agree with this conclusion. The scope of anthropology is surely one of the most extensive among all academic disciplines—it potentially covers all the peoples of the world. Since no one definition of culture can possibly cover the realities of such a complex and changing globalizing environment, I will first present a general, working definition of culture. This definition emphasizes that cultures are not fixed entities, but processes in which people struggle for meaning in a threatening political environment. The definition also highlights the fact that a culture tells members of a particular society how to *view* the world, how to experience it *emotionally*, and how to relate to one another and to people of other societies. The titles of the next seven chapters, however, give more specific or focused definitions that will then be explained.

Culture: general definition

    A culture is a pattern of meanings

- encased in a network of symbols, myths, narratives and rituals,

- created by individuals and subdivisions, as they struggle to respond to the competitive pressures of power and limited resources in a rapidly globalizing and fragmenting world,

- and instructing its adherents about what is considered to be the correct way to feel, think, and behave.

Theological Reflection

Scripture scholar Walter Brueggemann sees that postmodern deconstructionism and reflexivity can be a liberating force in the use of Scripture. Under the influence of modernity, he argues, we made biblical texts

46. Sherry Ortner, "Introduction," in *The Fate of "Culture": Geertz and Beyond*, ed. Sherry Ortner (Berkeley: University of California Press, 1999), 8, 11; see also Ortner's book *Anthropology and Social Theory: Culture, Power, and the Acting Subject* (Durham, NC: Duke University Press, 2006), 1–18, 107–28.

fit our orderly modes of knowledge and control. Deconstructionism allows the text to speak to us in all its prophetic radicality without our
imposing meanings on it.[47] What examples can be given in which, under
the influence of modernity, theologians have used biblical texts to fit
their orderly modes of knowledge and control? Anthropological reflexivity
calls theologians to be self-critical. They need to become aware of how
much their own personal and cultural needs unconsciously mold their
interpretation of theology and their desire to impose this uncritically as
dogma on others.[48]

47. See Walter Brueggemann, *Texts Under Negotiation: The Bible and the Postmodern Imagination* (Minneapolis: Fortress Press, 1993), 11.

48. See Delwin Brown, "Refashioning Self and Other: Theology, Academy, and
the New Ethnography," in *Converging on Culture: Theologians in Dialogue with Cultural
Analysis and Criticism,* eds. Delwin Brown, Sheila Greeve Davaney, and Kathryn Tanner
(Oxford: Oxford University Press, 2001), 41–55.

Chapter 2

Cultures as Webs of Symbols and Myths

The result of symbolic activity . . . is the attainment of emotionally experienced meaning.

—Thomas Fawcett, *The Symbolic Language of Religion*[1]

Myths mean the value impregnated beliefs that men [sic] hold, that they live by or for. Every society is held together by a myth system.

—Robert M. McIver, *The Web of Government*[2]

Symbols are as important to us as water is to fish. Without symbols we simply cannot converse with one another. In fact, we are in chaos! Symbols shape what we buy, the television programs we choose to enjoy, our responses to world events, our face-to-face communications, even our sense of identity. As Westerners we may like to think of ourselves as distinctly individualistic. We proudly choose the way we dress, even the cars we drive, in order to show our distinctive identity, but however outrageous our efforts, society does set symbolic limits to attempts to be unique. We are still expressing ourselves through symbols that are intelligible to society; otherwise we simply could not communicate.[3] The purpose of this chapter is to explain the nature and power of symbols, laying the foundation for an understanding of a particular type of symbol, namely myths or story symbols.

1. Thomas Fawcett, *The Symbolic Language of Religion* (Minneapolis: Augsburg Publishing, 1971), 34.
2. Robert M. McIver, *The Web of Government* (London: Macmillan, 1947), 4.
3. See Joy Hendry, *An Introduction to Social Anthropology: Sharing Our Worlds* (London: Palgrave, 2008), 93–109.

Symbols

Clifford Geertz emphasizes the fundamental role of symbols in his definition of culture. Culture is a "pattern of meanings embodied in symbols, a system of inherited conceptions expressed in symbolic forms by means of which men [sic] communicate, perpetuate, and develop their knowledge about and attitudes toward life."[4] A symbol is a "thing," for example, a place, an artifact, a material object our senses perceive; and it is able to convey a meaning, not just about itself but about all kinds of relationships. At the same time the meaning of a symbol is not a "thing," and it can only be understood inductively through the observation of many examples of its use by people.[5]

Because symbols are so much part of our lives it is difficult to analyze them and appreciate their enormous importance in our daily lives. To help readers reflect on their own experience of the power of symbols, I will narrate two personal events and then describe the nature, qualities, and types of symbols.

Discovering the Power of Symbols

Example 1

One day I was strolling down a road in the countryside outside Rome with a recently arrived friend from Australia. He was suffering from a severe attack of homesickness. Suddenly he gave a loud, joyful shout, rushed toward a tree, and physically embraced the trunk with his hands. This was most unlike him! What had happened to him? When I went up to him I immediately understood why he was acting in such a strange and embarrassing way. It was an Australian eucalyptus tree. My friend then remarked with obvious pleasure, "Now I am at home!"

Example 2

Recently I revisited my college in Cambridge University, Christ College, after many years away. I first stood right in front of the college gazing up at its coat of arms directly over the entrance. All kinds of energizing

---

4. Clifford Geertz, *The Interpretation of Cultures* (New York: Basic Books, 1973), 89.

5. See Mary LeCron Foster, "Symbolism: The Foundation of Culture," in *Companion Encyclopedia of Anthropology*, ed. Tim Ingold (London: Routledge, 1994), 366.

memories of my happy student days quickly returned: challenging intellectual discussions with tutors, good times with friends, stories of academic heroes such as Charles Darwin and John Milton. On entering the first court I recalled that as students we were forbidden to walk on the lawn; that was possible only for senior academics. In the ancient dining hall I saw the coat of arms of St. John Fisher, cofounder of the College in the sixteenth century. I felt proud to have been at his college, but then sadness intruded as I recalled fellow students who had died over the years. As I walked back through the main entrance I somehow felt taller because from this institution I had received many academic skills that have stayed with me throughout my life. These skills seemed to take on renewed energy as I pondered the uncertainties of aging.

Reflecting On the Incidents

When a culture dramatically disintegrates, or threatens to, people experience, as Berger reminds us, the darkness of meaninglessness, a crushing taste of chaos. My friend had been thrown suddenly into a totally foreign culture.[6] He had tasted the shock of chaos. Then suddenly he saw a symbol of home and his joy returned. Such is the power of a symbol. In my incident I had been pondering the approaching chaos of old age, but on my visit to my college I relived what it symbolized for me from the past, namely, the gifts of learning and the skills to keep moving forward. Symbols are reservoirs of memory.

A sign or symbol such as a word, image, or action is something that points to something else. It expresses meaning. The words "sign" and "symbol" are frequently used interchangeably, but they differ quite significantly. A sign only points to an object—for example, the arrow indicating the site of the supermarket. A symbol, on the other hand, not only indicates something but represents it in some intrinsic manner.[7] Understanding a symbol necessitates being involved or becoming involved in it. The moment I saw the coat of arms of my Cambridge college the past again became present. To my friend the tree trunk had become Australia itself. A cross would be only a sign for an unbeliever, indicating just an event in the past, but to believers it is a symbol because the cross calls them to become involved in the many lessons it teaches. To see the cross

---

6. See Peter Berger, *The Sacred Canopy: Elements of a Sociological Theory of Religion* (New York: Doubleday, 1969), 23.

7. See Carl Jung, *Man and His Symbols* (London: Aldus, 1964), 55.

as a symbol means, for example, that I might have to die to defend the faith, as Christ himself did.

Definition and Qualities

> ### Definition
>
> A symbol is any reality that by its very dynamism or power leads to (that is, makes one think about, imagine, get into contact with, or reach out to) another deeper (and often mysterious) reality through a sharing in the dynamism that the symbol itself offers (and not merely by verbal or additional explanations).[8]

There are three fundamental qualities to any symbol: the meaning, the emotive, and the directive. The meaning aspect is its cognitive quality; the symbol makes a statement about something that the mind is able to grasp. Second, a symbol has an emotive quality because it is able to touch the hearts and imaginations of people, evoking positive or negative feelings. The emotive quality of a symbol is thus able to *re*-present the object. At the sight of the coat of arms of my college I *re*-live the past, positive experience of student days. Third, a symbol has a directive quality. As a result of its cognitive and emotional impact I am directed to act in certain ways. The symbol of the tree moved my friend to run and hug it; the green lawn in my college was a symbol reminding me that students could not walk on it.

There are other qualities of symbols.[9] Symbols are said to be *multivocal*, that is, they gather many meanings over time. Take the coat of arms over my college gate and some of the meanings it evoked; many more could be added. Another quality is their *timelessness*. I had to think very hard to put dates to the events the symbol over the gate brought to mind. Because of their emotive quality, symbols have the ability to command the allegiance of people over a long period. Take the example of Abraham Lincoln's Gettysburg Address. Although it was delivered in 1863, it continues as a symbol of freedom to evoke powerful patriotic reactions among Americans. A symbol also has the quality of *polarity*; it

8. Definition by Adolfo Nicolas, SJ.

9. See Paul Ricoeur, "The Hermeneutics of Symbols and Philosophical Reflection," in *The Philosophy of Paul Ricoeur: An Anthology of His Work*, eds. Charles E. Reagon and David Stewart (Boston: Beacon, 1978), 36–58.

is able to evoke opposite meanings at the same time. The coat of arms in my college reminded me of many happy experiences, but it also brought to mind colleagues who had died over the last fifty years. Or take the example of the cross itself; it symbolizes simultaneously both the death and the resurrection of Christ. Sometimes symbols are described as models *of* and models *for*. The former describe clusters of symbols that convey the way things are; the latter indicate the ways people are expected to behave. Sometimes the same symbols have this twofold function. The men's suits on sale in the shop window symbolize what is stylistically acceptable today, but they are also endeavoring to convey a message to me personally that I must follow today's styles if I am to be socially acceptable.

Qualities of Symbols

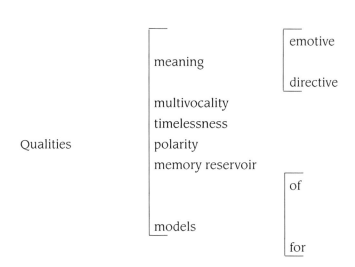

Figure 2.1

In summary, the effect of symbolic action is emotionally experienced meaning. Signs are concerned about visible and quantifiable experience, but symbols seek to draw us beyond the observable to a higher experiential, transcendent level of knowledge. Hence the role of evangelizers is not so much to turn objects into signs as to invite people to transform signs, such as the cross, into symbols.

Types

There many types of symbols, but it is useful here to describe some of particular importance.

Dominant and Instrumental

Dominant or key symbols are those that are clearly visible in a social situation and have meanings that are generally constant and consistent over time, such as a nation's flag. Instrumental symbols assist the dominant symbols to achieve their function. For example, a nation's flag may on important occasions be saluted with significant ritual dignity. This ritual is an instrumental symbol. A dominant symbol in my college is the coat of arms, and an instrumental symbol is the importance of its positioning over the entrance gate.

Summarizing and Elaborating

Dominant symbols can be arranged along a continuum between summarizing and elaborating symbols. Summarizing symbols compress meanings "in an emotionally powerful and relatively undifferentiated way."[10] Again, the coat of arms is an example. It stands for the college, but at the same time for me it also evokes many meanings that relate to my time as a student. Another example is the American flag, which represents the American way of life. However, the American way of life is a multifaceted collection of actions, thoughts, and feelings that can include such things as democracy, individual rights, military superiority, or just simple things like apple pie. The aim of elaborating symbols, on the other hand, is "to sort out experience, to place it in cultural categories, and to help us to think about how it all hangs together."[11] Elaborating symbols are fundamentally analytic. They help us to arrange and mark intricate ideas and feelings into understandable and communicable language and action. They give us categories to think about the ways in which the world is ordered. For example, when St. Paul likens the church to a human body he is using an elaborating symbol.

---

10. Sherry Ortner, "On Key Symbols," *American Anthropologist* 75 (1973): 1339.
11. Ibid.

Condensed and Diffuse

There can be no debate about the meaning of a condensed symbol. For example, a traffic stop sign means only one thing—stop or else! But the meaning of a diffuse symbol largely depends on different contexts and even the personal interpretation of individuals. Before Vatican II the symbolism of the priest was of a condensed type: the priest was the intermediary with Christ at Mass and other sacraments between people and God. After Vatican II the symbolism became diffuse: the priest is now in "the service of Christ the Teacher, Priest and King."[12] He must build and animate a community of faith as well as presiding at liturgical rites.

Personal and Public

A symbol is personal when an individual is not under any public pressure to adopt it. For example, a person may freely choose to have a body tattoo in today's Western society. A symbol is public, however, when social norms insist it be adhered to; for example, in precolonial days in New Zealand certain tattoos for Maori men were compulsory.

Representational and Presentational

Representational symbols bind together things that are different even when there may not be any natural linkage between the symbol and the thing symbolized. The relationship results from custom. For example, the color green on traffic lights sends the message "proceed," but the color could easily have been blue. Presentational symbols, however, are more than representative in a purely cultural sense; rather, they "participate in, or are similar to, the thing they symbolize."[13] There must be a real analogy between the symbol and that which to which it directs our attention. The map on the wall in the entrance hall of my college resembles the actual geographical situation of the buildings.

Presentational symbols are particularly important in religious matters and actions. Thus water and blood in rituals contain qualities that are inherently associated with purifying and new life, or with death and

---

12. Decree on the Ministry and Life of Priests (*Presbyterorum ordinis*), 1, in *Vatican Council II: The Conciliar and Post Conciliar Documents*, ed. Austin P. Flannery, new rev. ed. (Northport, NY: Costello, 1975).

13. James C. Livingston, *Anatomy of the Sacred: An Introduction to Religion* (New York: Macmillan, 1989), 70.

sacrifice. A presentational symbol in religion "points to and addresses a reality that is essentially transcendent, mysterious, and never fully plumbed."[14] It is only through symbols that we can meet ultimate reality in any meaningful manner. We say God is our Father, and this calls us to act as children of a loving Parent. The symbol of kingship biblically invites us to be loyal, obedient to, and respectful of God. When we speak of God one symbol can never be used to exclude others, because one symbol alone can never possibly portray the infinite presence of God. If, for example, we confine the symbol of God only to God's kingship, we are in danger of viewing God as a despot. Or if we exclusively say that God is just, we would exclude the overwhelming love and compassion God has for us in Christ. The exclusive use of one symbol fosters fundamentalism.

Body and Non-body Control

Cultures that significantly control people's freedom have very strict dress codes. For example, in the former Soviet Union spontaneous movements or unconventional dress for individuals were banned from all government rituals and public life in general. This is still the case in North Korea. By contrast, those symbols that express meticulous management of the human body and fixed coordination of many people were officially valued, for example the precisely coordinated mass military parades of May Day. In cultures where freedom is fostered, however, these symbols of rigid body control rarely exist. Hence in Western societies in general all kinds of spontaneous behavior such as hippie cults, communes, and sects are permissible.[15] To return to my college visit: as I looked around and noticed the dress of students, I became aware of how the culture of the college must have relaxed since my time. I knew this simply by observing that students no longer wear gowns to lectures, but one power symbol remains intact—students may still not walk on the lawns!

Polar Opposites

We commonly divide our lives into a number of separate or polar divisions, each marked by powerful, distinguishing symbols—for example work/leisure; home/workplace; white collar/blue collar; male/female;

---

14. Ibid.

15. For the development of this theme see Mary Douglas, *Natural Symbols: Explorations in Cosmology* (New York: Pantheon Books, 1970), 99–106.

kitchen/lounge room; public morality/private morality; church/state. That is, we tend to arrange our experiences according to a system of symbolic pairing. For example, we invite only very close friends into the kitchen and reserve the tidy living room for people we do not know well. Any infringement of these dichotomies can suggest disorder, danger, or pollution. It is not surprising, therefore, that unisex hairstyles and attire can still anger some people in Western cultures. The blurring of boundaries creates uncertainty, even the dreaded fear of chaos.

Interpreting Symbols

According to Dan Sperber symbols are uniquely noted for their mysterious quality of nonrationality. In his view symbolism arises from the human effort required to handle information of a kind that "defies direct conceptual treatment."[16] Neat, logical analysis of symbols is impossible. Geertz agrees. The analysis of culture is "not an experimental science in search of law but an *interpretive one in search of meaning*."[17] Semiotics is the art of putting ourselves in the shoes of others, our minds in their bodies. Geertz continues: "Doing ethnography is like trying to read . . . a manuscript—foreign, faded, full of ellipses, incoherencies, suspicious emendations, and tendentious commentaries, but written not in conventionalized graphs of sound but in transient examples of shaped behavior."[18] Unlike a written text, a culture is also constantly changing. Just when we think we have interpreted the meanings within symbols, new meanings have developed, so our interpretation is already out of date.

As symbols are cultural constructs, it is rare that any symbol is able to have a universally recognized meaning. A ring, for example, may symbolically indicate steadfast dedication when placed on the finger of a bride in a Western marriage ceremony, but among the Bangwa of the Republic of Cameroon a ring on the ankle of a woman shows that she has been a slave. The eucharistic bread and wine, symbolizing the real presence of the body and blood of Christ, may be spiritual food for Catholics, but this is a source of scandal to Hindus who interpret it as having cannibalistic qualities. A symbol, therefore, can only be interpreted when viewed in relation to other symbols that form part of the

16. Dan Sperber, *Rethinking Symbolism* (Cambridge: Cambridge University Press, 1975), 148.

17. Clifford Geertz, *Interpretation*, 5. Italics not in original.

18. Ibid.

same culture.[19] One rare example of a possibly universal symbol is the left hand connoting something fear-evoking, even at times evil.[20]

Pastoral Advice

- Symbols possess a density of meaning that words alone cannot encapsulate.

    Janine Roberts illustrates this by describing how residents of Dixie Valley, Nevada, reacted when they were forced by the military to leave their homes and land in order to make way for a target practice site. They held a symbolic burial of significant things in their lives that were now going to be lost: two articles of the Constitution, water from the artesian wells that kept the valley green, and a hip flask symbolic of the last drink one person would ever take in the Valley. It would be quite impossible to put into words alone the layer upon layer of meanings symbolized in these items.[21]

- Not all meanings of symbols are accessible, because they lie unarticulated, perhaps mostly unexamined in the innermost corners of people's minds; anthropologists variously call them "unconscious,"[22] "tacit,"[23] or "implicit."[24]

- The interpretations we give to symbols are "ours" because they may not fit the meanings intended by the people we are observing.

    When other people use words or act in certain ways that are familiar to us, we are tempted to assume that the meanings correspond to our own, but this may not be the case at all. Different people in the same culture are likely to differ when they try to

---

19. See Fiona Bowie, *The Anthropology of Religion* (Oxford: Blackwell, 2000), 40.

20. See Robert Hertz, "The Pre-eminence of the Right Hand: A Study of Religious Polarity," in *Right and Left: Essays on Dual Symbolic Classification,* ed. Rodney Needham (Chicago: University of Chicago Press, 1973), 3.

21. See Janine Roberts, "Setting the Frame: Definition, Functions, and Typology of Rituals," in *Rituals in Families and Family Therapy*, eds. Evan Imber-Black, Janine Roberts, and Richard A. Whiting (New York: W.W. Norton, 2003), 22–23.

22. See Rodney Needham, *Symbolic Classification* (Santa Monica, CA: Goodyear, 1979).

23. See Sperber, *Rethinking Symbolism.*

24. See Mary Douglas, *Implicit Meanings: Essays in Anthropology* (London: Routledge & Kegan Paul, 1975).

interpret their own public symbols. Any two Catholics may publicly state that they believe in God, and, because they use the same words it is assumed they "understand" each other. In practice their notions of what their belief in God means may radically diverge.

- There is a significant degree of subjectivity in our interpretations, implying the possibility of imprecision, of inexactitude, of ambiguity.[25]

The problems of an "interpretation of others' interpretations"[26] are immense. Little wonder that Geertz bluntly writes: "Cultural analysis is (or should be) guessing at meanings, assessing the guesses, and drawing explanatory conclusions from the better guesses, not discovering the Continent of Meaning and mapping out its bodiless landscape."[27] If we want to understand the meanings of other people's symbols we must be prepared to spend significant time listening and questioning. Even then we may misinterpret their meanings.

- Symbols with their variety of meanings are born because they respond to the subjective needs of people and their experience of life. If theology and liturgies do not relate to these needs they remain irrelevant.

Myths: Story Symbols

Whereas empirical language refers to objective facts, myth refers to the quintessence of human experience, the meaning and significance of human life.

—Rollo May, *The Cry for Myth*[28]

Myths are story symbols and mythologies are many interconnected myths. When I stood in front of the episcopal coat of arms of St. John Fisher in the dining hall of Christ College, I recalled a story of my first formal meeting with the Master of the college in 1960. "Sir," he said, "I

25. See Anthony P. Cohen, *The Symbolic Construction of Community* (Chichester: Ellis Horwood, 1985), 73.

26. Geertz, *Interpretation*, 18.

27. Ibid., 20.

28. Rollo May, *The Cry for Myth* (New York: Delta, 1991), 26.

want you to remember the great founders and alumni of the past. Think of John Fisher, cofounder and the one who brought Renaissance learning into this college and university, John Milton, Charles Darwin. These were men committed to excellence in learning. I expect the same of you!" It was a powerful, inspiring, but frightening memory. As I reflected on what the Master had said I became aware of how much this mythology had unconsciously influenced my life. This is the power of a myth and the ability of heroes or villains to make it visible in concrete ways.

Definition

- Myths are value-impregnated beliefs or stories that bind people together at the deepest level of their group life, and that they live by and for. Contrary to popular belief, myths are not fairytales or fallacies. A myth is a story or tradition that claims to reveal in an imaginative or symbolic way a fundamental truth about the world and human life. The truth is encased in a story simply because it is so powerful for those who accept it that it cannot be contained in any strictly technical or rational statement. In this sense myths are closer to poetry than to any other form of speech.

- Myths inspiringly and feelingly tell people who they are, what is good and bad, and how they are to organize themselves and maintain their feeling of unique identity in the world. Rollo May writes that "myths are like the beams in a house: not exposed to outside view, they are the structure which holds the house together so people can live in it."[29] Or they resemble the information contained in the DNA of a cell, or the program technology of a computer. A myth is the cultural DNA, the software, the unconscious information, the program that governs the way we see reality and act accordingly.[30]

Myths and History

Myths can be a mixture of remembering, forgetting, interpreting, and inventing historical happenings. But the purposes of myth and history differ; myth is concerned not so much with a succession of events as

29. Ibid., 15.
30. See Sam Keen, "The Stories We Live By," *Psychology Today* (December 1988): 10.

with the moral significance of these happenings.[31] A myth is a "religious" commentary on the beliefs and values of a culture. Rollo May describes it this way: "The myth is a drama which begins as a historical event and takes on its special character as a way of orienting people to reality."[32] Thus George Washington can be viewed in historical or mythological terms. As seen from the historical perspective, he is depicted as fitting into a definite time period, influencing and being influenced by events around him. If, however, he is evaluated as a person who exemplifies the virtues of honesty, inventiveness in the face of difficulties, and hard work, then we are measuring him by the founding mythology of the nation. Ultimately, a story that becomes a myth can be true or false, historical or unhistorical, but what is important is not the story itself but the purpose it serves in the life of an individual, a group, or a whole society. Myths simply allow people of different societies and subcultures to understand themselves and their world.

Mythologies Compared: Australia and the United States

Australia's founding mythology, unlike that of the United States, is very much due to its partly convict origins and the harshness of most of its countryside. The internationally known lyric "Waltzing Matilda" recounts in a fictional way the very heart of this mythology. There are two central characters: a "swagman" (vagrant) and a "squatter" (rich land owner). The swagman is discovered by the squatter stealing a sheep and the squatter calls in the "troopers" (police), who rush to apprehend the thief. Then the swagman jumps into a "billabong" (small lake) and drowns, but the story does not end there. The swagman actually wins! His ghost lives on to haunt the rich and powerful, reminding them that the real hero in Australia is the underdog (or, as it is now symbolically termed in Australia, "the battler").

One of the positive contributions of Claude Levi-Strauss to our understanding of mythology is his emphasis on polarities and the ability of myths to reconcile them.[33] In the mythology of democracy there are two complementary poles: the rights of the individual

---

31. For fuller explanation of this section see Gerald A. Arbuckle, *Violence, Society and the Church: A Cultural Approach* (Collegeville, MN: Liturgical Press, 2004), 7–13.

32. May, *The Cry*, 26.

33. See Edmund Leach, *Levi-Strauss* (London: Fontana, 1970), 54–82.

and the common good. The third quality, "fraternity," is the balance between these two mythological poles. For Americans fraternity means that the rights of the individual are to be respected even though the common good may suffer. In Australia it is the common good that must be emphasized even though individual rights are consequently restricted; this egalitarian interpretation is commonly summed up in the expression "Fair go, mate." The "mate" refers especially to those on the margins of society and the economy, society's underdogs. Consequently significant cynicism is directed toward people who show "squatter-like" qualities, that is, who dare to "put on airs" of superiority or artificiality. Any politician who forgets that the swagman remains the mythological hero to this day has no political future.[34]

By contrast, in the United States, since the rights of the individual take precedence, the individual retains, for example, the unqualified right to own guns despite the clear, tragic consequences to the community. It is a world made for capitalism and its expression—unrestrained competition, not collaboration for the common good. Not surprisingly, therefore, interest groups such as the medical profession, through their professional associations and major corporations, have been able to wield considerable unrestrained economic and political power. Marginalized people must solve their own problems. Any attempt by governments to redress the imbalance in favor of the common good is met with strong emotional opposition. Efforts at healthcare reforms have been branded as "socialized medicine," "government meddling," enough to condemn the most justice-based plans! It will be interesting to see how successful President Obama can be in his attempts to reform the health system. In Australia, however, with its emphasis on egalitarianism, not only is there universal healthcare but governments are expected to respond to the needs of people on the margins of society.[35]

---

34. See Bruce Kapferer, *Legends of People: Myths of State* (Washington, DC: Smithsonian Institution Press, 1988),121–208; Les Carlyon, *Gallipoli* (Sydney: Macmillan, 2001), 122–24.

35. See Gerald A. Arbuckle, *Healthcare Ministry: Refounding the Mission in Tumultuous Times* (Collegeville, MN: Liturgical Press, 2000), 65–76.

Qualities

Myths respond positively to five basic, interrelated needs. They tell us that we have a reason to exist, define for us a way of living that makes sense and is safe, provide a social and legal framework that allows us to live together in an orderly way, inculcate an inspiring sense of belonging and pride in our way of life, and are able to reconcile contradictory forces. There are, however, possible negative qualities of myths that are now to be described.

Exclusivity

People of the same culture commonly and unconsciously believe that their myths alone have validity; this can blind people to reality and foster prejudice and discrimination. The founding fathers of America had a very exclusive mythology of equality that did not extend past Anglo-Saxon Protestants. Many Americans might think that the potlatch feast in which Native American tribes in the Northwest of their country methodically destroy their wealth is senseless waste. They fail to see that they are doing the same thing every time they roam through shopping malls spending money on expensive and unnecessary extravagances.[36]

Conservatism

Myths give a sense of security and identity, but this can lead to an excessive conservatism when times demand radical changes. As Sam Keen comments, a myth "encourages us to . . . imitate the way of the culture's heroes, to repeat the formulas and rituals exactly as they were done in the old days." That is fine until radical change becomes necessary for survival, and then it is of little use "to walk into the future looking through a rear-view mirror."[37]

Manipulative Potential

To prevent the devastating effects of national chaos, every culture must maintain some level of order by encouraging a shared sense of transcendence and significance among its citizens, that is, a national mythology. This, however, can open the doors for political manipulation

---

36. For French examples see Charles Lindholm, *Culture and Authenticity* (Oxford: Blackwell, 2008), 103–7.
37. Keen, "The Stories," 11.

of power by leaders. Hitler's powerful subordinate, Heinrich Himmler, was able to develop a highly effective national myth of superiority based on a toxic mix of racial theory, primitive Teutonic pagan religion, and mass rituals.[38] Less serious was Fidel Castro's manipulation of Cuban mythology. Seeking to remove Cuban cultural dependence on Western art styles, Castro insisted that the rhumba should be promoted as the dance most characteristic of Cuban identity. This was a statement to the world that the revolution would correct the abuses of the past and that Cuban culture would embrace the sensual African legacy that had been previously suppressed.[39] Even in democracies, however, politicians and others can attempt to manipulate national mythology in their favor.

Drift Capacity

Drift takes place when myths change, degenerate, or disappear without any deliberate planning or even awareness by people that it is happening. It is sometimes said that the church, by its founding mythology, is not a democracy—it has never been and will never be one, and so Rome can justifiably ignore the values of participative or consultative leadership. This represents a myth drift. Not only is it contrary to the spirit of Vatican II, but it also goes against the original mythology of the church for a significant period of history. Historian Leonard Swidler concludes that the choice of bishops by clergy and people remained effective until the twelfth century. John Carroll, the first bishop of the United States, was chosen with Rome's approval by the priests of the country. As late as the beginning of the twentieth century fewer than half of the world's bishops were directly chosen by the pope.[40]

Residual Challenge

A *residual* myth is one with little or no daily impact on a group's life, but that at times can surface to become a powerful operative myth. Slobodan Milosevic, the Serb leader, manipulated Serbian public opinion in his incendiary speech of 28 June 1989 by invoking a residual myth of

---

38. See Jonathan Glover, *Humanity: A Moral History of the Twentieth Century* (London: Jonathan Cape, 1999), 317–27.

39. See Lindholm, *Culture and Authenticity*, 92–97.

40. See Leonard Swidler, "Democracy, Dissent, and Dialogue," in *The Church in Anguish*, eds. Hans Kung and Leonard Swidler (San Francisco: Harper & Row, 1986), 310.

humiliation when he recalled the defeat of Serbs by Muslims in 1389. The people responded with enthusiastic support. A more contemporary example is the global economic crisis. The public myth of capitalism is that unfettered market forces of supply and demand must regulate the world's economies. The residual myth based on bitter historical experience, however, is that this public myth leads to disastrous consequences; there must be governmental regulation to control unrestrained greed. This residual myth resurfaces in times of economic depression, as in the contemporary world financial crisis, but eventually the public myth may again prevail as the economic situation improves.

Polar Tensions

As myths are symbols, they contain within themselves polar opposite meanings. In the myth of democracy there are the polarities of the rights of the individual and the common good, but myths never tell us precisely how these polarities are to be reconciled in practice. In Vatican II the myth of the priesthood contains two polarities—the sacramental priesthood and the priesthood of all believers. Nowhere in the documents does the council spell out precisely *how* these polar opposites are to be balanced in real life; in fact, it simply could not do so. Where one pole is emphasized to the exclusion or neglect of the other, we have the seeds for conflict and fundamentalism.[41]

Theological Reflection

For communication to occur in theology and liturgy, the structure of the symbols must first be able to express something relevant to the culture of the people; otherwise what is said is meaningless. For example, many of the traditional Western symbols of Jesus, such as King or Judge, make no sense in the Asian context. Hence the Synod of Bishops of Asia recommended in 1998 that symbols such as the following be adopted: the Teacher of Wisdom, the Healer, the Liberator, the Obedient One.[42] In Australia the key Christian festivals, devised with Europe of the northern hemisphere in mind, have no clear connection with the nation's life and

---

41. See Gerald A. Arbuckle, *Refounding the Church: Dissent for Leadership* (Maryknoll, NY: Orbis Books, 1993), 39–43.

42. See Peter Phan, *Being Religious Interreligiously: Asian Perspectives on Interfaith Dialogue* (Maryknoll, NY: Orbis Books, 2004), 128–46.

rhythms.[43] Second, people must themselves be involved whenever their religious myths and symbols require changing. I am grateful for Vatican II, but as an anthropologist I believe it was culturally naïve. Interfering with a symbol and myth without involving the people concerned leads inevitably to unnecessary messiness, pain, and grief or chaos. This lesson has yet to be significantly acknowledged and accepted in today's church.[44]

43. See Gerard Moore, "Sacramentality: An Australian Perspective," in *Christian Worship in Australia: Inculturating the Liturgical Tradition*, eds. Stephen Burns and Anita Monro, 137–51 (Sydney: St Pauls Publications, 2009).

44. See Arbuckle, *Refounding the Church*, 42.

Chapter 3

Chapter 3

Cultures as "Not Dirt," "Pure," and Power Reservoirs

> Dirt [is] matter out of place. . . . Where there is dirt there is a system. Dirt is the by-product of a systematic ordering and classification of matter.
>
> —Mary Douglas, *Purity and Danger*[1]

Just before beginning this chapter I looked around my study, and what a mess I saw! Books and papers in disarray. "Ugh, something must be done about this before I can start to write." Once I had put things into their right places my peace of mind was restored and I could begin writing in earnest. The aim of this chapter is to explain how an apparently unimportant incident like this can have profound implications for our understanding of the nature and power of culture.

The fact is that a simple incident or object may point to what is at the heart of an entire culture. For Karl Marx it is the commodity that contains the secret of the entire capitalist system of production. Once we understand the ways in which goods are produced and exchanged, says Marx, we will discover the core of capitalism. For Durkheim an understanding of the simple totems of Indigenous Australians could lead to foundational insights into the elementary forms of all religions. For the philosopher-historian and sociologist Michel Foucault it is the often hidden, widespread violence of power. For anthropologist Douglas, however, the object of concern is everyday dirt. It evokes an attitude—"ugh!"—and demands a solution: "clean up!" What is considered dirty in some way or other

---

1. Mary Douglas, *Purity and Danger: An Analysis of the Concepts of Pollution and Taboo* (New York: Pantheon Books, 1966), 48.

pollutes or defiles what is clean, and it must be removed. An appreciation of what causes things to be called dirty or clean, Douglas argues, may uncover the deepest mysteries of the moral order itself, the reasons why some societies renew and reaffirm their fundamental collective feelings and beliefs while others do not even bother.[2] This chapter focuses on the insights into culture of Foucault and Douglas.

Power: Michel Foucault

Power in cultures, traditionally defined as the capacity to influence, takes many forms. *Position* power is the ability to use power flowing from the status of the person in an organization; *coercive* power is the ability to force people to act through fear of punishment; *reward* encourages a response by offering or refusing benefits; *personal* power is the capacity to influence because of personal qualities. In addition there are *unilateral* and *reciprocal* power. A person exercising unilateral power refuses to receive influence from others, so that dialogue is impossible. Reciprocal power, however, allows a person not only to influence others but also to be influenced by others; this form of power is integral to all genuine dialogue.

Disciplinary Power

While acknowledging these types of power, Foucault introduces an entirely new way of viewing power in contemporary cultures. He refers to "power/knowledge" to indicate that every search for knowledge is in fact a quest for power. Contrary to Enlightenment thinking, which assumed that knowledge leads to freedom, he asserts that knowledge results in domination.[3] As background to his postmodern views on the nature of power we need to recall that he distinguishes two overall historical developments in Western social and political life: the increase in political and state power and the emergence of new techniques by which power is directed at individuals at all levels of society. It is this second development that especially concerns him. Though he never explicitly refers to culture in his writings, he in fact deals with topics that are at the heart of every culture, namely power and "discourse."

2. See Robert Wuthnow, James D. Hunter, Albert Bergesen, and Edith Kurzweil, *Cultural Analysis* (London: Routledge and Kegan Paul, 1984), 85.
    3. See Michel Foucault, *Power/Knowledge* (New York: Pantheon, 1980).

For Foucault, power that is ubiquitous and insidious is predominantly *disciplinary*, but to understand this we need to first appreciate what he means by "discourses" and the central role of the human body in their development. For him a discourse is the organization of ideas and language that uniquely characterizes every institution.[4] It is a collection of specialized knowledge through which the controlling elite is able to discipline others. Power and knowledge in discourses "directly imply one another . . . there is no power relation without the correlative constitution of the field of knowledge." He continues: "the subject who knows, the objects to be known and the modalities of knowledge must be regarded as so many effects of these fundamental implications of power/knowledge and their historical transformations."[5] Since the eighteenth century the physical human body, he claims, has become the primary location of disciplinary political and ideological power, surveillance, and regulation. With the body and its actions in mind, the structures of the state, health departments, educational systems, psychiatry, the law, and so forth classify the limits of behavior and document activities, disciplining the bodies that violate the established boundaries in order to make them politically and economically valuable.

Example: The Medical Profession

Foucault illustrates his theory with particular reference to the historical development of the discourse of the medical profession, which is able to categorize bodies as deviant or normal, as hygienic or unhygienic, as controlled or requiring control. He writes: "[Medicine] set itself up as the supreme authority in matters of hygienic necessity . . . [It] promised to eliminate defective individuals, degenerate and bastardized populations." He goes further: "In the name of biological and historical urgency, it justified the racisms of the state . . . it grounded them in 'truth.'"[6] In his book *The Birth of the Clinic* (1975) he further develops his analysis of the relationship between disciplinary power and surveillance. He refers to the "anatomical atlas" that is the human body formed by the medico-scientific gaze. Since medical practices altered in the late eighteenth century, the adoption of such procedures as the physical examination,

4. See Michel Foucault, *Discipline and Punish: The Birth of the Prison*, trans. Alan Sheridan (Harmondsworth: Penguin, 1979), 27.

5. Ibid., 27–28.

6. Michel Foucault, *The History of Sexuality, Volume 1: An Introduction* (London: Penguin, 1979), 54.

the postmortem, the use of the stethoscope, psychiatry, radiology, surgery, the establishment of hospitals and doctors' clinics have all resulted in an ever-increasing power over the body. A person is expected to surrender his or her authority over his or her body to the medical profession, the supreme example of surveillance.

The surveillance power of medical knowledge, Foucault claims, is only a symptom of wider trends in the Western world. This power of surveillance and control especially resides in self-perpetuating cultural systems, and individuals become their watching agents. It is this power that is intensifying in all areas of life through an ever-increasing array of laws, rules, and rituals. We are ceaselessly under scrutiny by all kinds of people such as doctors, police, security guards, bureaucrats, and in recent years through the dramatic increase in closed circuit security television. In shops, workplaces, on highways, and in all kinds of public areas, surveillance can now occur throughout the entire day and year. Even if there is no surveillance, people still think someone is watching. Within the Catholic Church itself theologians and pastors experience this ever-present power of surveillance. For example, restorationists or fundamentalist Catholics are able to send an article or a sermon to a bishop or to Rome for evaluation with computerized speed, the target of their concern remaining unaware of the identity of the accusers.

Though Foucault's writings are often annoyingly obscure, his use of "discourse" helps us to consider power and culture without the academic baggage that has come to be associated with terms like "ideology." For example, "ideology" is apt to conjure up controversial Marxian terminologies such as class, modes of production, historical materialism, economic determinism. Marxists have traditionally claimed that their theories alone give the complete, unbiased truth about the social world, but Foucault's emphasis on discourses and their origins undermines such self-assurance. He questions the ability of any form of human knowledge to reach a complete and unbiased understanding of the ways people behave. We must be suspicious of people who are not prepared to have their assumptions of truth questioned.

Defining "Dirt": Mary Douglas

The question is: why are some things judged to be dirty and other things clean? Why are shoes considered dirty when deposited on the table, but clean when on the floor? It is the location that defines their dirtiness and its power to evoke a reaction. As Douglas writes: "Dirt is the by-product of a systematic ordering and classification of matter, in so far as ordering involves rejecting inappropriate elements."[7] This means that what is thought to be dirty is relative. Douglas comments: "It's a relative idea. Shoes are not dirty in themselves, but it is dirty to place them on the dining-table . . . it is dirty to leave cooking utensils in the bedroom . . . out-of-door things downstairs . . . . In short, our pollution behavior is the reaction which condemns any object or idea to confuse or contradict cherished classifications."[8] It is not just a question of factual location that condemns something as dirty or qualifies it as clean. Shoes are not dirty just because they are on the table rather than on the floor, but because they *should* be on the floor and *not* on the table. There is a moral quality to reality that renders the issue of classification, and mis-classification, also a matter of right and wrong. When we say that shoes should not be on the floor we are not only stating a fact about "the mechanical appropriateness of nature, but a moral evaluation of that order."[9] Dread of pollution is like fear of immorality or sin.

Classification and Impurity

Beliefs and reactions to dirt or pollution are not haphazard, but are in fact systematic and can be understood only within the framework of wider mythological categorizations. That is, food taboos are rarely isolated beliefs; they point to an underlying social structure into which they are inserted: "Defilement is never an isolated event. It cannot occur except in view of a systematic ordering of ideas . . . the only way in which pollution ideas make sense in reference to a total structure of thought whose key-stone, boundaries, margins and internal lines are held in relation by rituals of separation."[10] Any object or action that confuses or contradicts the classifications within a culture of what is clean is considered polluting and dangerous in social relations. Douglas illustrates her thesis by examining the foundation of Jewish dietary rules in the Old Testament decreeing certain animals either clean or unclean. The rules were constructed on a model of God as One, Complete, and Whole: "To be holy is to be whole, to be one: holiness is unity, integrity,

7. Douglas, *Purity and Danger,* 48; for a revised analysis of Douglas's culture models see her book *Cultural Bias,* Occasional Paper 35 (London: Royal Anthropological Institute, 1978).

8. Douglas, *Purity and Danger.*

9. See Wuthnow, et al., *Cultural Analysis,* 87.

10. Douglas, *Purity and Danger,* 41.

perfection of the individual and of the kind."[11] The animals that were considered unclean did not fit neat categorizations. Lacking completeness, they were "imperfect members of their class"[12] and could not be eaten. They included those that lived in the water but did not have fins and scales (eels, shellfish), birds of the air that at the same time lived in the water (gulls, pelicans). The pig was also unclean, for although it came within the category of cloven-hoofed animals, it did not chew grass like the edible goat and sheep. The likewise cloven-hoofed antelope, goat, and sheep were clean because they did eat grass.[13]

Some peoples at times, however, embrace oddities or anomalies rather than avoiding them. The Lele men of Zaire argue that if they always avoided what is anomalous they would never bridge the gap between the ideal and the reality in their society.[14] So by ritually eating an anteater, definitely classed as an anomaly, the men claim that they are temporarily breaking down the barriers between what is pure and impure in their lives and culture.[15]

Culture: Models[16]

On the basis of her conclusion that defilement is never an isolated happening, but is related to a particular cultural context, Douglas develops a fourfold set of culture models based on two variables, namely *group* and *grid*.[17] *Group* denotes the strength of the boundary surrounding a social group, while *grid* is concerned with the degree of rules, hierarchy, and social differentiation within it. Those cultures that are weak on both variables tend to be individualistic, whereas those cultures, for example some sects, that have strong group but weak grid have a robust feeling of collective identity and are egalitarian. Cultures of strong group

11. Ibid., 64.

12. Ibid., 55.

13. For a later development of these insights see Mary Douglas, *Leviticus as Literature* (Oxford: Oxford University Press, 1999), and her "Justice and the Cornerstone: An Interpretation of Leviticus 18–20," *Interpretation* 53 (October 1999): 341–50.

14. See Douglas, *Purity and Danger*, 170.

15. See ibid., 171; also Richard Fardon, *Mary Douglas* (London: Routledge, 1999), 96–99.

16. These models are an updating of those originally published in my book *Refounding the Church: Dissent for Leadership* (Maryknoll, NY: Orbis Books, 1993), 81–97.

17. See Douglas, *Purity and Danger*, 114–28.

and strong grid, such as the army and police, are noted for their formal rules and power, with little tolerance for disobedience. We now examine these four models in more detail.[18]

Strong Group/Strong Grid Cultures

In the strong group/strong grid cultures the boundaries of the group and the way individuals are expected to relate to one another within the boundaries are sharply defined. The modern definition of culture fits this model very well indeed, for the culture it depicts is internally and externally neatly unified and integrated. People are expected to fit into a tradition-based, bureaucratic, hierarchical, and patriarchal system that is presumed to have by right the monopoly over power and knowledge; dependency and conformity are the esteemed qualities. Within the hierarchical system, which is visibly reinforced by symbols of coercive power such as titles and attire, there will be obvious socially graded divisions such as classes and castes with specialized roles and inequitable access to economic and educational resources. To maintain conformity there are detailed, rigid, morally sanctioned rules, and to break them is to risk ritual pollution. The patriarchal hierarchical leaders' task is coercively to maintain the status quo. People feel under constant surveillance, fearing their misbehavior will be reported and punished; they are encouraged to bully those who dare to question and defile the status quo.[19]

If there is a religious mythology there will be a hierarchy of transcendent gods/spirits intimately concerned with the well-being of the culture and its stability. There are intermediary and more approachable spirits helping people to relate to the higher and more remote gods/spirits. The world is maintained in harmony by the gods/spirits who keep the evil forces under control, but people can allow those same powers to enter their lives through sin. Sin is the unconscious or conscious breaking of detailed rules established particularly to maintain the clarity of roles and boundaries within the culture. Sexual sins can be especially evil because if control over the body is broken there is real danger that the social body will be fractured also. There are rituals under the firm direction of officials to remove the pollution resulting from sin and to ward off evil forces endangering the predictability of daily life. Examples of cultures

---

18. For further explanation see Gerald A. Arbuckle, *Violence, Society, and the Church: A Cultural Approach* (Collegeville, MN: Liturgical Press, 2004), 27–28.

19. See Gerald A. Arbuckle, *Confronting the Demon: A Gospel Response to Adult Bullying* (Collegeville, MN: Liturgical Press, 2003), 65–94.

approximating to this model are the Israelites as described in the book of Leviticus, the Soviet Union, the Indian caste system, the pre–Vatican II church, prisons, armed forces, and hospitals.

Strong Group/Weak Grid Cultures

In cultures of this kind people have a sense of belonging to *this* group rather than to another; there is, however, a lack of clarity about *how* individuals are to relate to one another. There is an ideology of egalitarianism, but as the grid is weak there is considerable inner confusion over roles and access to scarce resources within the group. Officials may try coercively to reimpose an internal sense of order, but with little success. People will form together in loose, social, quasi-egalitarian units to compete more effectively for limited resources, but they are forever intensely suspicious of one another, fearing all the time that people will take advantage of them. They blame others for their problems. Suspicions eventually lead to feuding— that is, relations of mutual animosity among intimate groups in which resort to verbal or physical violence is anticipated on both sides.

Mythologically this world has no harmony. It is subject to all kinds of warring forces such as ghosts, evil spirits, and witches; it is a volatile world out of control in which evil forces and spirits aim to crush people indiscriminately. Sin is an evil affecting one's inner self far more than is the case in the previous model, which stressed an external state of pollution as a result of sin. Rituals are of two major types. There are public, coercive rituals of witch-hunting and political show trials against those branded for endangering group identity. The second category of rituals includes those at the grassroots conducted by unofficial sect or cult leaders in response to the people's need for meaning in the midst of fickle and evil forces that forever threaten them. These unofficial ritual leaders need to find the right formula, otherwise their intercessory prayers will be ineffective and they will lose their guru power.

Leland White argues that the evangelist Matthew's community illustrates some characteristics of this type; the members feel they belong to a community of the righteous marked off from the unrighteous. The egalitarian low grid qualities are evident in the dearth of formal power structures and the barring of rank or achievement status within the community.[20] The model can also help to explain traditional church life

---

20. See Leland White, "Grid and Group in Matthew's Community: The Righteousness/Honor Code in the Sermon on the Mount," *Semeia* 35 (1986): 61–89.

in the Philippines, Mexico, and South America. Popular religiosity provides the grid for millions of poor, with its saints and fiestas being a source of identity/security within a world subject to evil and unpredictable forces. Other examples could include the emergence of global Pentecostalism and the rise of religious and political fundamentalism, including restorationism in mainline Christian churches (see chap. 8).

Weak Group/Strong Grid Cultures

In these cultures people are sturdily egalitarian-oriented, individualistic, utilitarian, and competitive, but they have a very weak sense of belonging or of having obligations to the group. People obtain their sense of personal identity from submitting to and interiorizing the clearly stated norms and goals of their society's inner structure. Individuals form alliances with one another to provide better opportunities for competitive successes, but such alliances are very fragile since they are held together only for the self-interest of the individuals themselves.

Sin is just negligence or the making of mistakes through one's own fault in the personal mission to succeed or achieve one's destiny. It is the failure to take advantage of this or that relationship that will guarantee for individuals an economic, social, or political advantage. Power rests with successful business-organizational cultures, especially global, whose CEOs symbolize the secrets of achievement. More and more improved surveillance techniques ensure that workers are forever success-oriented. Morality in this type might be termed "Watergate," that is, "do everything to get ahead, without any concern for the common good, provided one is not found out." Among the high priests in this culture type are management and mass media consultants. Individualism and self-fulfillment are so encouraged, no matter what the costs to the group, that people will turn to any fad/magic such as astrology that offers them the secret of instant success.

Religion in this model will reflect the basic stress on the grid over the group. Since cosmic forces in whatever form do not intrude into people's lives, secularization flourishes; if god(s) or spirits do exist, they are befriended for the benefit of individuals in pursuit of material success. The society has the potential for religious—even business-oriented—millenarian movements, that is, enthusiastic crazes under the direction of charismatic leaders using their personal power to offer quick and "miraculous" shortcuts to the desired goals of the individual. These movements are generally short-term, but when they are at their peak their leaders (for example the radio orator and anti-Roosevelt/New Deal Fr. Charles E. Coughlin of the 1930s)[21] can rival or threaten the authority and power of the officially appointed leaders. Traditional religious rituals are critically assessed according to the utility principle: will they advance my position in society? If they feel right and useful, then let's accept them and see what happens. If success does not come, then turn elsewhere; God and spirits are therefore seen as "enablers in my journey toward success."

Example

Robert Bellah and others in their book *Habits of the Heart* seek to analyze the values of middle-class Americans.[22] One fundamental emphasis emerging in their research is a common acceptance of Lockean-inspired utilitarian individualism and a lack of consensus over values that bind people together for the sake of the group. This consensus deficiency is an extremely weak foundation on which to build a community in which individual rights are balanced by the legitimate requirements of the common good. Their description of American society conforms well to the weak group/strong grid cultural model—for example: vigorous individualism, a philosophy of self-fulfillment, a manipulative use of individuals or organizations to achieve fulfillment, and secularization.

Weak Group/Weak Grid Cultures

A culture that resembles this model is strongly egalitarian in social relationships and in gender, with minimum coercive power pressure from structures within and at the boundaries of the group. Generally communities of this type emerge only under the inspiration of some charismatic leader who denounces the oppressive rigidity of the group/grid traditions or structures of a dominant culture from which escape is sought. Dress codes and rigid rules of conduct based on tradition are considered irrelevant. Far more important is the inner conversion and effective commitment of members to the group's vision/values, resulting

---

21. See Mark S. Massa, *Catholics and American Culture* (New York: Crossroad, 1999), 90.

22. See Robert Bellah and others, *Habits of the Heart: Individualism and Commitment in American Life* (New York: Harper & Row, 1986), 111–24.

in what sociologically are termed intentional communities. There is government by direct democracy or consensus; the group is open to new insights, dialogue, and outsiders. Power is essentially reciprocal.

Personal identity according to this model comes from an awareness of one's self-worth and potential for change, not from a culture's traditional internal and boundary structures. Religion is highly personalized. A personal relationship to gods/spirits and to other people who have the same values as oneself is what counts and thus traditional rituals are unimportant unless they reinforce that sense of relationship or emerge out of the events of daily living, in which case they are very simple in structure. The world of nature and human relationships is inherently good, and if there are problems such as the abuse of the environment they are due to traditional group/grid structures.

Historical examples of this model are: the early Christian community in Jerusalem (see Acts 1:12); prophetic groups like religious congregations in the first stage of founding enthusiasm, for example, St. Francis of Assisi and his early followers and L'Arche communities; countercultural communities or communes through history, such as the commune movement in the late 1960s and the environmental groups of recent times; and religious communities at the authentic refounding stage. If fervor is to be maintained, members must face the challenge of building suitable structures and group identity that do not crush the original enthusiasm.

Theological Reflection

Only those people who assume that the church is a pure spirit can conclude that it does not exist in cultural forms. Theologian Henri de Lubac is right: "Like all human institutions, the Church has her exterior façade, her temporal aspect, often ponderous enough . . . . There is certainly nothing 'nebulous and disembodied' about her—far from it."[23] Given, therefore, that the church has a history and cultural expressions of its own building, the question is: of the above culture models, which one do the gospels call us to approximate to in order to find a new style for presence in a postmodern world?

A culture built on religious, social, and political prestige may have been acceptable in a previous age, and there were plenty of theologians

---

23. Henri de Lubac, *The Splendour of the Church* (London: Sheed & Ward, 1956), 114.

who even used Scripture to support that concept. But no longer. People are looking for Gospel witnesses who primarily use reciprocal power in their ministry.[24] One role of theologians is to be prophetic, that is, to ponder what is happening today in light of the gospel narratives and to reflect back to believers what they see. When some followers of Jesus pondered what he had said and done, they decided to follow him no longer: "This teaching is difficult; who can accept it?" (John 6:60). Truly prophetic theologians may experience the same isolating reaction, but Jesus will still be near and walking with them (Luke 24:15); they "will know the truth, and the truth will make [them] free" (John 8:32).

24. See the reflections by Yves Congar, *Power and Poverty in the Church*, trans. Jennifer Nicholson (London: Geoffrey Chapman, 1964), 135–57.

Chapter 4

Cultures as Stigmatizing Patterns of Social Exclusion

The option for the poor is not just a matter of *giving* to them, but of *receiving* from them.

—Jon Sobrino, *The Eye of the Needle*[1]

Discussions of welfare reform . . . too often fail to address a broader problem: a problem in the way that people who are not poor think about those who are.

—Mark Peel, *The Lowest Rung*[2]

Annually an estimated ten million people die of hunger and hunger-related diseases. Over one billion people must struggle to survive on less than one dollar a day and almost half of the world's children live in poverty. This clearly becomes a powerful breeding ground for armed conflict and terrorism. It is embedded in cultures in which inequalities of class structures, gender, age, and ethnicity foster new and complex types of poverty.[3] Yet these statistics of global poverty can only hint at the extent of the human suffering. Even in affluent countries like the United States there are significant levels of poverty that remain stubbornly persistent. Despite its widespread reality there is little agreement

1. Jon Sobrino, *The Eye of the Needle: No Salvation outside the Poor* (London: Darton, Longman, & Todd, 2008), 49. Italics in original.
2. Mark Peel, *The Lowest Rung: Voices of Australian Poverty* (Cambridge: Cambridge University Press, 2003), 10.
3. See Tim Butler and Paul Watt, *Understanding Social Inequality* (London: Sage, 2007), 116–34.

about how to define, measure, and analyze the connection between cultures and poverty.[4] The purpose of this chapter is to concentrate particularly on the relationship between poverty and cultures. Is it correct to speak of cultures of poverty?

Cultures of Poverty

Debate

It is generally agreed that any definition of poverty must take into account the social, cultural, and historical circumstances of people because any attempt to measure it only in terms of the lack of access to adequate income is too narrow an approach. Oscar Lewis, an American anthropologist, recognized this in the 1960s and argued that there is an identifiable culture of poverty among people who are economically and socially marginalized in a capitalist society. In order to survive they develop patterns of behavior characteristic of a particular culture: low aspirations, political apathy, disorganization, helplessness, and a belittling of what they consider middle-class values. As a consequence people who are poor foster devices that tend to perpetuate poverty, even if structural situations change. Lewis estimated that about twenty million Americans lived within such a culture.[5] Governments and voluntary agencies in these circumstances can do little to help, other than to provide relief food and other supplies. On the positive side his conclusions emphasized the relationship between poverty and people's attitudes and behavior. However, his thesis is correctly criticized because he based his analysis on the now discredited modern definition of culture, namely, that a culture is a unitary and internally coherent set of qualities shaping an *entire* group's behavior. Second, he assumed that cultures are static realities from generation to generation and that individuals can have little or no influence in breaking through the status quo.[6]

---

4. See Pete Alcock, *Understanding Poverty* (Basingstoke: Palgrave Macmillan, 2006), 4.

5. See Oscar Lewis, *The Children of Sanchez* (New York: Random House, 1961), and idem, "The Culture of Poverty," *Scientific American* 215 (October 1966): 19–25.

6. For a critique of Lewis's thesis see Charles A. Valentine, *Culture and Poverty: Critique and Counter-Proposals* (Chicago: University of Chicago Press, 1968); Mario L. Small and Katherine Newman, "Urban Poverty After the Truly Disadvantaged: The

Social exclusion

There are cultures of poverty, but because the term has been misinterpreted by Lewis and others, some academics especially in Europe prefer to use the expression "cultures as stigmatized patterns of social exclusion." People experience social exclusion when, for a variety of factors beyond their control, they are excluded from participating in key economic, political, and social activities in the society in which they exist.[7] The resources available to these people are so inferior to those commanded by the average individual or group that they are effectively excluded from acceptable living conditions and activities. The term "social exclusion" highlights the immaterial or dehumanizing effects of poverty resulting from this exclusion, such as the experience of powerlessness, shame and stigma, violence, denial of rights, diminished citizenship, and loss of self-worth.[8] Such consequences for people who experience social exclusion are patterns of behavior that can form identifiable cultures as understood in the postmodern sense. Ruth Lister, using Foucault's insights into power, terms these patterns the "relational" qualities of poverty to indicate that the wider society dictates who are poor and how they should behave. In particular, the manner in which they are referred to and dealt with by politicians, bureaucrats, the mass media, and other dominant groups powerfully affects the wider society's understanding of, and reactions to, people who are labeled poor.[9] These relational qualities will become clearer with the following explanations.

Describing Poverty

We can use the expression "cultures of poverty," therefore, provided the word "culture" is not used in its modern restricted homogeneous sense. In this discussion we will always bear in mind the dehumanizing qualities emphasized by the term "social exclusion." Because the nature and causes of cultures of poverty are so multifaceted, it will be helpful

---

Rediscovery of the Family, the Neighborhood, and Culture," *Annual Review of Sociology*, 27 (2001): 23–45.

7. See Tania Burchardt, Julian Le Grand, and David Piachaud, "Degrees of Exclusion: Developing a Dynamic, Multidimensional Measure," in *Understanding Social Exclusion*, eds. John Hills, Julian Le Grand and David Piachaud, 30–43 (Oxford: Oxford University Press, 2002).

8. See Butler and Watt, *Social Inequality*, 109.

9. See Ruth Lister, *Poverty* (Cambridge: Polity, 2004), 7, and Nancy Fraser, *Justice Interruptus* (New York: Routledge, 1997), 14.

to consider cultures of poverty under the following interconnected headings:

- poverty as income deprivation
- poverty as capability deprivation
- poverty as socially stigmatizing
- poverty as cultural breakdown
- poverty as a culture of violence

Poverty as Income Deprivation

An obvious quality of poverty is the lack of income. On the basis of income there is a distinction between absolute and relative poverty. *Absolute poverty* is defined by a set income measure below which people experience complete destitution and so cannot meet even *minimum* needs for health, food and shelter. The United States is by far the most unequal in the OECD (Organization for Economic Cooperation and Development) and the proportion of long-term poor is relatively high. It has one of the highest rates of poverty in the industrialized world, despite the fact that it has one of the highest average incomes.[10] In 2006, 36.5 million people, approximately one in eight of the population, in the United States were experiencing absolute poverty. In the same year the poverty rate for minors was the highest in the industrialized world, with 21.9 percent of all minors and 30 percent of African-American minors living below the poverty line.

Relative poverty, on the other hand, refers to the lack of resources needed to obtain the kinds of diet, participation in the activities and enjoyment of the living conditions and services that are widely accepted and generally obtained by most people in a particular society.[11] Those who experience this form of poverty have resources so far below those of others in society that they are effectively excluded from the ordinary living arrangements and activities that are considered socially essential.

---

10. See Jan Pakulski, *Globalising Inequalities: New Patterns of Social Privilege and Disadvantage* (Sydney: Allen and Unwin, 2004), 198-203, and Joel F. Handler and Yeheskel Hasenfeld, *Blame Welfare, Ignore Poverty and Inequality* (Cambridge: Cambridge University Press, 2007), 17–69.

11. John Pierson, *Tackling Social Exclusion* (London: Routledge, 2002), 9.

Statistics in 2002 reveal that approximately one in five Britons live in relative poverty and one in eight in Australia.[12]

Cycles of Poverty

People can become so imprisoned by their low income that it is extremely difficult to break through its crushing circumstances. We speak of a "cycle of poverty," simply because the factors referred to are *interconnected*. A family with a very limited income will commonly experience a poor diet, inadequate housing, restricted access to health and educational facilities, unemployment and underemployment because of a lack of qualifications and reduced energy levels.[13] Structural changes such as employment opportunities and specialized educational services are required for most to break the cycle, but few governments are prepared to be so proactive, at least over a long period. By way of example, in Australia's most populous state, New South Wales, in most disadvantaged and remote schools there are "disproportionate numbers of beginning teachers and [they] experience high rates of teacher turnover."[14] Little wonder that children in these areas are poor school achievers.

Poverty as Capability Deprivation

Amartya Sen, a Nobel laureate in economics, when defining poverty as the "deprivation of opportunities" or simply "capability deprivation," further clarifies the meaning of social exclusion. He believes that economic systems are to be judged successful when people have the capability needed to accomplish critical functionings.[15] These "functionings" may include basic physical needs like being nourished, being sheltered, and breathing fresh air. They may also involve more abstract realities such as possessing self-respect and dignity, sharing in the life of community, and

---

12. See Simon Burgess and Carol Propper, "The Dynamics of Poverty in Britain," in *Social Exclusion*, eds. Hills, Le Grand and Piachaud, op.cit., 44–61.

13. See Gerald A. Arbuckle, *Earthing the Gospel: An Inculturation Handbook for Pastoral Workers* (New York: Orbis Books, 1990), 58.

14. N.S.W. Government, "Building on Strong Foundations," reported in *Sydney Morning Herald* (4 April 2005), 6.

15. See Amartya Sen, "Capability and Well-Being," in *The Quality of Life*, eds. Martha Nussbaum and Amartya Sen (Oxford: Clarendon Press, 1997), 30–53.

being able to appear in public without shame. Everyone has the right to work, to participate in, and to contribute to society, and to grow intellectually, emotionally, and spiritually,[16] but those who are trapped in a circle of poverty have a restricted range of choices available to them.[17]

Pierre Bourdieu's insights into the nature of class in France further enlighten our understanding of capability deprivation.[18] In his view the Marxist thesis that economic inequalities are the foundation of classes is too restricted because symbolic and cultural elements are also significant in defining class structures. For him class depends on how individuals and groups use a variety of resources in their relationships with others. These resources are divided into different types of "capital"; it is the distribution of these types and the power attached to them that provide the foundation for the class structures in society. People without access to these types of capital experience capability deprivation. Classes develop on the basis of three chief types of capital: economic, cultural, and social. Economic capital includes income, wealth, and financial inheritance. Cultural capital[19] includes scarce attributes normally related to education such as knowledge of classical music and of classical literature and art as well as linguistic abilities. This capital is normally passed down from generation to generation and in this sense is difficult to buy or achieve. Social capital embraces the resources that come from social connections or group membership and is mainly acquired and possessed by different classes in different ways. For example, in traditional French working-class communities people often take care of one another's interests by helping to find employment for each other or by exchanging services (e.g., fixing a leaking tap in exchange for mending a punctured car tire). In upper social classes social capital has the same connotation, but it frequently works through arranging such matters as business contacts or looking after the interests of each other's children.

The actual amount of capital is gauged by the sum of economic, cultural, and social capital classes possess, while the makeup of capital is determined by the relative dimensions of the three types of capital.

16. See Mary J. Bane and Lawrence M. Mead, *Lifting Up the Poor: A Dialogue on Religion, Poverty and Welfare Reform* (Washington: Brookings Institute, 2003), 22–23.

17. See Amartya Sen, *Development of Freedom* (New York: Anchor Books, 1999), 87.

18. See Pierre Bourdieu, *Distinction: A Social Critique of the Judgement of Taste* (London: Routledge, 1984).

19. Bourdieu is here using "cultural" in the classicist or normative sense.

People with ample economic capital are well positioned to improve the composition of their overall capital: for example, a suddenly rich financier may spend his or her money to purchase highly valued art. Or, as Bourdieu explains, "the reconversion of economic capital into educational capital is one of the strategies which enable the business bourgeoisie to maintain the position of some or all of its heirs."[20] On the other hand, people who are economically poor have limited opportunities to achieve cultural and social capital.

Bourdieu's term "habitus" further helps to explain why upward mobility for people who are poor can be so difficult. Habitus is the socially formed and interiorized readiness of people to think, perceive, and act in certain ways (see chap. 1). For example, he argues, children of French working-class families are seriously disadvantaged if they try to "break into" the educational systems that are biased in favor of the habitus of the middle class. Middle/upper-class children learn to speak with what Basil Bernstein terms an "elaborated code" in contrast to a working-class "restricted code."[21] In addition, the privileged children are taught at home and school the "correct" mannerisms, values, and types of recreation unique to social classes. Little wonder that working-class children can be made to feel inferior and excluded by middle-class pupils and teachers.

Reflecting on the recreational habitus of different classes in France, Bourdieu in 1984 argued that working-class sports tend to be noticeably physical, even violent, such as boxing and soccer. Middle-class sports, by contrast, are far less physically demanding and rather emphasize the social networking that accompanies them, for example, skiing or golf. He further contends that in these dissimilar class habitus there are different approaches to the human body. The body is viewed by working-class people as an instrument to achieve some external purpose: for example, the person who digs drains must develop strong muscular skills. People belonging to the middle classes, on the other hand, perceive their bodies as the primary focus of shaping for aesthetic and social reasons.[22] From early childhood working-class children are socialized

20. Bourdieu, *Distinction*, 136–37.

21. See Douglas, *Natural Symbols: Explorations in Cosmology* (New York: Pantheon Books, 1970), xiii–xiv.

22. See Pierre Bourdieu, "Sport and Social Class," in *Rethinking Popular Culture*, eds. Michael Schudson and Chandra Mukerji, 357–73 (Berkeley: University of California Press, 1991), and Philip Smith and Alexander Riley, *Cultural Theory: An Introduction* (Oxford: Blackwell, 2001), 264–68.

to view their bodies in ways that reinforce their feeling of social exclusion from middle-class society.

Poverty as Socially Stigmatizing

A *stigma* is a culturally recognized quality that is used by people who hold power to stereotype and discredit others. A particular stigma disqualifies those so marked from full social acceptance. The stigma may be physical (e.g., a bodily deformity), mental, related to age (e.g., elderly), behavioral, or social (e.g., an ethnic group, the unemployed, people of low income). The identification of the stigma is used to reduce the person from a complex whole to a single, tainted, and discounted characteristic upon which all social interaction by the dominant power group with the person will be based.[23]

For example, in Australia poverty is generally seen as the victim's problem and not as a multifaceted cultural issue.[24] As Mark Peel, an authority on Australian poverty, commented in 2003: "Some politicians and public policy-makers [have] even created fictional stories to demonise welfare recipients; in the absence of sufficiently dramatic empirical evidence, fiction does just as well."[25] Likewise in the United States people who are poor, especially if they are single mothers, African-Americans, or Hispanics, are commonly demonized by governments. Poverty is the fault of individuals rather than of the structural realities of society. Welfare only makes people lazier. Therefore, if people are forced into work it is assumed that poverty disappears, when in fact it only increases.[26]

A stigma is a highly subjective issue, both for the stigmatized and for the stigmatizers, affecting the identity of people at the deepest level. Both groups can internalize the scripts that portray some with less-than-humanity and others with full humanity.[27] Shame is a most likely result

---

23. See Erving Goffman, *Stigma: Notes on the Management of Spoiled Identity* (New York: Prentice Hall, 1963).

24. See Alistair Greig, Frank Lewins, and Kevin White, *Inequality in Australia* (Cambridge: Cambridge University Press, 2003), 94.

25. Mark Peel, *The Lowest*, 172.

26. See Handler and Hasenfeld, *Blame Welfare*, 1–16; Pakulski, *Globalising Inequalities*, 157–81.

27. In 1976, in a study of attitudes of senior Maori college students in New Zealand, I found that 73 percent accepted the dominant culture's view of their inferiority by agreeing to the statement that "Maoris have above-average gifts for manual or semi-manual work." Teachers said that when these students of average

when the stigma of poverty is internalized.[28] People feel worthless, of no credibility, second-class citizens, even genetically inferior as human persons. Most of us at some stage experience some of these feelings, but people who are stigmatized by society, such as people who are socioeconomically poor, or those mentally ill, are made to experience these feelings every day of their lives. A sense of fatalism and hopelessness can grip them as their sense of self-worth and self-respect disintegrates. The psalmist describes the inner pain of people who have been socially marginalized because of their poverty: "You have caused my companions to shun me, you have made me a thing of horror to them. I am shut in so that I cannot escape" (Ps 88:8). People can give up trying to cope with the endless stigmatizing pressures of prejudice, poverty, unemployment; human dignity cannot be subjected to endless indignities and remain intact. As one Australian Aboriginal person declared with sadness: "Look at me—I'm colored and I'm dirty, drunken, lazy and irresponsible, like they say—that's my privilege, because I'm Aboriginal—I can do as I like, because that's what they expect of me anyway." Little wonder if at times this sense of hopelessness can be a catalyst for violent outbursts of frustration.

Consumption, Tastes, and Stigmatizing

Zygmunt Bauman, an experienced interpreter of postmodernity, writes that "the poor of a consumer society are socially defined, and self-defined, first and foremost as blemished, defective, faulty and deficient—in other words, inadequate—consumers."[29] Not only is it an issue of what goods they select to purchase but also their quality, for example new or second hand, branded or not, and their source, such as ordinary retailers or informal options like garage sales. In a British study of low-income families and their experience of the stigma attached to having to purchase cheap goods, it was found that "social identities are increasingly being defined by expenditure [and] . . . families can experience social exclusion in simple and painful ways."[30]

---

or above-average ability found their studies hard they would quickly lose confidence in themselves, saying: "What's the use! We Maoris don't have the skills anyway."

28. See Lister, *Poverty*, 117–23.

29. Zygmunt Bauman, *Work, Consumerism and the New Poor* (Buckingham: Open University Press, 1998), 38.

30. Augusta Stephenson, *Work and Welfare: Attitudes, Experiences and Behaviour of Nineteen Low Income Families* (London: Analytical Services Division of the Department of Social Security, 2001), 51.

Herbert Gans writes of "taste cultures" to explain why some groups of people prefer certain kinds of foods and clothing. He explains that taste cultures are "aggregates of similar people making similar choices, and aggregates of similar content chosen by the same people."[31] Individual tastes are to some degree formed by education and economic class. But the most sophisticated theory of taste cultures comes from Bourdieu. When analyzing the processes of demonizing people who are poor he draws attention to the profoundly symbolic power of taste. In his definition of the habitus of a distinctive class he significantly emphasizes the connection between emotions and culture. This habitus is "the system of durable and transposable dispositions through which we perceive, judge and act in the world," and these dispositions incorporate not only "learned thought and attitudes, but also modes of feeling—in other words, dispositions have both cognitive and affective components."[32] Cultural tastes of different classes classify themselves in oppositional terms: "taste is first and foremost the distaste of the tastes of others."[33]

Bourdieu illustrates how class interaction includes the domain of taste; the way that classes categorize themselves on the basis of taste is symbolically fundamental to maintaining class power. Groups with power regard their own tastes and lifestyles as superior, thus, for example, opposing high-priced brand clothing to cheap mass-produced items, golf to bingo. This, he writes, is an exercise of "symbolic violence," that is, a dominant group claims that a specific taste is legitimate while they hide the power dynamics that form the foundation of their strength. Their tastes are pure, while others are impure. This approach by Bourdieu is reminiscent of Douglas's analysis of the symbolic power of "non-dirt" and "dirt" when applied to cultural analysis. When classes define themselves as clean or pure they believe they have authority to control or oppress people whose tastes dare to differ from theirs.[34] Those who do not share the tastes of my class are inferior to me. Bethany Bryson, using Bourdieu's analysis, claimed that in the United States members of the middle class generally value "anything but heavy metal." They have a distaste for the melodic tastes characteristic of groups socially the most distant from them, such

31. See Herbert Gans, *Popular Culture: An Analysis of Evaluation and Taste* (New York: Basic Books, 1974), 582.

32. See Butler and Watt, *Social Inequality*, 173–74.

33. Loic J. D. Wacquant, "Pierre Bourdieu," in *Key Sociological Thinkers,* ed. Rob Stones (Basingstoke: Palgrave, 1998), 223.

34. See Pierre Bourdieu and Jean-Claude Passeron, *Reproduction in Education, Society and Culture* (Beverly Hills: Sage, 1977).

as the poor or working-class people who happen to enjoy heavy metal, and African-Americans, who prefer hip-hop and rap.[35]

Poverty as Cultural Breakdown

A culture provides people with a sense of identity, belonging, and security. Consequently they can be emotionally and psychologically devastated if their culture is dramatically undermined. For example, it is impossible to understand poverty among Indigenous Australians today if we ignore what some describe as a history of cultural genocide, the consequence of racism, lack of understanding, and neglect. They have passed as a people through almost every kind of negative experience short of total extermination.[36] Indigenous peoples in some parts of the world have materially improved their conditions, but, concludes Paul Havemann, their life chances and prospects for survival "as peoples, at present reflect 'nautonomy,' not autonomy."[37] Applying Foucault's notion of power, Havemann calls the barrier to revitalization "nautonomy," which he defines as a powerlessness embedded in the key sites of power, such as the legal, political, and coercive systems of the state, education, and welfare services.

Poverty as a Culture of Violence

Violence is about abusing *people*. It is not confined to physical violence, but it is also the creation of cultural conditions that materially or psychologically destroy or diminish people's dignity, rightful happiness, and capacity to fulfill basic material needs. For this reason we can speak of poverty as a culture of violence. Here are some examples of this violence in the Western world.

35. See Bethany Bryson, "Anything But Heavy Metal: Symbolic Exclusion and Musical Dislikes," *American Sociological Review* 61 (October 1996): 884–99.

36. See Henry Reynolds, "New Frontiers: Australia," in *Indigenous Peoples' Rights in Australia, Canada, and New Zealand*, ed. Paul Havemann, 129–40 (Oxford: Oxford University Press, 1999).

37. Paul Havemann, "Indigenous Peoples, the State and the Challenge of Differentiated Citizenship," in *Indigenous Peoples' Rights*, 470 .

1. Impact of neo-capitalism[38]

Over the last thirty years there has been a revival of nineteenth-century capitalism, the effects of which impact especially people who are poor. It is variously called "neo-capitalism," "neo-liberalism," even "market fundamentalism," because its theoretical foundations could not be questioned until the global economic meltdown beginning in 2008. Its ideological assumptions are: profit is the sole measure of value; greed is good when it fuels economic growth; sustained economic growth is the best way to distribute wealth; free markets, unrestrained by government interference, result in the most efficient use of resources; there need be only minimal concern for the environment; there should be lower taxation for the well-off and reduced government spending, especially for the benefit of people who are poor; trade unions ought to be broken up. Public institutions are to be pseudo-businesses. In the United States most policy makers have long considered healthcare an economic commodity that must be subject to the principles of supply and demand in the marketplace. Even in Australia, which has universal healthcare, health policy makers have gradually shifted their concern from equity and social justice to cost containment and, more recently, to cost-effectiveness.[39]

One common assumption of neo-capitalism is the false Social Darwinist supposition that the best adapted and most successful social groups survive, and have a right to do so, in a world of conflicting qualities. Taken to an extreme this implies that, consequently, the poor are not fit enough to survive.[40] Welfare services only make poverty worse and reduce the incomes of the wealthy. Hence there has been a "rolling back" of social and welfare services,[41] contributing to further inequalities and the emergence of the new "working poor." In the United States welfare reform did lead to a decrease in unemployment for single mothers, but its former

---

38. For a fuller development of the relationship between postmodernity and violence see Gerald A. Arbuckle, *Violence, Society and the Church: A Cultural Approach* (Collegeville, MN: Liturgical Press, 2004), 153–214.

39. See Hal Swerissen and Steve Duckett, "Health Policy and Financing," in *Health Policy in Australia*, ed. Heather Gardner (Melbourne: Oxford University Press, 1997), 33.

40. See John Wright, *The Ethics of Economic Rationalism* (Sydney: University of New South Wales Press, 2003), 123–37.

41. See Peter Saunders, *The Ends and Means of Welfare: Coping with Economic and Social Change in Australia* (Cambridge: Cambridge University Press, 2002), 181–83.

welfare recipients have fallen farther into poverty, earning less than they would have had on welfare.[42] The approximately 60 percent of the general population who are unemployed do not qualify for welfare benefits at all, which is especially tragic in times of economic recession.[43]

2. Normalization of violence

The gambling policies of governments such as those in Australia and the United States are an example of normalizing violence in cultures. Indirect taxation through poker machines falls excessively on people who are poor. A disproportionate share of problem gamblers are also drawn from the lower socioeconomic sections, and the socioeconomically disadvantaged geographical areas are particularly targeted by the companies owning these machines. Since the governments concerned gain financially significant amounts from gambling revenues they are not likely to change their policies radically in favor of people who are poor unless there is public pressure to do so.[44]

3. Affluenza

The ideology of neo-capitalism promotes the belief that higher and higher consumption of material goods will lead to a happier society. This is contributing to the personal and social disease in the Western world called "affluenza," an extreme form of materialism in which consumers overwork and accumulate high levels of debt to purchase more and more goods. This unbalanced pursuit of material goods results in various kinds of personal and social stress, anxieties, addictions, feelings of guilt and shame as people struggle "to keep up with the Joneses." The disease is so rampant that some term it "the all-consuming epidemic."[45] In these

42. See Pakulski, *Globalising Inequalities*, 200; for an overview of the social effects of welfare reform see *The Promise of Welfare Reform: Political Rhetoric and the Reality of Poverty in the Twenty-First Century*, ed. Keither M. Kilty and Elizabeth A. Segal (New York: Howarth, 2006).

43. See *The Economist* (3 January 2009), 26–27.

44. In 2002 approximately 13 percent of the total Victorian State Government (Australia) income came from poker machines. See www.salvationarmy.org.au/media/2002/02/02424.

45. See John de Graff, David Wann, and Thomas H. Naylor, *Affluenza: The All-Consuming Epidemic* (San Francisco: Berrett-Koehler, 2005), and Clive Hamilton and Richard Denniss, *Affluenza: When Too Much is Never Enough* (Sydney: Allen & Unwin, 2005).

circumstances we can expect little concern for people who are genuinely poor or for the care of the environment.

4. Not listening

Thinking about justice and how to achieve it begins by first listening to people who experience injustice.[46] Only in very recent times have researchers and government policy makers begun to include in their studies of the causes and relief of poverty the personal views and expertise of people who are poor. They were thought to have nothing to offer. On two occasions while researching on remote islands south of New Zealand I was marooned without food and shelter and each time I was instantly befriended by families. Despite their extreme poverty they cared for me for several days, asking nothing in return. For decades newspaper reporters and government officials had demonized the islanders as lazy and unintelligent, yet how wrong they were! Despite their extremely limited resources I found them caring and creative. If officials had listened to them with respect they would have discovered the real causes of their poverty and the way they could have moved forward in collaborative fashion.

Theological Reflection

The Scriptures, which are not against wealth as such but are opposed to the acquisitiveness and greed that are valued as "virtues" in neo-capitalist economics, call us, even in the rich Western world, to view all our actions through the lens of a "preferential option for the poor." There must be a willingness, while maintaining good stewardship, to risk not just our surplus, but even our capital resources in the service of people who are poor. Finally, we are called to listen to and to learn from people who are disadvantaged; Jesus Christ has a special love of people who are poor because, like him, they are powerless and rejected.[47] Theologians who fail to respond to these foundational faith imperatives can scarcely become authentic interpreters of the Scriptures.

---

46. For excellent examples of how this can be done see Anthony J. Gittins, *Where There's Hope There's Life: Women's Stories of Homelessness and Survival* (Liguori, MO: Liguori/Triumph, 2006), and Peel, *The Lowest*.

47. See Gerald A. Arbuckle, *A "Preferential Option for the Poor": Application to Catholic Health and Aged Care Ministries in Australia* (Canberra: Catholic Health Australia, 2008), 19–59.

Chapter 5

Chapter 5

Cultures as Narratives Negotiating Identities

> Now it is myth as narration that puts the present experience . . . into relation with the totality of meaning.
>
> —Paul Ricoeur, *The Symbolism of Evil*[1]

> At any given time . . . we are not just negotiating our localities or positions *vis-à-vis* race, class, gender, and nationality, but also positionalities within a geopolitical system.
>
> —Eduardo Mendieta, "Identities: Postcolonial and Global"[2]

One day a group of villagers in Fiji wanted to explain to me what membership in a credit union meant for them. Instead of a speech they sang a lengthy ballad (called *meke*), accompanying it with actions. They began by describing the coming of the missionaries and the discovery that Jesus Christ has saved them. Then they sang about how Christ saves them today through the arrival of a credit union in their village, for they have now learned to save money, avoid debt, and spend wisely. This simple incident illustrates the important distinction between myths, as explained in chapter 2, and narratives, which are the subject of this chapter. It also highlights one of the most important functions of storytelling, namely, its ability to bring some theoretical concept down to earth so that it can be grasped at several levels, by the heart as well as intellectually.

1. Paul Ricoeur, *The Symbolism of Evil* (Boston: Beacon Press, 1967), 171.
2. Eduardo Mendieta, "Identities: Postcolonial and Global," in *Identities: Race, Class, Gender, and Nationality*, ed. Linda Martin Alcoff and Eduardo Mendieta (Oxford: Blackwell, 2003), 409.

Myths and Narratives

Myths are the stories that make our lives intelligible in the *past*, but the retelling of these stories in light of *present* needs is what we call narrative. In narratives, myths from the past are applied to what concerns people today, and in the process the myths are enlarged, altered, or even discarded. As with myths, narratives are at the heart of cultures. For the Fijian villagers the coming of salvation through Christ is the myth, but its application to their particular experience of credit union is the narrative.

Every narrative has a plot or purpose that shapes its structure. That is, not only must a narrative be more than one thing following another, but some form of meaningful connection between events is necessary. The connection is provided by the plot of the narrative and the raconteur chooses how to do this, depending on the audience.[3] The plot is the vehicle whereby the overall purpose of the narrative is achieved. As Paul Ricoeur writes: "By plot I mean the intelligible whole that governs a succession of events in any story. . . . A story is made out of events to the extent that plot makes events into a story."[4] The plot in the villagers' narrative of the founding of their credit union was the mixture of song and action.

Narratives are:
• about creating identity in the here and now, all the while drawing on myths of the past;   • stories that recount in a variety of ways, such as images, music, gestures, but particularly language, a series of temporal events so that a meaningful succession is depicted, which is the plot;   • everywhere, to be found in all forms of human communication, so much so that human beings can be called "narrating animals."

Thus narratives are stories that are able to provide people with a sense of order, identity, and meaning within and beyond time. They are innately interesting because they entertain, enlighten, engage, provoke, validate, and reflect existence at the same time. The narrator is in control, so listeners are compelled to see reality from a different perspective, even if they do not agree with it. Even music, with its ability to evoke

---

3. See Anthony Kerby, *Narrative and Self* (Bloomington: Indiana University Press, 1991), 39.

4. Paul Ricoeur, "Narrative Time," *Critical Inquiry* 7 (January 1980): 171.

meaning and emotions in ways no words or pictures are able to do, can be a narrative in which the composer creates the plot through particular musical arrangements. Consider how Frederic Chopin imbues the musical plot of his "Military Polonaise in A" with his own nostalgic nationalistic feeling. The purpose of this chapter is to explain the links between identities and narratives, but we must first describe why narratives are particularly important in postmodernity.

Postmodern Identities

- One symptom of this postmodern age is the dramatic breakdown globally and locally of traditional identities and boundaries. The quickening movement of people, goods, and information has encouraged widespread anxieties. Unease over identity is nourishing ambivalent attitudes toward ethnic mixing, immigration, international investment, and supranational organizations. There is an increasing search by nations, minority groups, institutions, business firms, and individuals to redefine their identities in order to clarify what makes them unique in the global scene.[5] More and more people are asserting their difference or uniqueness. Thus when Greenland, despite its tiny population of fifty-six thousand and very limited income resources, voted in 2008 to loosen its ties with Denmark, the premier commented that at last Greenlanders could tell their own story to the world.[6] In the United States, Native Americans clamor to reaffirm the identity they fear is being lost, African-Americans hunt for their African origins, and white Americans revive the cookery and clothing styles that characterized their ancestors. Young people create languages, gestures, music, and clothing styles to distinguish themselves from older generations.
- Rarely is the search for identity without controversy. Sometimes it is violent, fueled by a fundamentalist escapism. Suicide bombers testify in ways we never expected to the power of identity and meaning in human lives. Disconnected in their storied worlds from wider significance, people become anxious, angry, even deadly. Most often the search for identity is peaceful, but it is always a painful and uncertain journey.

---

5. See Linda Martin Alcoff, "Identities: Modern and Postmodern," in *Identities*, eds. Alcoff and Mendieta, 1–8.

6. See *The Economist* (17 March 2007): 64–65.

Reflexive Identities

There is still the popular modern view, a further relic of Enlightenment thinking, that the self is an autonomous, stable, structural entity composed of factors and traits that "add up" to a total person without their active involvement and transcending their particular place in culture, language, and history.[7] However, it is increasingly obvious in this postmodern world that identity is a process of "self-engaging-with-context."[8] Take myself. My Australian passport defines me as born in New Zealand on a certain date, but there is more to my identity than this general statement. My specific identities are constantly changing, depending on the context. In certain contexts I am a religious, in others I am a priest, at times I am a New Zealander, at other times I am a patriotic Australian, at others I am an anthropologist, a lecturer. Individual identity is less and less a question of conforming to definite, set roles, and more and more an issue of trying to make sense of who I am through monitoring my own actions depending on the ever-changing context in which I find myself. It involves at times a complicated process of decision making in face of manifold social situations. It is as though I am constantly telling stories to myself to remind me of my identity at a particular time and in the particular context I happen to be in. Sociologist Anthony Giddens refers to this process as the "reflexive self," that is, a process whereby "self-identity is constituted by the reflexive ordering of self-narratives,"[9] a point to be further explained later in this chapter.

In summary, who we are is primarily to be found in the way we live day by day within a particular cultural context or environment, not just in what we think or say about ourselves. Identity is always a process of "being" or "becoming," never a final and settled issue. In fact, each individual or group of people occupies multiple and sometimes even contradictory identities, which interact and give the individual or group different options for action. It is an increasingly complicated and contentious process because relationships and power must be forever negotiated, owing to the ever-increasing speed of change both locally and

---

7. See Frank Johnson, "The Western Concept of Self," in *Culture and Self: Asian and Western Perspectives,* ed. Anthony J. Marsella, George Devos, and Francis L. Hsu, 91–138 (New York: Tavistock, 1985).

8. Thomas K. Fitzgerald, *Metaphors of Identity: A Culture-Communication Dialogue* (New York: SUNY Press, 1993), ix.

9. Anthony Giddens, *Modernity and Self-Identity: Self and Society in the Late Modern Age* (Cambridge: Polity, 1991), 244.

globally. For example, in a study of Northern Ireland Protestant and Catholic communities in the midst of conflict it was found that individuals are constantly having to negotiate definitions of themselves and other people during day-to-day interactions and storytelling.[10]

Cultural and Personal Identities

As for the individual, so for cultures. Until recent times social sciences interpreted collective identities also as relatively stable categories, related to such social groupings as class, ethnicity, gender, nationality, or race. It was assumed that each culture has a unique, unchanging, well-rounded identity or essence that transcends all changes and is independent of the wider context, and all individuals share cultural identity equally. However, as we have seen, this is not the case. In postmodernity, so far from being eternally set in some essentialized past, identities—whether cultural or individual—are subject to the ongoing interplay of history, culture, and power.[11] Cultures have been intermixing from time immemorial. Every culture is an ongoing hybrid creation. There is no such thing as a "pure identity" abstracted from social relations and history.[12]

Interconnecting Personal and Cultural Identities

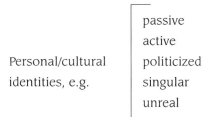

Personal/cultural
identities, e.g.

passive
active
politicized
singular
unreal

Figure 5.1

10. See Anthony D. Buckley and Mary C. Kenney, *Negotiating Identity: Rhetoric, Metaphor, and Social Drama in Northern Ireland* (Washington: Smithsonian Institution Press, 1995).

11. See Stuart Hall, "Cultural Identity and Diaspora," in *Identity,* ed. James Rutherford (London: Lawrence and Wishart, 1990), 225.

12. See Anselm Strauss, *Mirrors and Masks: The Search for Identity* (London: Martin Robertson, 1977), 164.

People have multiple identities (see Figure 5.1), but which one is chosen will depend largely on the particular cultural situation the person happens to be in. Harriet Bradley detects three types of cultural identity: passive, active, and politicized.[13] "Passive identities" are potential identities inasmuch as they originate from a series of relationships such as class, gender, ethnicity, but they are not at the moment being acted on. People are generally unaware of their passive identities unless a situation emerges in which they need consciously to define themselves according to particular relationships. For example, when I lecture in the United States I am not conscious of the fact that I have an Australian passport, unless of course I am at the immigration section at the Los Angeles airport. "Active identities" are those that individuals are consciously aware of, even though they may not continually use these identities. These identities can operate as a self-defense reaction or because people are being defined in a negative way through an experience of discrimination. For example, once in Belfast I was refused a taxicab ride because I am a Catholic priest. Women realize the importance of gender when they suffer discrimination simply because they are women. "Politicized identities," on the other hand, refer to situations in which individuals *constantly* regard themselves in terms of a particular identity. For example, the feminist movement has persuaded many women to assume a politicized female identity.

Finally, there are two particularly negative types of identity, namely, "identity disregard" or "unreal identity," and "singular affiliation."[14] "Identity disregard," popular with many economic theorists, assumes that people are totally unaffected by what is happening around them, but with one exception; they are narcissistic and single-minded in the pursuit of personal economic gain. Often they are referred to as "the economic man [*sic*]" or "the rational agent," a fantasy of the authors' imaginations. "Singular affiliation" is when individuals choose, or have imposed on them, one identity to the exclusion of any other and this can lead to dangerous forms of religious or political fundamentalism. For example, white supremacists in the United States, who destroy property and kill, claim this is lawful because God is calling them to keep their country "pure Anglo-Saxon."[15]

---

13. See Harriet Bradley, *Fractured Identities: Changing Patterns of Inequality* (Cambridge: Polity, 1996), 25–26.

14. See Amartya Sen, *Identity and Violence: The Illusion of Destiny* (London: Penguin, 2006), 19–29.

15. See Gerald A. Arbuckle, *Violence, Society and the Church: A Cultural Approach* (Collegeville, MN: Liturgical Press, 2004), 197–99.

The Clash of Civilizations

In 1996 Samuel Huntington, a Harvard political scientist, published his controversial book *The Clash of Civilizations*,[16] in which he argues that we have reached a phase in history, following the end of the Cold War, when the clash of ideologies has ended. In his view cultural identity will become more important in determining friendships within and conflicts between "civilizations." With the decline in the influence of Western nations the world will be dominated by six "civilizations": the West, Islam, a Confucian bloc, a Hindu bloc, Latin America, and eastern Orthodox Christianity. The "central focus of conflict for the immediate future will be between the West and several Islamic-Confucian states."[17]

For Huntington civilizations represent distinct cultural groupings of people, but this is where the author's thinking is seriously in error. His adoption of the discredited modern definition of culture—that cultures are rigidly discrete, homogeneous structures—undermines his thesis. For example, he wrongly assumes that everyone in Islamic countries shares the same values. It is true that religious and ethnic fundamentalism is on the rise, but there is little evidence that conflict is increasingly between blocs of "civilizations." For example, there are serious conflicts between Russia, Ukraine, and Georgia, which happen to belong to the same "civilization" according to Huntington's thesis. "Islam," according to the author, is monolithic, despite the fact that it consists of factions that are more hostile than mutually friendly. He overlooks the reality that the Chinese business elite are much more interested in the technical skills of Silicon Valley in California than in their Confucian past.

In summary, Huntington's theory is fundamentally naïve and potentially dangerous because it is built on a faulty understanding of culture.[18] Cultures are considered to have inflexible structures that determine the shape of his arguments. Supposedly homogeneous, consistent cultural profiles are played off against each other.[19] His thesis is a deliberate, demagogic combination of security interests and an unscholarly statement of civilizational (cultural) differences. As anthropologist Jan Pieterse

---

16. See Samuel P. Huntington, *The Clash of Civilizations and the Remaking of World Order* (New York: Simon and Schuster, 1996).

17. Samuel P. Huntington, "The Clash of Civilizations," *Foreign Affairs* 72 (1993): 48.

18. See *The Economist* (3 January 2009), 29.

19. See the critique by Dieter Senghass, *The Clash Within Civilizations: Coming to Terms with Cultural Conflicts* (London: Routledge, 1998), 1 and *passim*.

concludes, "it merges two existing enemy discourses, the 'fundamentalist threat' of Islam and the 'yellow peril,' and its novelty lies in combining them."[20] It is a perilous mix.

Identities Through Narratives

Given that contemporary identities are increasingly fragmented, blurred, and unstable, the key question is: how are people at the personal, group, and cultural levels to attain reassuring identities? Identities are clarified in one of two ways, didactically or experientially. When the didactic approach is used people are told who they are; this is the "mug" and "jug" approach in which learning occurs almost entirely at the intellectual level. The recipient of a preset identity is like an empty mug waiting to receive information poured into her or him from the source of knowledge, the jug. This is a passive method of learning in which people are not required to examine their own emotional response to identities handed down from above.

On the other hand, in the experiential approach people negotiate for themselves and others who they are and who they are not. Through storytelling, individuals write and rewrite the story of their selves and the many worlds in which they live. In describing this process, which is especially important in postmodernity, Giddens comments that "the narrative of self has in fact to be continually re-worked, and lifestyle practices brought into line with it," and in consequence "life-style choices are constitutive of the reflexive narrative of self."[21] Individuals are constantly reflecting through storytelling on their experiences in order to define their changing identities and create a sense of personal stability. As individuals construct stories from experience, so also do groups of all kinds: business organizations, communities, governments, and nations assemble preferred narratives that feelingly tell them who they are at this moment in time, where they come from, what is good or bad, and how they are to organize themselves and maintain their sense of unique identity in a changing world. There is a complex relationship between narrative, time, and memory, for we amend and edit the remembered past to fit with our identities and context at the present moment. For

---

20. Jan N. Pieterse, *Globalization and Culture* (Lanham, MD: Rowman & Littlefield, 2004), 43–44.

21. Anthony Giddens, *The Transformation of Intimacy: Sexuality, Love and Eroticism in Modern Societies* (Cambridge: Polity, 1992), 75.

example, when I talked to my aging mother about the thrills of flying in small one-engine planes in mountainous Papua New Guinea I definitely did not tell her about the dangerous nature of these flights. I prudently did a little editing!

"Metanarratives" and Identities

Jean-François Lyotard describes as grand narratives, or "metanarratives," theories that claim to give all-embracing explanations and draw on the authority this gives them. The grand narratives of the last two centuries, such as Marxism and capitalism, are no longer important because they have failed to achieve their visions.[22] In place of grand metanarratives there are "little narratives" celebrating variety and differences and making no claim to universal knowledge. Individuals and especially minority groups must be given space to tell their own different stories and we must concentrate, says Lyotard, on these little narratives as a way to stand up against the authoritarianism of grand narratives.

His claim that grand narratives have ceased to be important is somewhat discredited since we can observe the dramatic development of new grand theories such as religious fundamentalism and even market fundamentalism. However, Lyotard is right to the extent that there continues to be a dramatic rise in new small narratives such as an increase in ethnic consciousness and the ongoing vitality of traditional cultures. The speed of globalization and the questioning of Enlightenment assumptions of superiority have encouraged new ways of thinking about the human person and society. As Charles Lemert writes: "the destabilizing of the modern world is associated with a curious, but undeniable, energizing of identity as the topic of widespread political interest."[23]

---

22. See Jean-François Lyotard, *The Postmodern Condition*, trans. Geoff Bennington and Brian Massumi (Manchester: Manchester University Press, 1986).
23. Charles Lemert, *Postmodernism Is Not What You Think* (Oxford: Blackwell, 1997), 128.

Cultural Narratives

Discourse we tolerate; to story we attend.

—Klyne R. Snodgrass, *Stories With Intent* [24]

As has been explained, myth and narrative are two sides of the one coin. Narrative is the actual recounting of the myth, but within changing times and in the process of retelling the myth itself is altered or modified according to the circumstances of time and place. The following examples of different types of narratives within cultures will illustrate these points.

Narrative Types

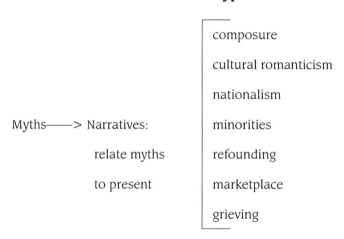

Myths——> Narratives:

  relate myths

  to present

composure

cultural romanticism

nationalism

minorities

refounding

marketplace

grieving

Figure 5.2

Narratives of Composure

Alistair Thomson concludes that "composure" is a suitable word to define a process whereby people through narratives try to accomplish a

24. Klyne R. Snodgrass, *Stories With Intent: A Comprehensive Guide to the Parables of Jesus* (Grand Rapids: Eerdmans, 2008), 1.

feeling of composure or peace about their past.[25] In 1915 Australian and New Zealand soldiers (subsequently called by the acronym "Anzac") suffered on the beaches of Gallipoli, in the Dardanelles, a crushing defeat at the hands of Turkish forces, due in no small part to the incompetence of British generals and politicians. Some ten thousand troops were killed and thousands wounded. Yet the public narratives of this event overlook these painful and tragic facts to emphasize instead the positive experiences of comradeship among the troops, their natural intelligence, endurance, personal bravery, and even the birth of the Australian national identity.[26] This is an image of the past that people can comfortably live with. Another example of narrative composure occurred recently in Japan. A competition was launched for the best essay to deny Japan's wartime role as an aggressor and sponsor of atrocities, and it was won by the then head of Japan's air force. In his revisionist narrative he writes that Japan fought a war of self-defense. Pearl Harbor was an American-laid trap. The author ironically ends his essay with the words: "for a country that denies its own history is destined to fall."[27]

Narratives of Cultural Romanticism

The term "traditional culture" is commonly used with respect by many indigenous peoples to refer to their cultures before colonization. However, the term is increasingly understood in postmodern anthropology as an invention constructed for contemporary purposes rather than a stable, objectively based narrative handed on from the past. To illustrate this point, anthropologist Allan Hanson focuses on the development of "traditional culture" among the indigenous people of New Zealand, the Maori.[28] The Maori have been reduced to second-class citizenship since the coming of British settlers in the 1840s. Resentment against this social and economic marginalization and a desire to be acknowledged as the original owners of the land have given rise to a narrative called *Maoritanga* (Maoriness). In this narrative New Zealand's white majority is negatively pictured as ruthlessly rational, individualistic, greedy, passionless, and mechanical.

25. See Alistair Thomson, *Anzac Memories: Living With the Legend* (Melbourne: Oxford University Press, 1995).

26. See Bruce Kapferer, *Legends of People—Myths of State* (Washington, DC: Smithsonian Institution Press, 1988), 121–47.

27. See *The Economist* (8 November 2008): 41.

28. See Allan Hanson, "The Making of the Maori: Culture Invention and its Logic," *American Anthropologist* 91 (1989): 890–902.

On the other hand, *Maoritanga* is positively presented as emotional, concerned for others, family-oriented, passionate, deeply spiritual, united with the land, and natural. The negative qualities of Maori life before and after colonization are ignored in this culturally romantic narrative. Anthropologist Roger Keesing writes of the romanticism involved: "Maori and Aboriginal Australian ideologues are engaged in reconstructing ancestral pasts characterized by Mystical Wisdom, Oneness with the Land, Ecological Reverence, and Social Harmony."[29] He then describes the way warfare and violence, including Maori cannibalism, are carefully edited out of this rewritten history. Violence against women, commoners, and slaves, along with cannibalism, were to be found in all parts of New Zealand. But new narratives, whether objectively true or not, aim to offer the Maori a romanticized alternative view of history that they can affirm as authentically their own. A similar narrative of nationalistic composure is to be found among indigenous Hawaiians. This narrative pictures pre-European life as "egalitarian, pious, and generous, ignoring historical evidence of hierarchy, oppression, and cruelty."[30]

Narratives of Nationalism

Sometimes individuals such as politicians seek to impose narratives of identities on people, selectively manipulating history for their purposes. What we believe to be traditions passed from generation to generation through the mists of time may actually have been deliberately invented by politically motivated people fewer than two hundred years ago. It is thought, for example, that Scottish people have all worn kilts and played bagpipes from time immemorial. But my lowland ancestors certainly did not, because it was all a political invention for nationalistic purposes in the early nineteenth century.

New nationalistic narratives can rapidly receive widespread support. Nazism is an example of "politicized identity," as earlier described, inasmuch as this cult demanded total allegiance from its followers. The Nazis, provoked by resentment of Germany's failure and humiliation after World War I, developed a narrative of the "pure German," untainted by the blood of "impure peoples" such as Jews, gypsies, homosexuals, intellectually handicapped, or black people.

29. Roger Keesing, "Creating the Past: Custom and Identity in the Contemporary Pacific," *The Contemporary Pacific* 1 (1989): 19; see also Roger Sandall, *The Culture Cult: Designer Tribalism and Other Essays* (Oxford: Westview Press, 2001), 3–17.

30. Charles Lindholm, *Culture and Authenticity* (Oxford: Blackwell, 2008), 132.

Less dramatic nationalistic narratives are common in today's post-modern world of confused identities. For example, the rise of a right-wing political party in Australia in the 1990s sought to redefine Australian identity fundamentally in terms of white Australian immigrants and their descendants, thus ignoring and denigrating Indigenous Australians and Asian immigrants. Similar efforts to redefine "Britishness" through narratives continue in the United Kingdom due to such factors as increased immigration from Islamic countries and levels of political devolution in Wales and Scotland.[31] In 1987 the Minister of Education proposed as a matter of urgency that a national curriculum be introduced in British schools to guarantee the continuation of an authentic British narrative and national identity. He stated: "There is so much distraction, variety and uncertainty . . . that in our country today our children are in danger of losing any sense at all of a common culture and a common heritage." He ends with this statement: "The cohesive role of the national curriculum will provide our society with a greater sense of identity."[32] At first sight these comments look logical and innocent, but the proposed national curriculum reflected an imperialist concept of a static Anglo-Saxon culture that had ceased to exist. The reality is that through immigration the ethnic mixture is significantly diversifying. Any curriculum must mirror this. Moreover, the qualities of the former imperial Britain were very much the construct of an upper-class system from which especially the working class was excluded. Contemporary "Britishness" is not something to be defined by one class or ethnic group.

Narratives of Minorities

Two examples illustrate the significance of narratives of minorities. In his speech in Chicago marking his success at the elections Barack Obama acknowledged that American voters had negotiated a new narrative of identity because they had elected the first African-American as president: "It's been a long time coming, but tonight, because of what we did on this day, in this election, at this defining moment change has come to America."[33]

Notting Hill, a London suburb, has the biggest annual urban street carnival in Britain, attracting around a million spectators of various

---

31. See *The Economist* (14 January 2007), 48–49.
32. Kenneth Baker, in *The Times Literary Supplement* (25 September 1987): 5.
33. Barack Obama, cited in *The Sydney Morning Herald* (6 November 2008): 1.

backgrounds, where the performers are mostly low-income African-Caribbean people from the West Indies. They are immigrants who came to Britain in the 1950s and 1960s and their descendants. At first the immigrants settled in Notting Hill, then a poor section of London, where they had to struggle against significant racial discrimination, even experiencing the violence of race riots. Over time they were forced to move elsewhere as the suburb became increasingly transformed into a high-income residential area. However, in the face of continued local opposition, they return annually to the streets of Notting Hill to experience "active identity," as described earlier in this chapter. In brilliantly colored masquerade parades and mas bands the participants use narrative themes such as Africa and the abolition of slavery. Africa before slavery is most frequently chosen because it is the imaginary homeland of West Indians. The plot in the narrative is the need to negotiate an identity in a hostile milieu; participants take an original myth about African origins and history and rewrite it to suit the contemporary scene. The carnival is thus a celebratory narrative of West Indian belonging and identity in the midst of a racially discriminatory atmosphere.[34]

Narratives of Refounding

Paul Ricoeur writes that narratives can evoke the revitalization of the moral imagination of people because of their singular power to revision reality. This is because narrative allows people to "try new ideas, new values, new ways of being-in-the-world."[35] The reader's world is suddenly questioned by the narrative. New and imaginative possibilities of being and acting are presented to them. What is found in the story's plot has the radical ability to "disturb and rearrange"[36] the reader's own relation to life. Listeners or readers are drawn into the raconteur's experiences; they are invited to enter the narrator's perspective on life and to participate in profound individual and cultural changes.

---

34. See Kimura Yoko, "The Notting Hill Carnival in London: A Study on Masbands, Masquerading Groups of an Urban Festival," *Japanese Review of Cultural Anthropology* 7 (2006): 85–96.

35. Paul Ricoeur, "The Function of Fiction in Shaping Reality," in *Man and World* 12 (1970): 134.

36. Paul Ricoeur, "On Interpretation," in *From Text to Action: Essays in Hermeneutics, II*, eds. Kathleen Blamey and John B. Thompson (Evanston, IL: Northwestern University Press, 1991), 6.

This describes the narrative of refounding, the process whereby people relive the founding mythology of a group and are so inspired by the experience that they imaginatively and creatively search for ways to relate it to contemporary life. When Blessed Mother Teresa told of her care of dying individuals she would return to the founding mythology of her faith, a story of Christ's compassion for people on the margins of society. This motivated her to change her own life. Many observers were so disturbed by her stories that they also felt impelled to alter their own lives and challenge society's neglect of disadvantaged people.

In his presidential inaugural speech Barack Obama reminds Americans of their founding mythology, in which God calls them to participate in a new Exodus, a new journey from the chaos of poverty and oppression to a land of promise. The nation is again in chaos, so Obama invites Americans to re-own this mythology and join him in the narrative of refounding the nation with the courage, imagination, and creativity of the original founders: " Our Founding Fathers, faced with perils drafted a charter . . . . Those ideals still light the world. . . . Starting today, we must pick ourselves up, dust ourselves off, and begin again the work of remaking America. . . ."

Narratives of the Marketplace

Successful narrative depends on the ability of storytellers to lead listeners gradually from what they already know and understand to new insights. This is evident in any flourishing advertising campaign in the American business world. The distrust of political dogma and/or any form of abusive power is integral to the founding mythology of the United States, so people who challenge such behavior become popular national heroes and heroines. These rebels venture out alone into the threatening world where they do battle against evil, articulate the problems ordinary folk experience in society, and quickly resolve them. Shrewd advertisers of products build on this mythology and focus on what the brand represents, not how the brand performs. Hence, in the 1990s advertisements for the Apple computer company emphasized the fact that its founders had rebelled against traditional computer systems, advertisements for Harley Davidson motor bikes stressed their links with outlaw bikers, Nike their connections with the African-American ghetto through rebel athlete Michael Jordan.[37]

37. See Douglas B. Holt, "What Becomes an Icon Most?" *Harvard Business Review* 81, no. 3 (March 2003): 43–48.

Identification with this rebellious quality in the American story is constantly exploited by the film industry with its fictional narratives building on the nation's founding mythology. In the Western film genre, as in *Shane* (1953) or *Cat Ballou* (1965), the central character is a strong, self-contained individual unknown to or not fully accepted by society, who has exceptional abilities that are used to defend the powerless against the evil actions of the villain. The once-rejecting society finally accepts the savior. American audiences identify with this type of person, otherwise the Western would not be so enduringly popular. But the narrative must be constantly updated. The plot remains the same, that of "the truly American hero," but the John Wayne of the traditional Westerns is succeeded by the Rambo movies of Sylvester Stallone. The vigorously individualistic, macho, physically strong, thoroughly self-contained and silent person, the "truly American hero," is center stage once more, destroying villains with modern firepower, using helicopters rather than horses, restoring the morale of the American people, and prepared to return at any time when needed to uphold the American way of life.[38] Rambo is succeeded by the high-tech Terminator movies with Arnold Schwarzenegger as the hero. The Batman movies, based on American founding mythology, are also regularly updated in order to maintain their relevance to audiences.

Narratives of Grieving

Narratives of grieving remain an essential precondition for the successful renewal of identity. Grieving is a process whereby loss is formally acknowledged and allowed to slip into the past, after which the future can be confronted with all its uncertainties, fears, and hopes. Frequently, however, groups that have been culturally marginalized experience significant unarticulated grief, that is, the accumulated sadness, fatalism, anger, and loss of identity resulting from their ongoing humiliation and rejection. Where grief is kept hidden and unprocessed in a community we can be sure that hopelessness will be a consequence. There is no energy for constructive change. Grief remains like a powder keg waiting to be ignited into all kinds of individual and community-destroying behavior. Ovid, the first-century Roman poet, well described the reality of unnamed grief: "Suppressed grief suffocates."[39]

---

38. See Gerald A. Arbuckle, *Earthing the Gospel: An Inculturation Handbook for Pastoral Workers* (Maryknoll, NY: Orbis Books, 1990), 39–41.

39. Ovid, *Tristia,* Book V, eleg. 1, 63.

The voices of many indigenous people calling for political and cultural reconciliation are a poignant example of narratives of grieving. The museums around the world that honor the victims of the Holocaust contain narratives of grieving. In both Old and New Testaments we see many examples of people who, once they began to recount the story of their grief, were able to discover new hope and new visions of society. For example, in the lament psalms the twofold dynamic of grieving is forcefully expressed, namely, the public declaration before God of loss with its crushing sadness and then the energizing identification of what is surprisingly new and hopeful in the experience of individuals or the nation, however faint this might be.[40] The public proclamation of grief can, however, be silenced either because people are too crushed to recount their sadness or because oppressive political powers fear that the public narratives of grief will threaten their own stability. Tyrannical governments particularly fear the public display of grief at funerals of their victims, for it is there that the narratives of sadness can energize people to further resist tyranny. For this reason public funerals of dissidents may be forbidden, as is the case in contemporary China.[41] Even in democracies governments can fear the public display of grieving. Such was the case in the United States under the Bush administration when the American people were forbidden to see on television the return of the coffins of soldiers killed in Iraq.

Theological Reflection

David Tracy defines theology as "the discipline that articulates mutually critical correlations between the meaning and truth of an interpretation of the Christian fact and the meaning and truth of an interpretation of the contemporary situation."[42] If theologians are not able to help people

40. For an understanding of the significant relationship between ritual and cultural change see Gerald A. Arbuckle, *Grieving for Change* (Sydney: St Pauls Publications, 1991); idem, *Refounding the Church: Dissent for Leadership* (Maryknoll, NY: Orbis Books, 1993), 180–200; and idem, *Healthcare Ministry: Refounding the Mission in Tumultuous Times* (Collegeville, MN: Liturgical Press, 2000), 271–341.

41. See Walter Brueggemann, *Hope Within History* (Atlanta: John Knox Press, 1987), 72–91.

42. David Tracy, "The Foundations of Practical Theology," in *Practical Theology*, ed. Don S. Browning (San Francisco: Harper & Row, 1983), 62; for an overview of Tracy's understanding of theology and correlation see his article, "The Uneasy Alliance Reconceived: Catholic Theological Method, Modernity, and Postmodernity," *Theological Studies* 50 (1989): 548–70.

relate the Christian fact to contemporary realities they end up talking only to themselves. This chapter reminds theologians that the most powerful method of relating mythologies to daily life is through storytelling in its many forms. The Scriptures are filled with examples. In the Old Testament, for instance, the prophet Nathan has to rebuke David for arranging the death of Uriah in battle so that he could marry Uriah's wife Bathsheba (2 Sam 11:12). Rather than confront David directly, Nathan tells a story about a rich man stealing a lamb from a poor man (2 Sam 12:1-25) and David is enraged when he hears what the wealthy person has done. David has unknowingly described himself. Then Nathan turns to David and says: "You are the man!" (2 Sam 12:7). David is mortified and repents. Jesus Christ follows this tradition of storytelling in his use of parables as his principal method of teaching and relating to audiences.[43] There is a lesson here for theologians.

---

43. See N. T. Wright, *The New Testament and the People of God* (Minneapolis: Fortress Press, 1993), 40.

Chapter 6

Cultures as Processes of Ritualizing Life

Ritual forms, like speech forms, [are] transmitters of culture . . . [and] exercise a constraining effect on social behavior.

—Mary Douglas, *Natural Symbols*[1]

[Ritual] is an aggregation of symbols . . . [and a] patterned process in time . . . [that] is transformative, [while] ceremony [is] confirmatory.

—Victor Turner, *The Drums of Affliction; The Forest of Symbols*[2]

In the midst of a workshop on culture for a group of executives in a healthcare facility I announced that the next lecture would be entitled "Ritual—Foundation for Creativity." My audience looked surprised. Ritual surely had nothing to do with health care! Most felt that ritual was synonymous with religion or with grand national events celebrating the traditions of the past. It had nothing at all to do with creativity, certainly nothing to do with industrial inventiveness. How wrong they were! I explained to them that my lecture would help them to see that without ritual they would be unable to communicate with each other and all creativity would cease. In fact, without ritual—an integral quality of all cultures—they could not remain human. The purpose of this chapter is to explain these statements.

1. Mary Douglas, *Natural Symbols: Explorations in Cosmology* (New York: Pantheon Books, 1970), 21.
2. Victor Turner, *The Drums of Affliction: A Study of Religious Process Among the Ndembu of Zambia* (Oxford: Clarendon Press, 1968), 2; idem, *The Forest of Symbols: Aspects of Ndembu Ritual* (Ithaca: Cornell University Press, 1967), 95.

Defining Ritual

General Definition

A ritual is any prescribed or spontaneous action that follows a set pattern expressing through symbols a public or shared meaning. Prescribed rituals vary from simple gestures such as shaking hands, greeting a person, bowing, to elaborate dramas such as a British royal coronation or the inauguration of an American president. Thus the expression "How do you do?" or "How are you?" as a routine method of starting conversations is a simple prescribed ritual of everyday interaction. Rituals can be spontaneous. For example, when a young man was tragically killed in a car accident on the street not far from my home, total strangers spontaneously placed flowers on the site. People unknown to the family of the deceased wanted to express symbolically to the bereaved their deep human sympathy for the enormity of the loss they had experienced.

It is the capacity of rituals to transform people and their environment, to resolve, prevent, and even cause conflicts that gives them their positive or negative power. Rituals have the power to evoke significant emotional reactions such as the joy of a birthday party.[3] Yet rituals can arouse a whole range of negative emotions, even violent ones. The annual summer parades of the Protestant Orangemen through Catholic suburbs in Northern Ireland's towns and cities can be perceived by Catholics as ritual acts of symbolic warfare, reminding them that their minority status will continue to be enforced.[4] Rituals may create a well-behaved school pupil or a brutal terrorist, a devoted employee or a dictator. Such is their power.

Categories of Definitions

We have just briefly defined ritual, but there are many divergent definitions simply because its qualities are so complex. Most definitions fall into one of two complementary categories: one group stresses the ordering function of ritual in a chaotic world while the other highlights its transformational quality (see Figure 6.1). Victor Turner, however, correctly gives priority to ritual as transformative. He writes: "Ritual is a transformative performance . . . not, in essence, as it is commonly supposed

---

3. See Roy A. Rappaport, *Ritual and Religion in the Making of Humanity* (Cambridge: Cambridge University Press, 1999), 258–59.

4. See Catherine Bell, *Ritual Theory—Ritual Practice* (New York: Oxford University Press, 1992), 197–223.

. . . a prop for social conservatism. . . . Rather does it hold the generative source of culture and structure . . . ."[5] Ritual does at times express and reinforce the existing order, but its primary purpose is ultimately to foster transformative individual and cultural change. Each category of definitions will now be considered.

Ritual types
- Ordering
- Transforming: social dramas

Figure 6.1

Ordering Rituals

> ### Definition
>
> Ritual, a form of storytelling, is the repetitive[6] spontaneous or prescribed symbolic use of bodily movement and gesture to express and articulate meaning within a social context in which there is possible or real tension/conflict and a need to resolve or hide it.[7]

An example is found in Western customs whereby people resolve or hide a tension/conflict between them by shaking hands. This is a stylized gesture of set form that outwardly at least conveys the meaning that peace has been restored. A game of football contains an intricate set of

5. Victor Turner, *On the Edge of the Bush: Anthropology as Experience* (Tucson: University of Arizona Press, 1985), 20; see Bobby C. Alexander, "Correcting Misinterpretations of Turner's Theory: An African-American Pentecostal Illustration," *Journal for the Scientific Study of Religion* 30 (March 1991): 26.

6. Sally F. Moore and Barbara G. Myerhoff note: "Even if [a ritual] is performed once, for the first and only time, its stylistic rigidities, and its internal repetitions of form or content make it traditionlike." See "Secular Ritual: Forms and Meanings," in *Secular Ritual*, eds. Sally F. Moore and Barbara G. Myerhoff (Assen and Amsterdam: Van Gorcum, 1977), 8.

7. See Robert Bocock, *Ritual in Industrial Society: A Sociological Analysis of Ritualism in Modern England* (London: George Allen and Unwin, 1974), 35–59.

rituals found in the rules of the game that must be observed by the players. If the rules are not observed there is chaos. Doctors operating in a hospital must follow certain procedures, that is, rituals, for the safety of their patients. All these rituals demand the use of bodily movement that symbolically articulates meaning in situations that are potentially capable of causing conflict or chaos.[8]

Functions of Ordering Rituals

Rituals do change in structure, in symbolic meaning, and in their social impact; new rituals can develop while older ones disappear. The following qualities of ordering rituals illustrate, however, that rituals do not change easily, sometimes for very good reasons.

1. Relieving anxieties

Ordering rituals are "defenses against anxieties"[9] through which we seek, establish, and preserve or celebrate order and unity for ourselves and society. Social life proceeds on a continuum between two possible imaginary opposing poles: absolute order and absolute spontaneity/chaos. There is an ongoing tension between these extremes with consequent uncertainty and fear, and that needs to be controlled in some recognizable action. The more tension there is in relationships, the more urgent it is to develop rituals that ease the anxieties.[10] When heads of state meet, considerable attention is given even to the smallest of details of diplomatic protocol for fear that a mistake will be interpreted as a slight to one or other of the national leaders. The very predictability and timelessness of ritual restore confidence in people that order can be established and maintained in a world of threatening chaos.

In other words, since social reality is too complex and ambiguous for the human person to deal with, there is an inborn desire to make it simpler and unequivocal, to build order where there is only the threatening uncertainty of chaos.[11] The more the uncertainty, the more urgent it is that the ritual be unequivocally clear. For example, when I want to

---

8. See Gerald A. Arbuckle, *Earthing the Gospel: An Inculturation Handbook for Pastoral Workers* (Maryknoll, NY: Orbis Books, 1990), 96–97.

9. See Isabel Menzies Lyth, *The Dynamics of the Social: Selected Essays* (London: Free Association Books, 1989), viii.

10. See Moore and Myerhoff, "Secular Ritual," 3–24.

11. See Robert Wuthnow, *Meaning and Moral Order: Explorations in Cultural Analysis* (Berkeley: University of California Press, 1987), 120.

turn on a busy highway I must indicate without ambiguity that I am about to change direction. If I fail to do so I am endangering not just my own life but the lives of others.

Examples[12]

- Today when hospitals, schools, or churches close, or when there are liturgical changes, even if the reasons are sound, there are often vociferous protests from affected people. No amount of logical argument will convince them that the closures are in their best interests. One significant factor behind these outcries is the hidden function of these institutions: they ritually exist to contain people's fear of death. Their closure reminds people that death is a reality.

- Anton Obholzer[13] explains this further with reference to hospitals. He writes that in the unconscious part of our being we have no sense of health, but we have a concept of the chaos of death. In order to control our anxieties over death we repress them into the unconscious. Various defenses are used, including the formation of assorted rituals that safely contain our anxieties about the unknown. All cultures deal with the anxieties evoked by death.[14] In Christianity death is seen as a transition to a higher life in Christ (1 Cor 15:54-55) and Christian rituals express this. With the growth of secularism, however, this fear of death is allayed by the rituals of hospitals and medical staffs, the postmodern substitutes for the churches and their ministers. As Obholzer notes, "our health service might more accurately be called a 'keep-death-at-bay' service."[15] There is a popular fantasy that hospitals and their staffs will shield us from death.

---

12. See Gerald A. Arbuckle, *Healthcare Ministry: Refounding the Mission in Tumultuous Change* (Collegeville, MN: Liturgical Press, 2000), 126–27.

13. See Anton Obholzer, "Managing Social Anxieties in Public Sector Organizations," in *The Unconscious at Work: Individual and Organizational Stress in the Human Services*, eds. Anton Obholzer and Verga Z. Roberts (London: Routledge, 1996), 171; see also Wilfred Bion, *Second Thoughts* (Beverly Hills: Sage Publications, 1986), 199–231.

14. See Gerald A. Arbuckle, *Change, Grief and Renewal in the Church* (Westminster, MD: Christian Classics, 1991), 25–28.

15. Obholzer, "Managing Social Anxieties," 171.

They will find the right medical ritual to solve moral diseases and aging. If they do not, they have failed in their task.[16]

• Sometimes a decision is made to have "simple rituals" when in fact it is important to have rituals with a multiplicity of symbolism. Jimmy Carter, United States President 1977–1981, publicly declared that rituals surrounding the presidency would be simplified. Hence he walked back to the White House after his formal inauguration rather than using the traditional motorized cavalcade; gold braids were removed from the guards at the White House, and the usual ceremonies ceased to accompany a president's formal entrance. In his attempt to become "one of the people" he lost significant popular appeal and was perceived as "lacking in charisma, the sacred aura, that presidents should have."[17] This illustrates the importance of Victor Turner's definition of ritual, that is: "prescribed formal behavior for occasions not given over to technological routine, having reference to beliefs in mystical beings or powers."[18] The United States as a nation, and the role of the president that represents it, is so complex that no technological language or purely intellectual statement by themselves can comprehend it. That is why the word "mystical" is used in the definition. The office of the president symbolizes the awe-inspiring quality of nationhood and the rituals surrounding it are holding back the anxieties of the people by reassuring them that all is well with the nation. To change these rituals arbitrarily is to unnecessarily evoke fear about the very stability of the nation.

2. Constraining behavior

One way to discover if an action is a ritual or not is to evaluate people's reactions to any attempt to change or ignore it. For example, if I refuse to obey a red traffic light it will not be long before I have an accident and/or the traffic police are at my door. The symbolism of the red light constrains me to act in a definite way. Again, if I fail to take a gift for a birthday party, people will at least nonverbally let me know that I have broken a ritual. Hence ritual can be defined as behavior "prescribed

16. Ibid.

17. David Kertzer, *Ritual, Politics and Power* (New Haven: Yale University Press, 1988), 182–83.

18. Turner, *The Forest of Symbols*, 19.

by society in which individuals have little choice about their actions."[19] Emile Durkheim in his major study *The Elementary Forms of Religious Life* (1912) argues that the primary purpose of ritual is *always* to constrain the behavior of the group so that it remains a coherent whole. As this book shows, however, this reductionist approach is unacceptable. Rituals can in fact generate conflict. Moreover, many games and play have no other purpose but the enjoyment of the participants.[20]

3. Defining boundaries

Rituals define boundaries, classifying who belongs and who does not. For example, on the day I received my Australian passport the simple public ritual clearly defined that I now had rights and privileges that non-Australians do not have. People become aware of the realities of inclusion and exclusion through ritual. In the ritual granting me Australian citizenship I became acutely conscious of the fact that I was "in" and some people in the reception hall were not, that is, they were still beyond the boundaries of Australian citizenship. The symbolic articulation and affirmation of boundaries through rituals increases people's consciousness of their community. This may help to explain why political activists often rationalize fruitless demonstrations by arguing that they have at least raised the consciousness of their participants to their own identity in the midst of opposing forces.[21]

4. Incorporating contradictions

Ritual, like all symbols, has the ability to manage both sides of a contradiction simultaneously and to support and contain strong emotions. Contradictions, such as ideal/real, good/evil, life/death, joy/sorrow, confront us at every turn of our lives. A retirement ritual marks the sadness of ending a career, but it also celebrates the joy of leisure ahead, not bound by the rituals of daily working. A wedding ritual contains within it the emotions of loss and joy. At the same time parents are losing a son or daughter but are also gaining a daughter-in-law or a son-in-law. The ritual of the Eucharist simultaneously contains the symbolism of the death and resurrection of Christ.

19. Joy Hendry, *An Introduction to Social Anthropology* (Basingstoke: Palgrave Macmillan, 2008), 75.

20. See Johan Huizinga, *Homo Ludens: A Study of the Play Elements in Culture* (Boston: Beacon, 1950), 13.

21. See Anthony P. Cohen, *The Symbolic Construction of Community* (London: Tavistock, 1985), 50.

5. Articulating myths

Myths and narratives are two sides of the same coin (chap. 5). Narratives are also rituals because they make the mythic values of a culture concrete and experiential. Edmund Leach describes their interdependence in this way: "Myth . . . is the counterpart of ritual; myth implies ritual, ritual implies myth. . . . Myth regarded as a statement in words 'says' the same thing as ritual regarded as a statement in action."[22] But the interdependence is even more dynamic than what this statement describes. True, narrative rituals are the outward expression of myths, but they also reinforce the power of myths and even change them, depending on the circumstances.

Rituals of Male Sport

The fact that male sport as ritual has developed with considerable rapidity since the late nineteenth century may help to illustrate these points.[23] The mythology underpinning the ritual is that of modernity: competence, science, intelligence, achievement, profit, patriarchal power, aggression. Modernity exalts the power of the machine and financial investment for the sake of profit. In commercial male sport we find the human body envisioned as a finely tuned machine capable of bringing investors an increasing amount of money through gate takings and advertisements, but at the same time there is a glorification of the physically powerful male body so popular in ancient Greece. Gad Horowitz speaks of hypermasculinity to describe the growing aggressive power of the male in sport in contrast to the dramatic weakening of public interest in women's sport.[24] The degree of aggressiveness that is permitted, even encouraged, in many male sports is so startling that we can speak of rituals of violence.[25] In a sense, concludes researcher Varda Burstyn, male sport has become "a religion of domination

---

22. Edmund R. Leach, *Political Systems of Highland Burma: A Study of Kachin Social Structure* (Cambridge, MA: Harvard University Press, 1954), 13–14.

23. See Varda Burstyn, *The Rites of Men: Manhood, Politics, and the Culture of Sport* (Toronto: University of Toronto Press, 1999), 21–32.

24. See Gad Horozitz, *Repression: Basic and Surplus Repression in Psychoanalytic Theory: Freud, Reich, and Marcuse* (Toronto: University of Toronto Press, 1977), 53–123, 182–214.

25. See Gerald A. Arbuckle, *Violence, Society and the Church: A Cultural Approach* (Collegeville, MN: Liturgical Press, 2004), 113–14.

and aggression constructed around a male godhead."[26] The more the rituals of male sport are presented, the more their inherent mythology of male dominance is reinforced; they feed each other with ever-increasing energy.

6. Denying reality

Rituals can be used to articulate denial through reaffirming order and cohesion when chaos is threatening. I was once working with a religious congregational leadership team and encouraging them to identify obvious symptoms of congregational disintegration and demise. For two days I was puzzled that the team lacked energy, holding back from naming reality until the leader formally stated: "I think we are concentrating on the negative! Our task is to have hope and be positive. What we need is a new apostolic venture into a foreign culture. We have the personnel." Suddenly the energy of the team rose. All agreed with him, despite the fact that the reserves of qualified manpower would never be available to staff the new missionary project. His narrative was a ritual of denial reaffirming the fantasy that all was well. Neither he nor his team could face the fear-evoking reality of congregational death.

7. "Models for"/"models of"

The function of "models for" rituals is to impose, reaffirm, and strengthen public conformity to the status quo. In the 1930s Adolf Hitler, supported by his ritual experts, ruthlessly created and manipulated public Nazi rituals to express his distorted mythology of Germanic racial superiority. "Models of" rituals exist where consensus does not have to be imposed but needs to be reaffirmed. For Americans the flag is a powerful symbol of national identity and its raising carries considerable ritual importance, especially in times of national tragedy. Following the terrorist assaults on the United States in 2001, the whole country was aflutter with flags; huge ones decorated the damaged Pentagon and sports stadiums, tiny flags were attached even to baby carriages. Their display was a ritual of defiance and reaffirmation of identity signifying that Americans would not be coerced into submission.[27]

---

26. Burstyn, *The Rites*, 23.
27. See Arbuckle, *Violence*, 13–14.

8. Achieving manipulation

The world of advertising is filled with manipulative rituals. The presence of a beautiful woman in an advertisement for a new car is an attempt by the producers to make the particular car more attractive to male buyers. Politicians are also adept in manipulating rituals for their political advantage. A member of Congress, for example, will deliver a speech on the floor of the United States Senate or House of Representatives surrounded by the powerful symbols of this national political shrine. The videotape of the speech, however, is for voters in the home constituency; it does not show that there are rarely any other congressmen in the hall.[28]

9. Enforcing compliance

When people externally comply with the demands of ritual it does not automatically mean they accept all or any of the mythology that underpins it. For example, when people attend a funeral in a Catholic church they will be motivated by a variety of reasons. They may be there out of personal respect for the deceased or in a spirit of solidarity with particular relatives of the deceased. They may be present simply because their status in society demands it and it would be a social offense to be absent. Whether they believe in the ritual of the Mass is not the issue.

Transforming Rituals: Social Dramas

Ritual is not just about maintaining order in relationships, but more importantly, writes Victor Turner, it is a "patterned process in time,"[29] that is at the same time "transformative"[30] because society itself is a process, not something static. Society is being repeatedly recreated out of the struggles, the social dramas, to settle the tensions between structure and *communitas*. Structure connotes everything in society that identifies differences, constrains people's actions, and keeps them separated in orderly ways. *Communitas* or "anti-structure," on the other hand, refers to the recognition of people's common humanity; if this is not accepted there can be no society. These complex statements will now be explained.

---

28. See Kertzer, *Ritual*, 108, and Barack Obama, *The Audacity of Hope* (New York: Crown Publishers, 2006), 14–15.

29. Turner, *The Forest of Symbols*, 95.

30. Ibid., 45.

Social Dramas

Turner calls the process of ritually recreating or transforming society[31] "social dramas." These range from the most extravagant ritual to quite commonplace exchanges such as a ritual of greeting or a smile. When a person greets another there is a built-in tension or uncertainty—will the person return the greeting or not? If the person positively responds, society is recreated; if the greeting is not returned there is a crisis in social relations. Reflecting on the dynamics of more significant social dramas, Turner notes that the normal pattern or order of society is temporarily suspended and the group is forced to reflect on its own behavior in the light of values inherent in their foundational myths or narratives, even if this means at times questioning the relevance of their values. The terrorist attack of September 11, 2001, evoked a social drama in which Americans reflectively rediscovered the energy-creating significance of their national founding mythology. "In other words," Turner had written earlier, "dramas induce and contain reflexive processes and generate cultural frames in which flexibility can find a legitimate place."[32] Ronald Grimes, a specialist in ritual studies, emphasizes the importance of these insights about social drama: "Before Turner ritual was [treated by theorists as] static, structural, conservative. After Turner, it is imagined as flowing, processual, subversive."[33]

Stages of Social Dramas

Rituals of large-scale social dramas typically have four phases (Fig. 6.2), each of which has its own characteristics and time span: breach, crisis, redressive action, and reintegration (or schism). A *breach* is a breakdown in social relationships. For example, when the Cold War developed between East and West after 1945 it destroyed the East-West alliance that had existed during the years of the Second World War. More recently there was the breach between the Western nations and Russia as a consequence of Russia's invasion of Georgia in 2008; this followed a period of cooperative relations after the breakup of the former Soviet Union.

---

31. The transformative nature of ritual is more fully explained in the author's book, *Laughing with God: Humor, Culture, and Transformation* (Collegeville, MN: Liturgical Press, 2008), 42–90.

32. Victor Turner, *From Ritual to Theatre: The Human Seriousness of Play* (New York: Performing Arts Journal Publications, 1982), 92.

33. Ronald Grimes, "Reinventing Ritual," *Soundings* 75 (1992), 22.

A *crisis* is an event resulting from a breach that cannot be ignored; the Berlin blockade by the Soviets was such an occurrence; another was the threat by Russia to place missiles aimed at the West as a consequence of the West's reactions to the Russian invasion of Georgia. The crisis phase is "usually one of these turning points or moments of danger and suspense when a true state of affairs is revealed, when illusions are dispelled and masks torn off or made impossible to don."[34] Factions or alliances develop to press for this or that strategy to resolve the crisis— some for the return to what was lost, others for a new set of relation- ships. If the phase continues, people are forced to take yet stronger stands based on what they perceive to be moral principles inherent in their mythologies. A war of words can develop.

The third phase, *redressive action*, is often a lengthy and complicated process. The crisis produces a feeling of chaos, senselessness, or mean- inglessness. This can be a most terrifying experience. People feel the need to discover meaning in what is happening, and so they are forced to reflect on fundamental myths that could guide them to resolution of the crisis. In this period of *reflexivity* there is a struggle to resolve the crisis through particular rituals, for example, recourse to informal arbi- tration, the law courts, revolution, and war. People generally experience considerable pain or emotional turmoil in this phase if their reflection is genuine. They are angered at what has happened, but the more they reflect on their mythological values, the more they discover that they cannot take refuge in past achievements or ignore the crisis.

The fourth phase, called *reintegration*, is characterized by the parties either resolving their differences with even a heightened sense of unity or breaking apart into *schism*. The Berlin blockade was overcome when the allies, led by the United States, after vocally resisting the Soviets, further reflected on the implications of their commitment to the mythology of democracy. Loyalty to the principles inherent in this mythology led to the concerted and successful creative effort to break the blockade. Concilia- tion with the Soviets did not eventuate, but instead a more deeply rooted schism between the East and West quickly developed.

---

34. Turner, *On the Edge of the Bush*, 215.

Life as a Social Drama

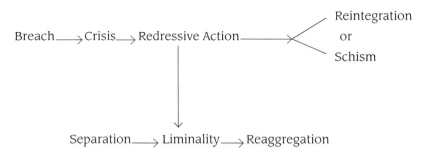

Figure 6.2

Redressive Action: Tripartite Stages

Turner concentrates his ritual analysis particularly on the tripartite stages of the third phase of social dramas, namely *redressive* action, as these stages are to be found in all kinds of human interactions. First there is the *separation* stage, in which people are symbolically reminded that they are about to break with the routine of everyday life with its predictable patterns of hierarchical roles and status (called *societas*). The second stage is *liminality*. Ideally this is the time during which people relate to fellow ritual participants and/or to deity/spirits in, at least symbolically, an undifferentiated ecstatic or shocked oneness that Turner calls *communitas*.

Examples

In July 1985 the pop musician Bob Geldof organized the Live-Aid concert in London to raise concern for poverty-stricken sections of the world and millions were able to participate through satellite television. Geldof described the spontaneous *communitas* scene in the London park: "There was a tremendous feeling of oneness on that stage. There had been no bitching, no displays of temperament all day. . . . Cynicism and greed and selfishness had been eliminated for a moment. . . . A lot of people had rediscovered something in themselves."[35] The shocked reaction of millions

---

35. Bob Geldof, *Is That It?* (London: Penguin, 1986), 310.

of people following the terrorist attacks in New York is another example. Class, racial, and religious distinctions ceased to have any significance. This period of often intense reflexivity can be a time of surprising personal and social creativity. As Geldof says, people are able to rediscover "something in themselves" through their reflections on their founding myths.

If in the liminality stage participants interiorize, or are reconverted to, their mythology, they feel the urge in passing out of liminality to recreate or transform the world. The status quo in which key societal values have been compromised will no longer be tolerated and this illustrates the potential power inherent in mythology and rituals. Mythologies that underpin rituals can help cultures to maintain stability in times of calm, but alternatively they can be subversively applied to new questions and issues in times of crisis, leading to new and creative responses. As Turner writes: "Ritual is a transformative performance revealing major classifications, categories, and contradictions of cultural processes."[36]

The liminality stage has such potential to subvert the status quo that individuals, organizations, and governments may deliberately erase it from rituals of social drama. For example, Charles Jackson, in reflecting on contemporary funeral customs in Western cultures, concludes that the denial of death "has become an art form and . . . dying is [presented] as an alien unnatural humiliation."[37] And Philippe Aries writes: "It is above all essential that society . . . notice to the least possible degree that death has occurred. . . . If a ceremony still marks the departure, it must remain discreet and must avoid emotion."[38] In terms of Turner's social drama model these Western rituals of death acknowledge the breach and crisis stages, but lightly trip over or ignore the reflexive phase. That is, the separation and liminality stages of the ritual process are skillfully avoided. The whole range of grief reactions among the bereaved—pining, numbness, anger, despair, guilt, questions about one's own mortality—are to be ignored. The cultural imperative is: reintegrate bereaved individuals and friends as fast as possible into life as though nothing has happened.

36. Turner, *On the Edge of the Bush*, 171.
37. Charles Jackson, in idem, ed., *Passing: The Vision of Death in America* (Westport: Greenwood Press, 1977), 242.
38. Philippe Aries, *Western Attitudes Towards Death: From the Middle Ages to the Present* (London: Johns Hopkins University Press, 1974), 90.

Another example, already referred to in the previous chapter, comes from dictatorial governments. The South African government under apartheid tried to prevent public funerals of dissidents for fear that people would use these rituals as the opportunity to question the status quo. Likewise the Chinese government effectively prevented public mourning for the students who had been killed in Tiananmen Square in 1989.

In the third stage, the rites of *reaggregation*, participants move back into the world of hierarchical status and roles (*societas*). This is a dangerous stage.[39] Douglas observes that on entering the reaggregation stage participants are "charged with power, hot, dangerous, requiring insulation and a time for cooling down."[40] They are so enthused by their transformative experience that they may want to change the world immediately. When confronted by the harsh realities of the status quo awaiting them, however, they can become so cynical that all attempts to be proactive are abandoned. I once observed a group of middle-level business managers who had been away in a rural conference center for a weekend's planning session. It had been a liminal experience for them. They had returned to their offices highly energized to transform their company into a dynamic operation, but a week later their passion had evaporated under a barrage of cynical comments from their superiors.

The following two case studies illustrate the tripartite stages of the redressive action phase of social dramas.

Case Study: Entertainment as Social Drama

By the mid-1990s Ireland as a nation was in a liminal stage of a national social drama. It was in the midst of an economic boom of such proportions that it became appropriately known as the Celtic Tiger. Ireland's traditional mythology included the realities of its chronic poverty and the tragedy of centuries of having to export its youth to seek employment overseas. Now Ireland had become both rich and a vibrant part of the global economy, necessitating for the first time the recruitment of workers from all over the world. What was to be its national mythology now? A creative, artistic narrative helped Irish people and outsiders answer this question. In 1994 a short, brilliantly presented performance, officially called *Riverdance*, won a Europe-wide television

39. See Gerald A. Arbuckle, *Change, Grief and Renewal in the Church* (Westminster, MD: Christian Classics, 1991), 32–37.

40. Mary Douglas, *Purity and Danger: An Analysis of Concepts of Pollution and Taboo* (Harmondsworth: Penguin, 1966), 117.

contest. Audiences in Ireland and internationally were captivated by its professionalism and relevance.[41] In a relatively short liminal space of time Ireland had embraced the postmodern mythology of a global economy resulting even in the commercialization of its entertainment industry. The secret of the show's success was its ability to name in ritual narrative form the radical mythological changes in the Irish nation.

Riverdance was advertised as a contemporary expression of the story of Ireland and its people, "a transformative moment in representations of Irishness and Irish dance."[42] Observers saw the show not just as a radical break with the way Irishness had been traditionally depicted, but as "an internationalized Irishness, an identity forged between the 'local' and the 'global' that reverberates with both past and contemporary dance forms."[43] It incorporated new and contemporary forms of dance such as Spanish flamenco, ballet, high leaps and jumps, and exaggerated horizontal actions across the stage. In addition, contrary to tradition, there was a tendency to sexualize particularly the female body in the performance. A further example of the ritual adaptation of Irish dancing to contemporary life was the remarkable use of technology. Small microphones had been inserted into the dancing shoes of the lead performers to ensure audiences in large halls would hear their hard shoe taps, a key quality of the production. The global aspects were significant. Prior to *Riverdance,* Irish dancing and music had been presented very much as leisure activities, but *Riverdance's* purpose now became financial profit as well as the expression of the new Ireland.

Case Study: Ritual Facilitates Mythological Change

This case study from Fiji illustrates that in the ritual of a social drama a mythological change can occur while its external expression remains unaltered. S*evusevu*, that is, the ceremonial presentation of kava, a mildly narcotic drink, is a pivotal ritual for all indigenous Fijians. The belief is that the age-old ritual must remain unchanged to ensure the stability and safety of the relationship between the supernatural and human society. The formal speeches at the liminal stage of the ritual reaffirm that Fijians live like a loving family and are always obedient to men of traditional rank and power. In a study done of the ritual in a rural village,

41. See Thomas M. Wilson and Hastings Donnan, *The Anthropology of Ireland* (Oxford: Berg, 2006), 92–103.
   42. Ibid., 96.
   43. Ibid., 95.

however, it was found that a significant shift in the mythology underpinning the ritual had occurred among its villagers there.[44] Villagers now feel threatened by three forces: the development of urban life among former villagers with its commercialism and individualism; the individualism and concern for making money of the different ethnic Indo-Fijians, who are descendants of immigrants from India in the nineteenth century and who live close by; and international tourists who come to see them participate in *sevusevu*.

Given these external pressures, villagers seek to bolster their self-image through *sevusevu*. In the ritual they claim that, *uniquely* in Fiji, they choose to forsake wealth in favor of better things such as loving each other, worshiping God, and serving the community. They are not like money-grabbing Indo-Fijians, international tourists, and their own Fijian cousins in the cities. During the *sevusevu* ritual they testify that they alone are loyal to traditional Fijian values. The reality is quite different. Villagers complain that there is much backbiting and suspicion, even accusations of sorcery, and dissatisfaction with traditional leaders among themselves, but this glaring contradiction between the ideal and reality does not bother them. The primary mythological emphasis now behind the ritual is no longer on traditional values but on their special identity as villagers within Fiji. They alone among all Fijians are protecting the culture in the face of disturbing internal and international forces.

Theological Reflection

In our postmodern world we are accustomed to seeing entire landscapes being destroyed and redeveloped over a short time. We can assume that the same destruction and growth can occur within cultures, that people's symbolic landscapes can be destroyed, the familiar sights, sounds, and routines in which people are nurtured can be obliterated overnight without particularly negative results for them. This is simply not so. Symbols, myths, and rituals are not replaced as quickly as buildings or landscapes or mass-produced as neatly as automobiles or toothbrushes. The uprooting of the inner framework of cultures, even when there is conscious and intellectual assent to what is happening, destroys the stable sense of belonging and people's individuality. All kinds of

---

44. See Karen J. Brison, "Constructing Identity through Ceremonial Language in Rural Fiji," *Ethnology: An International Journal of Cultural and Social Anthropology* 40 (2001): 309–27.

negative reactions can result. The reform of Roman Catholic worship was rightly mandated in 1963 by Vatican II and dramatic changes were initiated immediately. But there was little or no feeling for the complexity and dynamics of rituals, and serious mistakes were made. For example, churches were speedily redesigned, altar rails were withdrawn and statues destroyed, leaving people confused and angry.[45] Theologians and liturgists would do well to ponder the lessons of the following insensitive ritual change.

In a brief statement the Catholic bishops of England and Wales simply cancelled the ritual requiring Catholics not to eat meat on Fridays, as a small weekly mortification in memory of Christ's sacrifice on Calvary. The bishops exhorted Catholics to choose some personal act of sacrifice instead. Theoretically it was a good idea, but the bishops failed to realize that symbols and rituals have a multiplicity of meanings and are always adding more, while the external ritual remains the same. Migrant Irish laborers, alone and living in an atmosphere of cultural and religious prejudice, looked to rituals that would give them a sense of religious, personal, and cultural identity. Abstaining from meat on Fridays had become one of these rituals. But suddenly this ritual was destroyed and the immigrants, as well as many local Catholics, felt betrayed and confused. If the bishops had realized this they would have proceeded to initiate the change with far more cultural sensitivity and pastoral formation.[46]

45. See Gerald A. Arbuckle, *Refounding the Church: Dissent for Leadership* (Maryknoll, NY: Orbis Books, 1993), 42–43.

46. See Douglas, *Natural Symbols*, 37–53.

Chapter 7

Cultures as Multicultural Processes

Contrary to all those who think that the time to speak of multiculturalism is over, I think it is most timely and necessary, and that we need
more not less.

—Tariq Modood, *Multiculturalism* [1]

[The] problem of the twenty-first century will be the problem of ethnic
differences, as these conspire with complex differences in color, gender,
and class . . .

—Henry Louis Gates, Jr., *Loose Canons* [2]

The purpose of this chapter is to explain the meaning of the terms
"multicultural" and "multiculturalism," not an easy task. Multiculturalism, for example, has become "a buzzword with almost as many meanings as there are mouths to utter it." [3] One reason for the confusion
surrounding the meaning of the words is the assumption that they refer
exclusively to ethnic groups. In fact, the terms can be used in one of two
ways: broadly, to embrace all kinds of national subcultures, such as
youth subcultures, and narrowly, and more commonly, to refer to ethnic
groups. In this chapter two social categories, namely subcultures and
ethnic groups, will first be explained. Only then will it be possible to
explain the terms "multicultural" and "multiculturalism" with greater
precision and with particular reference to ethnic groups.

1. Tariq Modood, *Multiculturalism* (Cambridge: Polity Press, 2007), 14.
2. Henry Louis Gates, Jr., *Loose Canons: Notes on the Culture Wars* (New York:
Oxford University Press, 1992), xii.
3. Robert Hughes, *Culture of Complaint: The Fraying of America* (New York: Oxford
University Press, 1993), 111.

Subcultures

The term *subculture*, which refers to cultural patterns that make some segment of society's population symbolically distinct, is applied very widely to social groups including immigrant, ethnic, gender, and sexual groups.

Definition

A subculture is a method of defining and honoring the particular design and identity of different interests of a group of people within a larger collectivity. Thus subcultures consist of people, in tight or loosely connected groupings, who:

- share some common interests, values, tastes, and often specialist knowledge and linguistic jargon;
- adhere to the same rituals and pastimes to some degree or other;
- express their unity in some distinctive symbols such as dress; and
- may be known through an association with a particular geographical region.

The term is a particularly postmodern one, for it is a reminder that cultures are not homogeneous, but highly fragmented. Contemporary societies contain an ever-increasing diversity of subcultures, especially in densely populated urban environments—for example, trade unions, business clubs, youth groups, homeless people, jazz musicians, yuppies, campus poets, skateboarders, football fans, Punks, Hell's Angels, hip-hop, or rap.[4]

In every subculture there is always an element, sometimes strongly evident, of protest against the dominant culture of which it is part. The more people of the subculture feel threatened by the dominant group, the stronger and more vivid will be their symbols of protest and resistance. For example, the Catholic Church in the United States prior to Vatican II was the best organized and most powerful of the nation's subcultures. The more Catholics felt intimidated by prejudice and discrimination against them, the more they developed their own symbols of identity such as their own schools and hospitals.

---

4. See Peter Brooker, *A Concise Glossary of Cultural Theory* (London: Arnold, 1999), 208–9.

Sometimes the term *counterculture* is used to refer to a subculture in which people not only strongly protest against conventional ideas or behavior but are able to give an intellectual justification for their position. An example would be the youth-oriented counterculture of the 1960s that rejected the cultural mainstream as excessively competitive, self-centered, and materialistic. Also, hippies and other groups emphasized a cooperative lifestyle in which "being" and the capacity for personal growth ("expanded consciousness") became more important than "doing" or the possession of material goods.[5]

Youth Subcultures

Characteristics

Youth subcultures tend to function as loose-knit *scenes* rather than as formally structured organizations,[6] and membership is generally temporary, but some groups, for example biker gangs, are able to maintain the allegiance of their followers well into adulthood. These subcultures began to appear in countries with market economies around the mid-1950s as the gap between school and employment widened, thus delaying the need for students to face their responsibilities as adults.[7] Youth subcultures are especially rich in distinctive symbols and rituals against the adult world such as dress, hairstyles, and music.

The protest quality of youth subcultures against the adult world, as articulated in their symbols of identity, can at times be especially harsh. For example, the Beatles could attack the rigidity of school structures in their lyric "Getting Better" of 1967: "The teachers that taught me weren't cool—You're holding me down, turning me round—Filling me up with your rules." With their British working-class background and their creative musical professionalism the Beatles were well equipped to articulate anti-class sentiments in highly expressive rituals. Punks show their disdain for accepted middle-class standards with the juxtaposition of safety pins, bin liners, gaudy colors, and spiked hair. They believe that music should be as raucous and unsophisticated as possible, both to

5. See John J. Macionis and Ken Plummer, *Sociology: A Global Introduction* (Harlow: Prentice Hall, 1997), 112–13; Ken Gelder, *Subcultures: Cultural Histories and Social Practice* (London: Routledge, 2007), 5–26.

6. See Stephen Castles, *Ethnicity and Globalization* (London: Sage, 2000), 161.

7. See Sara Savage, Sylvia Collins-Mayo, Bob Mayo, and Graham Cray, *Making Sense of Generation Y: The World View of 15-25-Year-Olds* (London: Church House Publishing, 2006), 4.

annoy conventional society and to show that no one needs to be excluded from playing it. Biker gangs use the hated symbols of Nazi swastikas and army helmets.

Types of Subcultures

A whole range of types exists, sometimes closely connected to class structures, for example, the soccer tribes of Britain, which are directly linked to their working-class roots.[8] Skinheads first appeared in the late 1960s as a reaction to ethnic immigration and the growing acceptance of the gay culture, and punks in the late 1970s as a response to unemployment. The hip-hop or rap music subculture emerged in the 1970s from young African-Americans living in the slums of New York and then expanded nationally and internationally. It reflects a long history of black segregation and socioeconomic deprivation and is characterized by break-dancing, graffiti, particular dress styles, and a unique musical type.[9]

In more recent times researchers have identified four new youth subcultures noted particularly for their loose and flexible boundaries: the "Boomer Generation" (members born 1946–63), "Generation X" (born 1964–81), "Generation Y" (born 1982 onward), and "Net Geners" (born between 1978 and 1994).

- The Boomer youth subcultures, disillusioned with traditional institutions and authority structures, including the churches, are optimistic and idealistic about life, politically active, expecting immediate personal satisfaction.[10]
- Generation X subcultures are noted for their pessimism, viewing the Boomer subcultures as self-centered, fickle, and impractical. They are angry because they have been left with the social problems created by their predecessors: racial strife, homelessness, AIDS, fractured families, and government deficits. They yearn for a new spiritual eclecticism, respect for the environment, and tolerance between cultures.

---

8. See Gary Armstrong, *Football Hooligans: Knowing the Score* (Oxford: Berg, 1998), 156–74.

9. See Gelder, *Subcultures*, 114–21.

10. See Gerald A. Arbuckle, *Violence, Society and the Church: A Cultural Approach* (Collegeville, MN: Liturgical Press, 2004), 157–62; Rebecca Huntley, *The World According to Y* (Sydney: Allen and Unwin, 2006), 1–23; Peter Sheahan, *Generation Y* (Prahran: Hardie Grant Books, 2005), 2–105.

- Generation Y subcultures seemed to exemplify the early optimism, ambition, confidence, passion, and idealism of the Boomer years, but among them the latest communication technology such as computers, e-mailing, text-messaging, are taken for granted, linking them immediately with any part of the world. Theirs is a hybrid cultural world embracing influences simultaneously at the local and global levels, so much so that some theorists have called the subculture "glocalization."[11]
- Sociologist Don Tapscott has identified in his research on people born between 1978 and 1994 a new youth subcultural movement, the Net Geners, in which the qualities of Generation Y are more visibly and intensely present.[12] Members are smarter, faster, and more tolerant of diversity than their predecessors. They care strongly about social justice and are actively trying to improve society according to their lights; their role in the recent election of Barack Obama as president of the United States testifies to this. They value freedom and choice in all they do, scrutinize everything, and demand integrity and openness, including their ability to decide what to buy and where to work. They expect collaboration, and that everything will happen fast and with constant creative action.

Tapscott concludes that the Internet is producing an improved, more collaborative version of family life he calls the "open family." Parents increasingly acknowledge that young people have digital expertise they need but do not have. They also advocate that the most effective way to avoid misuse of the Internet by their children is to win their children's trust through honest conversation. Among the negative qualities of Net Geners is their disregard for personal privacy. For example, the posting of photographs of alcohol-fueled parties on the Internet, descriptions of drug use and other intimate matters is already causing an increasing number to fail job applications as employers are able to access this data.

---

11. See Ulrich Beck, *What is Globalization?* (Cambridge: Polity, 2000), 45-50.

12. See Don Tapscott, *Grown Up Digital: How the Net Generation is Changing Your World* (New York: McGraw-Hill, 2009).

Understanding Ethnicity

Ethnic Groups

Definition

Milton Yinger defines an ethnic group as "a segment of a larger society whose members are thought, by themselves or others, to have a common origin and to share important segments of a common culture and who, in addition, participate in shared activities in which the common origin and culture are significant ingredients."[13] That is, an ethnic group is defined as a gathering of people within a larger society having real or putative common ancestry, memories of a shared historical past, and a focus on one or more social markers, especially physical qualities such as skin pigmentation, particular customs, language, religion.

Ethnicity connotes individuals' sense of belonging to an ethnic group. Of course people will differ in their degree of commitment to an ethnic group; for some the links will be tenuous, for others strong. The intensity of ethnic identity is generally dependent on the attitudes of the dominant host group toward outsiders in their midst. If the outsiders approximate the culture of the host group, their own ethnic identity will slowly weaken, as is the case for Anglo-Saxon immigrants in United States or Britain. Negative reactions to outsiders by the dominant group intensify the outsiders' ethnic internal bonding, as is the case among contemporary Mexican Americans. This will be more fully explained later.

Qualities

There are several key qualities of an ethnic group. The most basic is *difference*, that is, people perceive themselves or are viewed by others as different. Historically, the tendency has been to assume that social markers were determined by the physical qualities of people. Thus the word "race" was applied to separate ethnic groups, but in recent years the term "ethnic group" has become preferable to counteract the implied or overt racism in the use of the word "race." The second quality is *memory*. Ultimately,

---

13. Milton Yinger, *Ethnicity: Source of Strength? Source of Conflict?* (Albany: SUNY Press, 1994), 3.

people feel they are different from other groups because of their origins, whether this is true or not.[14] Third, there is a *relational* quality, that is, an ethnic group is a subdivision of a larger cultural whole. For this reason it is impossible to consider an ethnic group separated from other groups or "at home" in a mainly monocultural state or society; for example, Koreans are not an ethnic group in Korea.

Types

Two types of ethnicity can be identified: involuntary (or ascribed) and voluntary.

1. Involuntary ethnicity

Involuntary ethnicity occurs when ethnic identity is imposed on a group of people from outside. There is little or no escape from this oppressive labeling; the us/them dichotomy that is always present in ethnic relations is especially strong. The dominant group ("us"), often out of fear of losing its position of power, pejoratively stereotypes the marginalized group ("them"). The oppression is institutionalized so that in key areas of life such as employment, housing, education, and social relations, people who are oppressed are excluded from equality with the dominant group. To develop and legitimize this discrimination, the in-group may brand the out-group as racially or culturally inferior. Such has been the fate of African-Americans, American Indians, black and colored people in South Africa under apartheid, Jews in Nazi Germany, and immigrants particularly from Muslim countries in contemporary Germany, Switzerland, and France.

Sometimes the confusing term *minority* is applied to an ethnic group, with the purpose of highlighting the subordinate or marginal nature of the group in relationship to the dominant political power. The ethnic group may in fact be numerically as large as, or larger than, the group with the political power; such was the case with the black population in South Africa and with Catholics in Northern Ireland.

People who are trapped in involuntary ethnicity have few choices about how they can define their identity. Their demands for equality of opportunity may lead them to seek radical forms of political self-determination as happened, for example, in the breakup of Yugoslavia into

---

14. See Jack D. Eller, *From Culture to Ethnicity to Conflict: An Anthropological Perspective on International Ethnic Conflict* (Ann Arbor: University of Michigan Press, 1999), 12–16.

the violently opposed nationalistic states of Bosnia, Serbia, and Croatia. In 1974 one Maori civil rights leader in New Zealand, protesting against institutional racism, vividly described his experience to me in this way:

> For over a hundred years we indigenous people have been told our way of life is inferior to [that of] the white settlers from Europe. Look at what has happened. We do the manual work in this country because we are told we are capable of little else. Now we demand the world recognize that we have a culture born of the struggle to survive through the centuries. Without it we are nothing, not human. The more we tell our own story, the more we feel stronger inside to stand on our own feet and demand respect. The more self-esteem we have, the more we feel we can give something of our uniqueness to others. We demand, and are getting at last, a say in the power institutions of this country. For too long we have had to depend on the good will of the whites to give us justice. No more. Many Anglo-Saxons in this country don't like it. Hard luck on them!

This comment illustrates two important practical axioms:

• Only from a position of cultural identity can a people move out with dignity and self-confidence to share with other cultures. The more people have the chance to articulate and share their stories, the more energy they will have to challenge the dominant power structures.
• Only if ethnic groups have access to power structures of a society such as political, economic, and educational institutions will the achievement of full ethnic self-confidence be possible.

Within the United States in the 1960s and 1970s these two axioms inspired protest movements among African-Americans. Negative stereotypes of inferiority had to be cast aside for blacks to elevate their sense of self-worth after two centuries of struggling to survive in a racist society. Hence the invention of the narrative "black is beautiful," the coining of the term "African-American" to indicate pride in cultural roots, the calls for controversial Black Studies programs within universities[15] and for affirmative action. Some African-Americans, convinced that the dominant political system could not be justly changed in their favor, preached separatism. For example, the leaders of the Black Muslims, calling for "freedom from contempt," planned for separate hospitals, schools,

---

15. See Gates, *Loose Canons*, 87–104.

industries, shops, but their ultimate goal was the granting of one whole American state for blacks alone.

Dangers of Ethnic Labeling

Here are some pastoral warnings:

- Ethnic groups, like cultures, must not be thought of as discrete, frozen in time, resistant to external influences, homogeneous, and without any internal conflict. That is, it is incorrect to consider ethnic groups as wholly resistant to other identities.[16]
- Members of ethnic groups must not be defined only by their origins and assumed to be behaviorally determined by them. Individuals in ethnic groups will have many identities, drawing on their ethnicity when occasions demand or require it.
- Not all members of ethnic groups and cultures share some unchanging essential characteristics. In fact, every ethnic group is a hybrid construction[17] from a wide variety of sources; an ethnic group is best thought of as a social process, with moving boundaries and identities that people collectively and individually draw around themselves in their social lives.
- Ethnic groups, in fact any social group, must never be reified as if they were inanimate things. Reification is "apprehension of human phenomena as if they were things . . . as if they were something other than human products—such as facts of nature."[18]

---

2. Voluntary ethnicity

Shortly after African-Americans in the United States began to demand respect for their history and origins, there developed what can be variously termed voluntary, symbolic, defensive, or backlash ethnicity among whites. Protests of self-righteous indignation still continue, especially as economic conditions worsen and the competition for employment intensifies. As a consequence of this defensive pluralism there are demands

---

16. Stuart Hall, "On Postmodernism and Articulation," in *Critical Dialogues in Cultural Studies*, eds. David Morley and Kuan-Hsing Chen (London: Routledge, 1996), 119; also see Steve Fenton, *Ethnicity, Racism, Class and Culture* (London: Macmillan, 1999), 10–27.

17. See Jan Nederveen Pieterse, *Globalization and Culture: Global Melange* (Lanham, MD: Rowman & Littlefield, 2004), 59–83.

18. See Peter Berger and Thomas Luckmann, *The Social Construction of Reality* (Harmondsworth: Penguin, 1967), 106.

for university programs in such areas as Irish, Jewish, and Polish studies. Similar but weaker reactionary movements exist in countries such as Australia, New Zealand, Britain, and Canada, whose governments have been fostering affirmative action programs for minorities. A Sydney taxi driver, talking about New Zealand immigrants to Australia, bitterly complained to me: "These spongers are taking our jobs. We are Australians and we are different from these lazy immigrants!" Logical or rational arguments do little to counteract such expressions of defensive ethnicity.

In summary, voluntary ethnicity means that, as a reaction to the growing identity demands by underprivileged ethnic groups, people feel the need to redefine themselves more precisely by asserting their own ancestral self-worth and their right to maintain their power position in society. This voluntary ethnicity of whites of European ancestry does not restrict their choice of a spouse, suburb, or friends, or affect their access to employment and political opportunities. But the socioeconomic and political consequences of being Asian, Hispanic, or black are real and frequently hurtful, obstructive, and unjust. These people are not free to choose their ethnic identity; its crippling boundaries are defined for them on the basis of skin pigmentation.

Multiculturalism and Ethnicity

Historical Background

Most governments that acknowledge ethnic diversity in their midst refer to their countries as "multicultural" societies and their official policies fostering respect for this diversity are designated "multiculturalism." That is, multiculturalism is a social doctrine that is a positive substitute for programs of assimilation; it recognizes the citizenship rights and cultural identities of ethnic minority groups and, more generally, it is the public endorsement of the value of cultural diversity.[19]

The term "multiculturalism" in particular now evokes strong emotional reactions among its supporters and detractors due in part to the failure to develop an agreed, precise meaning. For many conservatives the term has come to signify a very disruptive, unsettling, and dangerous force. For them diversity of cultures is something to be tolerated at best.

---

19. See Will Kymlycka, *Multicultural Citizenship: A Liberal Theory of Minority Rights* (Oxford: Clarendon, 1995).

Peace and order, they claim, existed in the past and will continue to exist only when a dominant group has insisted on conformity to their own monocultural ethos. Extreme liberals, for their part, also dislike the term. They claim that it implies either a bland "melting pot" or an assimilationist attitude that would remove all differences, or a situation in which cultural diversity is so emphasized that any unity between cultures does not or cannot exist.[20]

Multiculturalism has never been accepted in the United States and Europe to the extent that it has been in Canada, New Zealand, Australia, and to some degree in the United Kingdom. Sharp rises in immigration, the increasing fears of terrorist attacks by radical groups, and the growing tensions between Muslim minorities and dominant cultures that in recent times followed the terrorist offensives in the United States, Britain, and Spain, have moved the public discourse from multiculturalism to euphemisms of "cohesion" and "integration." In the 1990s, even before the terrorist assaults, there was generally a growing backlash against multiculturalism, even in countries where it has become an official government policy. In Australia, once considered "a laboratory for multiculturalism,"[21] under a Liberal/National Coalition government a vigorous political reaction has developed against the multicultural experiments. It has been the same in Canada. In Britain the head of the Commission for Racial Equality stated in 2004 that the country needs to discard its emphasis on recognizing cultural differences characteristic of multicultural education programs and accept instead a narrative of national culture. The leader of the Conservative opposition in Britain, David Cameron, declared in 2007 that the "creed of multiculturalism" had contributed to a "deliberate weakening of our collective identity."[22]

In the United States the political backlash against multiculturalism has expressed itself in a variety of ways; the growing antagonism toward equal opportunities for disadvantaged groups is a pertinent example.[23] And racism still lurks behind the rhetoric. When Republican politician Patrick Buchanan implored his audiences to "take back our cities . . .

---

20. Henry A. Giroux, "Insurgent Multiculturalism and the Promise of Pedagogy," in *Multiculturalism: A Critical Reader*, ed. David T. Goldberg (Oxford: Basil Blackwell, 1994), 336.

21. J. J. Smolicz, "Australia: From Migrant Country to Multicultural Nation," *International Migration Review* 31 (1997): 171.

22. David Cameron, *The Economist* (16 June 2007), 58.

23. See Roger Hewitt, *White Backlash and the Politics of Multiculturalism* (Cambridge: Cambridge University Press, 2005), 2–3, 151–56.

take back our culture and take back our country," the "our" in question signified the white population.[24] In the opening pages of Allan Bloom's monoculturalist *The Closing of the American Mind*, the author portrays the development of a Black Studies program at Cornell University as if Western civilization had just been destroyed by the Vandals.[25] Ultimately a major cause of the backlash against multiculturalism is the fear in the traditional holders of power that they will have to share their power with others. These power holders, while admitting other people are different, treat them with disdain, as deviations from their own "perfect culture," as people to be stigmatized.

Cultural Diversity Remains

Throughout modern history people have dreamed that ethnicity and nationalism would cease to exist. This fantasy reached new heights during the 1950s, when it was widely thought that the process of modernization would inevitably lead to the decline of intercultural differences and bitterness. Behind this dream was the Enlightenment vision of a common human civilization. Since the 1960s, however, the dramatic renaissance of ethnic diversity and the negative reactions it is evoking has destroyed this unreal dream.

Cultural diversity and its implications for governments, churches, and other organizations cannot be swept under the rug. There is an increasing desire for differences to be respected, especially by those with limited or no access to power. To counter the dominance of European cultural patterns, some supporters of multiculturalism are calling for Afrocentrism or Asiacentrism, that is, the dominance of African or Asian cultural patterns. They see this as a corrective for centuries of minimizing or altogether ignoring the cultural achievements of African or Asian societies. Many new immigrants in the United States are now rejecting the former melting-pot vision of the hundred percent American, but many more are refusing the idea of the hyphenated American, such as Chinese-American. Instead, they are defining themselves by transnational identities such as American *and* Chinese, American *and* Korean. Some want to obtain dual citizenship. Given the ease of travel and Internet

24. Patrick Buchanan, cited by Joe L. Kincheloe and Shirley R. Steinberg, *Changing Multiculturalism* (Buckingham: Open University, 1997), 219.

25. See Allan Bloom, *The Closing of the American Mind* (New York: Simon and Schuster, 1987), 27–43.

communication, many more remain actively involved, socially, politically, and economically, in their countries of origin.[26]

Dominant and Ethnic Groups: Power Relationships

Dominant groups that control economic, political, social, or religious power structures in society can relate to subcultures in one of two ways: *either* by oppressing them, for example, persecution of gay people in Muslim countries, the Falun Gong and Tibetan people in China; *or* by beginning a process of sharing power. This latter is an example of reciprocal power as described in chapter 3. Though this section will focus on the relations between dominant groups and ethnic subcultures (see Figure 7.1),[27] the theory can be applied to subcultures in general.

1. Power Held by Dominant Group

ANNIHILATION OR OPPRESSION

People of dominant cultures who refuse to share power with minority groups react in one of several ways: by policies of annihilation, coercive pluralism, or assimilation. Examples of annihilation are the British relating to Aborigines in Tasmania, the Dutch to blacks in South Africa in the nineteenth century, the Nazis to Jews.

ASSIMILATION

During the nineteenth century and well past the 1950s the melting pot metaphor was the most powerful characterization of ethnic relations in the United States. It was assumed that all immigrants must be thrown into the mainstream of American life, without concessions or supports, in order to pool their characteristics and develop a new amalgam or American culture. The reality was very different. No one was particularly interested in the customs and values of socioeconomically poor migrants. They were pressured for the sake of survival to adopt as quickly as possible the existing hegemonic Protestant Anglo-Saxon white culture. Many did not succeed and joined the ranks of those trapped in chronic poverty.

26. See Peter Kivisto, *Multiculturalism in a Global Society* (Oxford: Blackwell, 2002), 82.

27. See David Bennett, "Introduction," in *Multicultural States: Rethinking Difference and Identity,* ed. idem, 1–25 (London: Routledge, 1998).

A similar policy, variously called Anglo-Saxon conformism or Angliciza-
tion, characterized other English-speaking countries such as Australia,
New Zealand, and Canada.

Positioning of Power

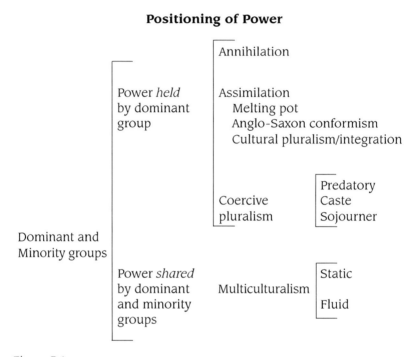

Figure 7.1

Cultural Pluralism/Integration

As the assimilative policies in several English-speaking countries in
the 1960s were not having the desired effects, a new approach called
cultural pluralism (sometimes referred to as *integration*) became popular
especially in the educational field. Core values of the dominant culture
were to be acquired, but ethnic subcultures could preserve values and
customs, provided these did not interfere with the dominant group's
core values. In Australia, for example, the policy in 1975 meant that
"immigrants would be expected to agree publicly that all things Australian are best, to be greatly interested in sport and not to work too hard,
and in return they would not be badgered if they privately practiced their

native culture."[28] A similar dynamic began to develop in other countries like Britain. In the United States the civil rights and countercultural movements signaled a shift from the prevailing assimilative governmental policies. At heart this policy of toleration of nonessential customs was merely an attempt to make cultural assimilation efforts a little less nasty or disruptive for migrants. The long-term aim remained the same, namely: ethnic minorities are encouraged to adopt all aspects of the dominant way of life.

COERCIVE PLURALISM

Some immigrant groups were considered "unmeltable" in the United States, and this was determined by definitions of race and religion. For example, Irish people, along with southern and eastern Europeans, tended to be portrayed in racial and religious terms and did not fit the category worthy and capable of assimilation.[29]

Lawrence Fuchs, when reviewing the history of policies in United States toward all "unmeltable" peoples, whether indigenous, involuntary migrants such as slaves, or immigrants from other countries, distinguishes three categories under the general title of "coercive pluralism," namely predatory, caste, and sojourner policies.[30] Indian tribes were considered to be "predatory," outsiders to be pushed aside because they obstructed European settlers. "Caste" policies refer to the slave trade and the subsequent history of prejudice and discrimination against African-Americans. "Sojourner" policies describe the government's relations to people such as Mexicans and Chinese in the nineteenth century, and later Latino and Asian groups. They were considered to be temporary residents providing cheap labor; they were given little or no legal protection. Even today millions of illegal migrant workers come within this category: they are people who exist to provide inexpensive labor and who are to be discarded in times of economic recession.

---

28. Martin Kovacs and Allan Cropley, *Immigrants and Society: Alienation and Assimilation* (Sydney: McGraw-Hill, 1975), 123.

29. See Peter Kivisto, *Multiculturalism in a Global Society* (Oxford: Blackwell, 2002), 43–52.

30. See Lawrence H. Fuchs, *The American Kaleidoscope: Race, Ethnicity, and Civic Culture* (Hanover: Wesleyan University Press, 1990), 80–127.

2. Power Sharing

MULTICULTURALISM

In the 1970s this emphasis on the intolerance of ethnic groups began to be increasingly challenged. By the 1990s the United Nations, particularly under the influence of the governments of Canada, Australia, and New Zealand,[31] rejected assimilationism and cultural pluralism for indigenous peoples in favor of multiculturalism. In a dramatic turnaround these three countries, unlike the United States, deliberately aimed to implement multiculturalism as a formal policy in which ethnic group rights were to be publicly promoted, though the implications of this policy often remained unclear.[32] As far back as 1971 Canada was declared a multicultural and bilingual country by the then-prime minister Pierre Trudeau: "Every ethnic group has the right to preserve and develop its own culture and values. . . . A policy of multiculturalism must be a policy for all Canadians."[33]

Many European countries, especially Britain, the Netherlands, and Sweden, began to follow suit: immigrants should be able to retain their distinctive cultures while they adapt to working and living in their new countries. Some assimilation would take place, but it should not be made compulsory. France has stubbornly continued to resist adopting multicultural policies. The melting-pot ideology has not as yet been seriously challenged from within, but the reality of poverty especially among immigrants, particularly Muslims, and their dissatisfaction with national monoculturalism will eventually force the French government to face the situation.

DEFINITION OF MULTICULTURALISM

Multiculturalism is a social system that claims to offer freedom of choice to those who desire to be culturally different in one or several

---

31. See Catherine J. Iorns Magallanes, "International Human Rights and their Impact on Domestic Law on Indigenous Peoples' Rights in Australia, Canada, and New Zealand," *Indigenous Peoples' Rights in Australia, Canada, and New Zealand*, ed. Paul Havemann, 235–76 (Auckland: Oxford University Press, 1999).

32. See Peter Kivisto, *Multiculturalism in a Global Society* (Oxford: Blackwell, 2002), 84–115; Mark Lopez, *The Origins of Multiculturalism in Australian Politics 1945–1975* (Carlton South: Melbourne University Press, 2000), 1–191.

33. Pierre E. Trudeau, quoted by John W. Friesen, *When Cultures Clash: Case Studies in Multiculturalism* (Calgary: Detselig, 1985),1.

aspects, for example, religious or political beliefs, occupation, styles of living, and ethnic identity. The model aims to remove the pressures that prevent subcultures like ethnic groups from using their cultural roots to develop their personalities and sense of group belonging. Bhikhu Parekh, an authority on multiculturalism, provides this working definition; although it focuses on ethnic groups it is increasingly being extended to apply to any subgroup in society:

> Multiculturalism does not simply mean numerical plurality of different cultures, but rather a community which is creating, guaranteeing and encouraging spaces within which different communities are able to grow at their own pace. At the same time it means creating a public space in which these communities are able to interact, enrich the existing culture and create a new consensual culture in which they recognize reflections of their own identity.[34]

This definition, therefore, embraces the following assumptions:

- Culture is to be understood in the postmodern sense (chap. 1), that is, no cultures are static, but all are *fluid*, and the boundaries of every culture are porous and open to change; members of subcultures differ in their commitment to values and openness to change.
- It rejects two popular classifications of multiculturalism: *demographic* and *holistic*. The former connotes that a particular society merely contains different cultural groups; the second means that a society values cultural diversity but gives higher priority to group-wide cohesion.
- It accepts the social philosophy of *political* multiculturalism that acknowledges the legitimate interests of subcultural groups within a society or an organization. Adequate politico-economic and educational structures must permit minority peoples *by right* to be fully involved in decision-making in matters that affect their lives.
- Multiculturalism is about sharing power, that is, in the process of negotiating a balance between cohesion and diversity members of traditional dominant power groups must be prepared also to make significant adjustments.
- Only from a position of cultural strength will members of ethnic groups be able to move out to contact other cultures with a sense

---

34. Bhikhu Parekh, cited in Goldberg, *Multiculturalism*, 335.

of self-respect and confidence. This is impossible as long as labeled groups of people suffer from poor housing, education, health services, and racial discrimination. Hence the need for much-maligned affirmative action programs that assume that merely removing legal obstacles to participation in decision-making is not sufficient to alter the behavior of the privileged majority or of the excluded minorities themselves; habits and attitudes encouraged by centuries of discrimination are not readily changed, even among people of goodwill.

• Through the process of power sharing, the dominant culture itself will be undergoing change, losing its overriding influence as a more overall hybrid culture slowly continues to emerge.

POLITICAL MULTICULTURALISM: PROBLEMS

Given that the theory of multiculturalism is still developing, it is understandable that mistakes continue to occur in its implementation. Here are some problems that have emerged:

Dialogue denied

If there is no power sharing there is no multiculturalism. In Britain, for example, the electoral process has provided ethnic groups with very little ability to be involved in making decisions in matters that deeply affect their lives. They must rely on the goodwill of the dominant white group to eliminate institutional prejudice and discrimination, to guarantee legal and civil rights, and to obliterate poverty. Moreover, there is no way of ensuring that this goodwill will be developed and maintained.

Culture misunderstood

A mistaken understanding of a culture or ethnic group has led to unfortunate policies by political multiculturalists. As already explained, a culture or ethnic group must not be defined as a homogeneous and cohesive entity frozen in time. Rather, it is a fragmented process with members at different levels of commitment and with several other sources of identity at the same time, such as gender, employment, recreation, and religion, all of which can powerfully affect the identity of individuals. There must be the freedom to choose whatever custom individuals feel is appropriate for them. They must not be forced to adorn themselves with an ethnic brand if they freely choose not to. The image given by tourist agents of indigenous Fijians is of smiling people, "always happy." In fact, employees at tourist centers have had to be "taught to smile in a Fijian way" in order to accommodate the tourists' image of Fijians. A serious deficiency of multicultural education in British schools has been the failure to avoid stereotypical images of unified and integrated minority cultures. Educationalists should rather have stressed the reality that all cultures are hybrid, constantly changing and experiencing internal divisions.[35]

Oppression reinforced

Governments can be blind to the injustices within migrant ethnic groups themselves, such as oppressive caste and class structures, and their failure to act can reinforce these forms of internal domination.[36] The government in British Columbia was accused in 2006 of ignoring traditional violence within the large Indo-Canadian population. Earlier there had been an acrimonious debate in Ontario over whether Muslims could use Islamic *sharia* courts to settle family disputes; the government finally decided against it. In Canada and elsewhere the practice of female circumcision and the custom of arranged marriages, with little or no consultation with the brides-to-be, are causing disquiet.

To prevent chaos, and this applies especially to multicultural countries, every national culture must at a minimum foster a unified identity by encouraging a sense of transcendence and worth among its members. That is, every government must cooperatively develop a persuasive and authentic unifying mythology for belief and action. Governments are now beginning to confront the fact that some ethnic groups and immigrants are refusing to respect some mainstream values of democracy, such as gender equality.[37] Getting the balance right between subcultures and a unifying mythology is not an easy task.[38] Sometimes governments overdo the requirements of uniformity to national values. Such has been the case in France, where female Muslim pupils were refused permission to wear traditional headdress to school. The government claimed religious particularism in schools threatens the secular rationality of education.[39]

---

35. See Hewitt, *White Backlash,* 126.

36. See Pariminder Bhachu, *Twice Migrants: East African Sikh Settlers in Britain* (London: Tavistock, 1985), 13–16.

37. See *The Economist* (18 November 2006), 47.

38. For an analysis of the complex interaction between principles of political multiculturalism in Western democracies and the religious expectations of Islamic immigrants, see Geoffrey B. Levey and Tariq Modood, *Secularism, Religion and Multicultural Citizenship* (Cambridge: Cambridge University Press, 2009).

39. See Fenton, *Ethnicity*, 207.

Second generation issues

Second-generation migrants may experience considerable difficulties in their adjustment to the host cultures. They must inhabit two cultural worlds at the same time: that of the school or the workplace, where they feel alienated, and that of the home, where they are thought by their parents to be abandoning the traditions of their ancestors. It is a dualism filled with tensions. The more parents insist on family traditions the more the migrant children feel alienated from the society they wish to adjust to, but that keeps refusing to accept them. Parents and children can be unable to communicate easily with each other simply because they no longer share a common language. Parents have been too busy working to learn the new language well, and the young, desperate to belong to their new cultural world, are often uninterested in learning the language of their parents. Young people may live in a kind of cultural "no-person's-land." Jawaharlal Nehru, first prime minister of India, describes how he experienced similar tensions of identity in his own life as he was educated away from the traditions of his country of origin: "I have become a queer mixture of the East and the West, out of place everywhere, at home nowhere. . . . I am a stranger and an alien in the West. I cannot be of it. . . . But in my own country also, sometimes, I have an exile's feelings."[40]

This helps to explain why young second-generation migrants may try to escape these identity tensions by joining gangs or organizations that are often anti-host society. For example, some young Muslims born in Britain and responsible for the suicide bombings in London in 2005 had bonded with the so-called "world Muslim nation" or *ummah*, which they felt was being persistently and unjustly harassed by Western governments. In these groupings they were able to find a much-needed sense of identity and support they could not find in Britain, their home.

Theological Reflection

Vatican II stated that "in the liturgy the Church does not wish to impose a rigid uniformity in matters which do not involve the faith or the good of the whole community. Rather does she respect and foster the

---

40. Jawaharlal Nehru, quoted by David Wilson, *Asia Awakes: A Continent in Transition* (New York: NAL, 1970), 56.

qualities and talents of the various races and nations."[41] The words "races" and "nations" are to be translated as "cultures" (see chap. 9). In this same document, the Constitution on the Sacred Liturgy, the council proceeds to list several levels of liturgical adaptation that are permissible in local cultures. This raises critically important pastoral questions such as:

> What is the culture of a particular country?
>
> Is it a culture oppressing subcultures within its boundaries?
>
> What if there are many subcultures or ethnic groups within the one parish?
>
> How is it possible to avoid domination by one or more ethnic groups during liturgical adaptation?
>
> How are both the unity of the parish and its diversity to be honored?
>
> Are pastors and teachers portraying minority cultures stereotypically as neat, unified wholes?
>
> How is the postmodern understanding of culture, with its fluidity, openness, and fragmentation, to be respected and welcomed while maintaining reverence for tradition?[42]

Unless the first principle of multiculturalism is rigorously adhered to, namely, that appropriate structures must be established to permit ongoing dialogue to occur between the parties concerned, there can be no answers to these questions.

Saint Paul fought hard in defense of ethnic rights at the Council of Jerusalem for this type of dialogue and succeeded, but he also defended the need for people to act for the wider common good: "There is no longer Jew or Greek, there is no longer slave or free, there is no longer male or female; for all of you are one in Christ Jesus" (Gal 3:28). When faced with this challenge, the pastoral team of a parish in New Zealand established a process of dialogue with representatives of thirty-six ethnic groups in their parish. As a result of the dialogue it was agreed that two complementary liturgical liminal spaces should be respected: private and public. In the private space people have the right to celebrate events such as weddings, funerals, and family rituals that respect their cultural

---

41. Constitution on the Sacred Liturgy (*Sacrosanctum Concilium*), 37, in *Vatican Council II: The Conciliar and Post Conciliar Documents*, ed. Austin P. Flannery, new rev. ed. (Northport, NY: Costello, 1975).

42. See Peter C. Phan, *Being Religious Interreligiously: Asian Perspectives on Interfaith Dialogue* (Maryknoll, NY: Orbis Books, 2004), 213–78.

diversity, but in the public space, for example at Sunday Eucharists, no sole ethnic group is to dominate, for it is here that the different ethnic groups are to celebrate their oneness in Christ: "But now that faith has come . . . you are all children of God through faith" (Gal 3:25-26).[43]

---

43. See Gerald A. Arbuckle, *Laughing with God: Culture, Humor, and Transformation* (Collegeville, MN: Liturgical Press, 2008), 143.

Chapter 8

Cultures as Patterns of Religious Symbols

> For communication about religion to take place, the structure of the symbols must be able to express something relevant to the social order.
>
> —Mary Douglas, *Natural Symbols*[1]

> Conventional, mainline religious groups may have fallen on hard times, but the curtain has yet to fall on faith, spirituality, and the quest for transcendence.
>
> —David Lyon, *Jesus in Disneyland*[2]

The purpose of this chapter is twofold: to explain that all religions, whatever their beliefs about the supernatural, are visibly expressed in cultural forms and, second, to identify four cultural models of Catholicism; particular attention will be given to the impact of postmodernity on Catholics.

Religion is extremely difficult to define; as with the word "culture" there are countless definitions of religion, with no agreement on one universal definition. Religion is like St. Augustine's comment on time: "If you do not ask me what time is, I know; if you ask me, I do not know."[3] Postmodernist Zygmunt Bauman is equally at a loss: "'Religion' belongs to the family of curious and often embarrassing concepts, which

---

1. Mary Douglas, *Natural Symbols: Explorations in Cosmology* (New York: Pantheon, 1970), 38.
2. David Lyon, *Jesus in Disneyland: Religion in Postmodern Times* (Cambridge: Polity, 2000), 137.
3. St. Augustine, cited by James C. Livingston, *An Introduction to Religion* (New York: Macmillan, 1989), 4.

one perfectly understands until one wants to define them."[4] Edward Tyler in the nineteenth century defined religion as "the belief in spiritual beings,"[5] but this is unsatisfactory as there are people whose apparently dedicated religious activities involve no spiritual beings. Buddhists are concerned, for example, with attaining a state beyond the spiritual, a state that does not require the intervention of a god or gods. A few years after Tyler, Emile Durkheim considered religion to be a kind of collective action in which society celebrates its own cohesive transcendent power over its individuals. But the purpose of religion is far more than just providing social cohesion.[6] As explained in the previous chapter, religious rituals can in fact create divisions and conflict.

Pierre Bourdieu: Religion

Bourdieu, an influential sociological theorist, concentrates on what he calls the "symbolic violence" of religion. For example, it is an act of symbolic violence to assert and inculcate into a people's vision of the world ("habitus," as it is termed by Bourdieu) that riches, not poverty, are a unique sign of God's love. The primary function of religion is then the legitimizing of the resulting social inequalities. For him it is the imposing of arbitrary forms and systems of meanings on people by the dominant powers in cultures so that the dominated do not recognize what is happening. The status quo is assumed to be normal and God-given and not to be questioned.[7]

Definition

The most influential contemporary definition among anthropologists is that provided by Clifford Geertz, who takes a phenomenological or experiential approach:

> A religion is a system of symbols which act to establish powerful, pervasive and long-lasting moods and motivations in men [*sic*] by

---

4. Zygmunt Bauman, "Postmodern Religion?" in *Religion, Modernity and Postmodernity*, ed. Paul Heelas (Oxford: Blackwell, 1998), 55.

5. Edward Tyler, *Primitive Culture*, vol. 2 (New York: Torchbook, 1891), 8.

6. Emile Durkheim's approach to religion is found in his book *The Elementary Forms of the Religious Life*, trans. Joseph Swain (New York: Free Press, 1965).

7. See Pierre Bourdieu, *Language and Symbolic Power* (Cambridge, MA: Harvard University Press, 1991), 5, 14, 210.

formulating conceptions of a general order of existence and clothing these conceptions with such an aura of factuality that the moods and motivations seem uniquely realistic.[8]

This definition contains no judgment about the existence or otherwise of the supernatural, because that is outside the scope of the social sciences. Religion defines in symbolic or mythological terms (see chap. 2) the nature and purpose of the world (what Geertz calls "models *of*") and how we are to relate appropriately to it by way of feeling and acting ("models *for*"). Symbols of any religion show that "a group's ethos" is able to be "rendered intellectually reasonable by being shown to represent a way of life adapted to the actual state of affairs."[9] Both the nature of the world and human emotions and motives are mutually confirmed and reinforced.[10]

Example

Using Gertz's definition of religion, Mark S. Massa explains why Senator Joseph McCarthy's anticommunist crusade in the 1950s was able to receive significant support among many Catholic Americans. As they watched with fear and sadness the persecution of millions of ethnic Catholics in Eastern Europe and the seeming loss of nerve by the American government to do something about this, they passionately (but wrongly) felt that their church's own consistent anticommunist stand made sound political sense. That is, their interpretation of their religion "rendered intellectually reasonable" McCarthy's strident political campaign.[11]

Three important conclusions follow from this definition of religion.

- Religions are not something purely otherworldly, because they are encased in cultures of their own making. Religions have their own cultures, influence other cultures, and are influenced by them.

---

8. Clifford Geertz, *The Interpretations of Cultures* (New York: Basic Books, 1973), 90.

9. Ibid., 89.

10. For a further explanation of the importance of Geertz's definition of religion see Carl F. Starkloff, "Inculturation and Cultural Systems," *Theological Studies* 55 (1994): 70–81; Talal Asad, "Anthropological Conceptions of Religion: Reflections on Geertz," *Man: Journal of the Royal Anthropological Institute* 18 (1983): 237–59.

11. See Mark S. Massa, *Catholics and American Culture* (New York: Crossroad, 1999), 62–65, 79–80.

Recall, for example, that the Catholic Church following the Peace of Constantine in the fourth century uncritically embraced the power structures and trappings of the imperial court.

• A religious culture must be able to respond to people's needs; otherwise it becomes irrelevant, a museum piece.[12] The Christian faith "must be rethought, reformulated and lived anew in each culture . . . and this must be done in a vital way, in depth and right to the culture's roots."[13]

• Since all cultures are inherently conservative and resistant to change, religious cultures are slow to be proactive when confronted with people's changing needs. They continue to address problems of the past or apply old, unworkable responses to contemporary issues. The consequence of this social drama is that either the religious cultures die or new movements emerge from within or from outside.

Catholicity: Culture Models[14]

The following are four culture models of Roman Catholicism. A model aims to illuminate complex social reality by highlighting emphases and downplaying details or nuances. Nuanced explanations of details are omitted to allow us to grasp a little more clearly what is in fact a highly complex situation. Any particular culture is then compared with the model to examine the extent to which it resembles that culture. In the application of models, however, the following cautionary comments are necessary. In a particular society it is possible for all the models to be observable at the same time, with one model being more influential than the others. Models, however, give the impression that cultures are static, their boundaries frozen, and that all within a particular culture are equally committed to its characteristics. Previous chapters show this is not the case. Cultures are not homogeneous (chap. 1); there are constant movements and tensions within all cultures. And within a short space of time a person or group may draw on one model and then on another, depending on the situation. For example, a person may opt for religious practices that

---

12. See Douglas, *Natural Symbols*, 38.

13. David J. Bosch, *Transforming Mission: Paradigm Shifts in Theology of Mission* (Maryknoll, NY: Orbis Books, 1991), 55.

14. These models draw on the insights of Mary Douglas as explained in chap. 3 and my publication *Refounding the Church: Dissent for Leadership* (Maryknoll, NY: Orbis Books, 1993), 80–97.

characterize premodern cultures one minute and then in the next minute commit to attitudes and behaviors that are postmodern.

Premodern Model

Premodern religious cultures consist of two levels: official, and unofficial or popular religiosity. At the official level the religion is rigidly hierarchical, patriarchal, rules of behavior are extremely detailed, and unchanging boundaries are firmly set and policed. As Mary Douglas has explained, the more a culture is threatened by dangerous alien forces the more it demands vigilance in guarding its boundaries. Orthodoxy must be maintained even in small matters. Dissenters who dare to question the status quo are polluters of "pure doctrines" and must be severely punished, even if the requirements of natural justice are broken in so doing. Dissenters are treated more severely than those beyond the cultural body because the maintenance of orthodoxy is more important than individual rights. At the unofficial level of premodern religious cultures people feel intimidated by evil spirits and manipulative sorcerers who need to be controlled through appropriate rituals. They feel the need to express their relationship to the deity and the spirits in very concrete ways and symbols, often accompanied by colorful dancing and music. Feeling or imagination is dominant, not rationality or intellectual analysis.

The culture of the official institution of the Catholic Church, especially from the Reformation to the Second Vatican Council (1962–1965), is an example of this premodern type. The church is a rigidly hierarchical and orderly system, patriarchal, with God the Father a distant and fear-evoking figure who is intimately concerned about even the smallest infraction of the religion's rules. Jesus Christ restrains the Father from punishing people, but the Father's role as the final judge of humankind remains in the forefront. Between this distant God and the people there are approachable saints who act as intermediaries and protectors. Liturgies are formal and under the direction of priests, with minimal, if any, direct participation by laity. As the world is evil and in danger of invading the church, those who question the theological and hierarchical status quo must be identified and marginalized. The image of the church is that of a fortress, powerfully protecting the faithful from the dangers of a threatening world.

At the unofficial level of the church, popular religiosity flourishes. "Popular religiosity" refers to beliefs and practices relating to supernatural or superempirical beings or powers that exist *independently* of, or are not officially sanctioned by, ecclesiastical authorities. Since people have recognized the need for all sorts of mediators or agents to intercede for them in a threatening world, it is not surprising that all kinds of devotions to Our Lady and the saints are so important in popular religiosity.[15] It is called *popular* because it is thought that this form of religion belongs to the "masses" or working class only, as opposed to the educated elite. But these descriptions are too restrictive. People of all classes may be deeply imbued with this form of religion. Individuals can be highly analytical in their social and business life but at the same time devoted to popular religiosity. Church officials, however, frequently disparage popular religiosity and seek either to destroy or domesticate it, often without success. The Latin American episcopate is more positive in its approach. The Latin American bishops write that at "its core the religiosity of the people is a storehouse of values that offers the answers of Christian wisdom to the great questions of life. . . . It creatively combines the divine and the human, Christ and Mary, spirit and body, communion and institution . . . intelligence and emotion."[16] John Paul II also spoke positively of the importance of popular religiosity for Catholics of all social and economic statuses in the United States in his Apostolic Exhortation *Ecclesia in America*, 1999.[17]

Modern Model

This religious type mirrors the wider culture of modernity with its sturdy commitment to values of egalitarianism, individualism, rationalism, utilitarianism, and competitiveness. In a culture of modernity people have a weak sense of belonging or obligations to the group. Individuals form alliances with one another to provide better opportunities for competitive success, but such bondings are very fragile since they are held together only by the self-interest of the individuals themselves. They break apart once more profitable interrelationships appear.

---

15. See descriptions by Eamon Duffy, *The Stripping of the Altars: Traditional Religion in England 1400–1580* (New Haven: Yale University Press, 1992), and *Popular Catholicism in a World Church*, ed. Thomas Bamat and Jean-Paul Wiest (Maryknoll, NY: Orbis Books, 1999).

16. "Final Document of the Third General Conference of the Latin American Episcopate, Puebla," in *Puebla and Beyond*, ed. John Eagleson and Philip Scharper (Maryknoll, NY: Orbis Books, 1979), 184–85.

17. See John Paul II, Apostolic Exhortation *Ecclesia in America* (22 January 1999), 16.

After the successive impacts of the Reformation and the Enlighten-ment, the Catholic Church withdrew into a citadel-like culture and ap-peared to remain untouched by modernity. However, the church as an institution was deeply but indirectly affected by modernity's emphasis on rationality and order. It encouraged a theology, condensed into orderly theological manuals far removed from the world of experience and feel-ing, in order to defend itself against the logical and rational arguments of Protestants. Scripture was used primarily to support preset theological positions.[18] Following Vatican II and the breakdown of the premodern structures of the church, Catholics in general became exposed to the full force of modernity and its values. Whenever this secular culture model is uncritically interiorized, Catholics accept only those beliefs and prac-tices that do not conflict with the mainstream values of the secular culture, manipulating the church to fit their personal aspirations. For them the church has become just another organization to be evaluated not in faith but by the requirements of utilitarian individualism.

Postmodern Model

Among the characteristics of postmodernity are: the refusal to consider that positivist and rationalist measures are the only criteria for knowledge (chap. 1); a readiness to use symbols from unrelated or eclectic sources; a ready openness to rejoice in spontaneity, superficiality, differences, and playfulness;[19] the centrality of chaos rather than order; a ready distrust of any myths or narratives that claim to have universal validity as opposed to individual and group narratives as the sources of different, even com-peting, identities; and cynicism toward traditional institutions such as the mainline churches and governments.[20] These qualities of postmodernity are profoundly affecting religious cultures in general. Among the distin-guishing qualities of postmodern Christianity are the following:

- The importance of experience rather than faith.[21] If God is "expe-rienced" in prayer, this is an assurance that whatever is said in the

18. See Gerald A. Arbuckle, *Violence, Society and the Church: A Cultural Approach* (Collegeville, MN: Liturgical Press, 2004), 119–24.

19. See James A. Beckford, "Religion, Modernity and Post-modernity," in *Religion: Contemporary Issues*, ed. Bryan Wilson (London: Bellew, 1992), 19.

20. See Arbuckle, *Violence*, 153–214.

21. See Paul Goodliff, *Care in a Confused Climate* (London: Darton, Longman, and Todd, 1998), 194–95.

Scriptures and by charismatic leaders is correct. Charismatics and Pentecostalists exemplify this approach. Major problems confronting society are ignored.

- Heaven is of little concern. People desire immediate solutions to their personal problems such as good health and wealth, hence the increasing emphasis on holistic healing such as New Age therapy remedies, and on the interconnectedness of the human/ecosystem.
- As a reaction to the scientific and materialist emphases of modernity there is a yearning for a spirituality, but there is often a vagueness about what it means.
- There is a remarkable eclecticism, a veritable spiritual supermarket in contemporary spirituality, with people drawing symbols and rituals from all kinds of sources,[22] failing to realize that they may conflict with Christian beliefs.[23]

Case Study: Catholicism and Postmodernity

The combined effects of the theological and cultural changes of Vatican II and the expressive revolution of the 1960s that significantly inspired the development of postmodernity have left Catholics breathless, lost in what seems to be an ever-increasing malaise. People feel stunned, overwhelmed with the speed of many social changes. They become exposed to movements and pressures they cannot understand. In an effort to restore order in the chaos there are fundamentalist movements, contrary to the vision of Vatican II, to return the church to its premodern mythology and authority structures.[24] Self-righteously, using their powers of surveillance, fundamentalists in the church identify anything they consider unorthodox and then harshly discipline the wayward. They assume that history must be put right and the church rescued from the "dangerous modernists" and returned to its "golden pre-Vatican II era."[25] They are highly selective about what is at the heart of the church's teaching, conveniently overlooking the social documents and concentrating instead on issues of lesser importance,

---

22. See Peter L. Berger, *The Social Reality of Religion* (London: Faber, 1969).

23. See Beckford, *Religion*, 11–23.

24. See Arbuckle, *Violence*, 203–14.

25. See comments by Patrick M. Arnold, "The Rise of Catholic Fundamentalism," *America* 156, no. 14 (11 April 1987): 298–302.

for example liturgical rubrics and matters of private sexuality.[26] At times Catholic fundamentalists are estimable leaders in the anti-abortion campaign, but wider issues of social justice are overlooked.

Fundamentalist movements, for example Communione e Liberazione, Neo-Catechumenate, Opus Dei, and Catholics United for the Faith, actively look to Rome to use its coercive power "to put the church right." Theologian Joe Holland prophetically commented in 1990 that the "new wave of postmodern lay communities are tempted to pursue a cultural strategy of classical restoration, rather than a postmodern regeneration." This strategy would "restore exclusively the classical transcendent and hierarchical disclosure of the masculine face of God." There would be an attempt "to reassert patriarchy as an authoritarian means of combating the disintegrating crisis of late modern culture." This approach to society would be done "predominantly in fear and resentment rather than in compassion and healing."[27] Time has proved Holland's analysis correct. Rome not only supports many of these fundamentalist-oriented organizations but itself appoints people such as anti-council bishops who then initiate movements with fundamentalist qualities. The overture of reconciliation in 2009 toward the four excommunicated schismatic Lefebvrist bishops, while a paternal act of mercy, is sending profoundly disturbing messages to the wider church. These bishops, publicly rejecting much of Vatican II, claim they have been seeking the lifting of the excommunication in order to work within the church for the restoration of a preconciliar style of Catholicism.[28] The fact that one of the four bishops has publicly questioned whether six million Jews died in the Holocaust has further fueled concern in the wider church.

On the other hand, many older Catholics, thoroughly educated in the council's theology of church and lay involvement, now view these restorationist movements with immense sadness and alarm. While Rome speaks of the need for dialogue and justice in the world, they see it as discouraging any reasonable critique of its

---

26. See Arbuckle, *Refounding the Church,* 53.

27. Joe Holland, "The Postmodern Cultural Transition: Its Challenge to the 'Vowed Life,'" Draft Background Paper to the Conference of Major Superiors of Men, USA (8 August 1990), 21.

28. See editorial "Not Yet Back in the Fold," *The Tablet* (31 January 2009): 2.

own structures, including its secretive methods of governing.[29] They search for priests and parishes that can speak to their needs according to the vision of the council. Others, feeling that the church no longer speaks to the realities of their daily lives, choose to walk away saddened and cynical or to join other religious groups.

Richard Gaillardetz, reflecting on the emergence of a new cultural type of lay Catholic in recent years, "the under-forty Catholics," describes their significant qualities.[30] They have a consumerist approach to their faith, choosing those beliefs and practices they feel make sense to them, but their commitment to the church as such is weak. He terms another type "Evangelical Catholicism," whose members earnestly search for a renewed sense of Catholic identity. They are quintessentially postmodern because they seek to construct from their own convictions a distinctive religious identity in a world of pluralist beliefs. This leads them to choose a variety of identity markers such as the Eucharist, Mary, the pope, and pre-Vatican II liturgical styles and dress. Not interested in critiquing the church's governing structures and authority, they lack the concern of Vatican II to enter into dialogue with the world or to be involved in social justice programs.

Case Study: Anglicanism and Postmodernity

The Anglican Communion also exemplifies many of the contradictory characteristics of contemporary postmodern religious groups: fragmentation, passionate exuberance, feeling over reason, fundamentalism. Anglicans traditionally emphasize a theological harmony between commitment to the Scriptures, tradition, and reason. But now the Communion is in danger of splitting because of two irreconcilable, different theological views concerning the nature and purpose of the church in the world. The evangelical fundamentalist wing of the church, which holds the Scriptures rather than tradition and reason as the foundation of their beliefs, claims that the world is inherently evil and the biggest threat to the church is secular humanism, which includes, for example, homo-

---

29. See Arbuckle, *Refounding the Church*, 16.

30. See Richard Gaillardetz, "Apologetics, Evangelization and Ecumenism Today," *Origins* 35 (19 May 2005): 9–15.

sexual freedom and women priests. On the other hand, liberal theologians hold that secularism is not an obstacle to the faith, for God
is working within the secular world. They claim that God loves
minorities, and the church should not judge or exclude them; hence
their support for women priests and gay rights. Very vicious verbal
infighting continues between the two sides, with the evangelicals
acting with the unrestrained verbal ferocity of fundamentalists demanding that they impose on the whole Anglican Church a uniformity of doctrine and practice.[31] At the same time the liberals are
struggling to prevent this from happening.[32]

Prophetic Model

This type of religious culture tends to emerge in reaction to authoritarian hierarchical forms of religion, often under the inspiration of a
charismatic person or persons. Relationships are strongly egalitarian
and the image of the church is that of a pilgrim people journeying with
Christ: brother, healer, savior. As many religious congregations in their
initial founding exemplify this type, they help to explain the qualities and
power of this model.

For example, St. Benedict of Nursia (ca. 480–547), founder of the Benedictine monastic movement, reacted prophetically to the feudal structures
within the civil and ecclesiastical institutions of his time. In opposition to
the individualism, materialism, and authoritarian abuse of power of these
institutions, Benedict offered an alternative vision of society founded on
the kingdom values of interdependence, love, and justice. The abbot's task
was to be persuasive, not coercive. Not only was he to be elected by all
the monks, he was to make important decisions only after listening to all
members of the community. Special consideration was to be given to
younger members because, says the rule, "the Lord often reveals what is
better to the younger. . . . If less important business in the monastery is
to be transacted, [the Abbot] shall take counsel with the seniors only."[33]

---

31. See Monica Furlong, *C of E: The State It's In* (London: Hodder and Stoughton,
2000), 334–35; Chris McGillion, *The Chosen Ones: The Politics of Salvation in the
Anglican Church* (Sydney: Allen and Unwin, 2005), 178–87.

32. See Peter Herriot, *Religious Fundamentalism and Social Identity* (London:
Routledge, 2007), 85–86.

33. *RB: The Rule of St. Benedict*, ed. Terence Fry (Collegeville, MN: Liturgical Press,
1981), 179–80.

Music historian John Shepherd argues that Gregorian chant as encouraged by the early Benedictine monasteries is itself prophetically countercultural in reaction to the hierarchical feudal structures within church and society. The pentatonicism of the chant was based on a nonhierarchical collection of tones in which there was no principal or root tone.[34]

A similar prophetic movement emerged under the inspiration of St. Francis of Assisi (1182–1226). He was shocked by the wealth and misuse of power within existing orders and the church in general. The poverty of Francis was not primarily personally ascetic; rather, it was to be prophetic and christological. As Christ had freely chosen poverty, thus revealing his humility, so also should Franciscans rejoice when they live among people considered of little worth such as the poor and powerless, the sick and lepers, and the beggars by the wayside.[35]

The model is helpful in understanding the rise and inner dynamics of prophetic groupings such as women's movements for equality of rights within the church, "churches from below," prayer groups, L'Arche communities, and Basic Ecclesial Communities (BECs). Bishop Francisco Claver, SJ, defines a BEC as "A community of believers at the grassroots level, which meets regularly under the leadership of a lay minister, to express their faith in common worship, to discern on their common living of the faith, to plan and act on common decisions regarding their life of faith in community, as community."[36]

Normally "churches from below" develop in reaction to the perceived poverty of Gospel values in society and/or the church. For many intentional communities, especially BECs, God in Christ is portrayed as a brother and a liberator, the one with whom the oppressed of this world can identify.[37] Theology becomes a "theology from below"—the result of people's reflection on their own narratives of life and experience in the light of the Gospel. Liturgies are participative, simple, and mirror the living faith experience of the members and the model of the church as a pilgrim in this world, a model so central to the theology of Vatican II. Every member has a particular role within the group; clerics are not

---

34. See John Shepherd, *Music as Social Text* (Cambridge: Polity, 1991); Philip Smith and Alexander Riley, *Cultural Theory: An Introduction* (Oxford: Blackwell, 2009), 150.

35. See Gerald A. Arbuckle, *From Chaos to Mission: Refounding Religious Life Formation* (Collegeville, MN: Liturgical Press, 1995), 13–21.

36. Francisco F. Claver, *The Making of a Local Church* (Maryknoll, NY: Orbis Books, 2008), 89.

37. See Aloysius Pieris, "A Theology of Liberation in Asian Churches?" *The Month* (September 1985): 231–39.

singled out for special status or influence beyond what their sacramental duties require of them.[38]

Catholicism, Pentecostalism, and Postmodernity

Pentecostal and charismatic Christianity worldwide have grown dramatically since the 1960s. In the southern hemisphere alone, by 2050 only one in five Christians will be non-Latino and white, as increasing numbers of Asians, Africans, and Latin Americans leave historically mainline Christian churches for the more recently introduced Pentecostal denominations.[39] From a total population in Latin America of 520 million, an estimated 170 million call themselves Pentecostals, charismatics, or members of independent, usually Pentecostal churches; 36 percent of Chileans belong to Pentecostal churches.[40] In Guatemala almost a third of the population is Pentecostal; in Brazil there are an estimated 24 million followers. Conversions continue with significant speed, mainly among people who are poor, but they are now spreading among the middle classes. Some now call this a new Protestant Reformation as the cultural monopoly of Catholicism continues to be weakened.[41] In Africa Pentecostalism is spreading twice as fast as Catholicism and shows three times the growth of other forms of Protestantism.[42] The impact of Pentecostalism among Hispanics in the United States is also increasingly significant. For example, though it is estimated that 68 percent of Hispanics are still Catholic, conversion to Pentecostal forms of religion continues to gather momentum.[43]

The zeal and courage with which converts witness to their faith[44] must raise serious questions for the mainline churches, and in particular

38. See Arbuckle, *Refounding the Church*, 90–93.

39. See Karen J. Brison, "The Empire Strikes Back: Pentecostalism in Fiji, *Ethnology* 46 (2007): 21.

40. See Ondina E. Gonzalez and Justo L. Gonzalez, *Christianity in Latin America* (Cambridge: Cambridge University Press, 2008), 271–96.

41. See Bernice Martin, "From Pre- to Postmodernity in Latin America: the Case of Pentecostalism," in *Pentecostalism: The World Their Parish*, ed. David Martin (Oxford: Blackwell, 2002), 106–9.

42. See John Micklethwait and Adrian Wooldridge, *God is Back* (New York: Penguin, 2009), 217.

43. See "Latinos and Religion: Separated Brothers," *The Economist* (31 July 2009): 31.

44. See Gonzalez and Gonzalez, *Christianity*, 274.

the Catholic Church. These churches are obviously not responding to the deepest desires of these converts. They are seen to be irrelevant.

Sociologist Bernice Martin offers reasons for the rapid spread of Pentecostalism in South America. The speedy transition from economic and social premodernity to capitalistic individualistic postmodernity is taking place in Latin America, for the most part without having to pass through the stage of modernity. Contemporary Pentecostalism, she claims, has become a significant vehicle for this process, not traditional Catholicism. There is a massive migration of the desperately poor from the rural areas to the cities in search of a new life, but they lack the traditional kin, class, and clientage support systems. Women are most vulnerable, for they have always suffered from the irresponsible *machismo* of their menfolk, domestic violence, alcoholism, and prostitution. The Catholic Church has preached against this for generations, recommending to women patience and recourse to Our Lady for consolation, but the problems have intensified in the massive slums of the megacities. Pentecostalism, on the other hand, promises to restore a moral order in the relationships between women and men and is having very visible success. It also preaches individual prosperity, if people but believe. Failure to move ahead in a capitalistic system is blamed on lack of faith and on bad spirits.

Case Study: The "Toronto Blessing"

The "Toronto Blessing" is an expression invented to describe the revival and subsequent phenomenon that began in 1994 at the Toronto Airport Vineyard Christian Fellowship (TACF), a Pentecostal church in Toronto, Canada. The *Toronto Star* described a session involving 5,300 people. Participants "collapsed, some rigid . . . some convulsed in hysterical laughter . . . [and] grunts so deep women recalled the sounds of childhood, while men adopted the very position of childbirth."[45] In her sociological analysis of TACF, Margaret Poloma argues that this revivalist movement is a reaction to the emotional sterility, materialism, and scientism of modernity. It provides a holistic view of the person: an integration of body,

---

45. Cited by Margaret M. Poloma, "The 'Toronto Blessing' in Postmodern Society: Manifestations, Metaphor and Myth," in *The Globalization of Pentecostalism: A Religion Made to Travel*, eds. Murray W. Dempster, Byron Klaus and Douglas Petersen (Oxford: Regnum, 1999), 364.

cognition, emotions, will, and spirit that has been destroyed by the consequences of the Enlightenment. It offers, she concludes, "a creative response to both the straight-jacket of modernism and the abyss of postmodernism."[46]

Martin identifies several weaknesses in the dominant Catholic Church that Pentecostalism has taken advantage of, namely, the traditional alliance of the church with the ruling elites, reliance on foreign priests, and the church's discouragement of popular religiosity following Vatican II. For the Latin American church the cultic trappings of popular religiosity together with the baroque untidiness of churches offended "the educated international opinion-formers of Catholicism as being in dubious aesthetic taste and obsolete theological fashion."[47] This over-intellectualized Catholicism has offended many of the poor, who found the plain washed church interiors, the weakening of pious respect for Mary, the expulsion of the colorful devotions and healing practices and the removal of the statues of their favorite saints too much to accept. Pentecostalism's approach is built on this denigrated traditional popular religiosity, especially its emphasis on healing and liveliness in worship, making people once more feel at home. Its democratic structure also allows people to feel they are actively participating without the controlling presence of the clergy. If a particular pastor becomes authoritarian, people can move away and establish their own worshiping group.

In summary, the secret of Pentecostalism's expanding success as a postmodern movement is:

- It has the ability to offer people *immediate* hope that there are solutions to their problems within the intense chaos of urban poverty; if there is no success they can blame the devil or their own lack of faith in the Spirit. Wealth is a sign of God's blessings. As one observer notes: "[Pentecostalism] doesn't oppose consumerism. It embraces it. It *imports meaning* into consumerism."[48]
- William Hewitt believes that among the reasons for liberation theology's lack of attractiveness in contrast to the success of Pentecostalism is its excessive intellectualism and its emphasis on distant

46. Ibid., 382.

47. Martin, *Pentecostalism*, 124–25.

48. Margaret Simons, *Now Faith, Money, Power: What the Religious Revival Means for Politics* (Melbourne: Pluto Press, 2007), 97. Italics in original.

goals.[49] It is the immediate promise of material achieve-ment through individual effort and the neglect of the group that highlights the postmodern quality of Pentecostalism. Liberation theology, on the other hand, emphasizes the fact that poverty cannot just be removed by individual enthusiasm and effort; structural change is also required. Without this structural change only a small minority can break through the barriers of poverty. Pentecostalists rarely challenge the injustices of national and global capitalism and for this reason, unlike liberation theologians, they are very acceptable to governments eagerly committed to economic rationalism.[50]

• Pentecostalism responds to individuals' yearning to tell and retell their personal story of salvation and their hopes for freedom from poverty and its associated evils. It is not based on rationalization and bureaucracy but on story, song, gesture and empowerment, enthusiastic release, and personal discipline.[51] Individuals no longer feel they are the passive receivers of complex theological or dogmatic narratives so characteristic of their experience of traditional Catholicism.[52]

• Although the new Protestantism insists that the man is the head of the family, and that women must obey their husbands, it also calls for men radically to change their aberrant immoral ways. In consequence, the double standard of sexual morality is theoretically abolished, resulting in mutual and equal responsibility between women and men.[53]

Theological Reflection

A positive quality of postmodernity is that chaos, not order, is at the very heart of the universe. And one of the most powerful images used

---

49. See William E. Hewitt, *Base Communities and Social Change in Brazil* (Lincoln: University of Nebraska Press, 1992).

50. See Donald E. Miller and Tetsunao Yamamori, *Global Pentecostalism: The New Face of Christian Social Engagement* (Berkeley: University of California Press, 2007), 183. For an example of uncritical support for the capitalist system in Australia by a Pentecostal Church see Margaret Simons, *Now Faith*, 55–97.

51. David Martin, *On Secularization: Towards a Revised General Theory* (Aldershot: Ashgate, 2005), 142.

52. See Peter Beyer, *Religions in Global Society* (London: Routledge, 2006), 147–52.

53. See Martin, *On Secularization*, 133.

by Y<small>HWH</small> and reaffirmed by the words and life of Christ is that of chaos itself. Having embraced the powerlessness of humankind in the paschal mystery, Jesus opens himself to the recreative energy of God the Creator, embracing chaos not for itself alone but as the way to the humanly inconceivable life of the resurrection (Phil 2:7, 9). The church is in the chaos of confusion that can be ignored, but can instead be embraced, as Christ has done. The new church of Vatican II values has yet to take confident shape, but restorationist forces refuse to let the old church go. If only the rich potential of this liminal darkness could be grasped, for "now is the acceptable time: see, now is the day of salvation" (2 Cor 6:2). This is a time rich in potentiality for refounding the church through the passionate collaborative efforts of people in touch with the anxieties and hopes of people who possess boundless faith, imagination, and creativity to bring the Gospel alive within this postmodern world. Conditions could not be better.

Chapter 9

Culture(s) in Ecclesial Documents and Theologians

> At all times the Church carries the responsibility of reading the signs of the time and of interpreting them in the light of the Gospel, if it is to carry out its task.
>
> —*Gaudium et Spes* 4[1]

The aim of this chapter is briefly to examine how some ecclesial documents and theologians define culture and cultures. If the definitions of culture are defective, theology will be uncertain or faulty. Theology is that which "mediates between a cultural matrix and the significance and role of a religion in that matrix."[2] Theologians must seek to discern where God is working and articulate a theology sensitive to the local culture. If their view of culture is a static one, their theology will be frozen in time and irrelevant. The church from the late seventeenth century, reacting against the Protestant Reformation, had become a cultural fortress, isolated from the world. The purpose of theology moved "from enquiry to *defence*, demonstration and 'proof.'"[3] Anything that did not support the theological status quo was seen as a threat to the integrated, unchanging, and thoroughly controlled worldwide ecclesiastical culture.

---

1. Pastoral Constitution on the Church in the Modern World (*Gaudium et Spes*), in *Vatican Council II: The Conciliar and Post Conciliar Documents,* ed. Austin P. Flannery, new rev. ed. (Northport, NY: Costello, 1975), 4.

2. Bernard Lonergan, SJ, *Method in Theology* (London: Darton, Longman and Todd, 1975), xi.

3. See Nicholas Lash, *Theology on the Way to Emmaus* (Eugene, OR: Wipf & Stock, 1986), 31.

The world could be changing, but there was no need for the culture of the church, and therefore theology, to change.[4]

There was an added problem during this period of the fortress church. It also accepted without question the classicist or normative notion of culture. As explained in Chapter 1, this definition of culture describes the process whereby people develop their intellectual, spiritual, and artistic qualities, and the actual intellectual and artistic achievements of people. The church saw itself as the guardian of the highest achievements of Western intellectual and artistic gifts. No other culture had anything of value to offer. Bernard Lonergan, SJ, (1904–84) summarized the impact of this conclusion on theology: "When the classicist notion of culture prevails, theology is conceived as a permanent achievement, and then one discourses on its nature,"[5] not on how it is to relate to a changing world.

If, however, we start with an empirical approach to culture, that is, the particular ways of living of a group of people as they search for meaning in the midst of constant change, inner tensions, fragmentation, and struggles over resources and power, the relationship between theology and culture changes.[6] Theology becomes "an ongoing process,"[7] no longer something static. Since there is such diversity of cultures, this process will result in many theologies.

Ecclesial Documents

Papal Expressions

In his Apostolic Constitution promulgating the first code of Canon Law in 1917, Pope Benedict XV summarizes the church's centuries-old classicist view of cultures beyond Rome in these words: "the Church was at pains . . . to abrogate the laws of barbarous nations and to reduce their rude customs to civilized form."[8] Pius XII in 1951 also used "culture" in the classicist sense, but with more sensitivity. He was promoting the

---

4. See Lonergan, *Method in Theology*, xi.

5. Ibid.

6. See Anna Green, *Cultural History: Theory and History* (New York: Palgrave, 2009), 1–10.

7. Lonergan, *Method in Theology*, xi.

8. Benedict XV, "Constitution 'Providentissima' Promulgating the New Code," in *A Commentary on the New Code of Canon Law*, ed. P. Chas Augustine, OSB, (St. Louis: B. Herder, 1921), 65; see also insights by Neil Ormond, *Introducing Contemporary Theologies* (Newtown: E. J. Dwyer, 1990), 3–22.

exhibition of what missionaries have achieved "especially in the field of culture" for distant peoples, "who sometimes boast a very old and highly developed culture of their own."[9] In 1953 the pope used "culture" in an empirical sense when declaring that "the right to one's culture and national character . . . are exigencies of the law of nations dictated by nature itself."[10] John XXIII, in his encyclical *Pacem in Terris* (Peace on Earth), 1963, when speaking of the "right to share in the benefits of culture," used the term in the classicist sense, but later, in adopting the expression "ethnic group," he was referring to culture according to its empirical meaning.[11]

Vatican II

In the documents of Vatican II and subsequent ecclesial documents "culture" is most frequently to be understood in its classicist sense.[12] The Pastoral Constitution on the Church in the Modern World (*Gaudium et Spes*) contains the most direct references to culture, but with confusing results. The authors use the classicist or humanistic definition; thus "culture" refers to "all those things which go to the refining and developing of man's diverse mental and physical endowments" (GS 53).[13] Then, in the same paragraph, they acknowledge its empirical meaning when they write that "'culture' often carries with it sociological and ethnological connotations." Overall, the emphasis in the document is on the classicist meanings of culture, but in a highly significant passage we read that evangelizers must "foster vital contact and exchange between the Church and different cultures" (GS 44). Here the reference is clearly to the empirical meaning of culture. The council ended in 1965 just as the postmodern revolution was beginning, but there is no intimation of this in *Gaudium et Spes*. If anything, the document assumes some of the optimistic ideas of modernity about capacity for human progress.

9. Pius XII, Encyclical Letter "On Promoting Catholic Missions" (1951), in *Modern Missionary Documents and Africa,* ed. Raymond Hickey, OSA (Dublin: Dominican Publications, 1982), 99.

10. Pius XII, in *Acta Apostolicae Sedis* 45 (6 December 1953), 794.

11. John XXIII, Encyclical Letter "Peace on Earth" (*Pacem in Terris*), 11 April 1963, 13, 43.

12. For analyses of the use of "culture" in Vatican II documents see Michael P. Gallagher, SJ, *Clashing Symbols: An Introduction to Faith and Culture* (London: Darton, Longman, and Todd, 1997), 36–55, and Phillip Tovey, *Inculturation of Christian Worship: Exploring the Eucharist* (Aldershot: Ashgate, 1994), 112–17.

13. See Charles M. Murphy, "The Church and Culture since Vatican II: On the Analogy of Faith and Art," *Theological Studies* 48 (June 1987): 317–31.

In the Constitution on the Sacred Liturgy (*Sacrosanctum Concilium*) the emphasis is on revising liturgical rites in order to encourage the "active participation in liturgical celebrations" of all the faithful (SC 14). The ritual should be simplified to make it more comprehensible: "The rites should be distinguished by a noble simplicity. They should be short, clear, and free from useless repetitions. They should be within the people's powers of comprehension, and normally should not require much explanation" (SC 34).

At first sight this is an estimable principle, but not all cultures appreciate "noble simplicity"; on the contrary, many value significant repetition as the best way to communicate meaning. Such is the case with a number of Polynesian and African peoples whose ways of communicating are filled with colorful symbolic repetitions. "Noble simplicity," therefore, can be offensive. The principle of liturgical reform behind the document is in fact the revival of the "noble simplicity" of Roman cultural values, which are now to be reimposed on the world church. While the document says there is room for "legitimate variations and adaptations to different groups, regions and peoples, especially in mission countries," nonetheless "the substantial unity of the Roman rite is [to be] preserved" (SC 38).

Anthropologists Mary Douglas and Victor Turner forcefully criticize this stress on "noble simplicity," complaining that reform is now to be dominated by rational criteria in which symbolism and mythology have little or no place (see chap. 1) and where the emphasis is to be on an intellectual understanding through the use of words, with little or nothing that speaks to the heart.[14] This is not to deny the importance of a sound theological or intellectual foundation for liturgy, but liturgy must be more than this. It must be able to touch the hearts of people in ways appropriate to their different cultures. Turner further complains that the reform is based on the outdated modern structural-functionalist definition of culture.[15] A functionalist approach to liturgical reform requires that liturgies must mirror the structure of the culture in which they are devised, but, as already noted, the reform assumes that the Roman culture with its emphasis on "noble simplicity" is the norm for all liturgies. No significant diversion from this is possible. Further, the purpose is that

14. See Mary Douglas, *Natural Symbols: Explorations in Cosmology* (New York: Pantheon Books, 1970), 4.

15. See Victor Turner, "Passages, Margins, and Poverty: Religious Symbols of Communitas," *Worship* 46 (August-September 1972): 392.

unity and harmony must prevail, even at the cost of legitimate diversity in ritual.

In 1986 the then-Cardinal Ratzinger was also highly critical of some of the renewal experiments in the liturgy.[16] The primary aim of the liturgy, he reminds us, is the worship of the Triune God, not the bonding of a community. When this is forgotten the liturgy becomes banal, primarily concerned with making people feel good. All members of the congregation are expected to be doing things together, such as singing and vocalizing responses. If not, there is no participation. Moments of silence, in which people can enter into a contemplative stance before God, must not occur. Ratzinger's criticism is valid, because those who overemphasize the bonding nature of liturgy are in fact adopting Emile Durkheim's view of religion. For Durkheim the primary purpose of music and chants is to generate collective emotional excitement or collective effervescence, not the worship of God.[17]

Paul VI

Under Pope Paul VI ecclesial documents begin to use the term "culture" more frequently in empirical ways. In both his first encyclical, On the Church (*Ecclesiam Suam*, 1964) and in On the Progress of Peoples (*Populorum Progressio*, 1965) he confines himself to the classicist approach.[18] However, in his pastoral document On the Pastoral Care of Migrants (*Pastoralis Migratorium*, 1969), his speeches while on overseas visits particularly to Africa,[19] and in his inspirational Apostolic Letter On Evangelization (*Evangelii Nuntiandi*, 1975) there is a sharp focus on the social and religious implications of the empirical definition of culture. *Evangelii Nuntiandi* contains several significant changes in the way culture is presented. Written in 1975 when cultural anthropology was beginning its revolutionary reinterpretation of culture, the document

16. See Joseph Ratzinger, *The Feast of Faith* (San Francisco: Ignatius Press, 1986), and Tracey Rowland, *Ratzinger's Faith: The Theology of Pope Benedict XVI* (Oxford: Oxford University Press, 2008), 123–43.

17. See Emile Durkheim, *Elementary Forms of Religious Life* (London: Allen and Unwin, 1968), 427.

18. See Paul VI, "Encyclical Letter *Populorum Progressio,*" in *The Gospel of Peace and Justice: Catholic Social Teaching since John XXIII*, ed. Joseph Gremillion (Maryknoll, NY: Orbis Books, 1976), 399.

19. See Aylward Shorter, *Toward a Theology of Inculturation* (London: Geoffrey Chapman, 1988), 206–21.

reflects something of this radical rethinking, particularly the semiotic approach of Clifford Geertz and even that of Claude Levi-Strauss. First, it no longer speaks of culture in the abstract sense but several times refers to "culture or cultures" (EN 20).[20] Second, it refers to the need to use a people's "language, their signs and symbols" (EN 63). There is also the hint that cultures must not be considered as homogeneous or static because evangelization will be ineffective "if it does not answer the questions [the people] ask, and if it does not have an impact on their concrete life" (EN 63). There is an undercurrent of some disquiet about the state of culture and cultures throughout the world (see EN 20, 63), but this would be the only acknowledgment of the chaotic influences of postmodernity. Given the fact that the letter was written in the mid-1970s it is surprising that postmodernity was so lightly treated.

John Paul II

From the beginning of John Paul II's pontificate he forthrightly focused on the fundamental importance of understanding and interacting with cultures as the prerequisite for effective evangelization. But it is not always clear how he was defining the term. Usually "culture" was used not in an empirical way, but according to its classicist definition. While analyzing the prodigious nature of the pope's pronouncements, Michael Gallagher, SJ, is able to distinguish three different ways in which the pope uses culture, although they may overlap at times: the classicist understanding, but often with a strong theological critique included; the sociological meaning of the term; and finally references in concrete terms to particular or local cultures.[21] An example of the classicist approach is his identification in 1980 of the dichotomy between "civilization of love" and the "culture of death."[22]

Examples of the empirical use of culture are evident in his encyclical Mission of the Redeemer (*Redemptoris Missio*, 1990).[23] When he uses the word "culture" in this document he follows the modern definition, that it is something frozen in time, homogeneous and resistant to external

20. See Paul VI, Apostolic Letter "On Evangelization" (*Evangelii Nuntiandi*), 1975 (Sydney: St Paul Publications, 1982).

21. See Gallagher, *Clashing Symbols*, 48.

22. See Tracey Rowland, *Culture and the Thomist Tradition* (London: Routledge, 2003), 36–37.

23. See John Paul II, Encyclical Letter "Mission of the Redeemer" (*Redemptoris Missio*), 1990 (Boston: St. Paul Books, 1991).

influences, but at the same time he frequently describes situations that are characteristically postmodern, such as the impact of megacities on cultural change, problems facing minorities, the threats to the environment (RM 37). In another encyclical letter, Apostles of the Slavs (*Slavorum Apostoli*, 1985), he emphasizes the part Saints Cyril and Methodius played in the development of Slavonic culture in the ninth century. While declaring these two saints the heavenly co-patrons of the whole of Europe, the pope uses the occasion to remind Europe that it owes its cultural identity to the founding Roman Catholic myth or story and emphasizes the importance of that myth for maintaining primal unity today. At no point does he refer to any fundamental crisis affecting the church or even to Protestantism.[24] He is using culture not in the empirical sense but as synonymous with intellectual and artistic achievements. Europe, in his view, is the model for the rest of the world of how these accomplishments can be attained through the interaction of the Gospel with cultures. As Aylward Shorter comments, the pope accepts the fact that cultures other than that of Europe exist, but he "places them lower down on the cultural scale."[25]

Confusion over the definition of culture is to be found also in documents from Vatican departments and episcopal statements. In 1994 the Congregation for Divine Worship and the Discipline of the Sacraments issued the Instruction, *Varietates Legitimae*, to provide more detailed pastoral guidelines for the correct adaptation of the liturgy. Adaptation, however, is to be understood in light of the modern definition of culture as an integrated and integrating whole. At the same time it describes changes and internal tensions within cultures that are distinctly postmodern, such as pointing out that a single country can contain many different cultures mainly due to immigration (VL 6, 49-50).[26] There is also an acknowledgment that singing among some peoples is "instinctively accompanied by handclapping, rhythmic swaying and dance movements" and that these "forms of external expression can have a place in the liturgical actions of these peoples" (VL 42). However, despite the frequent emphasis on the importance of local cultures in liturgies, the empirical culture into which all cultures must ultimately be assimilated is the present homogeneous, unchanging, and integrating ecclesiastical Roman

---

24. See Richard H. Roberts, "The Construals of 'Europe': Religion, Theology and the Problematics of Modernity," in *Pentecostalism: The World Their Parish*, ed. David Martin, 195–97 (Oxford: Blackwell, 2002).

25. Shorter, *Toward a Theology*, 233.

26. See the overview by Peter Phan, *Being Religious Interreligiously: Asian Perspectives on Interfaith Dialogue* (Maryknoll, NY: Orbis Books, 204), 227–32.

culture. The Roman rite is one very significant expression of this underlying culture. No substantial change in this rite, or in the culture of which the rite is but a visible expression, is to be allowed: "The process of inculturation should maintain the substantial unity of the Roman rite. . . . The work of inculturation does not foresee the creation of new families of rites; inculturation responds to the needs of a particular culture and leads to adaptations which still remain part of the Roman rite" (VL 36).

Statements like this assume there are no tensions and struggles for power within the ecclesiastical Roman culture. On the contrary, there has been and continues to be significant disquiet on the part of several episcopal conferences. They complain that their legitimate authority is being undermined by the centralizing authority of the Roman curial bureaucracy.[27] The fact that vernacular translations of liturgical texts, for example, must be submitted to Rome for approval is farcical, for there is no official person in Rome who knows complex languages such as the multiple tongues of Africa, Polynesia, and Melanesia. As Bishop Francisco Claver says, "the best judges of the correctness, even theological, of translations and texts are the faithful and clergy of the place where the language is spoken."[28] With evidence like this Nathan Mitchell is correct in stating that "it is difficult to erase the impression that [the document] seeks to *recentralize* decisions. . . . [That there is] continued Roman discomfort with the power granted Episcopal conferences . . . is evident."[29]

A description of three types of myth, namely public, operative, and residual myths (chap. 1), may help to explain the confusion within the document. A public myth is one that is claimed by those in power to bind a group of people together; an operative myth is what *actually* at a particular time gives people a cohesive identity, and this myth can and often does differ dramatically from the public myth. The residual myth is a myth from former times that potentially is capable of resurfacing as the operative myth, often on the initiative of those who have power to resurrect it. The public myth in the document is that "the liturgy of the church must not be foreign to any country. . . . It must be capable of expressing itself in every human culture" (VL 18). However, the operative myth is now the resurfaced pre-Vatican II residual myth, namely, that the unchanging

---

27. See the observations by Nathan Mitchell, "The Amen Corner," *Worship* 68 (July 1994): 371–76.

28. Francisco Claver, "Inculturation as Dialogue," in *The Asian Synod: Texts and Commentaries*, ed. Peter C. Phan (Maryknoll: Orbis, 2002), 101.

29. Mitchell, "Amen Corner," 371–72.

Roman culture must be imposed on all local churches as the integrating force for uniformity.[30]

At one point in the document there is some ingenuousness about the lack of need for inculturation in Europe: "In countries with a Christian tradition . . . it is not so much a matter of inculturation . . . but rather a matter of insisting on liturgical formation" (VL 8). This statement takes no account of the enormity of the postmodern cultural shifts that have occurred in Europe; it gives the impression that countries outside Europe such as those in Asia and Africa alone require the process of inculturation.

Two further documents illustrate the confusion over the nature of culture. In 1989 the International Theological Commission, under the presidency of Cardinal Joseph Ratzinger, published a document entitled Faith and Inculturation. It begins by summarizing the chapter devoted to the promotion of culture in the Pastoral Constitution on the Church in the Modern World of Vatican II. It then proceeds to use the word culture in the several different senses of that document, but with no reference at any point to the radical rethinking of the word in cultural anthropology since 1963. Like Vatican II, it acknowledges modernity with its "its undeniable progress in many cultural and material domains,"[31] but there is no reference to the realities of postmodernity and its impact on our understanding of culture. However, it is insistent that "We must develop a *capacity to analyse cultures*."[32] This indicates that the authors are aware of the urgency not just for theological research but for sound empirical analysis as well.

In 1999 the Pontifical Council for Culture, an important initiative of John Paul II in 1982, published a lengthy statement, Toward a Pastoral Approach to Culture. The authors' task is to examine "what is meant by culture,"[33] but they follow unchanged the confusing meanings of the word characteristic of the documents of Vatican II thirty-six years before.[34] However, the document does refer to critical postmodern cultural issues, for example the breakdown of cultural identity resulting from the

30. See Gerald A. Arbuckle, *Violence, Society and the Church: A Cultural Approach* (Collegeville, MN: Liturgical Press, 2004), 203–5.

31. See International Theological Commission, "Faith and Inculturation" (1988), published in *Irish Theological Quarterly* 55 (1989): 157.

32. Ibid. Italics in original.

33. Pontifical Council for Culture, "Toward a Pastoral Approach to Culture," *Origins* 29, no. 5 (17 June 1999), §2.

34. See ibid., §39.

movement of people from rural areas to cities and the rise of new religious movements.

United States Catholic Conference

In 1994 the Department of Education of the United States Catholic Conference issued a document called Principles for Inculturation of the Catechism of the Catholic Church, to offer catechetical and pastoral leaders guidelines for the implementation of the recently published *Catechism of the Catholic Church*. To assist in this aim it provides a "summary of the key principles of inculturation, pointing out some of the major challenges these principles face and offering concrete recommendations to carry out a truly inculturated catechesis."[35] Unfortunately, despite its good intentions, the document starts with a modern definition of culture, with its emphasis on homogeneity, namely that which "embraces the totality of the life of the group and the life of each individual who belongs to it."[36] At the same time, as in the documents already noted, it does refer to issues that are postmodern, such as the rise of religious sects, the growing variety of language and cultural groups in parishes, and the difficulties these present for evangelization. There is the clash between an unreal image of a homogeneous, all-embracing unity of culture as envisaged in a parish and the divisiveness and tensions evoked by these factors. As long as the document assumes the modern definition of culture is the correct one, then, at least unconsciously, diversity and tensions will be considered human aberrations.

Theologians

Bernard Lonergan rejected the Eurocentric classicist definition of culture in favor of an empirical one and sought to create a theology, based on new philosophical foundations, that could be intelligible to people in very different and changing cultures.[37] The highly respected theologian Hans Urs von Balthasar (1905–88), however, used the word

---

35. United States Catholic Conference, Department of Education, "Principles for Inculturation of the Catechism of the Catholic Church" (Washington, DC: USCC, 1994), 1.

36. Ibid.

37. See Lonergan, *Method*, 300–302.

"culture" in a classicist sense as synonymous with European intellectual and artistic achievements. He rejected a kind of Christian integralism that claims that Christian thinking has nothing to learn from any dialogue with human culture, as defined of course in the classicist sense. At the same time he refused to accept the claim that Christian faith is to be measured by the norms of human culture.[38]

For Karl Rahner, SJ (1904–84) theology may discover "its most significant dialogical partner not in philosophy but in the natural, psychological, and social sciences which shape people's self-understanding in the present."[39] Rahner severed his links with traditional theology of the church because it does not begin with the actual lives of men and women in the contemporary world. These people, not the church's dogmatic statements of faith, are to be the springboard for theological reflection; hence his focus was a pastoral theology that makes sense to people living their faith in the world. He was also sensitive to the fact that cultures are in rapid change and the world church needs to be urgently sensitive to this reality.

Rahner left no ambiguity about his rejection of a classicist Eurocentric culture when he wrote (in rather complex Rahnerian style):

> [One] can consider the official activity of the Church . . . and see clearly that despite the implied contradiction to its essence, the actual concrete activity of the Church in its relation to the world outside of Europe was in fact . . . the activity of an export firm which exported a European religion as a commodity it did not really want to change but sent throughout the world together with the rest of the culture and civilization it considered superior.[40]

Rahner was a postmodern theologian in the sense that he deliberately began his theology with the human person in the midst of rapidly changing cultural and contentious situations.[41] Though he did not formally

---

38. See David S. Yeago, "Literature in the Drama of Nature and Grace: von Balthasar's Paradigm for a Theology of Culture," in *Glory, Grace, and Culture*, ed. Ed Block Jr., 88–106 (New York: Paulist, 2005).

39. Ann Carr, "Theology and Experience in the Thought of Karl Rahner," *Journal of Religion* 53 (1973): 373.

40. Karl Rahner, "Towards a Fundamental Theological Interpretation of Vatican II," *Theological Studies* 40 (December 1979): 717.

41. See the interesting comments by Michael Purcell, "Rahner amid Modernity and Post-Modernity," *The Cambridge Companion to Karl Rahner*, eds. Declan Marmion and Mary E. Hines, 195–210 (Cambridge: Cambridge University Press, 2005).

discuss the nature of culture, he rejected as unreal the homogeneous and unchanging cultural model of the universal church. It is not only a divinely established church, but at the same time a very human multi-cultural process,[42] and subject to tensions of all kinds.[43] Because he recognized that cultures are filled with the diversity of individual and group myths, history, ways of speaking and communicating, he concluded that "there will no longer be any one single and universal basic formula of the Christian faith applicable to the whole Church and, indeed, prescribed for her as authoritatively binding."[44] This is an extraordinarily bold conclusion to make when so few in the church in 1974 would have been aware of the postmodern insight into culture.

Many of Rahner's successors such as Johann Baptist Metz, Gustavo Gutiérrez, Leonardo Boff, Elisabeth Schüssler Fiorenza, and Rosemary Radford Ruether follow his method. However, they begin their theological reflections not with humankind in general but instead with the evil and systemic injustice in particular cultural and historical situations. They develop specific types of theology. Metz, for example, recognizes the need to develop a theology that is praxis-oriented, which necessitates focusing on political power, a quality of all human actions that can be insidiously used even by theologians to oppress others. So Metz inquires "who should do theology and where, in whose interests and for whom?"[45] Liberation theology, as it has evolved under the leadership of theologians like Gutiérrez, is faith confronting the cultures of poverty in all its oppressive forms. It is a distinctly postmodern approach to culture. It recognizes not just the many-faceted aspects of poverty such as the manipulation of the power structures by people who are rich, but also the critical role of people who are poor as agents and subjects of change. This theology does not try to make people who are poor rich, or those who are rich poor, but "to guide the transformation of all human beings into new ways of being human."[46]

Feminist theology, which owes its beginning in significant ways to liberation theology and the writings of Foucault, first focuses on patriarchal

---

42. Rahner, "Towards a Fundamental Theological Interpretation," 718.

43. See Karl Rahner, *Concern for the Church* (New York: Crossroad, 1981), 143–53.

44. Karl Rahner, "Reflections on the Problems Involved in Devising a Short Formula of Faith," *Theological Investigations* XI (Darton, Longman and Todd, 1974), 233.

45. Johann Baptist Metz, *Faith in History and Society: Toward a Practical Fundamental Theology* (London: Burns & Oates, 1980), 58–59.

46. Rebecca S. Chopp, "Latin American Liberation Theology," in *The Modern Theologians* vol. 2, ed. David Ford (Oxford: Blackwell, 1989), 173.

power in cultures that make the fundamental assumption that males possess human qualities defining them as superior and dominant and females as inferior and passive. Feminist theologians aim to rebuild the fundamental theological symbols of God, male and female, creation, sin and redemption, and the church, in order to formulate these symbols in a gender-inclusive and egalitarian way.[47] Theologians such as Kwok Pui-lan and Mercy Amba Oduyoye highlight the particular patriarchal problems women in the Third World have to face. They must fight not only against the patriarchal assumptions imported by colonial powers, but also against beliefs of the men in their own local cultures who "create myths of homogeneous national and cultural identity"[48] in which women are second-class people. So Third World feminist theologians "have the double tasks of challenging androcentric myths and practices in their culture and in Christianity."[49] Ursula King concludes in light of these twofold tasks that the theme of liberation is more concrete and vivid in Third World feminist theology than in that of the Western world. Also the theme of "church as community" is much stronger among feminist theologians in the Third World than in the First World because church communities are often the first place in which women have the chance to reflect and speak openly about the patriarchal and cultural oppression they experience.[50]

Finally, there is a small group of contemporary theologians who are also aware of the postmodern understanding of culture and apply it in their theological reflections. Among them are David Tracy,[51] Peter Phan, Kathryn Tanner, Michael Gallagher,[52] Delwin Brown,[53] David Ford,[54] and

47. See Rosemary Radford Ruether, "The Emergence of Christian Feminist Theology," in *The Cambridge Companion to Feminist Theology*, ed. Susan F. Parsons, 3–22 (Cambridge: Cambridge University Press, 2002).

48. Kwok Pui-lan, "Feminist Theology as Intercultural Discourse," in Parsons, ed., *Cambridge Companion*, 27.

49. Ibid., 28.

50. See Ursula King, "Introduction," in *Feminist Theology from the Third World*, ed. eadem, 18–19 (London: SPCK, 1994).

51. See David Tracy, "The Uneasy Alliance Reconceived: Catholic Theological Method, Modernity, and Postmodernity," *Theological Studies* 50 (1989): 548–70.

52. See Gallagher, *Clashing Symbols*.

53. See Delwin Brown, "Refashioning Self and Other: Theology, Academy, and the New Ethnography," in *Converging on Culture: Theologians in Dialogue with Cultural Analysis and Criticism*, eds. Delwin Brown, Sheila Greeve Davaney, and Kathryn Tanner, 41–70 (Oxford: Oxford University Press, 2001).

54. See David Ford, *Theology: A Very Short Introduction* (Oxford: Oxford University Press, 1999), 12–15.

Nicholas Lash.[55] Tanner systematically analyzes the postmodern notion of culture and briefly explains that it opens up new vistas for theology, especially on how we are to view the purpose of theology, theological diversity, inculturation, and even Christianity's own cultural identity.[56] Phan skillfully summarizes the main insights of the postmodern understanding of culture and then shows that particular ecclesial statements on the reform of the liturgy are based on cultural anthropological research that is now inadequate.[57]

Theological Reflection

Paul Tillich (1886–1965), one of the most influential Protestant theologians of the twentieth century and a prophetic writer on the relationship between Christianity and culture, reminds us that "the unconditional claim of Christianity is not related to the Christian Church, but to the event on which it is based,"[58] namely the life, death, and resurrection of Jesus Christ. Everything ultimately must be judged by this event, including the cultures of churches themselves: "If the Church does not subject itself to the judgment [of this event] . . . it becomes idolatrous toward itself." Tillich then critiques the Catholic Church: "This is the tragedy of the Roman Catholic Church. Its way of dealing with culture is the result of its unwillingness to subject itself to the judgment [of this event] . . . ."[59] These are harsh words to hear. Is there some truth in them? How are theologians to react to them?

55. See Nicholas Lash, *Theology on the Way to Emmaus*, 3–33.

56. See Kathryn Tanner, *Theories of Culture: A New Agenda for Theology* (Minneapolis: Fortress Press, 1997).

57. See Peter Phan, *Being Religious*, 213–44.

58. Paul Tillich, "The Church and Contemporary Culture," *World Christian Education*, Second Quarterly (1956): 41.

59. Ibid.

Chapter 10

Jesus Christ, Social Dramas, and Inculturation: Lessons

> Jesus was . . . summoning his hearers to *be* Israel in a new way, to
> take up their proper roles in God's unfolding drama.
>
> —N. T. Wright, "The Mission and Message of Jesus"[1]

Inculturation is a dialectical interaction between Christian faith and
cultures in which these cultures are challenged, affirmed, and transformed toward the reign of God, and in which Christian faith is likewise
challenged, affirmed, and enhanced by this experience. When interacting
with members of his own complex culture and with people of other
cultures Jesus Christ fosters this dialectical exchange characteristic of
inculturation. As Jesus inaugurates the reign of God through proclaiming
the Good News of God's love for all, healing the sick, welcoming outcasts
(see Luke 4:16-21; Matt 11:4-6; 25:31-46), he is in fact at the same time
dialectically interacting with cultures and providing us with examples of
inculturation.[2] The purpose of this chapter is to analyze some of these
examples and to highlight some of the important qualities Jesus requires
in agents of inculturation.

Cultural Background

The modern definition of culture does not fit the world Jesus lives in;
in fact, the postmodern notion of culture best describes his environment.

---

1. N. T. Wright, "The Mission and Message of Jesus," in idem and Marcus Borg,
The Meaning of Jesus (London: SPCK, 1999), 36.
2. See Thomas Groome, "Inculturation: How to Proceed in a Pastoral Context,"
Concilium 2 (1994): 120–22.

There was nothing discrete, homogeneous, and integrating about his cultural world because it was filled with all kinds of tensions, fragmentation, and subcultural differences.

Jesus was born into a Jerusalem kingdom ruled by a king, installed and protected by the Roman empire. The culture of the Roman world in the time of Jesus was very much divided among a small, rich, politically powerful upper class that included representatives of the Roman colonial power; a relatively small intermediary class consisting of small landowners, craftsmen, and shopkeepers; then a large peasant population of tenant and subsistence farmers struggling to survive in harsh climatic conditions. Beneath the peasant class would have been slaves and the really poor and unclean such as lepers, the blind, the lame.[3] It was a precarious existence for the sizeable peasant population, pressured by difficult conditions for agriculture and the oppressive demands of their rich landlords and the political elite. Not surprisingly, therefore, when the disciples were unable to catch any fish, they knew they would go hungry (Luke 5:1-11; John 21:3-5). Then there was the religious structure that included the Pharisees and Sadducees. There was also extensive banditry, even of a potentially revolutionary kind, supported not only by peasants but also by some Pharisees and members of the upper class. And to further exacerbate these internal divisions and tensions there were the added pressures evoked by a complex cultural system of shame and honor affecting all relationships. Honor is a person's or group's sense of self-worth and the public, social acceptance of that assessment. Honor is the foundation of one's reputation, of one's social status in the community.[4] "To feel shame" means that mocking or stigmatizing by others is hitting home. It is that piercing feeling of worthlessness, of having no honor in society, that the psalmist describes in such vivid language: "All day long . . . shame has covered my face (Ps 44:15) . . . Insults have broken my heart, so that I am in despair" (Ps 69:20).

Jesus Uses Inculturation

Let us examine some examples of the ways in which Jesus by his preaching and example fosters the process of inculturation. He uses social dramas as occasions to instruct his followers about how his message

3. See John Stambaugh and David Balch, *The Social World of the First Christians* (London: SPCK, 1986), 68–81.

4. See Gerald A. Arbuckle, *Violence, Society, and the Church: A Cultural Approach* (Maryknoll, NY: Orbis Books, 2004), 79–87.

must challenge or affirm cultural values and rituals; for this they require appropriate qualities. As explained earlier, social dramas (chap. 6) begin with a break in relations between people or groups within a cultural situation, followed by a phase of mounting crisis or liminality. This is the stage of dramatic tension with highly uncertain outcomes. The final stage is marked either by reintegration of the disrupted group or by the formalization of irreparable schism between the conflicting people involved.

Inculturation by Listening

In the social drama of the healing of Bartimaeus, the blind beggar (Mark 10:46-52), Jesus spectacularly models by his actions and attitudes the way his followers, according to his concern for a "preferential option for the poor," must relate to people trapped in a subculture of poverty. The drama focuses not only on Bartimaeus but also on the crowd. Jesus and Bartimaeus are calling the crowd to believe in the Good News. The drama for them is: will they accept the invitation?

The drama begins with Bartimaeus "sitting by the roadside" (v. 46). In this one statement we have a description of two types of poverty. As a beggar Bartimaeus is caught in the poverty trap: no regular income, poor diet, little energy, and tempted to give way to fatalism. In addition he is blind. Because of his particular type of blindness he is stigmatized and socially excluded by society since he ritually endangers the clean. For his family and former friends he no longer exists. In the words of the psalmist, "I am . . . an object of dread to my acquaintances; those who see me in the street flee from me" (Ps 31:11). Without honor he is assumed to have sinned, and God is punishing him for this. The words "sitting by the roadside" symbolically describe this social exclusion and stigmatization. The only identity he possesses is that of a beggar, which is a very precarious one indeed.

The liminal stage commences when Jesus is passing by and Bartimaeus cries out for healing, addressing Jesus with a distinctive messianic emphasis: "Jesus, Son of David, have mercy on me!" (v. 47). The crowd do their best to silence him: "Many sternly ordered him to be quiet" (v. 48), but without success. People who are poor, especially those who are ritually unclean, must remain silent, accepting their shameful fate. This is a culture of violence—the dehumanizing of people—and no one questions it. The people in the crowd have followed Jesus and listened to his words on compassion and justice, but they remain blinded by their religious and cultural prejudice against people like Bartimaeus. How will Jesus react? Jesus will have none of this fundamentalist and violent nonsense as he calls Bartimaeus to his side and gently asks him what he desires: "What do you want me to do for you?" (10:51). Jesus actually listens to a poor person, contrary to the culture of his time. Bartimaeus replies: "My teacher, let me see again!"(v. 51). It is not just sight he is begging for. He is yearning to become a full member of society again, one who can freely contribute to society with a sense of pride and responsibility. By speaking directly to Bartimaeus—socially a non-person— Jesus breaks through the political, economic, and cultural barriers that entrap the blind man. By defying these stigmatizing, discriminating, and rigid customs Jesus allows Bartimaeus to rediscover his ability to be and act like a human person with dignity. In brief, there are four interconnected lessons in this drama that illuminate the heart of inculturation.

INCULTURATION IS PERSON-CENTERED

One gift of postmodernity is the call to refocus on the human person. Jesus exemplifies this in all his actions, so richly evident in his relationship with Bartimaeus. Jesus will not be distracted by the self-righteousness of the crowd around him: "Jesus stood still and said, 'Call him here'" (v. 49).

INCULTURATION IS A COLLABORATIVE PROCESS

Bartimaeus is in the liminal space of rejection by society. Jesus by his very presence, attitude, and actions inspires Bartimaeus to make an act of faith. He proves that his act of faith is authentic by refusing any longer to accept the cultural stigma that those who are poor must remain silent. When the crowd order him to stop he bluntly refuses to be bullied into silence: "he cried out even more loudly" (v. 48). The ultimate test of inculturation is willingness to act on the basis of faith. The focus at this point is on Bartimaeus, who by his actions is himself an agent of inculturation, challenging in collaboration with Jesus the crowd's culture that rejects people who are poor.

INCULTURATION REQUIRES SPIRITUAL AND HUMAN GIFTS

The gift most needed in evangelizers is the ability to listen and converse with people in a way that respects their human dignity. Listening is the gift of getting behind the words of another person, of entering

their hearts where words are ultimately unimportant. Hence inculturation cannot be something to be decided by outsiders without the full
participation of people within their own cultural settings. Jesus, the
evangelizer, enters into an empathetic dialogue with Bartimaeus, and in
the process critiques the culture that brands certain people as unclean
and to be avoided: "What do you want me to do for you?" (v. 51). Jesus
knows Bartimaeus is blind, and he could have acted without asking this
question of the victim, but that would have been an insulting action.
Jesus respects the dignity of Bartimaeus and knows that thinking about
justice begins by listening to those who know about injustice.

Liberation is an Integral Part of Inculturation

The incident shows that liberation is not something in addition to
inculturation but is an *integral* quality of the inculturating process.
Through his actions Jesus illustrates that the healing of poverty must be
holistic: social, cultural, economic, spiritual. Charity without the pursuit
of justice is not holistic. Jesus, therefore, reacts in two prophetic ways
to Bartimaeus's plight: he acts *for* and *with* the victim in order to break
the several imprisoning layers of poverty. By his actions Jesus is forcefully saying to the crowd that their prejudices contradict his teaching
about the dignity of every person. Every person has the right to be respected. In this, Jesus is an advocate *for* people who are oppressed by
the prejudices of society.

Jesus also stands *with* Bartimaeus. In listening to him he empowers
him to come forward despite his rejection by the crowd. By allying himself
with Bartimaeus, Jesus is himself risking a similar marginalization. He
lives what he is later to call his disciples to do: "for I was hungry and you
gave me food . . . in prison and you visited me" (Matt 25:35, 36). The
incident significantly ends with the description of holistic healing: "Immediately he regained his sight and followed him along the way" (v. 52).
No longer is Bartimaeus marginalized by society by being forced to sit at
the *side* of the road. Now through the collaborative action of Jesus and
Bartimaeus the once-rejected blind man is again a vital member of the
community. He has the right to walk unchallenged "along the way."

Inculturation Reaffirms Goodness in Mythology

The crowd's original exclusion of Bartimaeus illustrates that they
have forgotten a foundational mythological value of hospitality. The
Israelites, since they had been strangers in Egypt, were expected to show

hospitality in turn to strangers in their midst (Exod 23:9):[5] "You shall not oppress a resident alien; you know the heart of an alien, for you were aliens in the land of Egypt." "When an alien resides with you in your land, you shall not oppress the alien. The alien who resides with you shall be to you as the citizen among you; you shall love the alien as yourself, for you were aliens in the land of Egypt" (Lev 19:33-34). The prophets often speak of the duty of giving to the poor as an expression of hospitality, but their emphasis is primarily on its justice quality rather than on what today we would call philanthropy, that is, giving from one's surplus. Philanthropy, however, is also encouraged (Prov 3:27-28; 28:27). There is a strong emphasis on hospitality also in the New Testament; it is an integral part of Jesus' teaching and behavior (see Luke 7:36-50). Those who do not receive his disciples as guests are rejecting Christ himself (Matt 10:9-16).[6] Jesus insists in his conversation with the rich young man that to give *all* one's goods to the poor is a condition for becoming his follower (Matt 19:21; Mark 10:21).[7] The point he is dramatically making is that all goods ultimately belong to God and hence we must not be exclusively attached to them.[8]

Thus when the crowd turn against Bartimaeus they are forgetting the Jewish tradition and Jesus seeks to re-endorse this mythology. In the process Jesus is inviting the crowd, in imitation of the example of Bartimaeus, to make an act of faith themselves and reject their aberrant behavior. Jesus looks at the crowd and says to them, "Call him here" (Mark 10:49). Will they obey Jesus, or will they refuse? In this liminal moment they will either reject or accept Christ. The fact that the crowd immediately and enthusiastically call Bartimaeus shows that some at least are now prepared to challenge the culture of violence against people who are poor: "they called the blind man, saying to him, 'Take heart; get up, he is calling you.'" (Mark 10:49) Now the honorable thing to do is to follow Christ, even if this means suffering public shame at the hands of those who do not yet believe and are still prepared to stigmatize the poor as impure.

5. See Bruce J. Malina and Richard L. Rohrbaugh, *Social-Science Commentary on the Synoptic Gospels* (Minneapolis: Fortress Press, 1992), 244.

6. See Abraham J. Malherbe, "Hospitality," in *The Oxford Companion to the Bible,* ed. Bruce M Metzger and Michael D. Coogan, 292–93 (Oxford: Oxford University Press, 1993).

7. See John L. McKenzie, *Dictionary of the Bible* (London: Geoffrey Chapman, 1965), 21.

8. See Malina and Rohrbaugh, *Social-Science Commentary*, 244.

Openness to Learn

In one of the most touching incidents in the gospels, Jesus is called to evangelize beyond his cultural borders while journeying through the region of Tyre (Mark 7:24-30). Looking for privacy, he seeks shelter in a house, but a strong-minded woman, with a little daughter suffering from an unclean spirit, forces her way into his presence and falls at his feet begging him for a cure. The woman is a Gentile, of Syrophoenician origin (v. 26) and has heard people speak of Jesus. Not only is she a woman without honor in the Jewish culture, she dares to invade Jesus' privacy, disregarding the Gentile-Jewish cultural gap between herself and him. She is so determined that she also ignores the custom of not speaking to Jesus without a male patron.[9] This is the liminal moment in the drama not only for the woman but also in a startling way for Jesus. Will he put aside his Jewish cultural rejection of a foreigner and a woman?

Jesus strongly rejects her request, giving as an excuse the cultural tradition that Israel has priority in his ministry (Matt 10:5-6; 15:24). He uses the analogy well known in his culture in which children in a family are to be given food first, then what is left over is to be tossed into the streets for dogs (Luke 16:20). The Gentiles will have to wait until the people of Israel have heard his Good News. Then the dialogue takes a surprising turn. The woman will not be dismissed so easily. She actually calls Jesus to be converted by his own message, though this will mean publicly rejecting cultural norms of his society. Rather brilliantly she pushes the analogy about the dogs beyond what Jesus intends because she says that dogs under the table sometimes eat the children's crumbs while the children are still at dinner. Unlike the dogs outside the house, these do not have to wait. Impressed not only by her persistence but also by her surprising response, Jesus grants the request (Mark 7:29-30). Jesus puts aside cultural prejudices through the persistence of a woman. This is not the only time Jesus is successfully challenged to act through the tenacity of a woman (see John 2:12). The incident is also a reminder that to encounter those who are marginalized, evangelizers themselves must risk being marginalized. By challenging the cultural prejudices Jesus allows himself to be pushed farther toward the boundaries of his culture. What an example of humility to his disciples!

---

9. See Virgil Howard and David B. Peabody, "Mark," *The International Bible Commentary*, ed. William R. Farmer (Collegeville, MN: Liturgical Press, 1998), 1349, and Craig A. Evans, "Mark," *Eerdmans Commentary on the Bible*, eds. James D. Dunn and John W. Rogerson, (Grand Rapids: Eerdmans, 2003), 1081.

Inculturation Requires Dialogue

The description of Jesus speaking to the Samaritan woman at a well (John 4:1-42) is a particularly rich example of a social drama containing powerful symbols of prejudice. In the drama there are two clashing mythologies supporting two racially opposed cultures. This illustrates how, with the building of trust, dialogue can be the catalyst for the transformation not just of the woman but also of Jesus; here they both represent the two antagonistic cultures. Simple and ordinary circumstances of daily life such as eating, walking, and even a request for a drink of water often become social dramas of special importance for Jesus in his ministry of inculturation. They are transformed into moments of revelation and grace. This is to happen in the event at the well.

In the drama the separation stage is marked by a simple appeal to a stranger for water. Jesus is journeying through a part of Samaria with his disciples. Weary from his ministry, he pauses to rest beside a famous Samaritan pilgrimage site, Jacob's well (John 4:4-6). While the disciples are absent buying food, a Samaritan woman of doubtful morality appears and she and Jesus, now alone, meet, with Jesus taking the initiative in asking for a drink of water. This surprises the woman for two reasons. It is a dishonorable thing for Jewish men to greet women in public, and second, "Jews do not share things in common with Samaritans" (John 4:9). Jews look on Samaritans in a racist manner; they picture them as stupid, lazy, heretical, and a people possessed by the devil (John 8:48). John McKenzie, SJ, points out that there is "no deeper break of human relations in the contemporary world than the feud of Jews and Samaritans, and the breadth and depth of Jesus' doctrine of love could demand no greater act of a Jew than to accept a Samaritan"[10] as a brother or sister. Samaritan women had the additional stigma of being regarded as menstruants from birth, that is, inherently unclean.[11] Not surprisingly, therefore, it would later be a deadly insult to Jesus to call him a Samaritan (John 8:48). The Samaritans had similar degrading views of their Jewish neighbors. A Samaritan village would refuse Jesus and his disciples hospitality on their way from Galilee to Jerusalem (Luke 9:52). So, in this chance meeting between Jesus and a woman of such stigmatized cultural and personal origins, the questions are: how is Jesus to handle the situation? Will he and/or she end the process of dialogue that has just begun? Will Jesus continue to act dishonorably, contrary to the norms of Jewish

---

10. McKenzie, *Dictionary*, 766.
11. See Teresa Okure, "John," *International Bible Commentary*, 1468.

culture? In fact, they will proceed through the second stage of the social drama, the liminality phase, both showing extraordinary skills of storytelling.[12]

Jesus fosters an atmosphere of trust between the woman and himself, which is a fundamental requirement of inculturation, by letting her know he is aware of her private life (vv. 16-19).[13] With confidence established, there are two key matters Jesus wishes to explain to the woman: that knowledge of God is a gift likened to "living water" (v. 11), and the revelation of the true identity of Jesus himself (v. 14). Pleased with her trust in him, Jesus leads her to grasp these two realities through a conversational dialogue that is deeply respectful of her and of her ancestral and religious traditions, while at the same time plainly pointing out that worship will not be confined to a definite place either in Jerusalem or on the sacred Samaritan mountain, but within Christ himself (vv. 20-26).

Now the event enters the third stage of the social drama, the reaggregation phase. At this point the woman is so transformed and energized by her conversion to Christ that she leaves behind her water jug, a symbol of human thirst and affections that can never be satisfied without Jesus Christ, and hastens to share her faith with her kinsfolk. (vv. 28-30, 39-42). There is a quite humorous touch to this incident because Jesus incongruously uses as his messenger to these Samaritan people a woman whose marital history is well known to them. However, there is a second drama that has yet to begin, and it focuses on the disciples. When they return with food they react as Jewish men are culturally expected to behave. They are startled, even annoyed and ashamed, that Jesus is speaking to a woman, and a Samaritan one at that (v. 27). This should not be! They urge him to eat, but he replies in a puzzling way by saying that his "food is to do the will of him who sent me and to complete his work" (v. 34). By contrast with the enthusiastic Samaritan woman who has gained so much through her dialogue with Jesus, the disciples ironically give the impression of being uninterested in the dramatic nature of his words and do not seem to want to learn from the incident.

The events at the well reveal two important themes of the evangelist John: his particular theological emphasis and the missionary methods Jesus adopts in inculturation. The latter include beginning with the reali-

---

12. See J. Martin C. Scott, "John," *Eerdmans Commentary*, 1171.

13. Bishop Francisco Claver, SJ, has a short and helpful analysis of this incident from an inculturation perspective in his book *The Making of a Local Church* (Maryknoll, NY: Orbis Books, 2008), 116.

ties of everyday life, showing respect for people and their mythologies or traditions. Even when Jesus disagrees with them, as in the case of the Samaritan belief about where true worship is to take place (John 4:20-24), he does so in a culturally respectful manner. At the same time, inculturation also calls us to struggle against the entrenched obstacles of race, sex, and class that degrade people.[14] These lessons are also evident in the following incidents.

Inculturation Recognizes Diversities

Jesus is constantly on the move in his ministry. Not only is he often pictured dining and interacting with "sinners" and with people, including tax collectors, who are normally considered socially or religiously unacceptable, but also with professional people like Pharisees. As in many of his actions this table fellowship, or the manner in which he debates with representatives of the professional classes, becomes a way in which the kingdom is actually inaugurated.[15] But in every case he adapts his missionary methods to diversities and tensions inherent in the subcultures he is relating to.

In the following examples the dramas are initiated not by Jesus but by professional people, the first and second by Pharisees and the third by a lawyer. In his dialogue with Nicodemus (John 3:1-21) Jesus uses almost a debating and declamatory style that is characteristic of the professional class to which Nicodemus belongs. After a polite introductory comment, Nicodemus quickly draws Jesus into the liminal stage of the drama. He comes directly to the point of his visit by asking the question that is puzzling him: "How can anyone be born after having grown old? Can one enter a second time into the mother's womb and be born?" (v. 4). At one point in the lengthy interaction Jesus actually reproaches Nicodemus for his disbelief (v. 10). There is no indication in the text as to how the liminal stage ended. Did Nicodemus leave converted and energized by the dialogue or did the theological gap between Jesus and Nicodemus widen? But the fact that he would publicly speak in support of the rights of Jesus for a hearing according to the law (John 7:50), and that he would bring a large and costly quantity of spices for the burial of Jesus (John 19:39), gives the strong impression that a deep friendship did emerge from the dialogue.

---

14. See Okure, "John," 1469.
15. See N. T. Wright, *Jesus and the Victory of God* (London: SPCK, 1996), 148–49.

At another time Jesus is invited by Simon the Pharisee (Luke 7:36-50), who begins the drama by blatantly disregarding the courtesies normally accorded a notable visitor.[16] Guests were to be greeted at the door by the host, formally kissed, then have their feet washed by a servant, to be followed by water for the guests to wash face and hands prior to eating. Then a small amount of sweet-smelling ointment was given guests for their hair. Nothing of this is provided for Jesus. The liminal stage of the drama begins with the entry of a woman of shameful moral reputation who immediately begins "to bathe his feet with her tears and to dry them with her hair. Then she continued kissing his feet and anointing them with the ointment" (v. 38). The host is shocked by what is happening and it convinces him that Jesus is not a prophet, because if he were a prophet he would know of the scandalous background of the woman and immediately stop her, but he does not do so (v. 39).

Sensing the host's reactions, Jesus rebukes the Pharisee, but in an indirect, respectful way that is in accordance with custom. When he reprimands Simon he is simultaneously affirming the importance of the cultural forms of greeting guests. After telling a story about a creditor who cancels the debts of two people, Jesus asks the host "which of [the debtors] will love him more?" (v. 42). Simon gives the correct answer. Then, turning to the woman, Jesus praises her for her behavior, which contrasts dramatically to that of Simon. She recognizes who Jesus is and yearns to show her gratitude for having her sins forgiven. Simon fails to recognize Jesus and so does not even begin to appreciate the enormity of his discourteous behavior. In the reaggregation stage Jesus congratulates the woman for her faith: "Your faith has saved you; go in peace" (v. 50). The gift of faith is offered to Simon and his other guests, but they do not accept it, despite the culturally respectful efforts of Jesus. This is a reminder that the faith process of inculturation cannot be imposed. It can be offered, and accepted or refused.

Inculturation Through Storytelling

Storytelling is a critically important method of clarifying identity (chap. 5) and Jesus in his use of parables is the brilliant master of this pedagogical art. Probably this is his most important method of inculturation, and his approach remains as relevant today as in his own time. In

---

16. See Samuel O. Abogunrin, "Luke," *International Bible Commentary*, 1393.

more than forty parables[17] he adopts a traditional Jewish way of teaching but gives the parables his unique emphasis with dazzling imagination and creativity.[18] The parables are fictitious, often humorous stories about ordinary individuals and the down-to-earth realities of everyday life his listeners could readily identify with: the world of farming and fishing, of droughts and floods, of weddings and feasts, of rich landowners and restless tenants, of travelers banging on the front door at night, and of a widow challenging an unjust judge. It is a culture without superficial embellishment in which even the hero of the parable can be a pragmatic plotter (Luke 16:1-8) or a seemingly impulsive landowner (Matt 20:1-16). But there is a quality to the parables not usually found in everyday stories: the insights are dramatically new. They are subversive stories because they fundamentally challenge listeners to reorder and remold the cultural and economic reality around them. The writers of the gospels also illustrate that the parables have multiple meanings. For Matthew (Matt 18:12-14), the Lost Sheep functions to exhort church leaders to care for the weak in the community; in Luke it justifies Jesus' mission to the lost (Luke 15:4-7).[19]

The stories are of varying length and contain a meaning or message over and above the straightforward and literal, with an element of metaphor. Consider the parable of the foolish rich farmer (Luke 12:13-21) who wonders what he can do with an abundant harvest. He decides to pull down his existing barns and build larger ones to cope with the harvest, then sit back and thoroughly enjoy life. But this is a stupid decision. The harvest is already in the fields waiting to be collected and there is no time to destroy his storage sheds and build new ones. An audience of peasants, daily confronted by the enormous gap between rich and poor, would have laughed uproariously at the bumbling, wealthy farmer who now has no barns and a copious rotting harvest in the fields. Then suddenly the man dies (12:20). The lesson is simple: economic prosperity

17. About one third of the documented sayings of Jesus in the Synoptic Gospels are in the form of parables. See Brad H. Young, *The Parables: Jewish Tradition and Christian Interpretation* (Peabody, MA: Hendrickson, 1998), 7. The number of parables in the gospels is estimated to be as low as 35 and as high as 72, depending on the particular categorization by scholars.

18. See Arland J. Hultgren, *The Parables of Jesus: A Commentary* (Grand Rapids: Eerdmans, 2000), 1, and John Donahue, *The Gospel in Parable* (Philadelphia: Fortress Press, 1988), 3.

19. See Charles W. Hedrick, *Many Things in Parables* (Louisville: Westminster John Knox, 2004), 100–104.

may satisfy a person's immediate comfort needs, but everyone is ultimately to be called to account for how wealth is used.

Inculturation Through Functional Substitution

Functional substitution, a particularly important method of inculturation, is a process whereby over a lengthy period of time a Christian meaning is gradually substituted for a non-Christian symbol, myth, or ritual. It assumes that symbols (chap. 2) can only change their meanings slowly. It respects the dignity of people because, while they may intellectually accept a new understanding of truths or rituals, it takes much longer for their hearts to feel comfortable with them. Jesus uses this pastoral method throughout his ministry, while creating new symbols such as the cross and the Eucharist. For example, he preaches in the familiar synagogue and shows himself a good Jew by frequenting the temple. But at the same time, when he uses traditional religious symbols and rituals he endows them with new meanings; for example, at the Last Supper the traditional Passover meal is given a much richer mythological significance. He helps his listeners to discover what is good and to be retained in traditional Jewish mythological life, and what needs to be changed through the introduction of new meanings.[20] Another example of functional substitution is his resourceful use of parables, as explained above.

Theological Reflection

Saint James gives this advice: "let everyone be quick to listen, slow to speak" (Jas 1:19). How wise! In inculturation the most important quality of the evangelizer is the gift of listening, not teaching or speaking. What is the Spirit saying to us as we encounter not just other cultures but our own as well? In the above examples we see Jesus instinctively listening to people personally and to the cultural contexts in which they are living. At the same time he is a member of a particular culture containing many prejudices against outsiders, so Jesus must also be listening to himself to discover to what degree he is being affected by these prejudices. In the incident with the Syrophoenician woman he is being made publicly aware by her persistent intervention that he, in his humanity, is

---

20. See Arbuckle, *Laughing with God: Culture, Humor, and Transformation* (Collegeville, MN: Liturgical Press, 2008), 113–32, 134–35.

filtering information through his own prejudiced culture. A powerful example of humility for every evangelizer!

In biblical terms the word "listen" means to hearken to the expression of another's will, to respond to it and to comply with it (Matt 7:21; Mark 3:35; John 12:47; Rom 2:13). But in order to respond and comply we must also abandon those cherished values and customs not in accordance with God's will. Choan-Seng Song speaks of Jesus being in the womb of darkness as he struggles to let go, to respond to and comply with the will of the Father. His prayer in the terrifying darkness of Gethsemane reveals the degree of abandonment expected of him if he listens to his Father (Mark 14:36).[21] This darkness is shattered by the heartrending cry, "My God, my God, why have you forsaken me?" (Matt 27:46). This cry is the definitive break with the cultural expectations of his people, who so yearned for a human king. Letting go of what is culturally familiar to us in order to venture into the unknown demands abundant faith. Inculturation is not a human technique, but above all a journey of faith, a journey of listening and letting go (Rom 1:15-17).

21. See Choan-Seng Song, *The Compassionate God: An Exercise in the Theology of Transposition* (London: SCM, 1982), 92.

Chapter 11
Cultures as Challenges to Inculturation

> [We] still do not understand the inculturation process all that well.
>
> —Robert Schreiter, "Inculturation of Faith or
> Identification with Culture"[1]

There are two reasons for the reluctance among theologians to accept the challenge to dialogue with cultures, writes Robert Schreiter. In the first place, there are no adequate methodologies among theologians "to break through some of the conceptual logjams, and a lack of tools that can be used readily and easily" by practitioners of inculturation. The conceptual blockages are an inadequate understanding of culture and confusion about the meaning of inculturation. Second, there is the official unwillingness at the international and local levels of the church "to permit legitimate experiments in inculturation and to sanction successful experiments for ongoing use."[2] There is a general reluctance, especially among many Western ecclesiastics, to accept the fact that the interpretation of their faith is significantly molded by their own cultures. Their culturally conditioned understandings of the Gospel are then assumed to be synonymous with the kingdom of God itself.

Previous chapters have clarified the nature of culture in the postmodern context. This chapter will focus directly on inculturation: explaining the confusion surrounding the term and the reasons why ecclesiastics do not encourage experimentation, showing the importance of inculturation as social drama, and finally, exploring the complex relationship between syncretism and inculturation.

1. Robert Schreiter, "Inculturation of Faith or Identification with Culture?" *Concilium* 2 (1994): 17.
2. Robert Schreiter, "Faith and Cultures: Challenges to a World Church," *Theological Studies* 50 (1989): 758.

Definition

Since inculturation emerged as a theological term only in the 1970s, it is not surprising that there is still confusion about its precise meaning.[3] Inculturation as an expression was created in an effort to spell out two primary aspects of evangelization, namely, the object and the actual process of evangelization. Evangelization is to be directed at cultures; as Paul VI reminds us, "what matters is to evangelize human culture and cultures (not in a purely decorative way, as it were by applying a thin veneer, but in a vital way, in depth and right to their very roots)."[4] Consequently, inculturation is defined by Pedro Arrupe, SJ, as a process whereby the Christian faith becomes incarnated within "a particular culture, in such a way that this experience not only finds expression through elements proper to the culture in question, but becomes a principle that animates, directs and unifies the culture, transforming, and remaking it so as to being about a 'new creation.'"[5]

The word *faith* is used in defining inculturation in preference to Gospel or theology because faith connotes a twofold reality, namely, *what* we are called to believe by the Gospel and tradition and at the same time the *commitment* to act accordingly.[6]

Acculturation and Enculturation: Clarifications

Sometimes inculturation, a theological word denoting a faith-based process, is confused with *acculturation* and *enculturation*, both sociological terms.[7]

- *Acculturation* is the process of culture change in which contact between two or more culturally distinct groups results in one group taking over elements of the culture of the other group or

---

3. Among the clearest explanations of inculturation see the following: Aylward Shorter, *Toward a Theology of Inculturation* (London: Geoffrey Chapman, 1988), and idem, *Evangelization and Culture* (London: Geoffrey Chapman, 1994), and Anthony Gittins, "Beyond Liturgical Inculturation: Transforming the Deep Structures of Faith," *Irish Theological Quarterly* 69 (2004): 47–72.

4. Paul VI, Apostolic Letter *On Evangelization* (Vatican: Sacred Congregation for Evangelization, 1975), 20.

5. Pedro Arrupe, SJ, cited by Michael Amaladoss, SJ, "Inculturation and Internationality," *East Asian Pastoral Review* 29 (1992): 239.

6. See Schreiter, "Faith and Cultures," 745, and Francis V. Anthony, *Ecclesial Praxis of Inculturation* (Rome: Las, 1997), 99–101.

7. See Gittins, "Beyond Liturgical Inculturation," 48.

groups. For example, the sixth-century Sacramentary of Verona, which still forms the foundation for many liturgical prayers in the Roman church, introduced existing secular feudal notions of rank, honor and dignity into the rite of ordination, and together with it the notion of promotion through stages. Ministry thus came to be described in terms of an ecclesiastical career, each rank having its corresponding honors and dignity.[8] Acculturation, however, can be one stage in the inculturation process, as will later be explained.

- *Enculturation* is the conscious or unconscious conditioning occurring within the learning process whereby children or adults achieve competencies in their culture. So we can speak of an enculturation process whereby a person is introduced to, and learns, the practices of the Catholic Church, but it says nothing about whether or not persons and their actions are being transformed by their belief in Jesus Christ.

Often, and wrongly so, inculturation is made synonymous with the renewal of liturgical texts or practices. For example, a diocesan liturgical committee may legitimately decide to introduce some local customs into the liturgy to give it "cultural authenticity." It is then said that "the liturgy has been inculturated." This is not inculturation, though it may be a step in that direction. It is rather the acceptance of certain behavioral patterns by a particular cultural group, however estimable this might be, as directed by a particular diocesan liturgical committee.[9] The key test of inculturation is: are people's lives and cultures being transformed in faith? In fact, despite the extensive discussions and publications about liturgy and inculturation there is little satisfaction with the results.

Inculturation: Foundational Truths

Among truths of the Christian faith involved in the process of inculturation are the following:

---

8. See Theodore Klauser, *A Short History of the Western Liturgy* (Oxford: Oxford University Press, 1969), 32–37.

9. Ibid., 49.

1. The Holy Spirit is the source of all truth, no matter where it is found.

Certain church fathers such as Justin, Irenaeus, and Clement of Alexandria either explicitly or in an equivalent manner speak about the "seeds" sown by the Word of God in cultures.[10] Justin claims: "Everything good that has been said, no matter by whom, is Christian."[11] The Word of God is actively present, although in an incomplete way, in all cultures. This presence or glimmer of transcendence is the foreshadowing of the fuller revelation of Jesus Christ in the Scriptures and tradition. Whatever is good in cultures comes from the Spirit.[12] As Karl Rahner writes, "the very commonness of everyday things harbours the eternal marvel and silent mystery of God and [God's] grace."[13] John Paul II describes this foundational mystery of inculturation in these inspiring words: "Lying deep in every culture, there appears this impulse towards a fulfillment. We may say, then, that culture itself has an intrinsic capacity to receive divine Revelation."[14]

2. As no one culture has normative status in expressing the truths of faith, those truths are translatable into all cultures.[15]

It took a revelation from God for Peter to discover the fundamental truth that "no one cultural expression of [Christianity] is exclusive for expressing the fullness of the gospel."[16] Inspired by the Holy Spirit, early Christianity broke from its exclusive ties to Judaism. As Peter says: "I truly understand that God shows no partiality, but in every nation anyone who fears him and does what is right is acceptable to him" (Acts 10:34). Christianity then adopted in a highly effective way the dominant Hellenistic cultural framework of the Roman Empire as its missionary medium.

10. See Pontifical Council for Inter-Religious Dialogue and the Congregation for the Evangelization of Peoples, *Dialogue and Proclamation*, in *Origins* 21, no. 8 (4 July 1991): 125.

11. Justin the Martyr, cited by Leonardo Boff, *Church, Charism and Power: Liberation Theology and the Institutional Church* (London: SCM Press, 1985), 94.

12. For a fuller description of this mystery see Gerald A. Arbuckle, *Laughing with God: Humor, Culture, and Transformation* (Collegeville, MN: Liturgical Press, 2008), 111–13.

13. Karl Rahner, *Belief Today* (London: Sheed and Ward, 1973), 4.

14. John Paul II, Encyclical Letter "Faith and Reason" (*Fides et Ratio*), 1998, 71.

15. See Lamin Sanneh, *Translating the Message: The Missionary Impact on Culture* (Maryknoll, NY: Orbis Books, 2009), 74.

16. Ibid., 67.

Of this interaction John Paul II writes: "Christianity first encountered Greek philosophy; but this does not mean at all that other approaches are precluded . . . [but] the Church cannot abandon what she has gained from her inculturation in the world of Greco-Latin thought." He continues: "to reject this heritage would be to deny the providential plan of God."[17] When the faith is first preached to a culture, therefore, it is proclaimed through the medium of a human language and culture; there is an *intercultural* experience. But the principle of "the Gentile breakthrough" must always remain operative. Of course, for Roman Catholics no culture is the arbiter of divine truth. The ultimate interpreter is the church's teaching authority. Nevertheless, key questions like the following must be persistently asked:

- What is essential to the faith and what is accidental to the culture it happens for the moment to be clothed in?
- Can the truths of our faith be expressed more effectively through the symbols of the culture(s) being evangelized?

3. Inculturation must embrace all human endeavors.

Inculturation is not to be confined to liturgical issues. It includes the liberation, the freeing of a people and cultures from all forms of domination and injustice. This also applies to evangelizers themselves, who must develop the insight and willingness to abandon their own cultural expressions of faith that do not pertain to the heart of the Good News. But the unmasking of cultural domination, for example prejudices and discrimination, is an extremely difficult process. Hence it is imperative in these postmodern times for theologians to collaborate with the social sciences, whose role it is to uncover the positive and negative qualities of cultures.[18]

4. Inculturation is the call to relive the incarnation and paschal mystery.

Whenever inculturation is occurring, Christ is again becoming flesh and living among his people in symbols familiar to them (John 1:14). At the same time this faith experience calls people and cultures into the

17. John Paul II, "Faith and Reason," 72.

18. See Walter Wink, *Engaging the Powers: Discernment and Resistance in a World of Domination* (Minneapolis: Fortress Press, 1992), 87–104.

very heart of the paschal mystery itself—a process of dying to attitudes, values, and customs that are not in conformity with Christ's message and an embracing of what is new: "Do not remember the former things . . . I am about to do a new thing; now it springs forth, do you not perceive it?" (Isa 43:18-19).

5. The model of the church most suited to inculturation is that of the people of God.

Inculturation is not a process to be directed by experts alone; rather, it needs to be "an expression of the community's life."[19] The serious error following Vatican II was to entrust the renewal of the liturgy to scholars alone. The model of the church as the people of God is the most appropriate one to describe inculturation, for it focuses on the communal nature of the church rather than on its hierarchical or institutional aspects.

Inculturation, Dialogue, and Postmodernity

Contextual theology is the process of trying to understand the Christian faith in relation to a particular context. Stephen Bevans, SVD, has significantly and skillfully identified several models that are not mutually exclusive to describe this process.[20] I am concerned here with only two—the translation and anthropological models—and I argue in this book that the latter is the preferred model in the postmodern world of diversity.

Translation Model

This model stresses the paramount position of the Christian message; it assumes a supracultural Christian core that is in some way or other independent of cultural and linguistic expressions. The task of the theologian is merely to translate or adapt this unchanging Gospel message into idioms of different cultures. Since there is little or no concern to discover though a process of authentic dialogue those "seeds of the Word" already present in cultures, this model of theologizing is best

19. John Paul II, Encyclical Letter "Mission of the Redeemer" (Boston: St. Paul Books, n.d.), 54.

20. See Stephen B. Bevans, *Models of Contextual Theology* (Maryknoll, NY: Orbis Books, 1992).

suited for people who are already practicing Christians.[21] Three different types of the translation model can be identified.

- Superficial dialogue

  In the decades prior to Vatican II the terms "adaptation," "accommodation," and "indigenization" became familiar in papal missionary writings. These terms mean that an evangelizer, usually an outsider, decides to use this or that custom as a pastoral tactic, generally without consulting the people, in order to make the Eurocentric expression of the faith more locally acceptable. For example, the priest could add local symbols to Mass vestments to project a degree of local authenticity. The act of worship or theological expression can then appear, it is hoped, to the local people as *their* worship or theology. This allows for a superficial or token form of dialogue, but a genuine exchange is neither possible nor theologically necessary. In 1951 Pope Pius XII insisted that the evangelizer's "office does not demand that they transplant European civilization and culture, and no other, to foreign soil."[22] Despite these inspiring words, little could be done to stop the transplanting of "European civilization and culture" as long as local churches were forbidden to have authentic theological exchange between interacting cultures.

- No dialogue

  In the first type of translation some form of dialogue is possible, but not essential. However, adherents of this second type insist that dialogue is not only unnecessary but even dangerous to truth. This is the position of the followers of what is termed Radical Orthodoxy. Theological truth is confined to the church alone, as all cultures are inherently corrupt; thus any form of dialogue with cultures is theologically out of the question. Anglican theologians like John Milbank, Catherine Pickstock, D. Stephen Long, and Graham Ward are representatives of this view, along with some Catholic thinkers. Milbank believes that the theology of Vatican II has naturalized the supernatural, "reducing the transcendent to a

---

21. See ibid., 30–42.

22. Pius XII, Encyclical Letter "On Promoting Missions" (*Evangelii Praecones*), 1951, in *Modern Missionary Documents and Africa,* ed. Raymond Hickey (Dublin: Dominican Publications, 1982), 99.

dimension of our own human being."[23] He singles out the social sciences as especially dangerous. Liberation theology, for all its efforts to combat injustices, has given too much credence to these sciences and to the role of the state.[24] In her criticism of Long, Rosemary Radford Ruether goes to the heart of the issue when she points out that he "exaggerates Western history of thought into a dualism of normative truth . . . on the one hand, and fallacious modernity . . . on the other."[25] This simplistic dualism, with its sweeping demonization of secular movements, runs contrary to the fundamental reality of the incarnation. While not ignoring humankind's proneness to sin, nonetheless our faith in the incarnation tells us that goodness, no matter what its source, is a gift of the Spirit. What we see, and touch, the finite and the historical— all are capable of being instruments of the divine presence.[26]

• Dialogue with preconditions

A third group of theologians accepts the translation model and agrees that dialogue is an essential requirement of theological thinking. The group includes Karl Barth (and contemporary followers), Hans Urs von Balthasar, and Cardinal Joseph Ratzinger (later Pope Benedict XVI), but they insist that prolonged dialogue cannot begin until theologians have clarified and affirmed the uniqueness of Christianity. Theology must first be systematically ordered into a neatly bound whole and dialogue will not change this prestructured identity. Theologian David Tracy defines their position in this way: Catholic theology "needs to clarify and affirm its unique identity *as such* and not in correlation with the ever-shifting and dangerous contours of the contemporary situation."[27]

---

23. For a critique see Steven Shakespeare, *Radical Orthodoxy: A Critical Introduction* (London: SPCK, 2007).

24. See John Milbank, *Theology and Social Theory: Beyond Secular Reason* (Oxford: Blackwell, 1990), 101–40.

25. Rosemary Radford Ruether, "The Postmodern as Premodern: The Theology of D. Stephen Long," in *Interpreting the Postmodern: Responses to "Radical Orthodoxy,"* eds. Rosemary Radford Ruether and Marion Grau (New York: T & T Clark, 2006), 78.

26. See Richard McBrien, *Catholicism* (London: Geoffrey Chapman, 1994), 10.

27. David Tracy, "The Uneasy Alliance Reconceived: Catholic Theological Method, Modernity, and Postmodernity," *Theological Studies* 50 (1989): 554. Italics in original.

There are several dangers in this position. Unless theologians are able to be challenged by outsiders they can assume that accidental historical and cultural accretions are as important as fundamental dogmas. Second, and more important, the identity of Christianity is not something that transcends cultures, languages, and history. Identities can never be static. They must always be modified according to changing contexts (chap. 5). As Paul Ricoeur says, consciousness is not a given, but a task to be achieved.[28] As explained, John Paul II has spoken extensively on the need for inculturation (chap. 9), for example: "I have considered the dialogue with the cultures of our time to be a vital area . . . In order to evangelize effectively, it is necessary to have resolutely an attitude of exchange and of comprehension. The power of the Gospel must penetrate to the very heart of different cultures."[29] Bevans, however, concludes that John Paul II in his many references to inculturation is also primarily favoring this type of the translation model with its restricted acceptance of dialogue. Uppermost in the mind of the pope, says Bevans, is the need to preserve "the unity of the faith, and for him this can be accomplished only by emphasizing a primary universality of ecclesial communion and doctrinal expression."[30]

Anthropological Model

This model, significantly supported by the incarnational emphasis in the documents of Vatican II, especially The Church in the Modern World (*Gaudium et Spes*), highlights the need to dialogue with cultures in order to discover the "seeds" of the Word as the stepping stone to explaining the full Gospel of Christ. John O'Malley, SJ, argues that the council introduced a new style of discourse that is "more inclined to reconciliation with human culture than to alienation from it, more inclined to see goodness than sin."[31] Unlike the translation model, the anthropological model sets no preconditions for dialogue. For this reason it is especially

---

28. See Paul Ricoeur, *The Philosophy of Paul Ricoeur: An Anthology of His Work*, eds. Charles E. Reagan and David Stewart (Boston: Beacon Press, 1978), 170.

29. John Paul II, "Letter to Agostino Cardinal Casaroli, on Occasion of the Creation of the Pontifical Council for Culture," *L'Osservatore Romano*, English ed. (28 June 1982), 7.

30. See Bevans, *Models*, 44.

31. John W. O'Malley, *What Happened at Vatican II* (London: Belknap Press, 2008), 310–11.

relevant in today's postmodern globalizing world. It relies significantly on the social sciences and interreligious dialogue to uncover the presence of the Word acting within cultures.

Contemporary thinkers like Paul Tillich, Karl Rahner, Bernard Lonergan, Edward Schillebeeckx, and David Tracy follow St. Thomas Aquinas in emphasizing the urgency for dialogue through *correlation* with cultures. Their aim is "to correlate issues raised by Christian faith and practice with other approaches to those issues"[32] in the secular world. Tillich, for example, shows how religious symbols correlate with the basic questions people raise about the meaning of life in politics, economics, art, and science.[33] Correlation is possible only if theologians are prepared to enter into dialogue without any prestructured systematic way of relating Christianity to the world. Reflecting on the positive impact of postmodern thinking on theology, Tracy writes: "Theology will never again be tameable by a system. . . . For theology does not bespeak a totality. Christian theology, at its best is the voice of the Other through all those others who have tasted . . . the Infinity disclosed in the kenotic reality of Jesus Christ."[34] As the New Testament accepts many theologies, so must we; to be authentic in this tradition is "to be free and open to the totality of the Gospel."[35] To follow exclusively only certain paths is to remove ourselves from the possibility of dialogue with a postmodern world of diversity.

Obstacles to Inculturation

Confusion about Meaning

Several leading theologians have expressed critical views of inculturation. Aloysius Pieris, SJ, an authority on Asian non-Christian religions, argues that some explanations of inculturation assume a false dichotomy between culture and religion, with most unfortunate consequences in Asia. Inculturation is frequently interpreted as the insertion of "the Christian religion minus European culture" into an "Asian culture

32. David F. Ford, *Theology: A Very Short Introduction* (Oxford: Oxford University Press, 1999), 26.

33. See Paul Tillich, "On the Idea of a Theology of Culture," trans. William B. Green, in *What Is Religion?* ed. James L. Adams (New York: Harper & Row, 1969).

34. David Tracy, "Theology and the Many Faces of Postmodernity," *Theology Today* 51 (1994), 114.

35. Boff, *Church*, 77.

minus non-Christian religion."[36] But religion in Asia cannot be separated from culture. Moreover, inculturation in Asia has not yet been understood to embrace the desperate urgency for liberation from poverty.[37] He further comments: "Inculturation-fever might appear to be a desperate last-minute bid to give an Asian façade to a church that fails to strike roots in Asian soil because no one dares to break the Greco-Roman pot in which it has been existing for four centuries like a stunted *bonsai*!"[38]

Pieris is not against inculturation, but he is criticizing the neglect of in-depth theological reflection and the failure to do appropriate cultural analysis in Asia. Inculturation must focus on a Christology involving people who are poor and marginalized in Asia. In deeply moving words he writes that we have to learn how to "*discover* the Christhood of the Asian poor who, like Jesus, have no decent place to be born in (Luke 2:7), no reputable place to live and work in (John 1:46), no safe place in their own country to hide from oppressive rulers (Matt 2:13-14) or no honourable place to die in (Luke 23:23) and no place of their own to be buried in (Matt 27:59)."[39] If this Christology is recognized, Pieris says, the church *in* Asia will at last become the church *of* Asia.[40]

Father Peter Phan, also a missiologist with deep Asian roots, likewise correctly criticizes a superficial approach to inculturation. "Liberation without inculturation . . . sees humans simply as economic beings, while inculturation without liberation becomes an elistist, antiquarian quest irrelevant to people's lives."[41] He writes that "even the early attempts to 'inculturate' Christianity by missionaries such as Matteo Ricci, Roberto de Nobili, and Alexandre de Rhodes, as well as by Asian theologians, laudable as those attempts have been, amount to no more than trimming rather than transplanting the Christian tree" into Asian soil.[42] Stephen Bevans prefers to use the term "contextualization" because it includes "the realities of contemporary secularity, technology, and the

36. Aloysius Pieris, *An Asian Theology of Liberation* (Maryknoll, NY: Orbis Books, 1988), 52.

37. See Paul Knitter, "Foreword," in ibid., xiii.

38. Pieris, *Asian Theology of Liberation*, 53.

39. Aloysius Pieris, "Does Christ have a Place in Asia? A Panoramic View," *Concilium* 2 (1993): 43. Italics in original.

40. See ibid., 42–47.

41. Peter Phan, "Reception of Vatican II in Asia: Historical and Theological Analysis," *Gregorianum* 83 (2002): 276.

42. Peter Phan, "Jesus the Christ with an Asian Face," *Theological Studies* 57 (1996): 424.

struggle for human justice."[43] However, the term "inculturation" does embrace these realities and it continues to be more widely used among theologians than contextualization.

In 1995 Cardinal Joseph Ratzinger favored the word "interculturality" rather than inculturation.[44] There is confusion here because interculturality is technically a term of cultural anthropology, while inculturation is a theological term. As explained, interculturality, which is the initial contact between two cultures, is only the first, but critical, stage in inculturation. At this stage there must be a willingness to understand the other person's culture. If this is lacking, people cannot proceed to the stage of dialogue. Bishop Francisco Claver, SJ, an experienced cultural anthropologist in the Philippines, agrees with this conclusion, arguing that the neglect of this intercultural stage "killed—or at least delayed for centuries—the inculturation of the faith in Asia."[45] Back in the sixteenth century the Jesuit Matteo Ricci and his companions, on first making contact with Chinese culture and Confucianism, recognized the need for a lengthy and uncertain dialogue based on mutual respect. Given what they had learned at the intercultural stage, they understood that they could not impose on Chinese people a faith mixed with European values and customs.[46] Ricci's efforts were condemned by Rome in 1742, meaning that the hard-won victory by St. Paul at the Council of Jerusalem in favor of inculturation had been put aside. The evangelizing effort of the church in Asia and elsewhere would consequently suffer for centuries to come.

Continuing Centralized Control

Vatican II laid the theological foundations for the reemergence of a more flexible, apostolic relationship between the Gospel and cultures, the type of openness that had characterized the missionary life of the early church. The Word of God is actively present within cultures before evangelization;[47] the church is not to be a huge, uniform monolith of

43. Bevans, *Models*, 21.

44. See Joseph Ratzinger, "Christ, Faith and the Challenge of Cultures," *Origins* (30 March 1995), 681. He returns to this theme in his lecture reflecting on John Paul II's encyclical "Faith and Reason" (*Fides et Ratio*). See "Culture and Truth: Reflections on the Encyclical," *Origins*, 28, no. 36 (25 February 1999), 629.

45. Francisco F. Claver, *The Making of a Local Church* (Maryknoll, NY: Orbis Books, 2008), 121.

46. See George Minamiki, *The Chinese Rites Controversy* (Chicago: Loyola Press, 1985).

47. See GS 1.

Eurocentric cultural characteristics, but a fraternity of local churches, each of which seeks to give life to the universal church in accordance with the native genius and tradition of its own members;[48] bishops are "vicars and delegates of Christ" (LG 27), not of the pope, and are endowed with the appropriate authority to govern their dioceses; there must be a "vital contact and exchange between the Church and different cultures" (GS 44), so that through this dialogue and exchange local expressions of worship and theology may emerge; genuine dialogue requires that people be open to listen to one another, thus taking every means possible to learn about the cultures of the people to be involved in the dialogue.[49] These are the council's theological underpinnings for what we now call inculturation.

However, the restorationist movement in the church (as explained in chaps. 8 and 9), with its reaffirmation of pre-Vatican II structures and attitudes and an anti-world-culture approach, is obstructing inculturation efforts.[50] The document Inculturation and the Roman Liturgy, promulgated in 1994, exemplifies this restorationist approach by Rome. Early in the document it refers optimistically to inculturation as a "double movement" and says that the liturgy "must be capable of expressing itself in every human culture," but the same document significantly limits the powers originally given to bishops and episcopal conferences in matters of liturgical experimentation.[51] In 2001 Rome issued *Liturgiam Authenticam*, a document firmly asserting that Rome has the right to intervene in liturgical matters. It undermines what is at the center of Vatican II ecclesiology by centralizing power in the curia and by demanding that local cultures implement an essentially Roman form of worship.[52] The curia-centered control is not confined to liturgical matters but embraces all aspects that relate to faith and culture, including such matters as interreligious dialogue and social justice.[53] In 1979 Karl Rahner had sadly complained: "Do not the

48. See *SC* 35.

49. See the Decree on the Church's Missionary Activity (*Ad Gentes*) 22.

50. See Gerald A. Arbuckle, *Refounding the Church: Dissent for Leadership* (Maryknoll, NY: Orbis Books, 1993), 3–4.

51. See Congregation for Divine Worship and the Discipline of the Sacraments, "Inculturation and the Roman Liturgy" (1994), 1, 6, 47, 66; comments by Nathan Mitchell, "The Amen Corner," *Worship* 68 (July 1994): 369–76; and David N. Power, "Liturgy and Culture Revisited," *Worship* 69 (May 1995): 225–43.

52. See John L. Allen, "New Document Replaces 35 Years of Liturgy Work," *National Catholic Reporter* (25 May 2001), 13.

53. See Submission of Bishops' Conference of England and Wales to the 1985 Bishops' Synod, *The Tablet* (3 August 1985), 814, and Robert Schreiter, "Faith and Cultures: Challenges to a World Church," *Theological Studies* 50 (December 1989), 758.

Roman Congregations still have the mentality of a centralized bureaucracy which thinks it knows best what serves the kingdom of God and the salvation of souls throughout the world . . . [taking] Rome or Italy in a frightening naïve way as a self-evident standard?"[54] Forty years later the situation remains the same. Not surprisingly, Michael Amaladoss, SJ, director of the Institute of Dialogue with Cultures and Religions in India, concludes that "the process of inculturation is not making much headway in the Church today because it is mostly seen as the translation and adaptation of a pre-existent 'pure' gospel" that has a "privileged and normative expression in Judaic and Greco-Roman cultures."[55]

Case Study: Inclusive Language

In 1969 Rome published an official guide for translators of liturgical texts[56] in which the principle of "dynamic equivalence" receives substantial approval.[57] This principle gives priority to the message of the biblical text over its original linguistic form.[58] That is, in the translation of texts for worship priority is to be given to the cultural context. For example, two critical contemporary cultural issues are the changing role of women and the development of the English language as influenced by social change.[59] Both movements insist on inclusive language. We should expect to find these changes mirrored in the church's public worship. This is not the case.[60] Rome still continues to block efforts to have inclusive language in the liturgy.

---

54. Karl Rahner, "Towards a Fundamental Theological Interpretation of Vatican II," *Theological Studies* 40 (December 1979): 717–18.

55. Michael Amaladoss, "Liturgical Inculturation and Postmodern Culture," 2, http://eapi.admu.edu.ph/eapr007/amaladoss.htm.

56. See *Comme le prévoit*, 1969. English text in *Documents on the Liturgy, 1963–1979*, ed. Thomas O'Brien, 284–91 (Collegeville, MN: Liturgical Press, 1982).

57. See Anscar Chupungco, *Liturgical Inculturation: Sacramentals, Religiosity, and Catechesis* (Collegeville, MN: Liturgical Press, 1992), 43–47.

58. A point reinforced by Paul VI in *Evangelii Nuntiandi* (1975), 63.

59. See Mary Collins, *Worship: Renewal to Practice* (Washington, DC: Pastoral Press, 1987), 197–214.

60. In 2007 Rome granted permission to the Canadian Catholic bishops to use the NRSV.

Inculturation as a Social Drama

We are now able to look more closely at the stages of inculturation as a process (Figure 11.1).

Inculturation as Social Drama

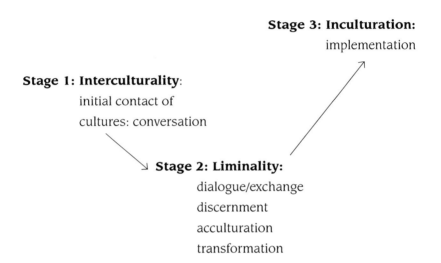

Figure 11.1

The process of inculturation follows the pattern of a social drama (chap. 10), although the stages may not always be explicitly delineated as now described. The first stage is interculturality,[61] which takes the form of an opening conversation. This initial stage is important because in it the parties to the conversation become aware that their cultures are different. A decision must be made by both parties either to stop or to continue the conversation. When the Samaritan woman and Jesus meet at Jacob's well they represent two different cultures (John 4:7-10). There is tension in the air. Jesus asks for water and the woman has to reply (v. 9). Then the crucial liminality stage with all its uncertainties begins and the conversation moves to a dialogue, that is, to a more focused form of conversation in which there is an open exchange of views (vv. 10-26).

---

61. I agree with Francisco Claver in his use of interculturality. See Claver, *Making of a Local Church*, 120–21.

A faith discernment is taking place. The parties now have a greater awareness of the presence and activity of God within themselves and in the world around them: "For we are what he has made us, created in Christ Jesus for good works, which God prepared beforehand to be our way of life" (Eph 2:10). Increasingly alert to God's presence the Samaritan woman realizes that her acculturation or acceptance of Christ's narrative must mean a change in her behavior. Is she prepared for this transformation? She must abandon attachment to aspects of her Samaritan mythology. She assents and immediately goes to share her joy with others. This is the inculturation stage.

Case Study: Option for the Poor

At a regular meeting of a management board responsible for several Catholic hospitals in the United States, the directors, who consist of successful businessmen and businesswomen, must decide either to buy a new hospital that would significantly improve the board's financial resources or to invest instead in a facility in a needy low-income suburb. If they choose the second option the board will have to subsidize its running costs, as the new facility could never pay for itself. The first alternative is more attractive from a financial and a prestige perspective. Initially board members favor this option—that is, until they begin a discernment process. Following their lengthy reflections on the Good Samaritan parable, which emphasizes the needs of people who are poor, the board votes unanimously to purchase the health facility.

I was asked to help the directors reflect on how they had come to their decision. Without being aware of it, they in fact had followed the tripartite steps of a social drama. Stage one, *interculturality*, was the awareness by the directors of a clash between two opposing mythologies: that of the business world, primarily focused on profit, and that of the Gospel with its emphasis on a preferential option for the poor. The *liminal* stage was characterized by dialogue and discernment. Directors agreed that their reflection on the parable was the key moment in their decision making. One director, skilled in contemporary research into the nature of poverty, had helped them to discover that immaterial consequences of poverty such as shame and loss of self-respect can be devastating for people. As a consequence of this realization other directors admitted that the suffering of the poverty-stricken traveler left on the roadside had a new meaning for them. They could see that an exchange had occurred between the mythologies of the business world and the Scriptures. Both had become enriched. The *acculturation* part of the liminal stage was the decision to choose the parable's primary concern for people who are disadvantaged. The actual buying of the hospital was the final *inculturation* moment.

Case Study: Family *or* Justice

In the mid-1960s I was researching the impact of credit unions on villagers in Fiji, a Third-World country. A credit union is a group of people who pledge themselves to save together and then lend their savings to one another at the lowest possible interest rates. There are strict accounting rules within a credit union: for example, family relationships must not dictate who can receive a loan or when it should be repaid. There is, however, an ancient custom among Fijians called *kerekere*, which is the practice of "borrowing" from kinsfolk at the will of the borrower in times of material misfortune. It had a distinctive beneficial role in a subsistence economy because it helped to spread consumption goods more evenly, but among people struggling to enter a money economy the custom was being abused. An official report noted that the custom now put "a premium on laziness and is often a serious or even disastrous drain on those Fijians who are endeavoring to accumulate and to invest."[62] I wanted to know if *kerekere* was being practiced in credit unions. Were people charged with assessing applications for loans being forced by relatives to agree to the requests, and did people renege on repaying loans on the basis of *kerekere*?

My research revealed that credit unions were not being significantly affected by the custom, the main reason being the ease with which villagers could integrate the lessons of biblical stories into the drama of their decision-making processes. It was not unusual for a spokesperson for a credit union to comment somewhat as follows:

---

62. O. H. K. Spate, *The Fijian People: Economic Problems and Prospects* (Suva: Legislative Council, 1959), 24; see also Gerald A. Arbuckle, "Economic and Social Development in the Fiji Islands through Credit Unions," in *Credit Unions in the South Pacific*, ed. Neil Runcie, 90–108 (London: University of London Press, 1969).

Yes, we are tempted to give way to the demands of *kerekere.* It is not easy. But Scripture tells us that we must behave with fairness to everyone, whether a relative or not. The stories that Jesus told are about being honest, and *kerekere* in a credit union is not being honest. It is hard to do this, because relatives can become very angry, but that is what Jesus wants. We Fijians traditionally hold that only people belonging to our tribes or clans are brothers. This is wrong, as we see in the Good Samaritan story.

The social drama in a credit union opened when the committee responsible for assessing applications for loans met. In the liminal phase the committee would have to assess the merits of the applicants for loans. Did the applications conform to the requirements of credit union? In the cases I examined there were identifiable stages: the intercultural clash between traditional village mythology and that of the Scriptures; dialogue; then the acculturation of the biblical mythology; finally the refusal to be influenced by *kerekere*, despite the anger of relatives, that is, inculturation. The refusal was the moment of inculturation.

Inculturation and Syncretism

Syncretism

Inculturation is social drama but it is also narrative. Narratives, as already described (chap. 6), are crucial agents that invest events with meaning, and as these events change, so do the narratives. In the drama of inculturation people are telling their stories of what it means for them to wrestle with the tension between their own cultural narratives and those of the gospels. At times syncretism is almost a predictable characteristic of this storytelling.

Syncretism evokes fear, particularly in those with authority within the institutional church. For example, the Vatican II document The Church's Missionary Activity (*Ad Gentes*) warns that any adaptation of the faith to local cultures must "avoid every appearance of syncretism and false exclusiveness" (AG 23).[63] Here syncretism is being used in its

---

63. See also the concern expressed by the Conference of Latin American Bishops at Puebla in 1979 (*Puebla and Beyond*, eds. John Eagleson and Philip Scharper [Maryknoll, NY: Orbis Books, 1979], 186, 241).

theological sense to mean an unacceptable amalgam of religious beliefs and practices, something to be identified and immediately destroyed by church authorities.[64] Yet anthropologically, syncretism as a quality of cultural change is largely inevitable.[65] At no point in time is there ever a pure Christianity. It has never existed and never will. The fact is that both the faith of Israel and the faith of the first Christian generations developed through processes of inculturation involving at times some syncretism in assimilating influences of other cultures.[66] It would take centuries of struggle for Israel to be clear about what was acceptable to God in the culture and religion of Canaan.

Syncretism is most likely to occur within the liminal stage of the inculturation drama as people evaluate the Christian mythology through the eyes of their own traditions. This is a lengthy and uneven process, and the people's narratives are forever changing. At the same time the mythologies and rituals of the local church must themselves be adapting to these changes if they are to be relevant to people. Pope Gregory the Great (540–604) provides a fascinating description of how slow this process can be and the wisdom and patience needed by representatives of the institutional church. In his advice to Abbot Mellitus, a fellow missionary of St. Augustine of Canterbury, the pope not only invokes the importance of functional substitution but also reminds him that the inculturation process is very slow. He is implicitly saying that syncretism is inevitable in the stages toward inculturation and that this is pastorally acceptable:

> The idols are to be destroyed, but the temples themselves are to be aspersed with holy water, altars set up in them, and relics deposited there. . . . In this way we hope that the people, seeing that their temples are not destroyed, may abandon their error and, flocking more readily to their accustomed resorts, may come to know and

---

64. See Louis J. Luzbetak, *The Church and Cultures: New Perspectives in Missiological Anthropology* (Maryknoll, NY: Orbis Books, 1988), 360; for clarifications and criteria for assessing authentic Christian identity see Robert J. Schreiter, *The New Catholicity: Theology between the Global and the Local* (Maryknoll, NY: Orbis Books, 1999), 62–83.

65. See Luzbetak, *Church and Cultures*, 360–61: Boff, *Church*, 89–107; and André Droogers, "Syncretism: The Problem of Definition, the Definition of the Problem," in *Dialogue and Syncretism: An Interdisciplinary Approach*, eds. Jerald Gort, Hendrik Vroom, Rein Fernhout, and Anton Wessels, 7–25 (Grand Rapids: Eerdmans, 1989).

66. See Silvia Schroer, "Transformation of Faith: Documents of Intercultural Learning in the Bible," *Concilium* 2 (1994): 3–13; Boff, *Church*, 92.

adore the true God. . . . . For it is impossible to eradicate all errors at one stroke, and whoever wishes to climb up a mountain top climbs gradually step by step and not in one leap.[67]

We, like Abraham, are called to let go of so much that is culturally familiar and comforting (Gen 12:1), and the journey will be uncertain, long, and at times tortuous.[68] Consider the drama of Jesus' relationship with Peter, one so close to Jesus yet so slow to let go. Simon Peter, with a burst of initial enthusiasm, "left everything and followed him" (Luke 5:11). Yet we quickly find Peter not understanding the words and intentions of Jesus (e.g., John 13:6-11; 18:10-11), still thinking and acting according to his former beliefs, sinking because he lacks faith (Matt 14:28-31), being vigorously rebuked as "Satan" (Mark 8:33). All the while Jesus is challenging, instructing, and waiting. Finally Peter's conversion comes, but with enormous pain (Luke 22:61-62). Jesus calls us not as pure spirits but as embodied in flesh and culture. This holistic conversion is a protracted and uncertain process of letting go.

The following case study from Papua New Guinea helps to clarify the highly complex process of Christian conversion in which syncretism is an integral stage in the cultural drama. It simply illustrates the fact that the inculturation process outlined can take decades simply because conversion to Christianity demands such radical changes in a people's traditional mythology. And of course, ultimate conversion is never certain.

Case Study: Melanesia

The people of Papua New Guinea, South Pacific, who belong to the cultural complex known as Melanesia, did not make any significant contact with the outside world until the late nineteenth century and for some tribes not until the mid-twentieth century. Traditionally Melanesian people distinguish between purely secular skills and "true knowledge." Purely secular skills are things that, given time, anyone can discover in the course of ordinary experience. By "true knowledge," however, the people mean the mastery of ritual, such as sorcery, the correct performance of which ensures the spirits bring them health and success in economic, social, and

---

67. Gregory the Great cited by Anthony Gittins, "Beyond Liturgical Inculturation," 62–63.

68. I researched in Papua New Guinea 1970–72. I am grateful for the insights of my late colleague and fellow anthropologist, Father Hermann Janssen, MSC.

political action. The spirits and human beings live together in a purely physical world and there is no distinction between the natural and supernatural; the power and actions of spirit-beings are as real and alive as the world we see. People believe that through the use of "right rituals" based on "true knowledge" they are able to manipulate the ancestors in their favor. If material wealth and power do not result, it is due to the fact that the wrong rituals have been used or they have been inaccurately recited. They do not question the underlying mythology. Millennial movements, called locally "cargo cults,"[69] are an integral feature of Melanesian cultures; these movements are built on the assumption that the ancestors will dramatically arrive in planes or boats bringing desirable produce *provided*, as always, people discover the correct rituals.

The long social drama of inculturation for Melanesian people begins when people first make contact with Christian missionaries. In this *intercultural* stage there is a period of initial apprehension, then enthusiasm that the contact will result in material benefits. There is enthusiasm akin to that Peter initially experienced in his conversion of faith. This is followed by the lengthy liminal phase in which it is possible to distinguish four stages of acculturation. The first is *ritualistic conversion*. People, believing that Christianity contains the secret knowledge, faithfully imitate externally the ways of missionaries in the hope that this will reveal the secret knowledge and the path to economic and political success. People abandon traditional rituals, for example ancestral cults, and enthusiastically adopt Christian rituals such as rosary beads and going to Mass. Despite the external changes the belief that ritual is the secret way to material achievement remains intact and unchallenged.[70]

The next stage of acculturation is *formal syncretism*. After some years people become disappointed that Christianity does not bring the results they are waiting for. The missionaries, they believe, are hiding the real secret knowledge from them and they begin again to fear the ancestors are punishing them for their neglect of traditional ways. A person's narrative lament summarizes this general

---

69. For helpful analyses see Kenelm Burridge, *Mambu: A Melanesian Millennium* (London: Methuen, 1960).

70. See Peter Lawrence, *Road Belong Cargo* (Melbourne: Melbourne University Press, 1967), 79.

reaction: "We worshiped the Christian God, where is the rice, the jeeps, nothing at all? We sent our children to the mission schools, where is the canned fish?" There is now a blending of traditional and Christian rituals, but the underlying traditional mythology remains unchanged, namely that the right ritual will bring results, if only it can be found. "Cargo cults" with their syncretistic qualities become common at this stage; people neglect or entirely abandon secular activities and give their full attention to the syncretistic rituals.[71]

The third stage of acculturation is *ritualistic secularization*. This involves a radical switch from the belief that the mixture of traditional and Christian rituals will bring the people the desired secret ritual knowledge. Now secular activities of government officials and foreign business people, not the Christian religion, contain the secret knowledge and people begin to imitate their behavior and ignore their previous syncretistic rituals. People abandon churches and Christian rituals. One person summarizes this stage: "If we follow the government laws and grow better coconut trees, the secret will be ours." There is a dramatic burst of enthusiasm for education, economic development, and involvement in government politics. As before, there is no change in traditional mythology, but only in the external ritual practices.

The last stage of acculturation is the decision either for a lasting rejection of Christianity or the conversion to Christian secularization. Christianity is no technology; God cannot be manipulated as people thought they could do with their ancestors. In Christian secularization Melanesians come to believe that they are instruments of Christ's incarnation and redemption within their own cultural milieu, the fruits of which are "love, joy, peace, patience, kindness, generosity, faithfulness, gentleness, and self-control" (Gal 5:22). Their task is to develop the resources given them by God for the benefit of all. Christian rituals and beliefs are not enough. Action must follow, and when this is happening the last stage of the drama is occurring, namely inculturation.

71. See ibid., 63–85.

Theological Reflection

While this chapter has shown that in theory Rome is open to the theological and cultural implications of inculturation, in practice, given the restorationist tendencies, it is not. It is not prepared to critique its own Eurocentric and patriarchal culture. Inculturation remains a dream as long as the institutional church is unwilling to accept the fact that it is now a global and multicultural reality in which the majority of its adherents have ceased to be of European origin. Inculturation is an arduous process, but it is an imperative of our faith, calling us to a cultural and spiritual conversion and to a pilgrimage to where we "do not wish to go" (John 21:18).

But the call of Jesus Christ is the same as that given to Peter: "Follow me" (John 21:19). We will follow if we "have faith in God" (Mark 11:22). We cannot foretell in advance what God may reveal about us and the cultures we must dialogue with, or how God will act. What we do know is that in order to begin, and remain in, the pilgrimage of inculturation we need to know who we are as church. Then we will begin to understand the essential and the accidental in our identity and discern what, as faithful pilgrims, we must courageously abandon.

Bibliography

Alcock, Pete. *Understanding Poverty*. Basingstoke: Palgrave Macmillan, 2006.

Alcoff, Linda M., and Eduardo Mendieta, eds. *Identities: Race, Class, Gender, and Nationality*. Oxford: Blackwell, 2003.

Amalodoss, Michael. "Liturgical Inculturation and Postmodern Culture." http:eapi.admu.edu.ph/eapr007/amalodoss.htm.

Aries, Philippe. *Western Attitudes Towards Death: From the Middle Ages to the Present*. London: Johns Hopkins University Press, 1974.

Arbuckle, Gerald A. *Earthing the Gospel: An Inculturation Handbook for Pastoral Workers*. Maryknoll, NY: Orbis Books, 1990.

———. *Change, Grief, and Renewal in the Church*. Westminster, MD: Christian Classics, 1991.

———. *From Chaos to Mission: Refounding Religious Life Formation*. London: Geoffrey Chapman, 1995.

———. *Refounding the Church: Dissent for Leadership*. Maryknoll, NY: Orbis Books, 1993.

———. *Healthcare Ministry: Refounding the Mission in Tumultuous Times*. Collegeville, MN: Liturgical Press, 2000.

———. *Violence, Society, and the Church*. Collegeville, MN: Liturgical Press, 2004.

———. *Laughing with God: Humor, Culture, and Transformation*. Collegeville, MN: Liturgical Press, 2008.

———. *A "Preferential Option for the Poor": Application to Catholic and Aged Care Ministries in Australia*. Canberra: Catholic Health Australia, 2008.

Armstrong, Gary. *Football Hooligans: Knowing the Score*. Oxford: Berg, 1998.

Asad, Talal. "Anthropological Conceptions of Religion: Reflections on Geertz." *Man: Journal of the Royal Anthropological Institute* 18, no. 2 (1983): 237–59.

Augustine, Chas. *A Commentary on the New Code of Canon Law*. St. Louis: B. Herder, 1921.

Barnard, Alan. *History and Theory in Anthropology*. Cambridge: Cambridge University Press, 2000.

Barthes, Roland. *Mythologies*. St. Albans: Paladin, 1973.

Bauman, Zygmunt. *Work, Consumerism and the New Poor*. Buckingham: Open University Press, 1998.

Beckford, James A. "Religion, Modernity and Post-Modernity." In *Religion: Contemporary Issues*. Edited by Bryan Wilson, 11–23. London: Bellew, 1992.

Bell, Catherine. *Ritual Theory—Ritual Practice*. New York: Oxford University Press, 1992.

Bennett, David, ed. *Multicultural States: Rethinking Difference and Identity*. London: Routledge, 1998.

Berger, Peter, and Thomas Luckmann. *The Social Construction of Reality*. Harmondsworth: Penguin, 1967.

Berger, Peter. *The Sacred Canopy: Elements of a Sociological Theory of Religion*. New York: Doubleday, 1969.

Bevans, Stephen B. *Models of Contextual Theology*. Maryknoll, NY: Orbis Books, 1998.

Beyer, Peter. *Religions in Global Society*. London: Routledge, 2006.

Bhachu, Pariminder. *Twice Migrants: East African Sikh Settlers in Britain*. London: Tavistock, 1985.

Bion, Wilfred. *Second Thoughts*. Beverly Hills: Sage, 1986.

Bloom, Allan. *The Closing of the American Mind*. New York: Simon and Schuster, 1987.

Blumer, Herbert. *Symbolic Interaction: Perspective and Method*. Englewood Cliffs, NJ: Prentice-Hall, 1969.

Bocock, Robert. *Ritual in Industrial Society: A Sociological Analysis of Ritualism in Modern England*. London: George Allen and Unwin, 1974.

Boff, Leonardo. *Church, Charism and Power*. London: SCM, 1985.

Bosch, David, J. *Transforming Mission: Paradigm Shifts in Theology of Mission*. Maryknoll, NY: Orbis Books, 1991.

Bourdieu, Pierre, and Jean-Claude Passeron. *Reproduction in Education, Society and Culture*. Beverly Hills: Sage, 1977.

Bourdieu, Pierre. *Outline of a Theory of Practice*. Cambridge: Cambridge University Press, 1977.

———. *Distinction: A Social Critique of the Judgement of Taste*. London: Routledge, 1984.

———. *Language and Symbolic Power*. Cambridge, MA: Harvard University Press, 1991.

Bowie, Fiona. *The Anthropology of Religion*. Oxford: Blackwell, 2000.

Bradley, Harriet. *Fractured Identities: Changing Patterns of Inequality*. Cambridge: Polity, 1996.

Brison, Karen J. "Constructing Identity through Ceremonial Language in Rural Fiji." *Ethnology: An International Journal of Cultural and Social Anthropology* 40, no. 4 (2001): 309–27.

———. "The Empire Strikes Back: Pentecostalism in Fiji." *Ethnology* 46, no. 1 (2007): 21–39.

Brown, Delwin, Sheila Greeve Davaney, and Kathryn Tanner, eds. *Converging on Culture: Theologians in Dialogue with Cultural Analysis and Criticism*. Oxford: Oxford University Press, 2001.

Brueggemann, Walter. *Texts Under Negotiation: The Bible and the Postmodern Imagination*. Minneapolis: Fortress Press, 1993.

———. *Hope within History*. Atlanta: John Knox, 1987.

Bryson, Bethany. "Anything But Heavy Metal: Symbolic Exclusion and Musical Dislikes." *American Sociological Review* 61, no. 5 (October 1996): 884–99.

Buckley, Anthony D., and Mary C. Kenny. *Negotiating Identity: Rhetoric, Metaphor, and Social Drama in Northern Ireland*. Washington, DC: Smithsonian Institution, 1995.

Burke, Peter. *What is Cultural History?* Cambridge: Polity, 2008.

Burstyn, Varda. *The Rites of Men: Manhood, Politics, and the Culture of Sport*. Toronto: University of Toronto Press, 1999.

Butler, Tim, and Paul Watt. *Understanding Social Inequality*. London: Sage, 2007.

Castles, Stephen. *Ethnicity and Globalization*. London: Sage, 2000.

Cenkner, William, ed. *The Multicultural Church: A New Landscape in U.S. Theologies*. New York: Paulist Press, 1995.

Chupungco, Anscar. *Liturgical Inculturation*. Collegeville, MN: Liturgical Press, 1992.

Clifford, James, and George E. Marcus, eds. *Writing Culture: The Poetics and Politics of Ethnography*. Berkeley: University of California Press, 1986.

Clifford, James. *The Predicament of Culture: Twentieth-Century Ethnography, Literature, and Art*. Cambridge, MA: Harvard University Press, 1988.

Claver, Francisco F. *The Making of a Local Church*. Maryknoll, NY: Orbis Books, 2008.

Congar, Yves. *Power and Poverty in the Church*. Translated by Jennifer Nicholson. London: Geoffrey Chapman, 1964.

Congregation for Divine Worship and Discipline of the Sacraments. *Inculturation and the Roman Liturgy*. Washington, DC: United States Catholic Conference, 1994.

Cohen, Anthony P. *The Symbolic Construction of Community*. Chichester: Ellis Horwood, 1985.

Davaney, Sheila Greeve. "Theology and the Turn to Cultural Analysis." In *Converging on Culture: Theologians in Dialogue with Cultural Analysis and Criticism*. Edited by Delwin Brown, Sheila Greeve Davaney, and Kathryn Tanner, 3–16. Oxford: Oxford University Press, 2001.

Department of Education, United States Catholic Conference. *Principles for Inculturation of the Catechism of the Catholic Church*. Washington, DC: United States Catholic Conference, 1994.

Donahue, John R. *The Gospel in Parable*. Philadelphia: Fortress Press, 1988.

Dotty, William G. *Mythography: The Study of Myths and Rituals*. Alabama: University of Alabama Press, 1986.

Douglas, Mary. *Purity and Danger: An Analysis of the Concepts of Pollution and Taboo*. New York: Pantheon Books, 1966.

———. *Natural Symbols: Explorations in Cosmology*. New York: Pantheon Books, 1970.

Dunn, James D., and John W. Rogerson, eds. *Eerdmans Commentary on the Bible*. Grand Rapids: Eerdmans, 2003.

Eller, Jack D. *From Culture to Ethnicity to Conflict: An Anthropological Perspective on International Ethnic Conflict*. Ann Arbor: University of Michigan Press, 1999.

Eriksen, Thomas H., and Finn S. Nielsen. *A History of Anthropology*. London: Pluto Press, 2001.

Farmer, William R., et al., eds. *The International Bible Commentary*. Collegeville, MN: Liturgical Press, 1998.

Fawcett, Thomas. *The Symbolic Language of Religion*. Minneapolis: Augsburg Press, 1971.

Fenton, Steve. *Ethnicity, Racism, Class and Culture*. London: Macmillan, 1999.

Fitzgerald, Thomas K. *Metaphors of Identity: A Culture-Communication Dialogue*. New York: SUNY Press, 1993.

Foucault, Michel. *The Order of Things: An Archaeology of the Human Sciences*. New York: Vintage Books, 1974.

———. *Discipline and Punish: The Birth of the Prison*. Translated by Alan Sheridan. Harmondsworth: Penguin, 1979.

———. *The History of Sexuality, Volume 1: An Introduction*. London: Penguin, 1979.

———. *Power/Knowledge*. New York: Pantheon, 1980.

Furlong, Monica. *C of E: The State It's In*. London: Hodder and Stoughton, 2000.

Gallagher, Michael. *Clashing Symbols: An Introduction to Faith and Culture*. London: Darton, Longman, and Todd, 1997.

Gaillardetz, Richard. "Apologetics, Evangelization and Ecumenism Today." *Origins* 35, no. 1 (19 May 2005): 9–15.

Gans, Herbert. *Popular Culture: An Analysis of Evaluation and Taste*. New York: Basic Books, 1974.

Geertz, Clifford. *The Interpretation of Cultures*. New York: Basic Books, 1973.

———. *After the Fact*. Cambridge, MA: Harvard University Press, 1995.

Gellner, Ernest. *Postmodernism, Reason and Religion*. London: Routledge, 1992.

Giddens, Anthony. *The Consequences of Modernity*. Palo Alto: Stanford University Press, 1990.

———. *Modernity and Self-Identity: Self and Society in the Late Modern Age*. Cambridge: Polity, 1991.

———. *The Transformation of Intimacy: Sexuality, Love and Eroticism in Modern Societies*. Cambridge: Polity, 1992.

Gittins, Anthony J. *Where's There's Hope There's Life: Women's Stories of Homelessness and Survival*. Ligouri, MO: Ligouri/Triumph, 2006.

———. "Beyond Liturgical Inculturation: Transforming the Deep Structures of Faith." *Irish Theological Quarterly* 69 (2004): 47–72.

Goffman, Erving. *Stigma: Notes on the Management of Spoiled Identity*. New York: Prentice-Hall, 1963.

Goldberg, David T., ed. *Multiculturalism: A Critical Reader*. Oxford: Basil Blackwell, 1994.

Gonzalez, Ondina E., and Justo L. Gonzalez. *Christianity in Latin America*. Cambridge: Cambridge University Press, 2008.

Green, Anna. *Cultural History*. New York: Palgrave Macmillan, 2009.

Grimes, Ronald. "Reinventing Ritual." *Soundings* 75, no. 1 (1992): 21–41.

Groome, Thomas. "Inculturation: How to Proceed in a Pastoral Context." *Concilium* 2 (1994): 120–33.

Handler, Joel F., and Yeheskel Hasenfeld. *Blame Welfare, Ignore Poverty and Inequality*. Cambridge: Cambridge University Press, 2007.

Hanson, Allan. "The Making of the Maori: Culture Invention and its Logic." *American Anthropologist* 91, no. 4 (1989): 890–902.

Havemann, Paul, ed. *Indigenous Peoples' Rights in Australia, Canada, and New Zealand*. Auckland: Oxford University Press, 1999.

Hebdige, Dick. *Subculture: The Meaning of Style*. London: Methuen, 1979.

Hendry, Joy. *Reclaiming Culture: Indigenous People and Self-Representation*. Houndmills: Palgrave, 2005.

———. *An Introduction to Social Anthropology: Sharing our Worlds*. Houndmills: Palgrave, 2008.

Herriot, Peter. *Religious Fundamentalism and Social Identity*. London: Routledge, 2007.

Hewitt, Roger. *White Backlash and the Politics of Multiculturalism*. Cambridge: Cambridge University Press, 2005.

Hewitt, William E. *Base Communities and Social Change in Brazil*. Lincoln: University of Nebraska Press, 1992.

Hills, John, Julian Le Grand, and David Piachaud, eds. *Understanding Social Exclusion*. Oxford: Oxford University Press, 2002.

Holt, Douglas B. "What Becomes an Icon Most?" *Harvard Business Review* 81, no. 3 (March 2003): 43–48.

Horowitz, Gad. *Repression: Basic and Surplus Repression in Psychoanalytic Theory*. Toronto: University of Toronto Press, 1977.

Huntington, Samuel, P. *The Clash of Civilizations and the Remaking of World Order*. New York: Simon and Schuster, 1996.

International Theological Commission. "Faith and Inculturation." *Irish Theological Quarterly* 55, no. 2 (1989): 142–60.

Jenkins, Richard. *Social Identity*. New York: Routledge, 2008.

Jenks, Chris. *Culture*. London: Routledge, 1993.

John Paul II. "Letter to Agostino Cardinal Casaroli, on the Occasion of the Creation of the Pontifical Council for Culture." *L'Osservatore Romano* (English edition), 28 June 1982.

———. *Mission of the Redeemer (Redemptoris Missio)*. Encyclical Letter. Boston: St. Paul Books, 1991.

———. *Faith and Reason (Fides et Ratio)*. Washington, DC: United States Catholic Conference, 1998.

Kapferer, Bruce. *Legends of People: Myths of State*. Washington, DC: Smithsonian Institution Press, 1988.

Keesing, Roger M. *Cultural Anthropology: A Contemporary Perspective*. New York: Holt, Rinehart and Winston, 1976.

Kertzer, David. *Ritual, Politics, and Power*. New Haven: Yale University Press, 1988.

King, Ursula, ed. *Feminist Theology in the Third World*. London: SPCK, 1994.

Kivisto, Peter. *Multiculturalism in a Global Society*. Oxford: Blackwell, 2002.

Kroeber, Alfred, and Clyde Kluckhohn. *Culture: A Critical Review of Concepts and Definitions*. Papers of the Peabody Museum of American Archaeology and Ethnology 47, no. 1 (Cambridge, MA: Peabody Museum, 1952).

Kuper, Adam. *Culture: The Anthropologist's Account*. Cambridge, MA: Harvard University Press, 1999.

Kwok, Pui-lan. "Feminist Theology as Intercultural Discourse." In *The Cambridge Companion to Feminist Theology*. Edited by Susan F. Parsons, 23–39. Cambridge: Cambridge University Press, 2002.

Layton, Robert. *An Introduction to Theory in Anthropology*. Cambridge: Cambridge University Press, 1997.

Lash, Nicholas. *Theology on the Way to Emmaus*. Eugene, OR: Wipf & Stock, 1986.

Leach, Edmund R. *Political Systems of Highland Burma: A Study of Kachin Social Structure*. Cambridge, MA: Harvard University Press, 1954.

Levey, Geoffrey B., and Tariq Modood. *Secularism, Religion and Multicultural Citizenship*. Cambridge: Cambridge University Press, 2009.

Levi-Strauss. Claude. *Mythologiques*. Paris: Plon, 1964.

———. *The Raw and the Cooked: Introduction to the Science of Mythology*. London: Cape, 1970.

Lewis, Oscar. *The Children of Sanchez*. New York: Random House, 1961.

Lindholm, Charles. *Culture and Authenticity*. Oxford: Blackwell, 2008.

Lister, Ruth. *Poverty*. Cambridge: Polity, 2004.

Lonergan, Bernard. *Method in Theology*. London: Darton, Longman and Todd, 1975.

Luzbetak, Louis J. *The Church and Cultures: New Perspectives in Missiological Anthropology*. Maryknoll, NY: Orbis Books, 1988.

Lyotard, Jean-François. *The Postmodern Condition*. Translated by Geoff Bennington and Brian Massumi. Manchester: Manchester University Press, 1986.

Malina, Bruce J., and Richard L. Rohrbaugh. *Social-Science Commentary on the Sypnotic Gospels*. Minneapolis: Fortress Press, 1992.

Malinowski, Bronislaw. *Freedom and Civilization*. London: Unwin, 1947.

Marcus, George E., and James Clifford. *Anthropology as Cultural Critique: An Experimental Moment in the Human Sciences*. Chicago: University of Chicago Press, 1986.

Marcus, George E. "The Passion of Anthropology in the U.S., circa 2007." *Anthropological Yearbook of European Cultures* 16 (2007): 29–55.

Martin, Bernice. "From Pre- to Postmodernity in Latin America: the Case of Pentecostalism." In *The World Their Parish*. Edited by David Martin, 102–43. Oxford: Blackwell, 2002.

Martin, David. *On Secularization: Towards a Revised Social Theory*. Aldershot: Ashgate, 2005.

May, Rollo. *The Cry for Myth*. New York: Delta, 1991.

McIver, Robert M. *The Web of Government*. London: Macmillan, 1947.

Metz, Johann Baptist. *Faith in History and Society: Toward a Practical Fundamental Theology*. London: Burns & Oates, 1980.

Micklethwait, John, and Adrian Wooldridge. *God is Back: How the Global Revival of Faith is Changing the World*. New York: Penguin, 2009.

Milbank, John. *Theology and Social Theory: Beyond Secular Reason*. Oxford: Blackwell, 1990.

Miller, Donald E., and Tetsunao Yamamori. *Global Pentecostalism: The New Face of Christian Social Engagement*. Berkeley: University of California Press, 2007.

Mitchell, Nathan. "Amen Corner." *Worship* 68, no. 4 (1994): 371–76.

Modood, Tariq. *Multiculturalism*. Cambridge: Polity, 2007.

Moore, Henrietta L. *Feminism and Anthropology*. Cambridge: Polity, 1988.

Moore, Sally F., and Barbara G. Myerhoff, eds. *Secular Rituals*. Assen and Amsterdam: Van Gorcum, 1977.

Mosko, Mark S., and Frederick H. Damon. *On the Order of Chaos: Social Anthropology and the Science of Chaos*. New York: Berghahn, 2005.

Murphy, Charles, M. "The Church and Culture since Vatican II: On the Analogy of Faith and Art." *Theological Studies* 48, no. 2 (June 1987): 317–31.

Needham, Rodney, ed. *Right and Left: Essays on Dual Symbolic Classification*. Chicago: University of Chicago Press, 1973.

———. *Symbolic Classification*. Santa Monica: Goodyear, 1979.

O'Leary, Daniel. *Begin with the Heart: Recovering a Sacrament of Vision*. Dublin: Columba, 2008.

Omerod, Neil. *Introducing Contemporary Theologies*. Newtown: E. J. Dwyer, 1990.

———. "A Dialectic Engagement with the Social Sciences in an Ecclesiological Context." *Theological Studies* 66, no. 4 (2005): 815–40.

Ortner, Sherry. "On Key Symbols." *American Anthropologist* 75, no. 5 (1973): 1338–46.

———. *Anthropology and Social Theory: Culture, Power, and the Acting Subject*. Durham, NC: Duke University Press, 2006.

Pakulski, Jan. *Globalising Inequalities: New Patterns of Social Privilege and Disadvantage*. Sydney: Allen & Unwin, 2004.

Paul VI. *Evangelii Nuntiandi* (On Evangelization). Apostolic Exhortation. Sydney: St Pauls Publications, 1982.

Peel, Mark. *The Lowest Rung: Voices of Australian Poverty*. Cambridge: Cambridge University Press, 2003.

Phan, Peter. "Jesus the Christ with an Asian Face." *Theological Studies* 57, no. 3 (1996): 399–430.

———. "Reception of Vatican II in Asia: Historical and Theological Analysis." *Gregorianum* 83, no. 2 (2002): 269–85.

———. *Being Religious Interreligiously: Asian Perspectives on Interfaith Dialogue*. Maryknoll, NY: Orbis Books, 2004.

Pieris, Aloysius. "A Theology of Liberation in Asian Churches?" *The Month* (September 1985): 231–39.

———. "Does Christ have a Place in Asia? A Panoramic View." *Concilium* 2 (1993): 121–30.

Pieterse, Jan N. *Globalization and Culture*. Lanham, MD: Rowman & Littlefield, 2004.

Poloma, Margaret M. "The 'Toronto Blessing' in Postmodern Society: Manifestations, Metaphor and Myth." In *The Globalization of Pentecostalism: A Religion Made to Travel*. Edited by Murray W. Dempster, Bryan Klaus, and Douglas Petersen, 363–85. Oxford: Regnum, 1999.

Pontifical Council for Culture. "Toward a Pastoral Approach to Culture." *Origins* 29, no. 5 (17 June 1999): 65–84.

Pool, Robert. "Postmodern Ethnography?" *Critique of Anthropology* 11, no. 4 (1991): 309–31.

Power, David N. "Liturgy and Culture Revisited." *Worship* 68, no. 4 (1994): 225–43.

Rahner, Karl. "Towards a Fundamental Theological Interpretation of Vatican II." *Theological Studies* 40, no. 4 (1979): 716–27.

Ratzinger, Joseph. "Christ, Faith and the Challenge of Cultures." *Origins* 24, no. 41 (1995): 679–86.

———. "Culture and Truth: Reflections on the Encyclical." *Origins* 28, no. 36 (25 February 1999): 625–31.

Ricoeur, Paul. *The Symbolism of Evil*. Boston: Beacon, 1967.

———. *Interpretation Theory: Discourse and the Surplus of Meaning*. Fort Worth: Texas Christian University Press, 1976.

———. *The Philosophy of Paul Ricoeur: An Anthology of His Work*. Edited by Charles E. Reagan and David Stewart. Boston: Beacon, 1978.

———. "On Interpretation." In *From Text to Action: Essays in Hermeneutics, II*. Edited by Kathleen Blamey and John B. Thompson, 1–20. Evanston, IL: Northwestern University Press, 1991.

———. "Narrative Time." *Critical Inquiry* 7, no. 1 (January 1991): 169–90.

Ruether, Rosemary R. "The Emergence of Christian Feminist Theology." In *The Cambridge Companion to Feminist Theology*. Edited by Susan F. Parsons, 3–22. Cambridge: Cambridge University Press, 2002.

Sahlins, Marshall. "Two or Three Things I Know About Culture." *Journal of the Royal Anthropological Institute* 5, no. 2 (1999): 399–421.

Sandall, Roger. *The Culture Cult: Designer Tribalism and Other Essays*. Oxford: Westview, 2001.

Sanneh, Lamin. *Translating the Message: The Missionary Impact on Culture*. Maryknoll, NY: Orbis Books, 2009.

Schreiter, Robert J. "Inculturation of Faith or Identification with Culture?" *Concilium* 2 (1994): 15–24.

———. "Faith and Cultures: Challenges to a World Church." *Theological Studies* 50, no. 4 (1989): 745–60.

———. *The New Catholicity: Theology Between the Global and the Local*. Maryknoll, NY: Orbis Books, 1999.

Sen, Amartya. *Development of Freedom*. New York: Anchor Books, 1999.

———. *Identity and Violence: The Illusion of Destiny*. London: Penguin, 2006.

Senghass, Dieter. *The Clash within Civilizations: Coming to Terms with Cultural Conflicts*. London: Routledge, 1998.

Shakespeare, Steven. *Radical Orthodoxy: A Critical Introduction*. London: SPCK, 2007.

Shorter, Aylward. *Toward a Theology of Inculturation*. London: Geoffrey Chapman, 1988.

Smith, Philip, and Alexander Riley. *Cultural Theory: An Introduction*. Oxford: Oxford University Press, 2009.

Snodgrass, Klyne R. *Stories with Intent: A Comprehensive Guide to the Parables of Jesus*. Grand Rapids: Eerdmans, 2008.

Sperber, Dan. *Rethinking Symbolism*. Cambridge: Cambridge University Press, 1975.

Stambaugh, John, and David Balch. *The Social World of the First Christians*. London: SPCK, 1986.

Starkloff, Carl F. "Inculturation and Cultural Systems." *Theological Studies* 55, no. 1 (1994): 70–81.

Tanner, Kathryn. *Theories of Culture: A New Agenda for Theology*. Cambridge: Cambridge University Press, 1997.

Tapscott, Don. *Grown Up Digital: How the Net Generation is Changing Your World*. New York: McGraw-Hill, 2009.

Tillich, Paul. "The Church and Contemporary Culture." *World Christian Education*, Second Quarterly (1956): 41–43.

Tracy, David. "The Uneasy Alliance Reconceived: Catholic Theological Method, Modernity, and Postmodernity." *Theological Studies* 50, no. 3 (1989): 548–70.

———. "Theology and the Many Faces of Postmodernity." *Theology Today* 51 (1994): 104–14.

Tylor, Edward B. *Primitive Culture*. 2 volumes. New York: Harper, 1871.

Turner, Victor. *The Forest of Symbols: Aspects of Ndembu Ritual*. Ithaca: Cornell University Press, 1967.

———. *The Drums of Affliction: A Study of Religious Process among the Ndembu of Zambia*. Oxford: Clarendon Press, 1968.

————. "Passages, Margins, and Poverty: Religious Symbols of Communitas." *Worship* 46, no. 7 (1972): 390–412.

————. *On the Edge of the Bush: Anthropology as Experience*. Tuscon: University of Arizona Press, 1985.

White, Leland. "Grid and Group in Matthew's Community: The Righteousness/ Honor Code in the Sermon on the Mount." *Semeia* 35 (1986): 61–89.

Williams, Raymond. *The Long Revolution*. London: Chatto & Windus, 1961.

————. *Keywords: A Vocabulary of Culture and Society*. New York: Oxford University Press, 1985.

Wilson, Thomas M., and Hastings Donnan. *The Anthropology of Ireland*. Oxford: Berg, 2006.

Wright, N. T. *The New Testament and the People of God*. Minneapolis: Fortress Press, 1993.

Yoko, Kimura. "The Notting Hill Carnival in London: A Study on Mas Bands, Masquerading Groups of an Urban Festival." *Japanese Review of Cultural Anthropology* 7 (2006): 85–96.

Index

Broth...
MAMBO

FINDING AFRICA IN THE AMAZON

J.D. LENOIR

with Phil Ceder, KutuKutu

Black Rose Writing | Texas

ISBN: 978-1-68433-877-1
PUBLISHED BY BLACK ROSE WRITING
www.blackrosewriting.com

Printed in the United States of America
Suggested Retail Price (SRP) $18.95

Brother Mambo is printed in Garamond

Cover design by Janice Shay/Pinafore Press

*As a planet-friendly publisher, Black Rose Writing does its best to eliminate unnecessary waste to reduce paper usage and energy costs, while never compromising the reading experience. As a result, the final word count vs. page count may not meet common expectations.

For
SaTchingTching
1943 - 2021

PRAISE FOR
Brother
MAMBO

"*Brother Mambo* is the best introduction yet to how anthropology is born in the field – its struggles, its joys, its strengths, its limits, and what it can and can not know."
–Gerald Sider, Professor of Anthropology Emeritus, PhD Program in Anthropology

"This is an excellent book for students and practitioners of anthropology, as well as for the intelligent reading public."
–Edward C. Green, PhD, former Senior Research Scientist, Harvard School of Public Health

"*Brother Mambo* is an amazing adventure that leads to an isolated group of Africans who as fugitive slaves reconstituted a society in the rainforest of Suriname."
–Dr. Charles W. Kegley, past President of the International Studies Association

"Lenoir and KutuKutu manage to cover delicate and complex subjects without lecturing or preaching. Their sense of humor, courage and curiousness kept me turning pages and wanting to know more."
–Ann Shortt, PhD, Superintendent, Fairbanks North Star Borough School District (Ret.)

Brother
MAMBO

"There are few things in life you can be sure of, except
Rain falls from the clouds,
Sun lights up the day,
And hummingbirds do fly."
–Benard Ighner

PREFACE

There was no turning back. I had just completed my courses at the Graduate Faculty of the New School in Manhattan and set off to conduct field research for a doctoral dissertation in cultural anthropology. It was early autumn of 1970 and my friends had thrown me a raucous send-off party. We were graduate students, but also comrades, having blocked Fifth Avenue and occupied the anthropology department for several days and nights to protest the Vietnam war. We were all Hippies of one sort or other, and despaired of seemingly intractable problems of Richard Nixon's America. I was headed to Guyana to study African cultural influences in that South American country. A two-year project, I figured; a welcome opportunity to finish the PhD in an idyllic tropic environment.

From the moment I walked down the wobbly ramp rolled up to the 707 in the Georgetown airport, nothing worked out as expected. Guyana would not have me rooting around their newly independent country doing research. I had to leave the country, but returning to New York was out of the question. The only option was to keep going, with no idea of where I would end up or what I would find.

Through a series of strange encounters and perhaps divine intersessions, I ended up on the muddy doorstep of Pamaka (pronounced Pah-MA-ka), an extraordinary community of Africans living on islands on the Maroni River, between Suriname and French Guiana. What I found was a people stolen some two hundred years ago from their villages in what is now the region of Ghana, Nigeria, and the Congo; then sold to Dutch plantation owners to work their South American colony. They had escaped the plantations and fled from troops and bounty hunters to form free settlements deep in the Amazon rain forest. They created a viable social, cultural, and spiritual order as fugitives banded together. Knowledge and traditions remembered from their disparate African origins informed their group concepts of self, life, death, afterlife, and the spirit world. It is in this sense that they are still Africans.

I had planned to spend two years living among the Pamakans to gather information for an ethnography and a PhD in cultural anthropology. The plan worked, except I never completely left Pamaka. This story is as much about what the Pamakans taught me about life and being a person as it is about them.

KATIE

There was supply and mail delivery to the village every week or two via the government long canoes that ran up the river from the Surinamese outpost in Albina. I sent word to Katie that I had a place all set up for us in this remote river island village and explained how to get here: fly to Paramaribo, get a bus to Albina and go directly to the district commissioner, tell him you are my wife. About three weeks later, she sent word that she had scheduled a flight and would get upriver as soon as she could. Katie and I had worked and traveled together in Vietnam war zones, so she was resourceful, and it helped that she was tall and beautiful, with chestnut hair that fell to her waist.

One early afternoon the main dock area of the village erupted in excitement. People, mainly kids, were hurrying to the landing where the government canoe had just arrived. The crowd was gawking and pointing at the boat as I rushed up—wearing only my jeans. Katie had arrived!

I pushed through the crowd to help her off the boat. We held a long embrace, and Langatabiki knew: "BaMambo's woman is here!" She traveled light so I grabbed her two bags. A third small bag contained a disoriented tabby cat—Daisy came too! I led Katie up the dirt (okay, mud) embankment of the landing where a clutch of villagers had gathered. They were awestruck. None of them had ever seen a human being like Katie—poised and upright like a runway model, long straight hair accenting vanilla white skin. And there was Daisy, too; she would be one of the few cats in the village.

As we got to the main village walkway, I addressed the growing audience to introduce my wife. Everyone had figured that out, of course, so I announced that her name was Katie. We could not move because of the growing crush of villagers wanting to get a closer look at Katie, and to touch her hair and her bare arms. One of the young women spoke up for her cohort of girls present: "She is 'S'Ayentina.'" The crowd murmured in collective appreciation. Her name was from then on 'S'Ayentina.' There was no literal interpretation of the word, it just was a name, a word that suited her perfectly.

Katie, or S'Ayentina, was ill at ease with all the attention; and it did not let up. There was a crowd of people, mainly children and young girls around her every step as we walked through the village. When we got to our thatched, dirt-floor A-frame with no furniture except a hammock, I opened my arms in welcome, "We're home!" I gave her a quick briefing on hammock sleeping: the trick is to go diagonal, and be careful not to let your feet, arms, or hands hang bare over side because of vampires. Yeah, vampires. No, not the garlic and stake thing, but disgusting little bats that will take advantage of an exposed limb to make a nick with razor-sharp teeth, and lap up the oozing blood quickened by their anti-coagulant saliva.

Katie was not impressed with the accommodations, not even B'Aleke's ornately painted and carved door interested her. We were not new to Spartan living from a year in Vietnam, several months in a microbus roaming through Europe and Morocco, and a battered tenement on Manhattan's Lower East Side in the 1960s. But through all our adventures, we generally had clean, fresh, sometimes hot—water, and showers in bathrooms. Here there was only the river. I had managed to get one of the weekly supply boats to pick up a one-burner propane stove and tank from a Chinese store in Albina, so I had a kitchen.

The house was more like an organic one-person tent, with absolutely no privacy from the neighbors. The place turned into a bedroom when you unrolled the hammock and strung it between the big horizontal sticks on either side that anchored the thatch. Daisy was nonplussed with the whole experience and was okay staying in her carry-on bag. I was so eager to talk with Katie in normal conversation (English!), to catch up and hear what she had been doing. I wanted to tell her of my capers in Guyana; Tolsie Persaud; my crazy mix-up of Surinamese ministers; the absurdity of Elvis Presley being a murderer; how I managed to get cooked food here, and, and…. She slowly looked around the dark, oppressively hot, barren little hut, with the slivers of light through the thatch spotlighting the dirt floor and gave me an intense "shut up!" look.

"I can't stay here," she said. She was dead serious and had clearly thought it through—it was not just the "here," she was through with *me*, and with *us*.

I was stunned, and stammered some ineffable "but's," and "why's." No, that was it; she had made her decision, and it wasn't just the accommodations. She could not, would not stay in our marriage. I did not see it coming; but appreciated her integrity to come all the way to Langatabiki to tell me directly. She stabbed me deeply with certainty and clarity, and it hurt terribly; but at least it was not in the back. We had had a wonderful love affair, travelled and done so many off-grid things together… I was devastated. That night was not the roll in the hammock with Katie I had anticipated for so long. I dared any bats to mess with me while I sat on a log in the dark going over and over in my mind what went wrong. Ultimately, I reconciled with myself that she was right to split. It was wrong for me to expect her, or anyone, to follow me in this strange journey with so many unknowns, aside from the privations. At least for me I had a purpose and goal—a PhD thesis, if I survived. There was also the unusual providence of my being here at all—I had to stay.

The supply boat would stop at Langatabiki the next day on its way back to Albina from its farther upriver destinations. She was off, leaving Daisy behind with me. I tried hard to keep a steady demeanor in the following days in front of the villagers. My neighbors were cool about my obvious loss; they sensed that she was gone for good, and were saddened by it. They continued to speak wistfully of S'Ayentina—how she looked and walked, her hair. They had fallen in love with her more quickly than I had.

That night after Katie left, I succumbed to a crushing loneliness that was frightening. I was alone in a strange land, and now alone in life! Was this adventure all a colossal mistake? Maybe a flight of male hubris? Even if I could have articulated these emotions in Pamakan, who would listen with a drop of understanding or empathy? No one around knew who I was as a person. There was no one to whom I could explain the smoldering terror of being so profoundly alone in such a strange and faraway place. I wondered if I could ever establish a legitimate social identity among these people in their own social and cultural context. Would I always be an oddity that they humor and put up with? In addition, I grappled with the Marxist anthropology dilemma of whether I could ever reciprocate by adding real social value to the people being chronicled for my doctoral degree?

I reviewed over and over in my mind how it was that I landed on this rainforest island on the river border of Suriname and French Guiana. The past three months had been a truly extraordinary journey with interventions so improbable and inexplicable that it became clear to me that I was guided here by something I did not understand. I had to shake off the terrors and do what I had come to do: be an anthropologist and document what I could learn about the Pamakans. I realized later just how much they taught me.

CHAPTER ONE

GETTING THERE

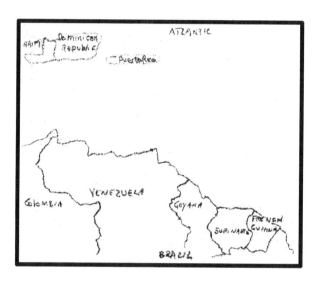

My adventure began three months earlier with a send-off party at our place in Manhattan's Washington Heights. The small apartment was packed with Katie's film friends and my graduate school colleagues. We were playing lots of Hendrix, still stung by his recent death. Joints were being passed around, and the dark air was heavy with sandalwood incense, a futile effort to mask the pot smoke. At one point, we turned off all the lights so a set designer friend of Katie's could show off his buzz bomb trick— dropping flaming plastic from the ceiling into a bowl of water on the floor. He had tied knots on plastic dry cleaner bags and fastened them on a clothes hangar held high over his head, like lumpy ropes on a fishing pole. When he held a lighter to the bottom of the rope, little drops of flaming plastic fell into the bowl making a weird, descending buzz till they plopped in the water. High, it is an awesome show; otherwise, pretty stupid to do indoors.

Daisy watched disapprovingly from one of her perches above the kitchen door. She was a little yellow kitten when Katie and I found her on the street about a week after we arrived in Manhattan. Our apartment had ceilings high enough to accommodate overhead cat ledges, which I built from scrap lumber and carpet remnants. That was Daisy's domain, looking down on us.

So, my new research plan was to find and document West African traditions of ritual and culture in rural communities in Guyana. Two years earlier I had entered the new graduate program in cultural anthropology at the New School for Social Research. The program was a perfect fit for me. The chair of the anthropology department, Stanley Diamond, was brilliant but unconventional, even radical. He was a self-described Marxist anthropologist, concerned not just with studying pre-industrial peoples but doing so with a clear examination of the controlling urban culture from which the observer came. Context mattered, as I planned to jet off to far corners of the world to observe and document customs and rituals of exotic people. Katie was working in a film company learning production and editing while I was in graduate school. The general plan was for us to work together, with her doing a documentary of the fieldwork.

I concentrated on West African religions and rituals since I was determined to do traditional field research. My interest in pursuing a degree in anthropology stemmed from time spent with Montagnards in Vietnam. I had worked in Vietnam for a year in the mid 1960s on a government contract researching the impact of the war on civilian populations in South Vietnam, and occasionally rode along with a CIA guy on his "rural development" visits to the mountain tribal people, or Montagnards as they were known there.

I was struck by how the Montagnards' lives seemed so much like I imagined Native Americans to have lived a few centuries ago. They wore loincloths, had a robust spirituality, and were self-sufficient. On each visit we would be invited into one of the long houses built high off the ground, to be seated before a big jug of rice wine. I enjoyed the rice wine, smoked from their pipes, and chewed the green leaves passed around in a hand-carved bowl. It was exhilarating to be in a forest village drinking palm wine from a communal vase, in a tree house that everyone lived in. This was a life to be revisited, just not in Southeast Asia in the middle of a war.

During my studies at the New School, I developed a plan to do research concerning certain ritual practices among the Igbo, an ethnic group in the Delta region of Nigeria. I had a fieldwork plan with funding through small scholarship grants and monthly GI Bill stipends that would cover about two years in the Nigerian delta area. There had been civil strife brewing in Nigeria over rights to oil revenues in the southeastern part of the country. Unfortunately, a few months before I was to leave for Nigeria, the Igbo became centrally embroiled in the conflict in Biafra. I needed to look elsewhere for field research.

The Nigerian civil war was an insurmountable problem; however, it was inconceivable for me not to start my field research project on schedule. I had committed to leave New York right after spring semester; Katie was to clear out the apartment and join me in about six months when I got situated. I began looking for Plan B. One of my professors suggested a study of African cultural influences somewhere in the Guianas in South America. None of my professors had any expertise in African American studies, but it seemed a reasonable alternative, if not well researched or planned. The Guianas—British, Dutch and French—are the small state entities on the northeastern coast of South America tucked between Venezuela and Brazil, just above the Amazon River. They are essentially three enclaves carved out of a corner of South America by British, Dutch and French colonists. These countries are more Caribbean than Latin. Guyana was British Guiana until independence from Britain in 1966. There were, I learned, rural communities in Guyana with significant African cultural influences, and Guyana was closer and, for the moment, more stable than Nigeria.

The party at our New York apartment was the big send-off for a two-year field research project in Guyana. I was the first graduate student to complete the full course of classroom study in the new PhD program in anthropology at The New School; I was leading the way for others working towards a doctorate through dissertation-based field ethnography.

When word went around the school that I was leaving to do field work in Guyana, the large, affable mailroom guy greeted me with a hug. From his accent and appearance, I knew he was from the Caribbean, Trinidad, I thought. He beamed, telling me that he was Guyanese and assured me that I would do well there. Then he leaned close to share a confidence, "Tolsie Persaud."

"What's that?" I asked.

"In Guyana, you go talk to Tolsie Persaud—he'll take care of you," he assured in a low voice, glancing away. I nodded an "okay, thanks," and made a half-hearted mental note.

I packed lightly and headed for JFK the next morning: a handbag with a few clothes and an ample supply of NASA space food. Having lived several months in a VW microbus, Katie and I learned to provision tightly and travel with essentials only. I carried a small, hard case with a Smith-Corona portable typewriter, the laptop of the day. I also brought along a tiny glass jar with a cork stopper filled with dirt. This was my personal talisman I had prepared as a way to connect with family roots. I had taken a short break from anthropology classes in New York to travel back to the long-abandoned farm in Oklahoma to collect some soil from underneath the big mulberry tree where I had spent countless hours as a boy. The long hemp rope swing my grandfather had tied was long gone, but I knew the tree intimately, and it seemed like an old friend.

PanAm had a weekly non-stop flight from JFK to Georgetown and back. Katie saw me off wistfully from our apartment. As I settled into the airport taxi I was bombarded with competing emotions of a sad goodbye to my love and best friend, and giddy exuberance of starting a long-anticipated adventure. We had a solid plan for her to meet me somewhere in Guyana in about six months.

It was exhilarating to clamber down the metal boarding ramp rolled up to the aircraft after the five-hour flight. The tropic air was welcoming, warm, and moist. There was a customs checkpoint just outside the small terminal building. The passengers had to line up about fifty yards from the aircraft to pass the outdoor immigration check. Most people on the plane seemed to be Guyanese and regular travelers on this flight, so the line moved quickly. The tall and imposing man standing at the podium was wearing a dark blue uniform with a very official hat set squarly on his head. His buttoned, white-collar shirt gave his dark skin a silhouette effect as my eyes adjusted to the bright sun. I handed him my US passport, which he studied for a moment. Holding my open passport with his right hand and leaning toward me with his left hand holding the front edge of his podium, he gave me a look that nearly knocked me backwards. "Business or Pleasure?" he demanded. There was not an ounce of human empathy in his expression or voice.

I was still exuberant to be on my first day as a field anthropologist, and I replied cheerily, "Pleasurable Business!"

He was not amused. "What *exactly* are you here for?" he asked disapprovingly, as he closely eyed my sparse luggage and thumbed through my passport full of visa stamps from Vietnam, Morocco, and about every country in Western Europe. I began to explain that I was an anthropologist and I was here to study African cultural influences…. He stopped me midsentence, "No, you can't just come here and do that. You must get back on the plane." He closed my passport and handed it back to me.

I should have been more sensitive to the Guyanese sense of nationalism, and suspicion of people like me with odd agendas. Since independence from Britain four years earlier, Guyana had been embattled with fractious turmoil between two major political factions, one that was widely believed to be backed by the CIA. Plus, I was not wearing the collared shirt and tie that had proven so effective in Europe and North Africa border crossings.

This was a jolting impasse. I had emerged from the PanAm 707 filled with joyful anticipation of launching my new career as a field anthropologist; and now I saw the plane being refueled ominously not far behind me. I had not even gotten into the terminal! This could not be happening!

"But I'm supposed to see Tolsie Persaud," I said to the uniform in a desperate grasp for something, anything.

The officer straightened up and studied me closely. "You know Tolsie Persaud?" he asked suspiciously. His demeanor changed from officious contempt to surprise and caution.

"Well, I'm supposed to see him first thing when I get to Georgetown," I said with faked confidence.

Everything changed at that moment. I was still clutching my passport to my chest when he reached over and took it back, and flipped to an empty page. With a perfunctory stamp and a notation, he handed it back, "You have two weeks," he said sternly, and motioned for the next in line.

I was shaken as I walked into the terminal, about the size of my small-town high school basketball stadium. A dozen or so men were hawking taxis, so I asked one of the least sketchy-looking characters if he could recommend an inexpensive boarding house in Georgetown. He said something which I understood to mean "No problem, mon," so I climbed in and held on, thankful to be leaving the airport on the street side. I studied the roadside from the back seat thinking there may be some sign or billboard mentioning "Tolsie Persaud." I had no idea of who this Tolsie was or what he was into, and did not want to start a Tolsie conversation with the already distracted driver speaking gibberish English.

After about thirty minutes lurching through traffic of cars, trucks, scooters, bikes and people, we reached a pleasant-looking white frame two-story house set back from the street. There was no sign indicating it was a boarding house, but it seemed okay. It was brightly painted white, had a big, lush green yard and head-high bushes surrounding an expansive front porch. Large open windows afforded light, and a slight breeze served as the air conditioning. The heat that was so welcoming to me getting off the plane had become oppressively hot and sticky. The house appeared clean and well maintained, if perhaps not in the best part of the town. The open trench gutter along the road was half filled with water and teeming with guppies—the kind you buy in plastic bags at the pet shop. I was greeted at the door by Miss Mae, a rotund, milk-chocolate-skinned woman wearing a colorful Aunt Jemima-style headscarf tied so the starched ends extended straight out several inches to the right side of her head. She said she had a vacant room on the second floor with a shared bathroom. Dinner would be served in the dining room at 6 p.m. sharp.

The residents of the house that I saw were Guyanese men in their twenties and thirties. All were Black Guyanese who seemed to have known Miss Mae for a long time. I was not troubled at being the stand-alone white guy in the house; however, it struck me that I had never been really alone among only Black people. 1950s Oklahoma was essentially segregated, as was my army, college, and travel experience in the early 60s.

While it was interesting being the only white guy in the house, my difficuly was communication! The local guys spoke an English I had never heard, and could not understand at all. I knew it was English because I could catch a familiar word or two in a conversation. That evening, after dinner of a sort of chicken stew over white rice, I tried talking with one of my new house mates:

"Hi, I'm John, from New York…"

"*Ah-mon, mi si yu na deh ja…*"

"Okay, yeah, well I'm here to learn about Guyana …"

"*Ya, yu gon sweet on jartong...*"

"Uh, yeah, and I'm going to go talk to a Tolsie Persaud…."

My new friend braced, leaned back just as the customs officer had done. "*Ya no is who Tolsie Persaud?*" he asked slowly and deliberately.

"Well, I'm supposed to go see him."

He stood up from the table, grabbed my arm, "*Le' we gaff—come wi me cyar….*"

Jonas, I think was his name, seemed like a basically good guy, about my age. Nothing alarmed me about him, and I thought if I could get him to slow down and enunciate better, I could make out what he was saying and learn more about Georgetown and Guyana.

I followed him outside to a beat-up, nondescript '*cyar*' parked on the street near the house. "*Getinn, getinn.*" He drove to a very different part of Georgetown, more ominous to me than our guesthouse neighborhood. Jonas was talking away; I discerned that he had friends I should meet. He pulled onto the grass, blocking half of the walkway in front of a line of small row houses with front doors set a few steps from the street—a tropical version of downtown Baltimore.

I stood close to Jonas as he knocked on a heavy wood door, with cardboard covering the small inset window. It opened slightly, allowing Jonas and someone to speak their apparent English. We were motioned into a tiny anteroom, and I began to doubt the wisdom of visiting a very strange place with a guy I didn't know and could barely understand.

Jonas opened a curtain framing the anteroom to expose a short hallway to a room with four intense men in their twenties, all very dark-skinned, two wearing t-shirts with jeans, two wearing only jeans. The back windows were open for air (otherwise one would suffocate in the damp, hot room), but heavy curtains closed off the outside light and view. It seemed that Jonas and I had interrupted an informal seminar or meeting, with the guys sitting in a sort of circle discussing something important. They looked back and forth at Jonas and me, clearly surprised to see a white stranger in their house. I smiled a "Hi guys!" and my long, frizzy hair and bushy beard sufficed as sort of a provisional access pass.

Jonas made an introduction that I understood to include several references to "New York" and "American." When Jonas finished, the mood of the room shifted to curiosity and careful welcome. "I'm a student from New York City," I offered gamely. One of the guys got right to the point in English delivered so that even an alien would understand: "You know about Rasta?" "Can you teach us about Rasta?"

Rastafari? There were no Bob Marley posters—indeed nothing at all—on the walls, and none of the guys had the hair or wore the colors. Other than living in New York City and liking the music of Bob Marley, my knowledge of Rastafarian culture and religion came from textbooks on cults. I didn't think present company was interested in an analysis of Rastafarianism as a messianic phenomenon. I begged off explaining that while there were plenty of Rastas in New York, I didn't really run with them. One of the guys asked how they treat their hair while letting it grow to dreadlocks. I had actually read about that somewhere, so I counselled that you should wash your hair, but only with pure water—no soap or shampoo for sure, and some say no saltwater. They all nodded in understanding, so I went on with some platitudes about Haile Selassie who was still Emperor of Ethiopia. And hey, I don't know, he *could* be the new Jesus. After some discussion in their private language, one of the guys went to the back of the room to return with a huge, cigar-shaped joint. He pointed to a bushel basket in the corner filled with loose marijuana leaves still on stems. It looked to be ready for processing and packaging. They were all quite proud of their product; the short one admiringly fired up the blunt and offered me the first toke.

The last thing I wanted was to loosen my brain moorings here, with these guys on stuff that was probably a lot stronger that any weed I had ever smoked, and a joint ten times larger than any I had seen, even in

Brooklyn! They were now cautiously friendly, interested in New York City and growing dreadlocks, at least as best I could make out. I was now in HOW.DO.I.GET.OUT.OF.HERE.ALIVE mode.

The smoke was indeed unlike anything I had experienced, and I was soon contemplating that these Rasta trainees could kill me and stuff my body in the trunk of their "cyar." I would never see Katie again; how would she even find me; who *are* these guys? My mind became turbulent liquid, reeling between terror, and the incredible feel of the fabric of this chair! The feel of the plank floor through my shoes! Wait, count your toes, hey, nobody I know knows where I am—*I* don't even know where I am; and who or what the fuck is Tolsie Persaud? This was heavy weed.

I was terrified and immobilized; it was all I could do to stay cool and quiet, and not bolt for the door. I complimented Jonas and the guys on the good smoke, "good shit, man," and announced that I had to get back to prepare for an important meeting tomorrow. I did not say I would be meeting Tolsie Persaud, but I thought they might think that, and if they thought I was meeting Tolsie, they would not kill me. I was so stoned and needed to get out of there. My brain in full manic, I guessed this Tolsie Persaud must be the Guyanese version of Jimmy Hoffa. Made sense for the customs officer to give me a couple of weeks to check in with the Boss, and these Rasta wannabees were probably one of Persaud's minor-league crews. Anyway, I was in way too deep to ask these guys, "Who exactly *is* Tolsie Persaud, and where can I find him?" I just had to get the hell out of there. One of the guys picked up a handful of weed from the basket and asked, *"Ya tink dis sell good in New York?"* I was working on standing up, both hands clutching the fat arms of the big chair, "It's really good shit," I swallowed. After a moment and a flash of survival inspiration, I said, "I'll talk with Tolsie." The guys were pleased, and excitedly congratulated each other like they had concluded a successful sales presentation.

Not sure of the details, but I did make it back to the guesthouse that night. I decided to let the Tolsie Persaud thing rest for a while. Last thing I needed was for this Tolsie character to come looking for *me*. Next day I took a city bus to the University of Guyana located a few miles from downtown Georgetown. Certainly, I would be received with professional courtesies as a visiting academic from New York City; after all, they had posted a faculty vacancy announcement for a position in the Social Sciences Department.

The university consisted of a large sterile, concrete building. The sparse and industrial campus had been open for about a year. There were no people carrying books in the hallways or grounds. "Where were the students?" I wondered. For that matter, there were no people around who appeared to be faculty members who I could approach and chat-up.

The South Asian woman guarding the social sciences department was more officious than the airport immigration officer. "No, I don't have an appointment, but I'm an anthropology doctoral candidate in town from New York and would like to speak with someone in the anthropology program." No appointment, no meeting. The soonest someone could see me would be in two days; I made an appointment.

I managed to avoid Jonas at the boarding house, as I prepared for my appointment with great expectations. Social sciences was a new program at the university, and it seemed they wanted to develop an anthropology department. I arrived on time and was ushered into the office of a very important social science professor, whose specialty was South Asian culture and the East Indian community of Guyana. It was clear after a minute or so of our conversation that he had no time for me, and even less interest in anything African Guyanese. My appearance and attire placed me more at home with the Rasta guys downtown than in his Faculty Club.

The professor was clearly put off by the effrontery of my informal inquiry about the posted faculty position, without having undergone the extensive application and vetting procedures. When I explained that I was interested in fieldwork, he reminded me that there was a strict government prohibition for foreigners like me to travel beyond the urban zone of Georgetown without special permits. He bid me an abrupt adieu without standing up from his desk. I headed back to the boarding house dispirited; my time and my options were running out.

It was midafternoon, and I could feel the air—heavy, hot, humid, organic. I sat on the big, unpainted wooden chair on the front porch to think of what to do. One thing was certain, I could not return to New York. The humiliation of slinking back after the big send-off was unthinkable. I sat alone on the porch cradling my chin, reviewing a list of bad options: Katie would see me a failure; the school would cancel my scholarship, my colleagues…

BZZZZZZZZZZZZZZZZZZZZZZZ…

"WHOA!" A huge insect thing flew right up to my face! I ducked and cowered in the chair…

WZZZZZZZZZZZZZZZ WZZZZZZZZZZZZ…

"Jeezus!" It would not go away! Was it a giant bumblebee? Can't be a bee, I thought—too big, too loud to be a bee. I peeked up; it was a hummingbird! Only slightly relieved, I sat up carefully as it hovered right in front of my nose. I had never seen a hummingbird in flight, certainly not one close enough to reach out and touch! I sat frozen as it started to do a vertical dance, wings buzzing like a crazy cartoon fan. What an amazing show I was being presented with! Somehow it became less frightening, despite bouncing in midair with a long, sharp beak close to my eyes.

WZZZZZZZZZZZZZZZZ WZZZZZZZZZZZZ… Up and down for a long ten seconds, then WZZZZAAAO, the bird made a left and vanished around the corner of the house, heading for the back.

I sat stunned. "What the hell was *that* about?" I wondered out loud. There were plenty of flowers in the bushes all around the house. Why would it buzz me, and look me in the eye?

WZZZZZZZZZZZZZZZ… It came BACK!

This time I did not duck. Just sat still. I kept thinking, "What is going on with this?" Again, the WZZZZ-up-and-down dance right in front of my face. Then, WZZZZZZAO, a quick exit to the back. My brain kicked into another gear: something was going on here. I was familiar with oracles and spirits animating animals from my graduate classes. Had something possessed this hummingbird? Was it trying to warn me of something, or tell me something?

WZZZZZ… He came back a third time and did another ten second up-down buzz dance for me, and WZZZZZZAO… back around the corner. "Okay, that's it!" I say to the empty front porch. It was clear that this hummingbird thing was trying to communicate with me.

I went into the house and found Miss Mae in the kitchen, "What's there?" I asked with grave urgency, pointing to the direction the hummingbird had flown away to. She looked at me as if I had lost my mind and shrugged. I persisted, "No really—that way," using my arm to indicate the direction of the hummingbird's flight to the back of the house, and way beyond. She saw I was earnest, and perplexed. Miss Mae leaned against the table, looked steadily at me. Her voice lowered, "That way," she paused with a nod toward my waving arm directions, "Suriname."

"Suriname? How would I get there?"

Miss Mae explained in the manner of a fairytale villager warning a naïf about the Dark Forest, "Well, you have to take a cyar to the river, then cross over." Her manner suggested she was guiding me to certain peril. "They different in Suriname," she cautioned. "They backward (pause) and do black magic." She did a little shudder and said the word, "*obia*." She turned and went back to preparing dinner, clearly uncomfortable with the conversation. I ran up to my room to pack and check out.

The taxi station near the main market turned out to be a scrum of random cars and vans that hustler-drivers fill up with people who want to go from downtown Georgetown to the same general destination anywhere in the country. I found one that was loading up to go eastward to the last town in Guyana, the river border with Suriname. It was only about $12 for a three-hour drive. The driver's business plan, however, was to cram at least eighteen people with luggage into a basic four-door sedan.

The one hundred-plus-mile ride along the Berbice Highway was a test of human endurance, with every discomfort imaginable. We arrived about noon at the market in Skeldon, the small border town on the Guyanese side of the Courantyne River. I went straight to the river to find a way across to Suriname. There were several small boats that, like the taxis, left dock whenever they were sufficiently loaded up with paying passengers. No customs officers were in sight to stamp me out and verify that I had left their country before my two weeks were up. I hope they think I'm still holed up in some Tolsie Persaud hideout.

CHAPTER TWO

SURINAME

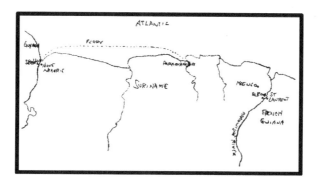

My arrival in Surinamese border town of Nieuw Nickerie had none of the drama of the Georgetown Airport. I just unfolded myself out of the boat taxi with my travel bag and typewriter. There was no immigration control in sight; the riverfront was bustling with the comings and goings of locals, from both sides of the river. My first order of business was to get some Surinamese currency, find a place to eat and get a beer. In border towns, you can always find money-changers on the street, so I traded my remaining Guyanese dollars for Surinamese guilders. I got directions for a lunch spot in downtown Nieue Nikerie. "Happy Snacks" was on a corner that afforded a view of the detached, wooden buildings along a main street. There were a few cars and small trucks that, as in Guyana, drove on the left side of the road. I could understand why they would do it in what was till recently *British* Guiana, but in *Dutch* Guiana?

I sat at one of the rickety plastic tables in the outside seating area, despite the afternoon steamroom/sauna effect of alternating rain and baking sun. There was no one else sitting outside, so I pulled my table and chair under a tree and settled in. Everyone I encountered on the Dutch side of the river border spoke an English that I understood—unlike that in English-speaking Guyana. I toasted myself with a cold Heineken—welcome to Suriname.

The beer was refreshing and holding the cold glass was familiar and comforting, so I mouthed a sincere and disquieting question to the half glass of beer, *Now what?* My Tolsie Persaud hall pass would be of no use here; and the hummingbird didn't make the trip out of Guyana.

As my mind was bouncing between wonder and despair, an old Gandhi-look-alike man walked up to my table in the shade and stood staring at me. I reflexively waved him away without eye contact, as one learns in New York to avoid panhandlers at sidewalk cafes. He stood still for a moment, so I gave him a "What!?" look. He was rail thin with deeply weathered skin; no beard but a shock of white hair. He stood erect, wearing beaten-down sandals, traditional floppy pantaloons, and a long smock that once was white. He leaned forward slightly and asked softly in South Asian-accented English, "May I sit with you a moment?"

The old man was very formal and polite; but his intrusion was annoying. I did not have any spare change to give him, and I did not want to share my moment. "Okay, have a seat," I said stiffly, not wanting to appear rude, or cause a scene on my first day in Suriname. The old man sat down, folded his hands on his lap and began: "I am from India, and as a Hindu, one must ritually bathe in the River Ganges at least once in your lifetime. It is important for the soul."

"Oh?" (I get it now, I thought. He's gonna make a pitch for money to go to India.) The old man continued, "But if it is not possible to wash in the Ganges, the next best thing is to be in the gaze of a holy man." He paused and went on: "I can see that you are a holy man. Thank you for letting me sit with you." With a smile, he stood, bowed slightly with hands clasped, and walked away.

"Whoa, what was *that* about?" I asked myself, probably out loud, as it filled my consciousness. Slouching back in the chair, "A holy man? Where could that have come from?" I felt like a jerk for assuming he was just a hustler. "Could this be some hummingbird-type message? What could it mean?" I was fascinated by this odd distraction from my where-to-now plight. How could I come across to anyone as a holy man? I was, indeed, in a special state of mind. Not only did I not really know where I was, beyond sitting under a tree on the western border of Suriname, it occurred to me (like when I was with the Rasta guys) *no one* I knew had any idea where I was. I got here following the directions of a hummingbird; now I was waiting for the next clue for where I go from here. Every sensory receptor of my body was on full-open channel. My complete lack of guile must have projected an exceptional insouciance to the old Hindu, whereas I was actually feeling stupid and vulnerable.

I had nearly finished my no-longer cold Heineken and ham sandwich when a boy about twelve years old came over to my table and welcomed himself in cheerful and reasonable English, "Hi Mister, you English?" He was slight and brown-skinned, wearing shorts, a school-type short-sleeve collared shirt, and flip-flops. His short hair was well groomed, and his English was remarkably good. Again, to my surprise, he did not ask for money. I must have looked like the most unusual and non-threatening white guy the locals had ever seen. My new, young friend, "Ronnie" he said, was curious about who I was and what I was doing in Nieue Nikerie. I bought him a coke. It must have been clear through our brief conversation that I really did not have a clear destination or purpose, other than to study African culture here. Ronnie had a solution: "You must come meet my sister!"

"No, no, no, no, I'm not interested in anything like that," I say, retreating from my quick assessment that this kid was legit. He persisted, explaining that his house was just around the corner, and that his mother was there along with his older sister. "My sister is smart—she can help you," he insisted. Having no better ideas, I agreed, gathered up my bag, and followed him to a small, single story frame house. It was, as he said, right around the corner from the restaurant. There, indeed, in a well-ordered living room was a young woman in her early twenties, introduced as his sister, Muriel. An older woman sat nearby, their mother, who mumbled a name.

Both women spoke halting but understandable English. They were polite and formal in their welcome; mother got up and made some tea, and we sat and talked about what brought me to Nieue Nikerie. I did not admit to them that I had followed a hummingbird; instead, I gave a precis of my research plan: African influences in South American communities.

Muriel and her mother both looked at me and said almost in unison, "You mean the 'Bush Negroes.'"

I was blank; I had never heard the term "Bush Negroes," and it sounded offensive, even coming from others of African ancestry. "They live in the interior, the bush, but you can see them in town," the mother explained. "You can tell they are Bush Negroes by the way they walk," she said as she went to the window to survey the street. "Come look! See two men walking there—Bush Negroes."

There were indeed two men walking along the other side of the street. Both were darker skinned than the African Guyanese and Surinamese I had met. "See how they walk," she insisted. I could discern only a slight difference in gait and posture, but I went along with her, "Oh, yeah."

"So how would I meet these people?" I asked. Again, the answer was obvious to the women, "You must go see minister Hosen in Paramaribo—he is the person in Suriname who knows all about the Bush Negroes. He is the one to help you."

That was it! I had my plan. There was an overnight ferry that went along the Atlantic coast of Suriname to the capital city of Paramaribo leaving in a few hours. It was an overnight run that would get me to Paramaribo in the morning. I would look up this minister, who I assumed led some large church mission work with the, uh, Bush Negroes. Missionaries and anthropologists generally are not a good fit, but this was a start.

The midnight boat to Paramaribo made the Guyana taxis seem like Manhattan black car service. The ferry was built for probably fifty people; there were easily 200 crammed on board. It was getting dark when we left, and in about fifteen minutes we hit rough, offshore seas. Soon everybody on board—*everybody*—got seasick. The air in the cabin was a suffocating perfume of diesel fuel and vomit. There was no access to an outside deck area; anyway, waves were crashing over the gunwales. Soon the cabin deck sloshed with a disgusting stew of seawater and puke. It was dark and unbearable; I found and squeezed my head through a small hatch that opened to an anchor chain locker on the forward deck. I huddled against the bulkhead all night, wet from the sea spray coming over the bow; but I could breathe.

We docked in Paramaribo at daybreak; again, no immigration checkpoint since it was a domestic ferry. I went straight to find a cheap hotel to shower and change clothes. Paramaribo was an interesting city with colorful wood frame, colonial-style buildings throughout. Even the office buildings of two or three stories were of wood construction. The tallest buildings were churches, an old synagogue, and government offices. Suriname was still a Dutch protectorate with a mutual assistance relationship with Holland, through which Surinamese managed their internal affairs. I would have relative ease getting into the country officially since an American passport was sufficient for a visa-free extended visitor-sojourn with the Dutch.

There seemed to be a balanced ethnic mix of hyphenated African, South Asian, and Indonesian people bustling about in the capital city. There were Chinese and Indonesian restaurants and shops all around, and a smattering of Europeans in cars. I got a room in a sketchy hotel near the center of the city, made a hurried recovery from the ferry nightmare, and about 10 a.m., I was downstairs asking the desk clerk if he knew of this minister Hosen.

"Minister Hosen? Sure, just take a taxi to his office."

This was starting to sound a little too easy, but I thanked him and went outside and hailed a taxi. "Can you please take me to see minister Hosen?"

"Sure, mon, no problem," the young cabbie said, again in clear English. "You go to see minister?" he asked.

"Ah, yeah, I hope to."

It was a short ride, but not to a church as I expected. The driver pulled into the driveway of a government complex and stopped in front of the most imposing building around. "No no, I want to see the minister, minister HO-sen!" I knew this was too easy.

"Minister Hosen—here. You go upstairs."

From the back seat I studied the building: the sign over the door read *"Ministerie Openbare Werken en Verkeer."* Under that: "Rudy H. Goosen, Minister."

"Ohhh! G-o-o-s-e-n is pronounced HO-sen?" I said out loud.

I sat back in the car, "I can't just go in to see a government minister like that!"

The driver, getting a little impatient, "Ya, you go wait in office—he talk to people."

I gave the driver a nice tip and climbed out of his family car that doubled as a cab, tucked in the clean shirt I put on that morning, and patted down my hair best I could. "Oh boy, here goes nothing," I muttered, and climbed the stairs to the *"Kabinet van de Minister van Openbare Werken en Verkeer."* He was the Minister of Public Works!

The reception area was a large, sparse waiting room with about twenty serious and anxious people sitting with folders and papers on their laps. It felt like a public health clinic. I checked in with the well-dressed receptionist and said, with the most official aire I could manage, that I was an American graduate student and would like to speak with Minister Goosen. I hoped not to betray my chagrin at thinking ten minutes prior that I was coming to visit a missionary. She took my name and politely asked me to take a seat. As I waited with the others, it seemed that each had some issue, perhaps about land rights or permits. I learned later that many were there just to ask for a government job. I also discovered that the minister regularly sets aside mornings to listen to anyone with a grievance, looking for government assistance, a job, or just an audience.

After about an hour, the receptionist motioned for me to approach: "Minister Goosen will see you now." His office was a large room with a couple of windows and bare walls. The minister was a tall, light-skinned man of African ancestry, late forties, with short, light brown hair that seemed naturally relaxed with a combed part. He wore the ubiquitous white, open-collar, short sleeve, smock-type cotton shirt with buttons improbably on the left and right side vest pockets. He welcomed me from behind a large, wooden desk that appeared organized despite various stacks of papers and folders. Formal and gracious, "What can I do for you?" he asked in perfect English. I learned later that he had been an executive in Alcoa and managed Suralco, the large subsidiary bauxite mining operation in Suriname.

I presented my best pitch about researching West African religious and cultural influences in communities in the New World. And added that I was particularly interested in working with the Bush Negro people here in Suriname. I thought to myself how my pitch and demeanor would be different if I *were* talking with a missionary preacher. He listened, nodded slightly, and seemed receptive. "Our Bush Negro people would be perfect for such research. But what would *they* get out of it? How would our people benefit from your work here?" he asked. That was a question straight out of Marxist anthropology! But, in two years of graduate study I never had to confront the issue, or answer the question in real, practical terms.

"Well," I said, "I would work to teach *them* as they taught *me*—it wouldn't be just one way." I was searching for an example of what the hell I could teach these people. Just then the Minister offered: "Start with language. You will have to learn their language, so teach them English as you go along. Would you agree to that?"

"Absolutely!" I must have gushed. This guy was good!

"There is a fellow here who can get you started—Petrus Domini. You can meet him in the waiting area; I'll send him over. Best of luck." The Minister signed off with a seated but sturdy handshake, and added that I should go to the ministry of education, next building over, to get a long-term study visa.

CHAPTER THREE

PETRUS

There were only a few people remaining in the waiting room when I returned from my audience with Minister Goosen. I was quietly ecstatic at having a real shot at legitimate and interesting research among the Bush N..., uh, People in the Suriname interior. I was uncomfortable with the term "Negro" and started considering alternate terminology. Before I could sit back down, a tall, very dark young man about my age, dressed improbably in an ill-fitting, navy polyester suit, white shirt, and tie approached, having entered the waiting room through a side door. He walked directly to me, extended a long arm for a vigorous handshake, "I am Petrus, Petrus Domini."

When close to him, I saw that his skin was coal black and glistening. Who wears a suit here where air conditioning is almost science fiction? I thought. His coarse half-inch-tall hair was clean cropped above his ears. He had no sideburns, so his hair formed a round cylinder around the top of his head. He smiled broadly, revealing gold-trim caps on his front teeth.

"You American?" he said/asked in unstable English.

"Yes, I am!" I say. "The Minister said that we should talk."

"I am Petrus Domini; I am *Ndjuka*; I want learn English," he explained carefully, ignoring the others staring at us in the waiting room.

"That's the deal," I say. "I will help you in English, and you help me with Bush…, the Bush language."

"*Ndjuka*," he corrected me before I screwed it up, emphasizing EN-djuka.

I instantly liked this very oddly erect and formal *Ndjuka* in a suit and tie. We made a plan to meet at my flophouse hotel that evening and go to a bar to start our mutual studies.

Petrus showed up at the hotel desk still in his suit and tie. He greeted the desk clerk who he seemed to know, and we walked to *TakTaki*, a neighborhood bar not far from the hotel. Our forum was a bare wooden table with benches, essentially a picnic table. Petrus greeted the bartender who he also seemed to know, and immediately a brown, one-liter bottle of the local Parbo beer and two empty pint glasses were plunked on the table. Petrus had an eighth-grade working foundation of English, and was eager to practice for vocabulary, context, and nuance. His manner was easy, which softened his intensity. He did not loosen his black tie, so my mind wandered around the visual if he were wearing sunglasses and a black fedora. I finally settled on the idea that he was like a local politician, since he seemed to know everybody he encountered.

Petrus was, in fact, a young man in a hurry to somewhere. He had ambitions; I just was not sure what they were. He had some sort of soft position with the ministry, a political patronage gig, or internship for the Ndjuka perhaps. His demeanor was to look and act European, but the gold trim on his front teeth distracted his all-business image. With me it seemed he was working on an American persona. The first issue he brought up suggested a direction of his ambition: "What means, 'United We Stand, Divided We Fall?'"

So, this was not going to be idle guy talk over beers till we got hammered. I scrambled to come up with a simple but cogent explanation of the phrase, "united we stand." He listened intently as I tried to explain that the original colonies of America joined together to make a nation of united states. He became animated when I added how, later, the labor movement used the slogan to unite workers and form unions. Petrus then asked about the song. I had not thought of the tune, "United We Stand, Divided We Fall" by the Brotherhood of Man, which had been released as a record about the time I left for Guyana. I was surprised that he knew it. He liked the political solidarity connotation of the lyrics; I thought it was just a love song about two people sticking together.

When it was my turn to ask the question, I wanted to know, "What do you call people like you, you know, bush people?" He thought for a minute and then laid out a basic human schema of Black Surinamese—the Amerindians, South Asians, Javanese, and the Dutch were of no concern. To Petrus there are two kinds of Black Surinamese: city people and bush people. City Blacks were the ones who kept working the plantations as slaves until emancipation. When slavery ended, they kept working and got paid, went to school, and took all the good jobs.

He looked around the room, pointing by making a smooch pucker with his lips toward the people in the bar, all of whom seemed to be city Blacks. He went on, "The bush people left plantations to live in the jungle. The bush people stayed in the forest after the end of slavery because they had no opportunities elsewhere." Petrus explained that city Blacks will say the bush people left the plantations because they were lazy and did not want to work; so, let them stay in the bush. Bush people, he explained, think city people keep up the plantation system by excluding bush people from the urban society.

"So, the Djuka were one of the original free settlements in the forest—and do I call people like you *Djuka*?" I asked. He seemed slightly uncomfortable with my use of the term Djuka—maybe it was my pronunciation.

"We are all '*nenge*,'" he explained. "'*Nenge*' means 'people' so I am an '*Ndjuka nenge*.'"

"You say 'EN-djuka' with an 'N?'" I asked.

Petrus leaned over the table with a little left-right glance to share a confidence. "'*Djuka*' is word used by some people to put us down. A lot of us escaped from the big Jewish plantation; people who did not like us called us '*dju ka*.'" I did not quite get it until he added, "'*Ka-ka*' mean 'shit.'" It started to make sense to me why Ronnie's sister and mother in Nieue Nikerie had spoken of Bush Negroes almost as if they were aliens.

Over the next few weeks, I sought out every book and article I could find for a more fulsome understanding of the history of Africans in Suriname. And now that I had the blessing of the minister of public works, I began introducing myself around Paramaribo to meet people from whom I could learn more about the social and cultural landscape. The Surinamese tourist bureau showered me with reading material and photographs, and put me in contact with professional people in Paramaribo eager to talk about their community and country. The American embassy staff was particularly helpful in widening my circle of contacts. One person I met through the embassy was a Surinamese with an encyclopedic knowledge of who-was-doing-what in the country. I never sought to confirm it, but it seemed likely that he was a local CIA asset.

So, Petrus' beer hall description of the distinction between city Blacks and bush Blacks was stark, understanding that it was the perspective of one unhappy with the inherent inequality. The broader view of events and circumstances that divided (and continue to divide) the Black population between city and bush people is a picture unique to Suriname.

Europeans began settling in Suriname in the mid-seventeenth century. During this period, there were various independent attempts at colonization by English and Dutch settlers. The first successful colonization was in 1650 when a British ship brought the first African slave laborers to work sugar cane plantations. The new colony included a large plantation settlement of Portuguese Jews. Suriname changed from English to Dutch control after the Second Dutch-English War in 1667. I found it ironic that part of the Peace of Breda included the trade between the British and the Dutch: Suriname for Manhattan.

The geography of Suriname had much to do in shaping the nature of the plantation rebellion and resistance in the colony. The plantation fields were located along the coastal plain, which extends only 50 to 100 kilometers southward from the Atlantic coast. Beyond this agricultural region is a belt of marshy secondary wood, which blended quickly into the rain forest that covered almost ninety percent of the country. The river avenues into the interior were not considered navigable by the colonists because of rapids and waterfalls. The rain forest itself was considered inhospitable, and worthless for plantation farming.

Independent settlements of escaped slaves were common throughout slave-based colonies in the Caribbean and the mainland of South and North America. The people of these free settlements were referred to as "maroons" by outsiders, from the Spanish *cimarron* (livestock which reverted to a wild state.) The free settlements in Suriname launched a tradition of an escape alternative to plantation slavery in that colony. As the plantations and the African laborer population grew, so did the free settlements.

In the eighteenth century, there appears to be a consistent ten percent of the substantial African population of Suriname living in free settlements. These settlements were a constant threat to the security and efficiency of the plantation industry. The colonists enacted extreme punitive sanctions (floggings, mutilation, and slow death) for the "crime" of escape, organized military expeditions against the free settlements, and offered bounties for returned escapees.

Despite efforts by the colonists, the free settlement Africans became more organized, and increasingly launched raids against plantations to get iron implements and women. Military countermeasures were generally unsuccessful and became progressively more costly and dangerous, from malaria as well as combat. The colonial military forces were not able to contain the free settlements, or stop further plantation escapes. In the 1760s, the Dutch attempted to come to terms with the free and independent groups of their former slaves. The colonists designated three major groups of free settlements as "tribes"—the Ndjuka, Saamaka and Matawai—and began to negotiate peace treaties with them.

What Petrus did not go into with me was the subtle distinctions between the different free settlement groups. The Ndjuka were one of the original free settlements who, as part of their agreement with the plantation owners, promised to capture and return any future Africans who escaped into the bush. This created a distinction between the original free settlements and the later plantation escapees, who had to hide from the Europeans *and* the cooperating "treaty" groups. I learned much more about this dynamic later.

CHAPTER FOUR

THE FREE SETTLEMENTS

Our beer-soaked language lessons were going well. I was getting a crash course on the history of Africans in Suriname through the books and research material I could find through the library, the American Embassy, and the Suriname government offices. I found people in Paramaribo who would translate key historical and ethnographic texts from Dutch to English. Petrus added context and nuance to what I was learning about who the bush people were, where they lived, and how they interacted with the outside world. What he did not want to talk about was how the five groups now view each other. This was to be a critical point of my research, but I did not want to press Petrus on a subject that he was reluctant to discuss, for whatever reason.

The slave labor of Africans was critical to the success of the colonization of Suriname. By 1687, there were approximately 600 European settlers and 4,000 Africans in the colony. Over the next fifty years, the plantation system flourished such that by 1738, four hundred separate plantations had been established along the coastal belt, with 57,000 Africans imported to work them as slave laborers. There were no manifest slave rebellions in Suriname, despite an unusually high ratio of Africans to Europeans. The resistance to plantation slavery in Suriname took the form of escape and formation of fugitive enclaves in the forest. When the Dutch took over Suriname from the British, there was already a free settlement of several hundred Africans occupying the forest region south of the plantation area.

By the treaty arrangements of the 1760s, the Dutch sought to freeze the escape-to-freedom option by recognizing established groups as official and granting them limited manumission. The plantations offered regular supplies of iron tools, cloth, salt, and such; in return, the "official" Free Settlers were obliged to return any slave laborer who thereafter sought to join them, and to actively assist the colonial forces in capturing free settlements not covered by the treaty. The three recognized groups were to serve as a militia arm of the colony in quelling slave rebellions and actively hunting down unauthorized escaped Africans. The colonists sweetened the deal by granting bounties for any future escapees returned to the plantations.

The differences among the distinct bush populations today stemmed from this treaty between the plantation colonists and the three originally recognized free settlements. Through the agreement, the three groups—or "tribes"—gained limited freedoms within their interior forest area.

Despite the treaty, African slave laborers kept fleeing plantations, but now were forced to create secret settlements away from both the plantations and the recognized settlements, because of the agreement to hunt down and return subsequent escapees. The most intense threats to plantation security occurred in the decades after the peace treaty, when small groups of non-recognized settlements formed in the no-man's-land between the plantation fields and the deep forest lands of the official settlements. These groups raided the plantations aggressively for supplies and recruits.

After the abolition of slavery, the government added two groups as officially recognized free settlement groups—the Aluku and the Pamakans. About 150 years later, the five groups continue to occupy designated areas of the forest interior along major rivers, and manage their internal affairs. A sixth group, the Boni or Aluku, settled on the French side of the river border of the two countries. I was not able to learn the nature and depth of the inter-group differences until much later, when living it. Suffice that with Petrus, the history of the original recognized groups versus the fugitive settlements was an awkward topic for conversation.

Petrus was gaining confidence in American English and did his own research on all things American. From me, he wanted to understand how Americans talked and what they talked about. I tried explaining common idiomatic expressions in my rudimentary Ndjuka. I got through "double speak," "chickens coming home to roost," "fair weather friend," and so on. The American sports analogies (home run, hail mary) were more difficult, since he had no understanding whatsoever of baseball or football. Explaining "catch 22" was impossible. We spoke nothing of the war in Vietnam, assassinations, and the protests that nonetheless seemed to be the major topic on the evening BBC radio news broadcasts.

Over the course of a few weeks, Petrus and I came to understand each other fairly well, and we became good friends. He was clearly on a quest to overcome whatever he felt were the limitations of being Ndjuka, and to be seen as an urbane political leader. He never articulated what his goals were; I hoped that he would go beyond wearing a tie and adopting European and now American affectations. The more I got to know Petrus, the more I realized we were both very much alike in our pursuits. We were like actors working to develop and adopt a character different from who we were; we were just going at it from opposite directions. I wanted to be able to speak and act like an Ndjuka as much as he wanted to become like an American. One evening Petrus showed up wearing a pair of new, imitation Levi jeans and a t-shirt. I did not say anything, but he was dressed exactly like me!

CHAPTER FIVE

OTIS

Petrus explained that the local Parbo beer was made from rice not hops like Dutch beer. Whatever, I know that it must have had low alcohol content because we drank a lot of it over our evening sessions and still remained reasonably lucid. We would walk into TakTakie and grab a table, and instantly the waiter would bring over a liter of Parbo (called a "*juggo*") and two glasses, then ceremoniously open the bottle as if to show that it had not been refilled. When guys (I never saw women there) came by our table to say hello, they would always bring a glass with them, which Petrus would always top off from the table juggo. When the juggo got close to empty, the waiter would appear and replace it. There was no check; at the end of the night, the waiter would just say how many juggos we went through and we would leave cash on the table. On occasions when we would order rum, the waiter would bring a full bottle and fresh glasses to the table. The rum charge would be the waiter's estimate of how much of the bottle was consumed.

One evening Petrus said he wanted to take me to a bar outside of town where I could meet some of his friends. He hailed a passing car that pulled over and told the driver where he wanted to go. He and the driver quickly agreed on a price, and we were off. When I asked why we didn't take a taxi, he explained that any car that has only a driver is available for hire—you just need to make sure you get the price confirmed before you get in.

The bar was a good distance from downtown, with a very different vibe. There were no streetlights on the road leading up to it, but lights and music from the place lit up the surrounding area. I followed Petrus into an open-air patio crowded with young, very dark-skinned men in the standard slacks and t-shirts, sitting and standing around a few tables. The place was animated by loud conversation and fun, jumpy Calypso-ish music. There was no band or DJ, just a soundtrack, I guessed. I stayed close to Petrus as he worked through the crowd, greeting nearly everyone he passed as if they had gone to high school together. As a tall, skinny white guy with crazy hair and a beard, I stood out in this crowd, and many gave me a second look as we made our way to a back table. The place reminded me of the Army beer joints full of boisterous young men, except everyone here was black. Not just black but dark black like Petrus, and all seemed incredibly fit in their tight t-shirts.

We sat down and got our juggo. Petrus said this place is a favorite of Ndjuka guys who live or work in and around the city. We were soon joined by four or five guys who crowded around our table. Petrus was clearly pleased to introduce his new *"Merican"* friend to his buddies. I was certainly an oddity in the place, and apparently the only American guy they had ever met up close.

Petrus was in high spirits as he showed off his trophy pal. He explained to the group that I was teaching him the real story of America. The guys pressed in closer, studying me carefully and talking excitedly among themselves. The closer the group crowded the table, I was able to determine the source of the distinctive smell of the room. It was a cologne I had not smelled before: a not unpleasant sweaty mix of bay leaf and coconut oil. One of the guys leaned over the table to look straight at me. In slow, deliberate English, he asked me, "What it mean, 'Papa's got a brand-new bag?'"

All the guys got quiet and were looking at me eagerly. Apparently, this was a question that had been really vexing them, and finally they had a Merican to resolve the matter. The music at the place was a mix of calypso and reggae so the godfather-of-soul-thing caught me by surprise.

Not only was I discomfited in the smothering company of intense, half-drunk, very black strangers in a strange bar, I never once had given thought to the meaning of "papa's brand-new bag." I looked for Petrus and he was nowhere around. I tried to remember the words to the song, and I hummed it my head. "Well," I leaned into the table for serious effect, and in slow English explained, "'Bag' does not mean a bag or sack," I indicate, holding up my arm like holding a tote bag. They clearly had figured that much out already, so I quickly continued, "He got a new woman; then he is happy, he make a new dance." I got inspired: "'Bag' means everything: woman, dance, clothes, feeling."

The group fell into animated discussion that I could not begin to understand. Smiles and knowing looks suggested that the Merican was cool—"Papa's got brand new bag" was peppered through their excited conversations. Petrus was still nowhere around. I sat stroking my glass and topping off empty glasses thrust onto the table with the juggos that kept coming, trying not to look terrified. The team reassembled their huddle around the table again. They got quiet as the one with the sort-of English resumed being the interlocutor: "Why EL-vis kill OH-tis?"

"What?!" I was not expecting this. "Why Elvis Presley killed OH-tis, Otis Redding?" I asked back, incredulous.

They were not buying that I didn't know. "Ya, mon—OH-tis too good. Better than EL-vis!" All the guys got into the boisterous affirmation that EL-vis murdered OH-tis. They wanted details, a confirmation from a Merican who surely knows the real story.

"I don't know about the Elvis and Otis thing," I beg off waving my hands for additional effect. While the notion that Elvis Presley was responsible for the death of Otis Redding was new and preposterous to me, I did not want to appear to be defending white Elvis who, they were convinced, caused the death of their hero, OH-tis.

Petrus finally reappeared at the table. The lesson sessions between myself and Petrus had been conversations with an almost formal tone, as Petrus was usually in his suit and always acting professional. I grabbed his arm to pull him close to say in his ear, "Let's get the fuck out of here." I don't think he was familiar with the adverbial emphasis, 'the fuck,' but he got my drift. We counted up our juggos and put money on the table. As we were leaving, one of the guys put his hand on my shoulder, "You know Brook Ben-ton?"

"Brook Benton—yeah! Very good!" I look back with a little thumbs-up. "I don't *know* him, though," I add for the record. To myself, "Brook Benton?"

I was glad to be in the dark back seat of a guy's car taxi on the way back to downtown Paramaribo. Petrus was quiet. I muttered out loud, "Elvis killing Otis Redding! That's crazy!" Petrus remained silent for a minute. Then out of the darkness, "OH-tiss was too good. EL-vis (searching for the right English word)... jealous."

I let it drop.

CHAPTER SIX

AJUMA KONDEY

Petrus was a coastal Ndjuka; that is, from the settlements east of Paramaribo along the Cottica River which runs parallel with the Atlantic coast. Several Ndjuka villages in this area were accessible by road and reflected far more urban influences than the isolated inland forest Ndjuka villages. I was itching to get out of Paramaribo and explore, so Petrus agreed to take me to his native village to meet his father. The next day, he arranged for us to go to Moengo Toppoe and Ajuma Kondey, where his brother and father live, respectively.

During my first weeks in Paramaribo, I had gotten to know an odd group of American and European ex-pats living (or hiding out) on the margins in Suriname. None of this crowd would give a credible account of how or why they ended up in Paramaribo. Each clearly had a get-out-of-town story that fell into a mutually understood don't-ask-don't-tell protocol. Some lived in rooms or small apartments; a few guys had moved in with local women. Mark and Norma were a couple of stoners who told me they were just dropping out of New York for a while. They were on something of a magic carpet of excellent pot with a trove of cassettes. I had no trouble fitting in with this crowd; I looked like a hippie and my story of being expelled from Guyana resonated. No one tried to pry into how I escaped, or what I had been in for. I was comfortable crashing with these fellow marginals, and it got me out of the grungy hotel.

• • •

After a quick morning tea and biscuit at a sparce apartment in downtown Paramaribo—rented by a British guy who said his name was John—I straightened up the couch and stuffed my clothes in a bag. John said he did odd jobs and drove a delivery truck, but was otherwise not forthcoming as to why he was there. His Black Surinamese girlfriend, Karla, spoke perfect English and seemed to know everything going on in the city, and everyone doing it. They were interesting and enigmatic, and a valuable resource to me in a new city environment.

On a pre-stamped, fold-up airmail post, I jotted a quick note to Katie that I was heading for the bush as an anthropologist. It had been a couple of months since I left New York with no communication between us. I was in full lean-forward adventure mode and had not figured out how to receive mail in Suriname. None of my off-grid friends had reliable telephones, and international calls were crazy expensive. My parents had grown accustomed to my long absences with no contact. I left Oklahoma the minute after high school graduation and kept on going. But it was so wrong (no, idiotic), it turned out, to assume that Katie would just know that I missed her and thought of her everyday.

I found Petrus standing in the crowd just outside the main market where the cars-for-hire, vans, and buses parked. He stood out, being relatively tall; I was glad to see that he ditched his suit for the trip. We pushed ourselves onto a van going east. There were at least thirty people already onboard the bus with seats for only sixteen. The two-hour ride included an improbable ferry trip to cross a "river" about forty yards wide for an extra charge. The bus went only as far as Moengo, the company town of Suralco, the mining operation that Minister Goosen used to manage.

Suralco was the massive Alcoa subsidiary bauxite mining company, the face of America for many Surinamese. The mining enterprise was self-sufficient, with farms and transportation systems, including its own railroad. Suralco-produced milk was the best in Suriname. The dairy and beef cattle operations were favorite attractions for school trips from all over Suriname. Employee housing was well built and well laid out, like American lower middle, middle, and upper-middle-class partitioned suburbs. Laborers were housed in small houses laid out in straight lines and square blocked streets—all houses were identical. Middle and upper management lived in differentiated and distinct houses and districts. These houses were arranged on curved roadways. Upper management lived on the hill. The only apparent problem perceived by the Ndjuka was that the company ignored them. Moengo is within the traditional territory designated for the officially recognized free settlement Ndjuka. The Ndjuka complain that when Suralco moved their mining operation there around 1900, the company ignored them and brought in urban Blacks to fill employment positions.

Petrus had friends in Moengo who provided us with lunch and a motorbike to go the twenty miles further east to Ajuma Kondey. Petrus greeted several people as we took a quick run around Moengo on the motorbike. Later, as we got within ten miles from Ajuma Kondey, Petrus greeted virtually everyone we encountered along the road as "uncle," "aunt," or "cousin." Ajuma Kondey is Petrus's home village, situated in a shallow but steep valley at the bottom of which is the Coermotibo River. Petrus took me to his father's hut and introduced him to me as D'Aladi. D'Aladi shook my hand and spoke to me directly to say that his name was *Opalani* (airplane). Petrus gave me a don't-mind-him look, so I continued to refer to him as D'Aladi.

D'Aladi was in his mid-70s, thin, and a little frail; his grey hair highlighted what I had not noticed before, having little interaction with Black people—his dark skin was losing luster. Unlike the young guys at the Parbo bars whose skin glistened, D'Aladi was turning grey all over. Aladi lived in a twelve-by-eight-foot wood and thatch hut that he shared with Tetay, a ten-year-old boy. Tetay was vaguely related to D'Aladi as a grandnephew, but the old man treated him like a servant. D'Aladi addressed Tetay very sternly, and directed just which morsel of leftover food he could have. Tetay fetched and assisted in household and personal chores. D'Aladi seemed pleased that the plan was for us to stay in Ajuma Kondey for a few days, and mustered a stern paternal admonition that if I am living with him in his house, I must not accept any food or rum from any other people in the village. Petrus explained later that D'Aladi is particularly concerned with people who have evil intensions towards him, and particularly any special guests of his.

Petrus took me on a walking tour of Ajuma Kondey, a village of about seventy small houses, mostly wood planks, packed earth floors, and thatch roofs. Petrus introduced me to everyone we met. He would explain that I was learning the language to make a book about Ndjuka people. People stared at me; kids and old women marveled at my beard. They liked the beads I was wearing around my neck—BB-sized, dark red ceramic beads I got at a Chinese shop in Paramaribo. When I strung the beads on dental floss for a necklace, I anointed them with the Oklahoma soil from my medicine jar by marinating them overnight in a slurry of Okie dirt and rum. I had no recipe or conscious reason for consecrating the beads other than to mark a connection between the previous me, as a child, and the current me on an uncertain journey.

My attempts at the formal greetings in Ndjuka provided great entertainment around Ajuma Kondey. I was uneasy talking with bare-breasted women; I was familiar with bare-breasted women from books and film, but this was my first actual experience standing directly in front of women whose breasts were looking at me.

• • •

Petrus and I washed up and swam a bit in the river while Tetay and two friends held our clothes. The kids seemed ready and available for any errand. Aladi had prepared the tin of ham that we brought from Paramaribo. I believe a neighbor sent over the rice. As we ate, Aladi closed the door, another apparent precautionary step against something untoward being sent in from the outside.

People we met through our tour kept telling us of a dance in the village that night. I was elated with the prospect of a full-fledged bush ceremony my first night. The dance, however, turned out to be the music of the local rock band, Apollo 11, pronounced "Apollo Elif." Petrus and I put on clean clothes for the dance; I passed on Petrus' offer of his bay rum-smelling cologne. The party started around 8 p.m. on an open slab of concrete, about twenty-five feet square, in the center of the village, with open sides and a tin roof. There was a concession stand with beer, soft drinks, and food at one end. The cost was one guilder (about fifty cents) to get access to the concrete dance floor. A ribbon lapel pin showed you have paid. The dance was well attended, and Apollo Elif was better than I had feared. The band was an energetic group of young Ndjuka musicians: two electric guitars, two cowbells, two shakers, a drum set, a home-carved conga drum, two trumpets, and two singers.

When the band started, most dancing on the concrete involved teenagers, girls dancing with girls, and groups of boys danced together. Younger kids danced and played on the dirt. Most older people were just spectating, dancing to themselves. Everyone was dressed up; no girls were bare-breasted at the dance. More people came later, and more bought access ribbons to the dance floor. Boys and girls began pairing off to dance. By midnight the dance floor was jammed; everyone was into it. Everyone now moved close to the dance floor edge and women danced together in a loose line. Men danced singly with loose orientation to the women. The band maintained a steady pace till 2 a.m. with only short breaks. They played different songs, but each tune has the exact same calypso rhythm and beat. Two hours in, the tunes started sounding alike to me, but still great fun with everyone present—kids, parents, and grandparents—all totally engaged in the show.

The next day Petrus and I took the motorbike to visit his brother, Renee Atolensi—his missionary-given name—who owned a popular roadside café in Moengo Toppoe, a few miles from Ajuma Kondey. The hand-written sign over the door read, "LETH THEM TALK." Renee welcomed us with a warm greeting; he served up beer and food. It was part grocery store and deli, with open cans of sardines, cooked corn on the cob, flat hard cassava bread, neat pyramid stacks of oranges, tiny finger bananas, regular bananas, and plantains. Petrus sampled just about everything in the store stock. A cat, puppy, and two baby peccaries roamed the floor. Renee was delightful, and very curious about the relative geographic and population features of the United States and Suriname. He found it inconceivable that I came from a city a hundred times the size of Paramaribo, and was astonished that people in New York do not know about Suriname or the Ndjuka people. Renee seemed to think Petrus was going to leave me there with him, so he said he would be happy to help me with language and getting settled into village life. I thanked him best I could and said that I may come back at another time.

We next went to another beer-soft drink shop to meet "Big Boy," the proprietor. He was a well-known local bandsman, with instruments and sound equipment stacked throughout his shop. He was a massive fellow in his middle or late 30s. Big Boy was friendly to a fault, continually strumming an old guitar labeled with large crayon letters, "THIS MACHINE KILLS." His place was decorated throughout with crayon writings on the walls: "Otis Redding," "United We Stand-Divided We Fall" and "Jesus is a Soul Man."

Big Boy served up soft drinks and went back to his guitar. Shortly, Petrus began singing to Big Boy's strumming. Petrus had a good voice and knew all the songs. After a few tunes, Big Boy brought out the Parbo. I had been nervous about this first-time overnight venture into the interior, even though I was with Petrus. There were still many unknowns about my new best friend, but all my concerns faded into the vibe of guitar strumming and singing! I felt welcome among friends who I had known for less than an hour, and would have joined in if I had known the tunes.

We headed back to Ajuma Kondey that evening and Aladi showed us to a vacant house near his. Neighbors provided a kerosene lamp, table, and two chairs. After bathing in the river, Petrus and I prepared hammocks and mosquito nets. He assumed I was incapable of stringing a hammock, so he started with mine. I had not told him that I spent a year in Vietnam and was experienced in tying hammocks with mosquito nets, but I wanted to avoid any Vietnam talk, so I thanked him for setting the hammocks.

After breakfast of tea, Wonder Bread, and canned ham, Petrus and I made another slow tour of Ajuma Kondey. During this trip, I came to appreciate Petrus as a natural politician—consistent and sincere in his ambition to advance. We met a group of boys clearing tall brush from an area with machetes. Petrus joked with them that they should get a power mower for the job. They joked (sort of) back that maybe he should help them. Petrus was wearing shoes and socks, a clean yellow shirt, and trousers with a crease. One of the boys playfully tossed Petrus a machete which fell at his feet. Petrus responded by raising his ever-present ballpoint pen aloft and announcing, unperturbed, "*This* is my machete!"

Everyone in Ajuma Kondey was interested in Petrus' American friend, and seemed greatly amused at my language attempts. People were genuinely well-disposed with me, and perhaps a bit flattered that an American from New York came to live in Suriname to learn their language and customs. Petrus explained to almost each family that I was a student and almost a professor. He embellished occasionally that I will be a big professor in America when I go back. I blushed as the listeners looked at me with puzzled awe. But I was troubled by the Marxist asymmetry that infused my studies at the New School. Here I was, able to be in this place—*their* place—and to examine their social and cultural behavior through *my* conceptual framework. I wondered how my rural Oklahoma hometown would receive a very dark-skinned, 28-year-old African who showed up and announced in pitiful English that he wanted to learn the language and report to his people about Okie cultural practices.

Petrus and I caught a bus back to Paramaribo that afternoon. I felt accomplished at what I had learned, the people I had met, and mostly that I had survived the outing without embarrassing Petrus, and without incurring lasting trauma to my sense of self. I felt one step closer to becoming a field anthropologist.

CHAPTER SEVEN

COOTIES

Encouraged by my first foray into the countryside with Petrus, I started making overnight visits to Ajuma Kondey on my own, staying in the vacant hut next to Aladi's. I was generally recognized and well received as I walked around the village. People would gather outside their houses and call me over for a round of greetings, comments about my beard, and the beads I wore. As people became more familiar and my language capability grew, a key topic became, "Where is your wife?" "When is she coming?" "What's her name?" One day a group of women asked (jokingly, I think) if I wanted a wife until the one in America comes. I laughed. The next day another group of women insisted with more bawdy humor that I should take a woman as a stand-in wife until my own arrived from America. I took this as a compliment, but it was becoming a little awkward. "Oh no, she is coming soon," I explained, and moved on.

The four-hour van trips between Paramaribo and Ajuma Konday were tortuous. I would have to change to a local van in Moengo and I soon became adept at elbowing for space. I noticed again and again a peculiar little van ritual where one taking a vacated section of a seat would slap the seat vigorously before sitting down. I once asked Petrus what's with the seat slapping when people get into a van or a bus. "Oh, it send away any stuff people put on the seat," he explained matter-of-factly.

"Stuff?" I ask. "What kind of 'stuff' would someone put on a seat?"

"You know," he explained as if to a pestering child, "some people have things that other people don't want to get; you scare off by slapping the cushion."

I thought I got it and said out loud but as a joke to myself, "something like cooties."

Petrus perked up, "What is 'cooties?'" he asks, dead serious.

I waved it off, "Nothing, nothing; just a silly little thing."

Petrus, now looking at me intently, insisted, "Who get cooties? What cooties do? Where you get cooties? How cooties work?"

I had never thought of cooties as a concept and could not begin to explain it, particularly across a still large linguistic and cultural gap. The more I demurred, of course, the more Petrus was convinced he was on to something. He got animated and the questions tumbled out, half in English, half Ndjuka, insinuating something dark going on. "Why you not want to tell me about cooties? Is cooties a secret that white people keep from Black people?"

"Stop it!" I exclaimed, exasperated. "It's just a game children play with each other."

We spoke no further of cooties, but Petrus gave me an unmistakable "I'll-find-out-sooner-or-later" look. It occurred to me later that Petrus was making a connection between cooties and the malevolent spirits that D'Aladi was obsessed with in Ajuma Kondey.

• • •

Petrus and I kept up our evening sessions at *TakTaki*, and one day he showed up holding an official looking envelope.

"Here's your letter from the Minister!"

The one paragraph letter was in Dutch with imposing official stamps over the minister's signature. Petrus translated and explained that it was a letter of introduction to the commissioner of the Marowijne District—the large region along the Dutch side of the Marowijne (Maroni in French) River border with French Guyana. The district encompassed the territories of the Ndjuka, Pamaka, and Aluku groups. Further south, inland near the Brazilian border, were isolated Amerindian villages. The letter asked the commissioner to facilitate my two-year study among the bush people of his district. This was my ticket to the real interior—to becoming the anthropologist I wanted to be.

I would get a bus to the district capital the next morning.

CHAPTER EIGHT

ALBINA

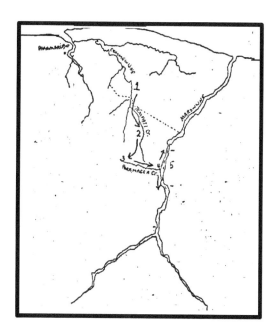

Albina is the river port on the border of French Guiana. I was by now accustomed to the overcrowded, cootie-laden vans that transported villagers and their cargo of pots and pans, reams of cloth, children, and woven bamboo cages of chickens and ducks along the coast. I was looking forward to the extra hour's ride to Albina. Albina had an odd charm to it—a miniature port town with a mash-up of Blacks (urban and bush), Chinese, Javanese, East Indians, and Amerindians. The approach by road was a winding downhill affair that made for a dramatic view of the town and the river, as the van lurched around the last curve. The center of town featured a cluster of two-story frame structures with shops on the street level and living space, or storage or whatnot, on the top floor. The civic center building housed the post office and the district commissioner's office.

The waterfront is what set Albina apart from any other place I had seen so far. The structures of downtown Albina were only about 100 yards from the bank of the Marowijne River (the French call it the Maroni). There were scores of riverboats at the shore; some tied to wooden docks, while some were pulled up so that the bow came to rest on the gradually sloping bank. There was an active coming and going between Albina and St. Laurent on the French side, about a one-mile crossing at that point. The transport routine was familiar; boatmen would hawk for passengers and launch only when the boat was filled to overcapacity.

What I found remarkable about this port town was that all of the boats were dugout canoes! Canoes, yes, but not the one or two-person rowing canoes of Ajuma Kondey's creeks. The canoes of the Marowijne River were large, masterfully designed, colorfully painted and carved single-tree vessels with powerful outboard motors. These riverboats in Albina ferried fifteen to eighteen people at a time, along with cargo, up, down and across the mile-wide river.

I took in the vibe from the waterfront for a short while, and then went straight to the district commissioner's office to present my letter of introduction. I did not have to wait long; the commissioner was in, but I still had to wait outside until he was ready to see me. He was professionally polite, but unpleasant. I greeted him formally and handed him the letter from the minister, which he only glanced at, "I heard you were coming," he said in educated English.

He relaxed in his chair and studied me suspiciously. "I know who you are," he said with smug assurance.

"Really?" I was impressed.

"Yes, I know you are CIA, but I do not care."

"Oh?" I say. I had heard this a lot since my stint in Vietnam. I also learned that protests and denials of any CIA connection simply confirmed the contrary, so I just shrugged and shook my head. "I'm an anthropologist," I say.

"Of course!" he exclaimed, smiling. "Look, we have nothing to hide. All that is in the interior here are Bush Negroes and Indians. Have a good time." (Little did either of us know at the time that a serious revolt against the government would be launched several years later from this interior district.)

With that, he turned his chair towards the window overlooking the big river, "There is a supply boat going upriver in a few days—check back for the schedule. They will take you." Meeting over.

The minister's letter was not specific other than I was to be allowed to conduct research in the interior of this large district that borders French Guiana. A Dutch anthropologist couple, Thoden and Ineke van Velzen, were already working and living among the Ndjuka far upriver in Dritabiki, so I would not likely be taken there. The Boni people had villages along the river, but they were all situated on the east bank—the French side. That left the Pamakans, an exciting opportunity since in my quick research in Paramaribo I found no published ethnographies on the Pamaka people.

The Pamakans were a relatively small group and not well known or documented. They had gone through two escape episodes: first was the escape from the plantations to clandestine camps near the fields from which they would raid for supplies and new members. In the late 1760s, when the Ndjuka, Saamaka and Matawai groups became allied with the plantation forces through their peace-for-manumission accord, the Pamakans had to escape further south far into the rain forest. They created secluded camps along a western tributary of the Marowijne River, the Pamaka Creek, about eighty miles from the Atlantic coast, and far from the main river. They remained completely hidden until slavery was eliminated and they were no longer subject to bounty hunters. When they emerged from hiding, they became known as the Pamaka Creek people.

I got a room at the no-star, but aptly named Riverview Hotel, and headed for the nearby Javanese restaurant, the only restaurant in Albina. The menu was "bami" or "nasi." ("You want chicken rice or chicken noodle?") The sturdy Parbo juggo with glass landed on the table as if by default. I must have looked like a regular juggo guy by now.

The government boat would not be ready for a few days, so I settled into Albina. One afternoon I jumped on one of the big motor canoes that ferried locals back and forth to St. Laurent under the customs radar. The contrast between the British, Dutch, and French Guianas was striking. St. Laurent du Maroni had the post card, nineteenth century French Provincial architecture centered around abandoned prison buildings— just as described by Henri Charriére in *Papillon*. It was exhilarating to find a French restaurant, with a menu, French bread, and red wine! Plus, they drove their cars on the right side of the road!

After a few days, the hotel desk clerk told me that the government supply boat would be leaving the following morning. I made sure I had essential provisions—clear sugar cane rum and bags of Dutch tobacco to facilitate my welcome.

Early next morning I found the official long boat being loaded up on the dock near the commissioner's office. The canoe was at least thirty feet long and powered by a 40 horse-power outboard. It was a sturdy, heavy craft. The hull was the traditional one piece of wood about two inches thick, stretched open to a four-foot beam at the center. Essentially, a motorized tree-trunk flying a Dutch flag. Two up-river Ndjuka men were loading it carefully to balance the cargo of boxes and bags fitted around a barrel of diesel fuel; I was the only passenger. One of the men operated the motor and steered, standing in the stern. The other stood in the bow area to navigate and watch for rocks just under the water. I sat in the center exhilarated as the Albina skyline faded in the distance.

The river was beautiful but menacing, with a fierce current and rock formations that would spring up everywhere along the way. There were no navigational markers, buoys, or lights—you just had to know the river. About one hour out, the river changed from a deep, tide-influenced waterway to a fast, rocky, and raucous affair. The boatman standing in the bow directed the motorman to zigzag around large rocks to find channels through rapids. The terrain along the shore was like nothing I had experienced. Very soon after we left Albina, the banks on both sides became impenetrable green walls of trees, bushes, and vines. From a distance, it looked like one continuous stretch of giant broccoli plants compressed side-by-side, about forty feet high. Very occasionally we would pass a small clearing where someone had carved out a notch in the broccoli wall and set up a small camp with a thatch hut or two.

No one spoke during the four-hour trip. I was anxious, expecting to be dropped at a Pamakan village, but not really certain where I was being taken, or if anyone was expecting me. Just beneath my fascination with the river and its green palisade, I could not decide whether I should be giddy or terrified. This was a brash experiment in trust: trust in the basic human decency in those I would encounter in the forest settlements, and trust in my ability to adapt and survive. I felt a confidence though, maybe because of the hummingbird and the old Hindu guy. And knowing that the women in Ajuma Kondey were ready to provide me a temporary wife! At this point I was committed and felt oddly self-assured. No matter how insane this adventure was it seemed clear that I was being led by strange events and odd coincidences that got me this far.

CHAPTER NINE

LANGATABIKI

I had packed all my NASA space food sticks, so about three hours into the trip I grabbed one from my bag for lunch. About one o'clock that afternoon the boat steered toward a large island that had several inhabited camps along the bank. There was a large clearing with a few canoes, both large and small, sticking out from the mud shoreline at the up-river end of the island. The motor man steered the bow onto the sloping shore so the bow man could jump off and tie up.

"You go here," the motor man said to me, pointing to the dozen or so thatch huts just beyond the dock area.

"Where are we?" I asked in Ndjuka.

"Langatabiki," he said perfunctorily. They were going to offload the barrel of fuel for the village generator, then keep on going upriver.

A group of people had gathered at the top of the dock area to see who had just come in. The boatmen spoke briefly to one of the men present, pointing with a wave at me. It did not take them long to roll the barrel onto the mud. I watched as the two boatmen backed out and pointed their big canoe with the Dutch flag upriver without a wave. I stood still as the sound of the big Evinrude faded, leaving an eerie quiet from all machine or electric sound.

I knew Langatabiki was the principal village of the Pamaka people, and home village of the paramount chief, Gaaman Cornelius Forster. A small crowd had started to gather and watch as I walked slowly but deliberately up from the boat dock to the village area. Kids were darting about in feigned, or perhaps actual fear; women stopped what they were doing in front of their huts to stare. The women wore only the colorful wrap-around *pangi* skirts. I was struck by the careful, complex, and distinctive braid patterns of their hair. Each woman's hair was unique; focusing on braid patterns was a useful way to not appear to be gawking at their bare breasts, although I had almost gotten accustomed to the diversity and beauty of women's breasts from my travels to Ajuma Kondey.

A man wearing a colorful loincloth approached. I initiated the formal greeting in Ndjuka, "*Oh mitie oh, Da.*" The crowd tittered as loincloth guy looked at me in disbelief, not saying a word. I repeated an abbreviated opening line of the greeting, "*Oh mitie.*" He looked at me incredulously, then offered the response line, "*Oh mitie eh.*" The ice broken, sort of, I said to him in my best Ndjuka that I was here to visit the Pamaka people. By then the crowd had grown to a few dozen people, few of whom were wearing shirts or tops—women included. A man in khaki shorts came up—a man of authority it seemed—as the others made way for him. He stood about ten feet away from me and offered a stiff greeting. This little formality done, I explained that the district commissioner had sent me here so that I could learn from the Pamaka people; and asked, if the gaaman was in?

The district commissioner and gaaman references worked. The welcoming party buzzed in discussion, and the khaki shorts man said yes, that I must see the gaaman. He led me and the growing entourage into the village proper, and up to a large thatch house built off the ground on poles. He motioned for me to wait a distance away while he went ahead. Meanwhile every eye in the village was staring at me. All activity had come to a stop. I was a spectacle not to be missed.

After about five minutes, a much older man in long khaki pants and white shirt emerged from the house. He was wearing a fedora! The crowd's focus shifted momentarily from me to Gaaman Forster. He was a robust man, slightly stooped with age and hard work, probably in his mid 60's. There was a distinct air of deference in the crowd with his presence. He smiled at me and motioned for me to come forward. I did the most formal greeting in my repertoire, with hands clasped and looking at the ground. This display amused the crowd, and the Gaaman seemed pleased. He motioned for me to sit at a low, elaborately carved wooden stool someone had scurried up with.

Pamaka and Ndjuka dialects are very similar; still I struggled and awkwardly explained anew that I was in Suriname to learn the language and ways of the African people living in the interior. I told him that I had spent a few weeks with the Ndjuka people in the Cottica River area.

Feeling a shift in the reception, I quickly added that the district commissioner had sent me to Langatabiki on a government boat at the behest of Minister Goosen (which I pronounced deliberately, HO-sen.) I then presented him with the bottle of rum that I had picked up in St. Laurent. It was the largest item in my bag, having ditched the typewriter in Paramaribo. Gaaman Forster was gracious, and offered a genuine welcome to Langatabiki, even though I understood his commentary to the crowd suggested he felt some risk in taking in this strange stranger.

I was relieved and delighted to have his blessing, however conditional it may be. The Gaaman spoke to the khaki shorts guy, who I learned later was TiTiban, the *kapiten* or lineage chief of the neighborhood where the government boat dropped me off. TiTiban led me along with an entourage of curious villagers to B'Aleke's house that was temporarily vacant. He said it would be okay for me to stay there for a while until B'Aleke returned. I gave him a cloth bag of Dutch tobacco. He smiled, despite his best efforts to be officious, and left.

B'Aleke, I learned, had no woman at the time. His house was modest to a fault, with the living space of a walk-in closet, without a single piece of furniture. The horizontal wooden poles that framed the thatch roof and walls were perfect, however, for tying a hammock. The steep angle of the walls limited access to all but the center of the place. The front and rear walls were handhewn planks of bare wood. The remarkable feature of the place, of course, was the door. The exterior of the door (the only door) was intricately carved with a complex, interwoven design, which was highlighted with bright red, black, and white paint. It was a work of art that I spent time admiring and trying to analyze any symbolic meaning. I could not figure out what it represented, but I thought Katie would like it.

I approached one of the older boys in the group watching my every move, and asked delicately where one would use the bathroom, or get water for anything. He laughed nervously and motioned to the river. My new place was about fifty feet from the riverbank, so I scoped out a path to and from. A quick visual survey of the village brought home another uncomfortable reality—where the hell was I going to eat? There were no Bami restaurants, no Chinese shops, no juggo joints, nothing! I had enough NASA snacks to last a day or so, but I needed a quick food plan.

One of the most influential books I had read in my anthropology course work was Marcel Mauss's *The Gift*. Mauss had posited the theory that human social order was founded on the practice of reciprocal gifting. He theorized that the giving of a gift creates an obligation for the recipient to reciprocate with a gift in return, and relationships build from there. I was not concerned with the rest of Mauss's theory about how complex social organizations were built around this principle of gift reciprocity—I was hoping it would get me something to eat.

The crowd of villagers had winnowed to mainly children and young men and women who had taken up vigil outside of my new hut. It was dark inside, so I unpacked my bag outside by the door. They seemed fascinated with my trove of space bars; I ate one very openly to show that they were edible, and quite tasty. I then started handing them out to my audience. Many took the strange packages and ran to their houses in the neighborhood. They appeared surprised and delighted with my gesture; meanwhile, I was thinking about my utter lack of food options.

The vigil in front of my little house thinned out to about six kids as the sun began to disappear behind the forest wall. It must have been around 6 p.m. Since we are about four degrees above the Equator, sunset and sunrise occur virtually the same time year-round. There was no sitting stool nearby, so I drug up a log to sit on in front of my designer door.

The houses in the distinct neighborhoods of the village were close together so I could see my nearby neighbors as they went about their evening routines. These houses, or huts, were small and dark, so the families lived mostly outside in front of their house using the interior as a bedroom. Every few houses shared a fire pit that was constantly burning or smoldering. The outside activity was oriented around the fire pits, even though most of the houses had propane or charcoal stoves for cooking. There were streetlights of sorts on poles along the main path some distance from my cluster of huts. Where I was, the only source of light when it got dark was the various fires by the huts.

I had not sat long when a young teenage boy came walking quickly and deliberately toward me. I remembered him from the earlier space food give-away. Now he was carrying something gingerly in front of him with both hands; it had a cotton cloth draped over it. He came up and stretched his arms forward. He did not say anything, but motioned clearly with a combination of head gesture and pooched lips to take it—this was my dinner!

I held in my hands the most magnificent plate of warm food in the world, having eaten only a couple of space bars all day. Moved almost to tears, I thanked the kid and asked his name. He looked down and smiled, "KutuKutu." A slight hand wave indicated the house he had come from. His mother, MaDennie, was standing by their fire pit looking on. I waved in appreciation to her as my new delivery friend took off. Under the cloth was a mound of rice topped with two pieces of stewed fish, splashed with an oily gravy. A spoon was thoughtfully included. This was the most memorable and enjoyable meal I have ever had. I made silent, solemn thanks to Professor Mauss, wherever he was.

CHAPTER TEN

THE WAKE

I finished my first meal and went to the river to wash the dish and spoon, and to wash myself. I returned the dish to my neighbor and thanked them again. They told me that MaBodie, Gaaman Forster's sister, had died recently and that there was to be a gathering that evening near her house in a different part of the village. I asked if I could attend, they gave me an "of course" look and pointed to where it would be.

I went back to my hut and tied the hammock at one end and rolled it up for easy flop later. When I heard singing, I followed others walking in the direction of the voices, an open area behind the Moravian church building. This was going to be shoestring fieldwork; I had no camera, and only a cheap cassette tape recorder, with no place to buy new batteries. My plan was to soak up whatever I could through my senses and take notes.

A group of about forty people had gathered, mostly standing, and some sitting on hand-carved stools. The Moravian preacher, a Black Surinamese from Paramaribo, led a group of boys singing hymns from a hymnal. The Gaaman and his wife were there, along with the two *kapitens*, chiefs representing lineages of the village. More people gathered until the crowd reached seventy or eighty people.

The dead woman's body was wrapped in cloth, and still in her house just next to the gathering. I was struck by the realization that here you cannot call 911. You cannot call anyone to come take care of a problem such as crime, trauma, sickness, or death. Here you have to deal with life events yourself. The Pamakans were well practiced in self-sufficiency from many years of isolated fugitive existence.

The boy choir dutifully sang the words of various hymns in rote *a capella*. It was like a memorised catechism, devoid of any hint of soul, gospel fervor, or even a hint that the boys knew or cared what they were singing. The hymnal was the work of Protestant missionaries who had translated Christian hymns into Surinamese, the lingua franca spoken only in the urban areas, but understood throughout the country. The boys sang the words of different hymns to what sounded like the same tune for nearly two hours. I was disappointed, thinking that it was going to be difficult to discern African influences here.

I was standing toward the back of the crowd. People in the front would sing along with some of the hymns, but people in the back of the crowd near me grew restless and eventually rowdy. The head kapiten stood and admonished the crowd that this was a solemn occasion, and they should be respectful and quiet. The crowd in the back was not chastened by this admonition, and in a few minutes, I heard a quick *d'dum, dumdum, d'dumdum*. Someone behind me had a drum! There was some commotion in the darkness behind me, and the head kapiten stood again and angrily announced that Gaaman does not want drums or dancing.

The back crowd only grew more restless, and the drum continued to interject a *d'dum* here and there. The preacher abruptly concluded the program, bade the gathering good night and left; the Gaaman and his wife left a few minutes later. At that point, the head kapiten said that people were free to switch to traditional songs and storytelling ("*matos*"), but PLEASE no drumming or dancing. Then the party started.

One man stepped up and started calling out a *mato*, one of the well-known stories of Anansi the spider, a tradition of trickster versus tigers and other dangers. I could not follow the story line with my rudimentary Pamakan language skills, but knew that Anansi stories were African fairy tales similar in kind to European tales of Cinderella and Little Red Riding Hood. The story itself is familiar to the audience and here, simply provided a vehicle for the song and dance of the party. After a few words into the story, someone in the crowd called out, "I was there!" The storyteller asked, "Wha'd you see?" to which the caller launched into singing, which was immediately joined by the entire crowd. This singing was classic African call-and-response, with one person calling out a lyrical phrase and the rest responding in chorus.

The mato singing went on for nearly an hour without drums or dancing. At one point, however, the drums just erupted and people began dancing. Four men brought to the front intricately carved drums fashioned out of tree trunks, slightly shorter than congas but with a similar sound. The crowd became animated with the drum rhythm; as the drums warmed with the infectiously repeated beat, people would step forward to dance individually. The dancers would sway with the drums, knees bent slightly for intricate footwork; arms extended to the front with their hands gracefully pantomiming the dance. This was not Africa, but these folks looked and sounded like the tribal groups of Africa I had studied so much about in graduate school!

People were singing and dancing, and the drums took over the night. Then I heard more commotion, this time from the front of the crowd. A small group protested the drumming and dancing, and an argument interrupted the festivity. I watched transfixed from my back-row distance, still very much the anomaly, and not understanding most of what was being said—and none of what was being sung.

I was exhausted from the boat trip, and unfamiliar with the village layout, especially in the dark. I left the ceremony sometime after midnight and made my way back to my hut, unrolled my hammock and listened to the drumming and singing in the near distance. The dynamic between the two groups at the ceremony was fascinating. I did not fully understand what it was, but I knew at that moment I was in the right place. There was something going on between the Moravian Church hymn contingent and the traditional, African-type ritual drummers and dancers. This suggested to me some very real tension between Christian thought and practice, and Pamakan concepts that were clearly based on traditional African belief systems. I had my first lead for the subject of a research project.

CHAPTER ELEVEN

BaMAMBO

During my first couple of weeks in Langatabiki, I worked out more regular trading arrangements with neighbors for meals. Water from the river was close by, and I began to settle in, remembering to use the river as bathroom downstream from where you and others wash and get drinking water.

Nights were daunting at first. It was pitch dark, B'Aleke's thatch hut had a distinctive smell, there were sounds of human interactions from the neighboring huts, and I struggled to find a good sleep position in the hammock. One night I was startled awake, frozen in fear by the eeriest sound I had ever heard. It was coming from the forest just across the river. As a farm kid, I was familiar with night sounds of coyotes, owls, and such; and I knew scary noises in the dark from Vietnam. This was other worldly, but with an animal sense to it. It sounded like a blizzard wind in the middle of trees in one specific part of the forest. But there was no wind; I was terrified! My panic eased when the sound did not come any closer, and faded further into the forest after a few chilling minutes. First thing in the morning I asked a neighbor what that was in the bush last night, trying not to sound completely stupid and naïve. "Oh, it was a bunch of howler monkeys that got stirred by something—get used to it."

Once I had my food, lodging, and night terrors under control, I had to get to work as a field cultural anthropologist. First order was to gain proficiency in the language. Their dialect was very close to that of Ndjuka, so I had a start. I had no Petrus with our beer joint language lab here, so I decided to learn Pamakan as if I were growing up in it. There was still a great deal of interest in just who I was and what I was doing, so I always had an entourage, mainly children, shadowing me. I started with the youngest. Kneeling or sitting on a low stool, I would hold my nose and ask with word and expression, "What is this?" Then ear, mouth, hand, and so on.

The kids delighted in this exercise, and soon I got fairly good with Pamakan idioms relating to body parts, dogs, chickens, trees—anything I could touch or point to. For intangibles, such as sunrise/sunset and fast/slow, hot/cold, I moved on to the pre-teens. Soon I had worked up to teenagers and basic concepts like love, fear, anger. The ritual greetings were essentially the same as the Ndjuka formalities I learned in Ajuma Kondey; however, I picked up important Pamakan nuances of the protocols of greetings among the villagers. A missed or improper greeting could easily be taken as a slight, or even an insult.

I followed the best I could as men and women went through the daily rituals. I could not just stand there silent, I also had to express my greeting with people met on the paths or by their house.

The day would begin with "*O wekie oh*," announced to any adult met for the first time in the morning of the day.

The person greeted would stop and respond with, "*O wekie Eh.*"

Person A would then ask, "*O doe ing?*"

Person B would respond, "*O doe ing eh, o sefi doe ing?*"

Person A: "*Oh doe-in baa.*"

This formality would take at least a half minute, then be followed with unstructured chit chat about where the person was going, how people were feeling, and so on. Weather was hardly a topic of conversation as it was monotonously consistent. There were no Pamakan words for hurricanes or tornadoes—they did not happen here. Only when this meaningless conversation was completed could you get on with what you were doing or where you were going. This scene played out a dozen or more times each morning with essentially the same people every day. There was a rhythm and ritual to it with the persons involved stopping what they were doing, and looking past each other while speaking. Eye contact was not proper, even offensive where a young person greeted an elder. The young greeter looked at the ground in the presence of an elder.

During the day and early evening hours, a similar greeting ritual would be performed when meeting someone for the first time, or even if you had gone through the morning greeting ritual earlier with the same person!

Person A: "*Oh mitie oh.*" (Hello)

Person B: "*Oh mitie eh, y dai?*" (Hello, how are you?)

Person A: "*Mi dai ba Baala/Ti/Da/Sissa/Tia/Ma' Y sefi dai?*" (I'm good, how are you Brother/Uncle/Father/Sister/Aunt/Mother?)

Person B: "*Mi dai mo?*"(I'm fine)

At this point the formalism gives way to expressing actually how you *are* doing or where you are going. This day greeting would be followed again with obligatory chit chat while standing still; young people talking with elders remain looking at the ground.

One morning a group of women inquired as to why I do not have a bush name. The "Mister John" thing was not working for anyone.

A moment later the choice was made for me: "*Mambo. Mambo! ou e gi yu a ning. Yu na Mambo,*" (Mambo! We give you that name. You are Mambo!)

Everyone smiled and repeated the name. I was not sure what to say in return. Was this an honorific gift of welcome and acceptance, or were they putting me on? What does "Mambo" mean, anyway? Despite my slight hesitation, I took it as a genuine gesture, and, what the hell, "Mambo" sounded kind of cool. I thanked them with the sincerest remarks of gratitude I could come up with, mixing English with my rudimentary Pamaka.

That afternoon I greeted another group of women I passed on the way to the river. "*O mitie o*," I call out, and am greeted in return, "*O mitie ey, Baala*." Free Settlement people address one another with a general kin designation. These kinship address terms are appropriate to the generation and sex of the addressees: young men and women through their twenties are referred to by all as *baala* ("brother") and *sisa* ("sister"); those in their thirties and forties are *tiu* or *ti* ("uncle") and *tia* ("aunt"); and elders are *da* ("father") and *ma* ("mother"). This was the first time I was referred to as *Baala* (Brother). Cool! I was from that moment on "*BaMambo*"—Brother Mambo.

The next day I had a chance to speak with Gaaman Forster. I was eager to tell him that I was given the name Mambo. He raised his eyebrows, cocked his head, and smiled broadly; the ever-present group of people who gathered around such conversations tittered. I learned later that here in the river area where most canoes are outfitted with outboard motors, the term "mambo" refers to canting the motor forward to shoot a water tail high in the air behind your boat—basically acting badass on the water.

CHAPTER TWELVE

KUTUKUTU

I was in an emotional shock after Katie showed up just to tell me our marriage was over and then leave. Katie and I met when she joined the research branch of the university where I was working during my last semester. She was on an internship from Antioch College—tall, lithesome, edgy, clever, and adventurous. In bearing, posture, and persona, she was so very different from the Delta Gamma girls I knew; and had a head start on the 60s fun-and-flowers scene. We fell in love instantly, and married in 1966 just after graduation and a wild courtship of only a few weeks. Our marriage was an exuberant, rolling adventure. We were sure we were the inspiration for the Beatles White Album cut, "Why Don't We Do it in the Road," (someone *was* watching us!).

Here in the village now, it was terrifying to be so thoroughly alone in such a strange and isolated spot of the world without my love and best friend, and with no prospect of support or companionship. What sustained me was the imperative to learn about the dynamic behind the hymn singers and the drummers from the first night's funeral ceremony. To get to that point, I knew I first had to learn the language well beyond basics to understand the history and cultural norms of the Pamaka.

KutuKutu, the kid who brought me my first meal, became invaluable to me as an information resource and translator—and soon a young friend. KutuKutu was very bright and had a wonderfully cheerful disposition. He explained that he was so adorable as an infant his mother named him Kutu twice. He and I began to explore the corners of Pamaka, and with his help I got more confident with the language, and became acquainted with all the residents of Langatabiki.

After Katie left, KutuKutu became a regular presence in my hut, and good source of local knowledge. He was fourteen, and in the last session of the sixth grade at the Moravian Church school, the final level of schooling available in the village. One day he told me proudly that he had completed his exams and was technically graduated. So, what are you going to do now? I asked him. He had no plan, and few options. Without much thought, I suggested that he work with me. I would pay him 10 guilders a week (about $5), plus food and English lessons. KutuKutu was excited, but he and I visited with his mother and father to confirm their permission with the arrangement.

His father, TiBaya, was a *basia*, a lineage leader and an accomplished hunter, wood carver and orator at the formal meetings (*kuutu*). Both parents were happy that KutuKutu would be working with me, and TiBaya sat him down and launched into a stern, HR orientation: never be late, always do what you say you are going to do, and be very careful of others who may be driven by jealousy.

KutuKutu started the next morning, showing up at 6:30, an hour early. I cooked up a pot of coffee to get us started. We were going to spend the day going over language related to kinship, and where different Pamakan lineage groups lived along the river islands south of Langatabiki. I offered KutuKutu a cup of strong black coffee, which he eagerly accepted and feigned to like. As we were enjoying our morning coffee, a group of his former classmates came by the hut on their way to school to see how KutuKutu was doing in his first job. One asked KutuKutu if he was going to start smoking now that he was out of school and all grown up. I joked that he was drinking coffee, and that was a start. No one got my coffee reference, so I explained that in America, the old people say that kids do not drink coffee since it stunts their growth. KutuKutu, self-consciously short, lurched and spewed the coffee out of his mouth. He dumped out his cup and sat stricken, giving his friends a great laugh. I quickly added that I didn't think that the story was true, and that it was just a ruse to discourage young children from drinking coffee, for whatever reason. Not convinced and taking no chances, KutuKutu swore an oath never to drink coffee again.

Once I began to settle into village life, I was able to arrange for my mail to be sent to the District Commissioner's office in Albina, and the Chinese store owner privately agreed to cash my checks if I spent most of the money at his place. Through this arrangement, I bought KutuKutu a pair of shoes, and he wore them proudly every day.

KutuKutu's work with me set him apart from mates his age, and he was quick to suspect problems. After a few months, he came to my hut particularly early one morning and in a high state of anxiety asked if I had moved his shoes. I had not touched his shoes, and asked what the problem was. He said he placed his shoes outside the door of his parent's hut where he stayed last night. This morning, his shoes were not where he had left them, but in front of my door. I had no idea of how his shoes would have transported from one hut to another, but KutuKutu was distraught. He threw the new shoes in the river fearing that there was some malevolent spirit involved. I knew better than to make some comment about cooties.

CHAPTER THIRTEEN

THE MAP

Langatabiki is a river island surrounded by dense forest. I had lost track of north/south-east/west spatial orientation points, so I started asking anyone who would listen questions about where we were in relation to, well, everything. It became apparent quickly that their territorial orientation was explicitly longitudinal, along the river. There was no use for north-south, east-west cardinal references. The Pamakans viewed their territory as the length of river between the two falls, *Tapu Dang* and *Boli Mofu*. There were no established limits regarding the lateral (east-west) extent of the land area. Virtually all Pamakans live at the river's edge, and only rarely did anyone travel beyond a few miles overland or spend a night in the forest. Only men on special hunting trips or prospecting expeditions would ever sleep in forest camps away from the river. Overnight camps on long river trips are made along the riverbank wherever possible. Essentially, the lateral territorial limits are fixed by the distance one can walk to and from swidden fields for a day's work.

One of the standard research tools of ethnography is a map of how kinship and marriage relates to the physical layout of a village. I started this social-spatial project by walking around with a notebook sketching the huts in the neighborhoods of Langatabiki. KutuKutu was to supply the names of residents I did not know yet, and add details about their lineage affiliation. I would, over time, determine who lived where throughout the village, and analyze any familial rules at play regarding where people lived. KutuKutu came back one day very upset. He had been confronted by an older man who told him he heard I was collecting names and writing them down. KutuKutu explained that the man forbade him and me from writing down his name. If I wanted to know his name, I could hold it in my head like everybody else. I told KutuKutu that it was not a problem; I could just use the guy's initials.

The following day, KutuKutu was still alarmed by the name-writing matter. He said more people are telling him not to write their names for me. I started interrogating KutuKutu about this problem of writing names. He insisted he did not know, but I kept on him, and he finally admitted that people were afraid that I will write their names down on a book, return to America, and prepare witchcraft against them.

Later that day, I was inside my house and heard people talking excitedly just outside my door. This was more than the usual group of kids that followed me constantly, these were grownups. KutuKutu ran to get his father as I stepped out to see what was going on. The group of about twelve people was agitated and shouting angrily at me. I was dumbfounded, and they were talking so fast and excitedly that I could not understand what their issue was. Thankfully, KutuKutu returned in a short minute with his father, TiBaya, who stepped up and shielded me from the angry crowd, and walk-pushed me backwards into the house.

TiBaya was forceful with me, but genuinely wanted to calm the situation. "The pictures!" he insisted in Pamakan. I struggled to understand, so he imitated me drawing pictures of houses on my notepad. Ah, it was my diagram or map of the neighborhood and the writing of names at issue. But he kept saying something about airplanes and indicating the sky. I showed him the neighborhood map I had completed with the layout of the houses. He studied it intently for several minutes, while the crowd maintained a noisy, ill-spirited vigil.

Suddenly TiBaya smacked my map with the back of his hand and turned quickly and took the notepad back outside to the crowd still outside my hut. He shouted for everyone to calm down and be quiet. When they settled down, he spoke waving my map over his head. He then invited each to examine my map closely, which most did. With the inspection of the map, and much discussion, the crowd's fervor abated, and people started walking away. TiBaya came back into the house and explained the situation to me in repeated and simple terms so I got it right.

In slow Pamakan, "They think you are preparing for the village to be bombed," he explained. My eyes could not have opened wider in astonishment.

"Bombed?" I asked aloud, in English.

"Yes, but you put your *own* house on the map. I showed them," he explained, pointing to the little hut symbol where we stood. "Nobody bombs his own house!" he explained, like a lawyer telling his client how he won him a major reprieve.

I was speechless, and at a loss as to how to express gratitude. He ripped the map pages out of my notebook which I had worked on for about a week, went back outside and with some fanfare, tore them into little pieces which he gave to KutuKutu to throw into the river. I came out of the hut while TiBaya addressed all still gathered, "Let this be the end of this—no more pictures, and no more talk of witchcraft or bombs." I agreed publicly, but was annoyed at the setback in my research plan, and deeply troubled that my new neighbors suspected me of plotting to kill them all with an air raid.

The neighborhood got back to normal after a couple of days, and I got a better understanding of the map matter. The government had recently started evening broadcasts on an AM frequency a one-hour program in the Ndjuka language. The program featured scratchy messages between people in the interior and those along the coast. The few people in Langatabiki with transistor radios would listen every evening, and pass along any messages for Pamakans.

The radio program announcer would read about five minutes of world news that he pulled from a wire service. The news at that time was filled with accounts of American B-52's and tonnage statistics of bombing raids over Vietnam. It occurred to me that the district commissioner's boatmen may have told people here that in Albina they all knew that I was American CIA spy, just pretending to be an anthropologist. Someone in Langatabiki perhaps connected the dots of an American showing up and mapping houses in the village: "*We're next!*" I would have been thrown to the Piranhas, except that TiBaya, my lawyer, had convinced them that no one would put his own house on a bomb map.

On my very first day in Suriname, I was mistaken for a holy man by the old Hindu at the restaurant. Here they saw me as a war criminal plotting to bomb their village. The difference seemed to be in my sense of purposefulness. I appeared "holy" when I did not know quite where I was, and had no clue about where I was going, or what to do when and if I got there. I was seen as highly suspect and dangerous when I stepped into the mind-set of a field anthropologist, making maps and taking names. It was clear that I needed to drop all pretentions and just learn to be a Pamakan like a child would.

I gave up on the idea of walking around with a clipboard, and resorted to writing notes in the evenings in the hut. KutuKutu and I would spend time sitting with older people listening to their stories, and gently posing questions about family history: who is related to whom, and where they live. We would work with men clearing fields and house-building projects, and just sit and listen to learn their stories. For me it was a good way to build an understanding of how they think about life (past, present, and future), hunting, fishing, sickness, and death. Soon I would be able to start piecing together the mystery of the dueling factions of hymns and drums at the wake of the Gaaman's sister.

CHAPTER FOURTEEN

CHURCH

I had been on the island for a couple of weeks when one day I caught a ride with a couple of guys from Langatabiki who were taking a cargo canoe for a day run to an upriver camp. I had seen these men in the village, but did not know them; but sure, I was welcome along for the ride. I sat near the motorman who asked me straight away in Pamakan, "Do you go to church?"

"Nah," I said, thinking nothing of it.

He responded optimistically, "Oh, you pray to God at home then?" When I shrugged that question off with, "No," he looked shocked, and gave me a *what-kind-of-person-are-you* look. I explained calmly that in America, many people simply do not go to church, and probably don't pray.

The motorman was nonplussed and protested loudly enough to include the other boatman in the bow, "But, if you don't pray to God, you must pray to the devil!" To make sure the other boatman understood the dilemma unfolding before him, the motorman repeated loudly, "He doesn't pray to God, so he must pray to the devil!"

The forward boatman looked at both of us. *Whaaat?*, he asked with his expression. I lightened the mood by explaining to them that I learned to pray in the Ndjuka fashion in Ajuma Kondey. They thought that was funny and left the discussion at that.

When we arrived back at Langatabiki later that afternoon, the motorman came over to my hut after he had secured the boat. There was the usual group of neighbors hanging around, and the motorman announced gratuitously that BaMambo doesn't pray to God, so therefore he must pray to the devil. Most people laughed, some didn't. One of the Gaaman's sons, Dirk, in his early twenties, came over to me and asked with the sincerity of the converted if I went to church. "No, I do not go to church!" I said, getting a little tired of the subject. Dirk persisted with a follow up, "Have you been baptized?"

"Maybe as a child I was baptized, but I really don't remember," I told him. Dirk then recited a line from the Moravian hymnal that he had learned at the church school, to the effect that he who is not baptized will not know the kingdom of heaven. He added that he was sad for me if I had not been baptized. I told him not to worry, that I will learn and participate with Pamakans in prayer, in both obia and church contexts. It was thus made clear to me that the Moravian mission was a large influence on Pamakans, at least some of them. This provided a logical starting point to understand the hymns versus drums dispute at the wake. I decided to go to church.

I learned that around 1915, a Moravian pastor moved to Langatabiki and began baptizing Pamakans. By this time also, a Roman Catholic missionary priest was seeking converts in the area, and bitter disputes continually marked the relationship between the two competing Christian missions. The Roman Catholic mission station was established up-river several years later; first at the village of Badatabiki, then at its present location near Nason. The priests who established and later maintained the mission have all been Dutch except for a period in the 1940s. The Protestant and Catholic missions have kept a spirit of competition, each striving to out-provide the other with school and health services. The Catholic mission built a professionally staffed clinic and a six-grade boarding school; an airstrip was under construction in 1972.

The two churches approached their evangelical missions differently, however. One of the Roman Catholic priests with long service among the Pamakans explained his church's orientation toward mission work as one which sought to convert Pamakans within a context of respect and tolerance for their traditional culture. He said the role of the priest was to try to teach basic Christian doctrine. He added that if a Pamakan accepts the concepts of one supreme god as maker of heaven and earth, and that Jesus Christ is man's mentor on earth for eternal life, he or she would be baptized and considered a Catholic.

The priest explained that the mission appreciated the importance of the traditional beliefs and culture to the Pamakans, and that it would take many generations for Christian principles to become manifest in most aspects of the culture. Indeed, some of the most respected obia specialists and spirit mediums I met described themselves as Roman Catholic, *Lomsu*.

The Protestant Moravians' view of their mission and Pamakan cultural traditions was markedly different. The more comprehensive and urgent messianic mission of the Moravians impacted the lifestyles of the downriver church people more so than that of the upriver Catholics. A Moravian pastor who spent several years in residence in Langatabiki described Pamakans, and traditional free-settlement Africans in general, as living in fear of evil spirits. For salvation, he explained, they must reject all pagan customs and live a Christian life.

The plight of TiBaila illustrated for me how the Moravian mindset differed from the traditional in the source and nature of illness. TiBaila had been attending lessons for Moravian confirmation, but began missing the sessions. Although he maintained church attendance occasionally, he gave up his ambition to become confirmed as a member. One day he fell seriously ill with painful and difficult urination. His condition grew worse, and he went to Albina for treatment. The man's family saw the illness as an ancestor-led reckoning for his having prepared a bush medicine to abort a young woman from the neighboring village of Pikien Tabiki. The Moravian church nurse said that he had kidney stones and a venereal infection. Gaaman Forster said the reason for his sickness was God's retribution for his discontinuation of confirmation lessons, and for wearing dirty clothes to church on Good Friday.

The Moravian church was the most imposing structure in Langatabiki—a large, standard frame-and-tin-roof affair, complete with standalone steeple and cross. Inside, there were rows of benches that would accommodate about 100 people. The mission included a resident pastor from the black population in the city. The pastor served as preacher and schoolteacher. Later pastors brought their wives and children to serve as a model Christian family.

The Moravians provided an early link with coastal "outside" communities for Pamakans. As a Moravian communicant, one could travel to coastal towns and have a place to stay on church grounds. The mission at Langatabiki expanded a few months after I arrived to include health services. A Dutch nurse would stay in a room at the clinic for periods to serve as the "doctor."

The mission continued to provide the major regular contact with the city through occasional boat service and a small airplane that would fly in periodically, using the soccer field as a runway. The school had six grades, where boys like KutuKutu learned rudimentary arithmetic, reading, writing, Bible stories, and church songs. Girls rarely attended, only staying one or two years before returning home to help with child rearing, household work, and preparing for motherhood in their mid-teens. The instruction was in the official language of Suriname: Dutch.

Pamakans who become communicants of the Moravian mission must renounce traditional sacred institutions. The Moravian church people are encouraged to go to the clinic for childbirth under sterile conditions and the nurse's supervision. In the clinic environment, it is, of course, cumbersome and impractical for people to observe the eight-day seclusion of mother and infant. The significance of the introduction and naming ritual, *pu-a-doo*, is diminished, with baptism used as a substitute ceremony.

Soon after a child is born, the parents are required to arrange for its baptism into the church. This requires selecting an appropriate baptism name (i.e., European or Biblical first name and family surname) and a godparent.

In one such session I attended, the preacher explained that the baptismal washing marked the child as a Christian who, as such, must continue the Christian life through school attendance and confirmation into the church. The mothers were told that no obia medicines would be able to take effect on their children's bodies after the baptism, so they must be raised completely within the Christian attitude.

Regular Sunday church attendance was expected of communicants. Those who missed church consistently were sought out and encouraged to attend. I watched one man admonish a woman who had missed a few services. He loudly told her that she had better start coming to church because the earth was going to come to an end some day without warning.

Each Sunday morning was announced by the church bell at 6 a.m. At this first bell, everyone was expected to rise, wash, and straighten out their house and grounds. The second bell was at 8 o'clock, which signaled everyone to change into Sunday clothes, meaning European styled pants, collared shirt and shoes for men and boys, dresses for women. Only on the annual Emancipation service were people allowed to wear traditional dress of loincloth *kamisas* for men and pangi skirts for women. As the 9 o'clock bell sounded, the Sunday service began promptly with a hymn. There were no musical instruments, so all singing was a capello. Strict composure was observed in church; fidgeting children were sternly scolded by adults, or the preacher. The congregation was seated in order according to age, sex, and church standing. The Gaaman sat directly to the right of the pastor on the elevated pulpit facing the congregation.

The congregation itself was separated into seating sections of adult male communicants, adult males, schoolboys, schoolgirls, adult women, and adult women communicants. The hour-long service followed the published liturgy and included several hymns, a collection plate, and a sermon. The language used in church services was a formalized style of the Suriname lingua franca. This specialized form of church creole was phonologically distinct from the Pamaka language and was only used in the Moravian church context.

One of the most consistent topics of the Sunday sermons was the invalidation of traditional concepts of ancestors and deities, which the preacher called "ghosts." One Moravian preacher told me his sermons seek to instill a fear of God as more powerful than the fear of evil spirits. At one service the preacher highlighted his sermon with the hypothetical: "Ancestors are simply dead people; if they were so smart and powerful, why are they dead?"

The sermons regularly emphasized the duties of citizenship and the rightful authority of government officials. Each Sunday liturgy outlined the structure of governmental authority with the order of blessing and the relationship of God, government, and citizen:

> *(Pastor) Bless the kings and elders of all lands, look after them well. Bless the elders of our country too, our dear King/Queen. Bless our paramount chief and all the elders of the council, guide all of their work, make them do Your will, and keep them from all evil, so we can live in peace and guide our lives under them, and we can walk in your path without trouble.*

July first was celebrated by the church as Emancipation Day. This was the one event of the year in which people were permitted to wear traditional clothing to church. The Emancipation Day service had no litany, but involved the recollection of stories of slavery by an elder, followed by a recitation by the preacher of the important role of the Moravian church in bringing about the emancipation of slaves.

The relative prosperity of the downstream capital village, Langatabiki, was obviously a result of its position as seat of the paramount chief and the Moravian mission. The national government and the Moravian church were the principal sources of wage labor in the area; both sponsored major construction projects and maintained small staffs in the territory. The government and the Moravian church both regarded the Gaaman as the sole agent of the Pamaka people, and scrupulously conducted their local affairs through him. One result of this arrangement was that nearly all jobs were held through the favor of the chief. The Gaaman directly appointed most of the coveted civil service positions in the area (i.e., village electrician, official boatman, scribe, etc.) and advised the Moravian mission in its hiring practices. Occasional outside sources of employment, such as ore or balata exploitation companies, tended to seek the favor of the Gaaman by referring calls for workers through him. When I learned how the Gaaman served as a union boss, I understood why KutuKutu's father presented him with a juggo and three bottles of soft drink to mark my hiring of KutuKutu. This patronage power of the Gaaman assured a loyalty to him, and acceptance of the church by beneficiaries, current and future. It was clear that the Moravian mission controlled entry to the market economy, and the price was renunciation of traditional beliefs and practices. It was a bargain that only a few Pamakans accepted at the time.

CHAPTER FIFTEEN

THE INTERVIEW

Around forty to fifty people tended to show up at the Sunday church services, but there seemed to be only a few dozen Pamakans who were committed congregationalists. The minister's sermons were incessant lectures about the hoax of ancestors and other "ghosts." The sermons consistently belittled the notions of spirits other than the Christian Trinity. The fact that the minister harped so much on the necessity to turn away from traditional concepts and beliefs suggested there were significant aspects of Pamaka culture that the church was still struggling to quash. The first thing I had heard about Suriname in the Georgetown boarding house from Miss Mae was the ominous warning: they do obia there, and

Surinamese obia was far more dangerous and secretive than the voodoo of Haiti.

Shortly after I arrived in Langatabiki, and after the bomb scare, I got directly acquainted with obia as spirit and process. I was called to a large thatch hut in the downriver part of Langatabiki. This was a little unusual, since I was not familiar with the eight or ten people sitting closely on low stools. KutuKutu was nowhere around. The tiny beams of sunlight through the thatch provided the only light inside.

Everyone there knew who I was, and that I was trying to learn about life in Pamaka. The woman host welcomed me and explained that an obia was coming and motioned to a young woman sitting quietly on a stool slightly apart from the others. The host asked me if I would stay and observe. It was a big deal for me to be included; I did not bring a stool so had to stand, but melted into a corner to get as out of the way as best I could manage.

The ceremony was being led by an older woman with several pangi cotton cloths draped over her bony shoulders and arms, and a red cloth tied around her head hiding most of the thick grey braids woven tightly to her head. She began to chant softly and sing; the others joined in response mode to the song. The leader placed one of the brightly colored pangi cloths over the young woman's head like a shawl. With more chanting and a period of highly stylized, one-way conversation between the leader and a presence I could not see, the young woman lurched out of the stool and began writhing on the floor, knocking off her cloth head covering. The spirit had entered her body. She contorted unnaturally with serpent-like movement, and began to speak in an unnatural voice in, what seemed to me, no language at all. The leader was kneeling on the ground close to the young woman listening to the odd sounds she was making.

The old woman called for an egg; the spirit is hungry she said. Someone handed her a chicken egg and the old woman held it with two fingers, just off the ground in front of the possessed young woman's mouth. I watched in amazement as the young woman lunged for the egg, took it in her mouth, and swallowed the thing whole! It did not seem like she chewed it at all.

The young woman, now serpent, pulled herself up from the ground holding onto the leader. Still making the strange, non-verbal sounds, she started looking about the room. The leader translated, "There is a different presence here." The young woman stood and looked straight at me. There was no focus, no eye contact, but everyone in the room was looking at me intently. The woman's serpent eyes seemed to dwell on the maroon-colored beads I had begun wearing since my first week with D'Aladi in Adjuma Kondey.

"Oh boy, now what?" I thought, and began to worry. The young woman as snake, or *vice versa*, looked me over with un-seeing eyes; her body swayed slightly for what seemed an inordinately long time. When she/it finally began to speak, it was a deep, manly voice uttering word-like sounds that broke through the susurration. Her words made no sense to me, and I doubted that anyone else in the room could understand the words. The old woman handler translated: "The spirit found the different presence (long pause) and it is not bad." The crowd reacted with nods and quiet discussions; most seemed pleased. I exhaled in relief. After a few more moments the young woman's body shuddered violently; the old woman helped her back to the stool where she sat quietly, looking exhausted. The snake spirit had left her.

The room returned to normal, with people talking with each other while some comforted the young woman still slumped on a stool. I politely excused myself and walked outside.

"Holy Shit! Was I just vetted by a snake?" I asked myself. I could use a cold juggo about now, I thought as I walked back to my place. Meanwhile, word went around the village quickly that BaMambo had been checked out and cleared by a powerful obia.

After this session and gaining the spirit serpent's blessing, people (that is, adults) seemed more comfortable with me around their neighborhoods. Some began to see me as a resource. In one instance, I was sought out as the only person who could read the English instructions on the jar of lye a young woman had bought in Albina. She and her friends had gotten burned, literally, trying to straighten her hair rubbing the lye paste on her head. It was hard for me to explain the application process (and the necessity for rubber gloves), so she finally asked me to just do it for her. I did a decent job but made it clear that I did not want to do any more lye applications. Thankfully, the processed hair look never caught on in Langatabiki.

Importantly, I was better able to use the more relaxed and welcoming sit-down sessions to delve into the basic anthropologist questions of how they define themselves, beyond their name. What does it mean to be a Pamaka person? The history and experiences of slavery were central to their sense of self. Being the only white person many of the Pamakans had ever sat and spoken with, I was sensitive to tread slowly with this topic. KutuKutu sitting next to me gave people an important level of comfort. The two of us ultimately learned much.

TiBaya, KutuKutu's father, became my initial go-to source for answers and wisdom. Ever since he won my acquittal for the bomb map, he was a steadfast friend who helped me find my way through Pamaka history and thought. KutuKutu's mother and father were both well respected in Langatabiki, and KutuKutu was an impressive young man who had spent the past six years in the Moravian missionary school. There was a sense among elders that KutuKutu needed to be educated on *Pamakan* history and tradition to balance the church indoctrination.

Teaming with KutuKutu became a winning solution for access to people and information. The two of us spent days and evenings observing and participating in tasks, from mundane chores to high ritual, and sitting on little, short stools with people and asking questions. For me, this process of learning was consistent with how I learned language basics from children, and then worked up to concepts in sessions with teens and older people.

I accelerated the way a young Pamakan learns to become an adult; I wanted to get up to speed with KutuKutu. At this point, a few months in, I had begun to think of myself as a functional teenager in my understanding of the language and basic assumptions and requirements of daily life. I had been attending Sunday church services, and KutuKutu had gone through the church elementary school. The church's dismissive view of pagan practices was clear. What we both needed was an overview of the deeper concepts which oriented the *traditional* Pamakan understanding of their origin, their place on the planet, how they explain disease and death, and mark other major life events.

CHAPTER SIXTEEN

GOD

KutuKutu started spending more time with me and soon brought his hammock over to B'Aleke's hut. We would cook meals together in my kitchen which consisted of a camping stove and some borrowed plates and utensils. There was basically one cooked meal at midday, coffee or tea with bread in the mornings, and a light fare of leftovers—corn on the cob roasted in the fire pits (delicious!) and such—for supper. During the day, there were generally ample sources of bananas, mangoes, and palm nuts. The main meal was invariably either a mound of rice or a bowl of *kwaka*, cassava milled and roasted to a consistency of grape-nut cereal. The rice or kwaka would usually be topped with a piece of fish, chicken, or wild game stewed with any onions or sweet cassava available. The stew would provide ample gravy sauce from the pot that would stretch the servings. Special treats included fried plantains, boiled sweet cassava, and a sort of sponge cake called *pom*. It was considered a delicacy, but I found it too sweet for more than a bite or two. KutuKutu once proudly showed me how to cook *bakka booyon,* another bush delicacy that tasted like flat, heavy, tasteless pancakes.

I bartered for and bought rice and kwaka, and we were generally able to catch a fish or get a piece of chicken or a large fish from neighbors. On good days when someone shot a peccary or other animal, we could get a good portion for a couple of meals. Potatoes and lettuce became memories. KutuKutu showed me how to find grubs in palm nuts that had fallen out of the trees. The grubs are good as fish bait, and the palm nuts themselves were great snacks.

Some of my most rewarding moments came while just sitting with village chief D'Ayambe when he and a couple of old guys would get together in the afternoons. They would sit on low stools to talk at length about village affairs. At the beginning of a session, D'Ayambe would pull out a small glass jar, like a blue Vicks Vapor Rub container. He would carefully massage the contents with his thumb, then pour about a teaspoon sized dollop of black juice onto the palm of his other hand. With a quick inspection of the juice, the old man would lean forward and put the juiced palm up to his nostrils, and snort the juice, working his palm side to side to cover both nostrils, and get all the juice up his nose. A rag was always handy to wipe hands and face. The guy with the jar would pass it to the next, and sit silently for a minute, blinking his eyes that would turn completely red. Then the next old man would start the process anew of working the mixture with his thumb.

KutuKutu dismissed this practice as an old man's game. I could not resist taking a shot, so at the next session I asked D'Ayambe about the Vicks jar. Like a sorcerer with an apprentice, he walked me through preparing the potion. It starts with Dutch pipe tobacco, *"Blakka T'Tei"* they called it (literally, black rope.) They buy the tobacco in Chinese shops in town. It is packaged in a foil-type pouch labeled as pipe tobacco, but I never saw anyone smoking a pipe. D'Ayambe then let me in on his secret ingredient: ash from a particular hardwood. He picked through the fire in front of his house that never went out. Finding the right log, he scraped off a pile of ashes, which he ground to a fine powder. A healthy, three-finger pick from the tobacco pouch goes into the Vicks jar first, then add the ash powder, working it with fingers. Finally add just enough water to moisten the glob so that when you press with your thumb you can squeeze out the tobacco-ash nectar that looks like watery molasses. This is the premier cru; you can add water to keep the juice coming for several hits.

Of course, I had to try it. The old chief approved my technique, which I had down from studying him and his buddies. With a nice pour from the jar, I examined my palm cradling the tobacco sauce that looked like reduced-prune-juice. Any pieces of tobacco or wood ash would have to be removed. I had never snuffed anything up my nose before, but how hard could it be? I buried my nose in my palm and snorted the juice in earnest shifting my palm from the left to the right nostril.

The rush was immediate! My body became a bag of liquid nicotine— I was overwhelmed with the instant taste of nicotine in my mouth and tongue; my skin tingled; my eyes were burning and probably red. It seemed like my hair was trying to shoot out of my head. I had a flashback of experimenting with smoking cigarettes in high school; this was like having smoked a pack of Luckies all at once.

It took a minute or two before I could even talk. With all the faked composure I could muster, I handed D'Ayambe his Vicks jar, and thanked him. When he and his snuff buddies got together a few days later I was offered a hit on the Vicks jar. I was honored to be included, but I passed.

Listening sessions like these were critical for KutuKutu and me to learn pre-Moravian Pamakan concepts. After the heaven-and-hell sermons of the missionary, I wanted to learn what they thought about god. Traditional Pamakan thought did not dwell on a monotheistic god as creator of things. There was no sense of what god would look like, or a locus such as a heaven or hell where a god or a devil could be found. Indeed, their sense of god was that it is remote and really doesn't *do* anything. People referred regularly to god in daily life through expressions such as "god willing." "God is there," is a common expression of reassurance in moments of uncertainty. But their concept of god was just that—an ethereal and detached notion.

The Pamakan concept of god is not one of a heavenly presence and the creator of all things; rather, god represents the *process* of nature and life. To live the god life is to live in harmony with others while on earth. Since there is no word for or concept of "accident," normalcy and good things happen in life through the god-sense of order and process. Bad things happen when there is disorder in the god realm, invariably caused by bad actions of the living.

When misfortune strikes, that means one is in discord with the god process. Someone with a problem must make amends with the spiritual order of the god process, or the problem will get worse. Making amends begins by determining what is the nature of the discord in the god sense— what is wrong here?

To the Pamakan, slavery was the hell from which they had emerged in the remembered past. Their involuntary removal from Africa (*Nenge Kondey*) was *slafu*, which is regularly translated as "slavery." Linguistically, the term was important in conveying the sense of the recollection: "slafu" is phonemically close to, and in most cases interchangeable with, "*stafu*" (punishment). Slavery was very much considered as punishment, a fall from the African grace. The reasons of the fall were unclear, but there was no question that it was at the hands of white people. The most significant and humiliating feature in Pamaka accounts of slavery was that white men caught them in their own homeland.

Pamaka elders such as D'Ayambe, TiYan, and others, I think, were encouraged by the easy rapport between KutuKutu and me. After a few sessions of storytelling, they felt comfortable talking with me about white people. It was an awkward subject, but these men acknowledged ruefully that white people used force, ruse, and the corruption of other Africans to capture them and bring them to Suriname. This was seen as a primal disgrace and remains a factor in considerations of relationships with Europeans. An almost standard prefatory comment on discussions of white-Black relations remembers, "They caught us, they won us with smarts, we are the low ones."

Once, during a several-day traditional burial ceremony in the forest, a man confided a frustration not previously discussed with me: "White people have the earth. Every manufactured thing you can see, the tin cup here, the airplane, is made by white people. How do they do it? God must have given them the smarts."

The only myths I learned which related to god and first man were less about how man was created, than how Blacks and whites ended up separate and unequal. The stories, on the order of self-deprecating humor, are not that god favored whites over Blacks; instead, they believed that disequilibrium on earth is a result of the original Black man's own doing.

In the first-times, god had two sons, one black and one white. At one point, god decided to send his sons to earth to fend for themselves. He instructed them that on earth he would place two large chests which would be theirs for their sojourn as mortals. Each son was to take one chest, and as the black son was the elder, he had first choice. The first son examined the sealed chests and found they were identical on the outside, but one was much heavier than the other. Thinking that the heavier one contained more riches, he chose it, leaving the light one for his white brother.

They opened their chests and found that the heavy one contained nothing but iron work tools: picks, axes, shovels, and sledgehammers. The white son's light chest contained pencils, papers, and books. This then became the legacy of god's children on earth, the black man his heavy iron tools of work, the white man his books and papers of control.

Another such story was that in the first times, all people on earth were black:

One day god pointed out a pond of water and told them if they bathed in the pond, their skin would turn white. Many people started running to the pond, others scoffed saying it was a trick and watched and laughed as others jumped into the pond. After a while, the scoffers saw that the people who had bathed in the pond were actually turning white! By the time they realized it worked and rushed to the pond, they found that it was dry except for puddles of water remaining on the bottom. Unable to bathe, they stood on the wet mud at the bottom of the pond and patted the remaining water with their hands. That's why, the story concludes with confirmation: black people are tan only on the palms of their hands and the soles of their feet.

The traditional Pamaka world, I learned, has no god, satan, heaven, nor hell in the Christian sense. A Pamakan is forever, manifest as a living being or as a spiritual ancestor. Ancestors—and only the good ones—are family members who have transitioned to the spiritual realm and act as key intermediaries between god of good order and the living. This was the stuff that kept the Moravian missionary pastor up at night. He explained to me at one point that the belief in ancestors were pagan superstitions, ghosts that had to be suppressed.

CHAPTER SEVENTEEN

PAMAKAN

The next big question after *What is God?* was *What is a Pamakan?* This was a complex subject with no clear answer. My interpretation, after hours of listening and observing, was that the primary symbol defining a Pamakan is the *Sweli*. The Pamakan Sweli was the tangible link with their African origin, and represented the nucleus of their identity.

The Sweli was, and in 1970s remained, a small collection of objects believed to have been carried from Africa by those who survived the passage to Suriname and processing into the plantations. The sacred bundle became their central spiritual oracle that was carried into the forbidding forest to guide escapes. For Pamakans, their Sweli led them out of harm's way, initially from the Dutch colonial military, and ultimately from both the military and the other free settlement groups that agreed to seek out and return non-recognized freemen. The Sweli represented Pamakan unity and survival.

The Sweli was a carry oracle, in the sense that the bundle was secured to the center of a wooden pole or narrow board that was carried on the heads of two men, one at each end. The most respected elders posed questions to the oracle and it replied by "moving" its porters forward for affirmative or backward for negative. The Sweli could indicate direction and point out certain people and places by moving its porters in the proper direction. Also, it could reveal displeasure by sending its bearers in a circle.

The Sweli served as an oath of trust among strangers who fled the plantations together. The most significant property of the Sweli in the early days as fugitives is said to be its ability to forewarn the approach of outsiders to the Pamakan settlements. When the Sweli would alert Pamakans to an imminent approach of colonial military, they would abandon the settlement immediately. In addition, the Sweli would be consulted on directions of travel and various courses of action.

The Sweli remained as the Pamakans' constitution—the symbolic manifestation of who they are, and how they survive. When the group achieved officially-sanctioned status in settlements along the Marowijne, the Sweli oracle took on a new role. It continued to represent and maintain the identity and integrity of Pamakans, but the threats changed. The existential dangers facing Pamakans were no longer from the colonial military and their mercenaries. Rather, dissention and problems within Pamaka were more likely generated or imported by Pamakans themselves.

The Sweli began to be credited with some deaths and certain diseases. Anyone who attempted to bring into the Pamaka community any supernatural device for personal gain faced the possibility of sickness and even death brought on by the Sweli. For example, the *Baku* is a pernicious spirit that can be obtained in the city and used for personal gain among Pamaka kinsman. (When I learned about the Baku, I thought this is what Petrus suspected I was hiding from him: cooties as the white man's Baku.)

If a Pamakan engaged external powers, like a Baku, that would offend the Sweli and subject the offender to suffer an illness, or worse. The Sweli is thus regarded as the protector of the group against foreign forces, and the sentry against inimical influences in social relations.

Shortly before my arrival in Langatabiki, a young man had fallen ill and went into a psychological withdrawal. He remained in a small hut without speaking to anyone for over a year. Later he began to speak but with only occasional coherency. The man was about twenty-five, and said to be very unsuccessful with women prior to his illness. His case was put to divination which revealed that the Sweli caused his troubles because he had gone to the city and purchased an obia preparation which would empower him to attract women against their will. The Sweli revealed that this was not a good obia to be brought from the city to the Pamaka community.

The Sweli alerts to the presence of evil generated from within the group, as well as from without. One such problem is what they call "*mandi*," which I translated as holding a grudge in your heart against a kinsman. A sure sign of a mandi is when someone abandons something in disgust or anger. This is a fairly common reaction in dealing with theft or misuse of food and material possessions. In social relations, one can show mandi by withdrawing from a relationship out of vexation, or abandoning a claim or position out of disgust or frustration.

An example of mandi was explained to me as when a guy discovers that someone has stolen one of his two or three canoe paddles, and he throws away the remaining ones "for the thief," that guy subjects himself to the punishment of Sweli. Everyone will agree that anger is justified in such a case, but to abandon or destroy material property in the passion of anger against another is to call the attention of evil supernatural forces against the culprit. So, even though one is justified in his anger, to attract malevolent forces against another is tantamount to witchcraft, and is a transgression of the Sweli.

The ultimate mandi is suicide, a serious transgression of the Pamakan oath, or Sweli, which must be reconciled through significant libation to the oracle. While I was on the river, suicide threats and attempts were not unusual in the course of serious disputes. If one is successful in suicide in the heat of a dispute, there is the real possibility that the spirit of the deceased will be a long-term problem for the matrilineal family of the opponent. It makes sense in a perverse way that if all else fails, one can always get the last word in a quarrel and possibly cause the death of your adversary, and/or his or her kinsman, by killing yourself "for them."

One domestic dispute involved a woman leaving her man after a series of quarrels. She returned to her matrilineal village and announced that she was no longer to be considered his woman. Weeks later she entertained a suitor who was then confronted and severely beaten by the former husband and two of his brothers. The woman's family was outraged, and reprisals were threatened. It was the aggrieved woman who raised the stakes of the matter when she dramatically took a drink from a bottle of Clorox and announced loudly for all to hear that she would die for the former husband's indignities and that her spirit would trouble his family forever after. She recovered after induced vomiting by a Macaw tail feather inserted deep down her throat. Her former husband's matrilineage elders quickly convened a council meeting to seek reparation and resolution of the dispute.

CHAPTER EIGHTEEN

THE SWELI

The existence of competing factions among the Pamakans was clear to me from the hymns-versus-drums dust-up during the funerary rite I saw my first night in Langatabiki. The casual answer to the question, "What's going on here?" would be that one group, the hymn singers, were "church people," and the drummers were "catholic people." A church person was one under the sway of the Moravian ministry located in Langatabiki, while a catholic was basically a non-church person, or traditionalist. The more I learned about the differences between the church and catholic people, the fault lines became deeper and more complex. The church/non-church distinction followed an upriver versus downriver trajectory, and a long-standing political dispute over lineage rights to name the paramount chief.

Just as the elders of Langatabiki, the *Antoisi,* linked their authority to the Moravian mission, the expression of political opposition emerged in a religious idiom. Elders of upriver villages, the *Asaiti* lineage, articulated their legitimacy through an association with the Roman Catholic Church and a reaffirmation of traditional cultural practices.

Before I understood the full significance of the upriver-downriver, Catholic-Moravian, *Asaiti-Antoisi* differences, I was invited to participate in an annual cleansing and renewal ceremony at the Sweli sanctuary about one hour upriver from Langatabiki on the Pamaka Creek. I was cautioned to not tell KutuKutu or anyone from Langatabiki about the ceremony. It was to be kept hidden from church stalwarts. I packed my hammock and was picked up by boat to join others gathering from the upriver villages at a small tributary of the river. The ceremony was to re-consecrate the Sweli, the sacred bundle believed to have been carried from Africa by the original Pamakans.

The ceremony lasted three days and involved formal speeches by elders to discuss the spiritual state of the people, and to call attention to individual cases requiring divination and blessings. Women had prepared food for all, and everyone (except me) brought bottles of rum and beer that were collected and displayed in two large piles—one for the old year and one for "praying for life" in the new year. The rum offerings were consecrated with white clay, *pemba,* and stored for consumption at the evening dances and libations at the shrine.

We were all called together on the afternoon of the third day to be cleansed with a ritual wash that would prepare us for the new year by shedding the dirt of the past year from our bodies. There was much drumming, and people were singing and dancing sporadically. The mood seemed different to me. I had the sense that the spirit realm was close, and particularly energized. A small group of men brought a freshly cut tree trunk to a clearing and hoisted it onto a stand of branches tied together with stripped vines. The log, about three feet long, had been hollowed out to form a large bowl in the shape of a dugout canoe. It was heavy; not only was it a large part of a tree, but it was filled with a liquid potion prepared from special leaves, bark, and roots for this occasion. It looked to me like a giant mojito slurry.

There was great excitement and a palpable sense of anticipation as folks lined up to be cleansed. I was pulled into the single file line about seven or eight people back from the bowl. Two men I did not know attended to the urn and stirred the potion with calabash bowls. They wore particularly fancy loincloths, with pangis draped over their necks and down their backs. They had an eerie ghost-like appearance as most of their bodies was covered with a white chalk substance, *pemba*. The participants were excited. The mood intensified with a near fury of drumming and ritual language incantations as the first person in line stepped forward to the wooden urn. When one of the attendants poured the medicine over his head and shoulders, everything got really crazy. I watched frozen as the first communicant lurched into a frenzy. His arms flailed and his legs danced some crazy thing until he collapsed to the ground, jerking as if having a bad seizure. No one seemed surprised or concerned. He lay jerking as the next man in line stepped over him to approach the urn. The same thing happened! The second man spun out of control, arms flailing as he whirled around like a helicopter until he too fell to the ground jerking violently. The line was moving up, and everybody getting the wash was completely losing it.

I looked around to see if I could discretely duck out of this line. No, the line was a serious commitment, moving ever closer to this now scary bowl of what-the-hell. When I was motioned forward, I had to step over writhing bodies of people who had just been washed. When one of the bowl priests took a scoop of the wash from the gourd and poured it on my head and shoulders, I was thinking hard to just be cool—hold on, don't freak! I had an immediate sensation of weightlessness in my shoulders such that I felt I could fly. I could see why the people in line had collapsed into a private frenzy; there was a distinct physical effect of the wash. I did not fall down but walked around in tight circles moving my shoulders up and down involuntarily, maybe even jerking. I thought I might be able to take off.

I later wrote of this experience to one of my thesis professors who had an expertise in ethno-pharmacology. His explanation was that the wash was likely a strong batch of organic atropine made with belladonna roots and and plant types of the Deadly Nightshade variety. These potions were the stuff of medieval spells, and what enabled witches to fly. "Don't drink it!" he said.

This literal high wore off after about ten minutes. It took me a while to sort out what had just happened, besides getting washed with a potion that medieval witches used for flying. I had been accepted, perhaps initiated, by the traditional branch of Pamakans. Living as I did in Langatabiki, I thought everyone would assume that I was part of the church people. This was a big breakthrough for me to have gone through this cleansing ceremony at the Sweli.

Once a level of trust was reached, Pamaka elders seemed to enjoy telling me and KutuKutu the "first times" stories of the escape. It became apparent early in the story sessions that the fundamental feature of being a Pamakan is that they are a people formed in revolt against slavery. They persevered as hunted fugitives in an inhospitable forest by the grace of divine guidance from Africa (meaning the Sweli, whether they said the word or not.) This not-too-distant history oriented how Pamakans saw themselves apart from everyone else, including Ndjuka and other free settler groups.

Getting to the basic anthropology stuff, I learned that family distinctions within Pamaka stemmed from the escape from the plantations. The free settlement Africans, who only later became known as Pamakans, began forming camps near the plantations from which they escaped: Hantros (*Antoisi*, in the African vernacular), Hazard (*Asaiti*), and a third, the *Molo*, from the Molonhoop plantation. These original plantation-related forest camps formed the kinship identity that persisted today and oriented Pamakan society. After one identifies as being a Pamaka person, he or she identifies as an Antoisi, an Asaiti, or a Molo person.

During the initial fugitive period, each camp maintained clandestine contact with the slave laborers remaining at their former plantations. There were certain essential items that could not be duplicated in the jungle, such as machetes, axes, and cooking pots. Small groups would return to the plantation fields to raid work areas or, more commonly, to infiltrate and arrange for specified items to be smuggled out.

One story often repeated was that of the pre-arranged raid. Freemen scouts would secretly contact the still captive Africans working the plantation fields and agree on a time and place for a raid of a work party. On the day of the raid, the captive Africans would supply themselves to the max as they set out for the fields where they would be "ambushed" by the freemen. In the confusion, all the tools and food supplies would be justifiably abandoned and lost. Occasionally, the enslaved African willing to take the risks would join the raiding party with the tools and food supplies they could carry. All Pamakans seem to know the story of how a woman from the Antoisi plantation who had particularly long hair would each day conceal stalks of seed rice in her braids. In the work area, she would secretly remove the rice and place it in a cache that would be picked up by freemen later that night.

Everything changed in the late 1700s when the plantations struck the peace agreement with the Ndjuka, Saamaka and Matawai free settlement groups. The truce agreement required the Treaty freemen to hunt down and return any Africans who were not part of their groups. At that point, the Antoisi, Asaiti, and Molo free settlements had to escape farther into the forest, out of reach of the free-settlement groups cooperating with the plantation owners. This second escape took them far deeper into the forest, out of range of the plantation fields, tool supplies, and new recruits.

Material survival was a matter of ingenuity and, as every storyteller pointed out, divinely inspired invention. The Sweli oracle, the bundle of small items said to have been brought from Africa, was used as a carry oracle that literally guided them through the forest and delivered them from a wide variety of evils.

The Antoisi, Asaiti, and Molo people settled along an isolated tributary of the main river, later known as Pamaka Creek. In this isolated sanctuary, the *Antoisi*, *Asaiti*, and *Molo* groups formed separate camps, which became their family identity. Even as one community of fugitive freemen, each of the three plantation (*pandasi*) groups maintained a distinct identity from each other in terms of family origins and camp geography. Each maintained its identity as a plantation cohort or *lo*.

With the abolition of slavery in Suriname, this group of fugitive free-settlement people emerged from isolation in the early 1900s and became known as the Pamaka People. By coming out of the isolated tributary to the Marowijne River, the Pamakans confronted a new swirl of challenges: the authority of a colonial nation state, a market economy, and the proselytizing Moravian church mission. Christianity served as an initial and pervasive medium of contact with the outside world. The active competition of Roman Catholic and Moravian missionaries for converts among the Pamakans also provided a convenient context to articulate and promote existing internal differences.

I resisted protesting to TiBaya that my bomb map would have shown just what the elders were telling us: that the plantation origins persist in identifying one's kin group, and where you live. The *lo*, originally an escape group from a common plantation, is still the maximal territorial domain among Pamakans. Their first free settlements were, in a sense, alternate plantations of the same name. Later, when the Pamaka settlements came out of hiding along the Pamaka Creek and moved to islands on the Marowijne, they divided up their new territory to reflect the three separate plantation groups: Antoisi, Asaiti and Molo. Ultimately, the Marowijne territory became divided into thirds, with each plantation group being associated with the river region around the three villages of Langatabiki, Nason and Loka-Loka.

I learned eventually that the fission between the hymn singers and drummers within Pamaka was baked into the group at its formation. The Pamakans have an origin story of a struggle of good versus evil. Two of the original leaders, Boni and Amawi, are said to have had extraordinary powers from their African origins. The evil leader, it is told, abused his powers for self-gain to the point of killing the paramount chief in order to assume the title through lineage succession—he was Amawi, an Antoisi. To that point, the paramount chieftaincy was determined through matrilineal succession within the Antoisi lineage. The assassination of the Gaaman was a huge shock to the entire group, and after a great counsel with ancestor divination, it was determined that not only did Amawi have to give up the title of paramount chief, but his lineage would also not be able to name his successor. The Asaiti would become the lineage of the paramount chief.

In the last years of the nineteenth century, when the Asaiti Gaaman died, the Antoisi moved to reclaim the chieftaincy, arguing that the censure was not permanent but only for one generation. A delegation of Antoisi elders travelled to Paramaribo and petitioned the colonial government to grant the Pamakans formal recognition as an official free settlement group, with the same status as the treaty tribes of Ndjuka, Saamaka, and Matawai. According to Antoisi oral historians, the national government acceded to make Pamakans an official free settlement group and presented the Antoisi's designated leader, Apensa, with a uniform and staff of office as the first Pamaka Gaaman appointed and recognized by the government.

Despite the Asaiti objections and accusation that the chieftaincy was stolen from them by what they regard as chicanery, Gaaman Apensa returned to Langatabiki triumphant. He marked the beginning of a new era by proclaiming that Pamakans have "come out of the forest" and were now part of the Suriname government. He solidified this move by formally accepting the Moravian Brotherhood as the official church and religion of Langatabiki. He proclaimed that Pamakans must become a Christian people and encouraged everyone to be baptized by the new Moravian missionary.

The Antoisi Gaaman thus became the recognized link between the Pamakans and the state government. And since Pamakans were now officially Christians, Apensa claimed there was no basis for succession based on pagan rituals of divination. In a departure from the Moravian calls for patrilineal families, he decreed that the chieftaincy would still follow the principle of matrilineal inheritance, but remain strictly within the Antoisi group.

The upriver lineages, Asaiti and Molo, pushed back against this takeover as theft, but the Antoisi alignment with the Moravian Church solidified their position. As a counter move, the upriver lineages embraced the Roman Catholic mission in an attempt to match the clout of the Antoisi-Moravian alignment.

The Catholic mission accommodated traditional practices, while the Moravians sought to suppress them. This original dispute over leadership succession was the basis for the continuing divide between upriver Asaiti and Molo villages and downriver Antoisi of Langatabiki, the traditionalists versus the church people.

To mark this out-of-the-jungle transition clearly in everyone's mind, the Antoisi Gaaman Apensa held a final Sweli ceremony at the mouth of the Pamaka creek. As Gaaman, he was chief priest of the Sweli oracle. He took the sacred oracle back to the Pamaka Creak and praised it for having delivered them safely through the difficult times in the jungle. He then sent men to carry the oracle far into the forest, where he said it should remain hidden forever. Other materials of the Sweli oracle, such as the exceptionally long, sacred *agida* drum were thrown into the river. A new cemetery for Moravian Christians was established on the island of Langatabiki to replace the traditional burial grounds along the Pamaka creek. According to the new Antoisi Gaaman, there would be no necessity to return to the region of the loway ancestors.

So, it appeared that this annual ritual at the not-so-secret Sweli site was a rebel movement in defiance of the Antoisi Gaaman's banishment of the Sweli and the Moravian minister's repeated condemnation of Sweli as a pagan rite. The Pamaka Sweli was indeed alive and well, if partially concealed in a forest grotto and celebrated annually by traditionalists, and now me.

This acceptance of me by traditionalists provided insight into who the drummers and dancers were that first night at the wake. The Moravian preacher, the Gaaman, and the few congregationalists at the wake were clearly irked by the drumming and left when it started. But it was becoming clear to me that, except for a relatively small core of church adherents, Pamakans were traditionalists. A colleague, Edward Green, was living among the Matawai in Central Suriname at the time and related a story that illustrated the surface acceptance of Christianity. The Matawai, like Pamakans, had been aggressively worked by Moravian missionaries to the point that the Matawai were considered Christianized.

He told me how late one evening, a young child went missing and the entire village mobilized in frantic search. When the child was discovered—hungry but unharmed—early the next morning, everyone attributed the child's safe return to the work of the ancestors. All praise focused on the spirit realm of ancestors. In a real-life crisis such as this, Jesus was simply not a factor.

CHAPTER NINETEEN

UPRIVER-DOWNRIVER

The river above the falls was swift and rocky. Rapids and falls all along the river continually changed the navigational characteristics according to the seasonal variations in rainfall and water levels. It required a special type of boat and considerable skill, teamwork, and intimate knowledge of the seasonal channels to travel along the upriver waterways. With few exceptions, only Amerindian and free settler boatmen are able to navigate the river beyond the falls. The district commissioner, the mission stations, police, and the periodic Dutch and French military patrols still relied on the freemen boatmen to transport them and their supplies beyond the first falls of the Marowijne.

Understandably, one of the most engaging projects of men was to build a boat. Every part of these boats—essential to life on an island—comes from the forest. The first step is to select a suitable hardwood tree and make a clearing around it for a forest workshop. You chop down the tree and begin trimming the log to the size boat you want. The log is sliced lengthwise to remove the top third of the trunk. This is a difficult task, as the wood is hard and the communal saw has been worn down over many trees. Even more difficult and time consuming is the process of hollowing out the tree trunk to make it like a huge bowl. It's like slicing a 24-foot, rock-hard banana lengthwise and digging it out to the peel.

When the center of the tree trunk is hollowed out completely, the ends are tapered to a closed point. This hollowed-out tree is then heated with a controlled fire along the underside. The fire's intensity is carefully regulated by fanning or tamping with palm branches, so the tree is softened but not burned. When the hollowed tree trunk is uniformly hot, the sides are pried apart with fork-shaped tree branches to open it from a "U" shape to a parenthesis lying flat on its back. When the right shape is reached, the tree trunk is braced with cross boards and allowed to cool. This is the hull of the boat, which must then be dragged to the river edge where gunwales, seats and sometimes a frame canopy will be added, and it will be outfitted with an outboard motor.

I needed a boat, and arranged for a long-term loan of a solid 15-foot dugout, sturdy enough to accommodate an outboard motor. With a few months of accumulated GI Bill stipends, I was able to buy a used 25-horsepower Evinrude. This afforded me a freedom to visit villages and camps up and down the river. It also added immensely to my standing as a man—I could handle the boat through the moderate rapids between the Pamaka villages.

• • •

KutuKutu and I had become known generally as Langatabiki people, despite my having been washed in the secret upriver Sweli grotto and my efforts to avoid any sense of partiality. One day the upriver-downriver antipathy took an ominous turn in an otherwise typical fight over a woman. The matter spread beyond the two men involved, and led to the aggrieved man gathering a posse of his kinsmen to beat up the interloper. The dispute here, however, involved an upriver group beating up a downriver man. The initial beating was followed by a retaliatory brawl, with the downriver man getting his relatives together to beat up the upriver guy. This affair escalated over a few weeks into a declaration of war of the upriver people against downriver people. Word went around Langatabiki that there was an armada of upriver battle boats on their way to attack Langatabiki and beat up *all* the young men there.

I told KutuKutu to stay in the house, and asked B'Ampata, one of the Langatabiki guys preparing himself for the fight, "Where does BaMambo fit in to all of this?" There was a sort of Geneva Convention protocol for Pamakan fights: no weapons are to be used. Even if there was little chance of getting hacked up by a machete, the idea of being pummeled by a gang of enraged young men was unpleasant.

B'Ampata was reassuring, "Don't worry, they know if they hurt BaMambo, the sky will darken with American airplanes."

"Uh, yeah—maybe," I said, glancing skyward. I turned and walked quickly back to my house hoping to conceal my utter chagrin at cashing in on the notion, apparently still lingering, that I was some American bomb spy.

The upriver armada never showed up in Langatabiki. Perhaps they did not want to tempt the American war machine—the daily radio broadcast to the interior continued to report aerial bombing in Vietnam with precise tonnage statistics. Or maybe they remembered me as the helicopter guy at the Sweli wash. I learned that the festering dispute was resolved through intervention of lineage elders and a proper ritual consultation with ancestors.

The escalation of the otherwise routine fight reflected a simmering have/have-not resentment of upriver *vis* downriver people. One consequence of the Moravian-traditionalist difference had been a stark economic disparity between Langatabiki and the upriver communities. The Pamakan transition from a completely subsistence and barter system to an increasingly cash economy was rapid, and generally restricted to Langatabiki. Pamakans talked of the first man to buy an outboard motor for his boat. This was around 1955, when TiSobo returned to Langatabiki from a long balata collecting expedition. He later opened the first "store" in the front of his house and announced this new venture by going about proclaiming that "city life has come to Langatabiki." There was strong resistance to his charging twice the cost of canned sardines and warm soft drinks than what one would pay in Albina. A consequence was that his entrepreneurship was widely denounced, and he was accused of having introduced witchcraft to the village. Later when his canoe foundered in a rapid and he drowned, it was common knowledge that his death was "retribution" by offended ancestors. There was still no store in Langatabiki in the early 1970s.

Wage employment opportunities had gone disproportionately to the Langatabiki congregationalists of the Moravian church, and those favored by the church beholden to Gaaman. In addition, the traditionalists of the upriver villages were under-represented in the wage labor market due to their differing priorities of work and family. Traditionalists often complained that coastal employment precluded full attention to ritual matters. They pointed out that employers allowed only a few days off to attend to the death of a spouse, parent, or child, and no time off at all for related rituals with the death of others of one's lineage. A man, they said, was constantly forced to choose between requirements of his job and fundamental responsibilities of his family. So, while the traditionalists found cultural responsibilities incompatible with marketing a person's time for work, the Moravians were accommodated by expedited and routine burial ceremonies and exempted from the need to explore causes of illness or death through protracted ancestor divination.

Access to the cash economy was a feature far more evident for Moravian-affiliated Pamakans in Langatabiki than for traditional Catholic upriver communities. The drift from subsistence to a market economy was led by the paramount chief and the Moravian church. In Langatabiki there were several houses with wood plank flooring and corrugated tin roofs. Even though thatch provided better insulation properties, a tin roof indicated the house belonged to someone of modern means. One must pay for tin roofing, meaning the builder has a cash income. Thatch must be gathered in the surrounding forest. It takes time to find the right leaves, weave them into the right sized bunches, tie them close together onto long bamboo poles, which in turn are tied from the bottom up to the roof frame. This is not something a man with a job has time for.

The physical differences between the village of Langatabiki and the upstream, more traditional villages were evident. Through the long-term settlements of spouses and sojourners, Langatabiki in 1973 had grown to nearly 150 houses and over 550 residents, twice as large as Nason and three times the size of Loka-loka. The remaining seven upriver villages averaged around 100 residents each. But the most prestigious feature of Langatabiki was its electricity. On most nights, "streetlights" would illuminate the main path until about 10 p.m. The lights, generator, and diesel fuel were compliments of the national government and the good offices of the Moravian church. The Moravian mission even provided an incipient skyline, with its modern, two-story boarding school dormitory and clinic. Tin roofing and outboard motors could be found in upstream villages also, but there was virtually no rival to the village of Langatabiki.

The Catholic mission to the Pamakans was established some distance across the river from its host community of Nason. Consequently, the village could not incorporate any of the facilities, such as the electric generator, into village lifestyles. Langatabiki, by contrast, had a comparatively active nightlife, with young people gathering under the light poles to talk, or to dance to drums or portable cassette players. Langatabiki kids would not consider longterm residency in any other village, citing boredom and lack of cash employment as main reasons.

CHAPTER TWENTY

THE CYCLE OF BEING

Drumming is serious business in the forest; it is the orchestra that accompanies song and ritual, and in certain contexts, is a means of ceremonial communication that includes ancestors. A few of the men in Langatabiki had drums that they kept in the back of their huts. The drums were works of art, made by hollowing a roughly two-foot section of tree trunk to a slight conical shape, about twelve inches in diameter at the top, and sixteen to twenty-four inches at the base. Each was unique in appearance and artwork, and readily identifiable with the drummer who cut the tree and made the instrument. The drums were intricately carved with geometric designs; the leather skin was tightened and held in place by five or six pegs that could be adjusted by hammering with the base of your palm. I loved these drums and learned that each had a distinctive sound that people recognized. KutuKutu knew basic drum themes, but did not share my enthusiasm here, perhaps a result of the Moravian schooling that drumming was pagan.

I watched the drummers closely during the all-night ceremonies. Their drums were an extension of themselves, and not to be trifled with. The drummers would occasionally share drums among themselves, but kids did not play with them, and no woman was to touch the skin of a drum. I memorized the basic rhythms of the dances and singing, hard not to do at three in the morning after the drumming had been nearly constant since sundown. Many nights I would practice alone on upside-down buckets.

One evening, I was sitting with the drummers as they were setting up for an all-nighter to mark the end of the mourning period for a widower. As they tuned up the drums and began to warm up, BaYoni motioned for me to sit at his drum and try it out. It was early, and people were just starting to gather, so I gave it a shot. Two other guys were playing so I joined in, keeping it as quiet and light as possible. Soon, I was into it! I was keeping up with the guys with the basic beat—nothing fancy, but in the groove (or at least close to it). The other drummers looked at me and smiled. We jammed for maybe ten minutes, which felt to me like a gig at the Apollo. I was transformed, but of course way out of my league. I handed the drum back to BaYoni who gave me an approving nod. A woman came over to joke politely about the new sound from the drums. It must have been a sight: a skinny, blue-eyed, bushy-bearded white guy in jeans and t-shirt banging out among the real African drummers, in loincloths barely covering their perfectly sculpted bodies.

The ceremony had marked the end of the mourning period for TiBodo, and the release of his deceased wife's *yorka* from his care. The next day, TiYandoley came over to my hut to say hello. He seemed impressed, not so much with my drum skills, but that I would take an active role in the ceremony at the risk of humiliation. It would have been inexcusable to mess up the drumming on this ritual occasion. TiYan, as I came to call him, revealed himself over a short time to be one of the smartest men I have ever known. He had a keen mind, with a temperament and demeanor that made him wise. In his mid 50s, with a couple of grown children, he was exceptional at all the things men do: hunting, carving, building, and storytelling. He lived alone in a well-built thatch house in Langatabiki. KutuKutu later told me that he had a woman in an up-river village, and children here and there.

I enjoyed and benefited from the friendship of TiYan and was fortunate that he welcomed my interest in learning about Pamakan thought and concepts. KutuKutu and I spent hours with him discussing life and death, and the world around us, both physical and metaphysical. As our conversations progressed, TiYan accepted me as worthy of a deeper level of understanding of Pamaka. He invited KutuKutu and me to sit with him and listen as he explained an extraordinary concept of the nature of human existence as a cycle of being.

The three of us sat on little stools in TiYan's dark hut one afternoon. He began by explaining that each person exists in both the physical incarnation (slapping his bare chest with both palms), and in a metaphysical being called the *yorka* (arms held out with palms towards his body.) He added that while your body is alive, your yorka plays no special role and normally receives no attention. An exception, however, is spirit possession, which is a special instance where your living being takes on a yorka in addition to your own. There are a few people, he explained, whose physical and metaphysical beings are close together, which can result in that person having exceptional powers. He looked at KutuKutu, explaining, these are the people who are *lepi*, literally meaning "ripe." These were matters that KutuKutu had certainly heard about, but never got such a deep explanation.

Each person is a unique combination of an *akaa*, a *toney*, and a *nenseki*, TiYan explained. The akaa is the life spirit that infuses the newborn infant with its first breath. One's akaa is unique and particular to each original life on earth. Your akaa is your consciousness; it is that aspect of a person that appreciates pleasure and endures pain.

TiYan had unusually light brown eyes that signaled his intent and mood. He looked particularly serious in warning that an akaa can be lost or entrapped when away from your body, and so must be treated with some consideration. He said that during sleep, your akaa leaves your body and encounters experiences that provide the stuff of dreams. He warned that it is dangerous to be awakened abruptly—your wandering akaa may not get back in place. He looked at KutuKutu and sort of jokingly told him not to mess around and startle BaMambo, particularly if he is sleeping. The problem, he said, is that you can lose your akaa and a witch may capture it. When someone loses an ability to speak coherently, it is a sign that the person has lost their akaa, unless a tree has fallen on his head.

TiYan shifted around on his stool, and continued, "Your *toney*," he explained, "is where you came from." As he went on, I understood that each person has a geographic locus that can be determined through divination. He did not dwell much on the toney, saying that people have a general idea of their toney through dreams and by taste preferences. For example, if you prefer fish over meat, you are a water person; vice versa, you are a land person. I was confident that I was understanding everything TiYan was saying, but I was going to review it all carefully with KutuKutu as soon as we got back to our place.

TiYan then took the seminar to a different level for me. "Part of your being," TiYan said, "is the *nenseki*. The nenseki is the ancestor in you." He explained that you can discover who is your nenseki by divination, or, informally, through personality traits, physical characteristics, or dreams. People want to know the identity of their nenseki because childhood diseases are often the result of the ancestor, as nenseki, agitating for recognition and attention. Any cure will require addressing the issues of your resident ancestor. About now, the thought crossed my mind, sitting in a dark thatch hut on a stool a few inches off the ground, that this would probably make total sense if I had smoked some weed.

I understood the definitions of one's component parts: your physical body with an akaa (your consciousness); your toney (your geolocation preference); and your nenseki (the particular ancestor animating your being.) I was struggling to understand how all of this works together. TiYan, ever patient, laid it out so a child could understand. He explained that a person lives on earth for four complete lifetimes. In your first go-round in life, you live as a unique incarnation of akaa, toney and nenseki. When your physical body dies, the akaa returns to the spirit realm while your toney and your nenseki simply expire. But you maintain a presence among the living after death, however, in the form of your yorka.

So, your yorka is your metaphysical self. Both KutuKutu and I leaned in a bit to understand where he was going. When you die, you, as yorka, remain near your corpse and can be consulted in divination using either your body or a bundle of your hair and fingernails. As yorka, you remain involved in the affairs of the living matrilineal kin as ancestor. In death where there is a surviving spouse, your yorka has a special locus with your spouse (usually in a basket) and is tended to daily with food and drink libation throughout the year of mourning.

Your yorka, then, is part of the ancestor order responsible for maintaining the good order of the living lineage, and especially you. After your physical being dies, and if you pass judgment of your living relatives, your yorka will return to the physical world as nenseki by passing into the womb of a woman kinsman during pregnancy. This initiates your next go-round as a walk-around life form.

I was starting to get it. Existence as an ancestor yorka and the possibility of reincarnation as nenseki are your rewards of not being perceived as a witch by your kin in your previous physical incarnation. If at judgment on your death you were found to be a witch, you would not be accorded the burial ceremonies. Instead, your dead body would be thrown away in a remote area of forest. This would be your final end; no mourning, no mention of your name ever again, no libation paid to you as an ancestor, and no chance to return to a living being as nenseki. This system of distinct aspects of your life made sense to me as a logical and effective conceptual order of life: you will enjoy several lifetimes in various configurations, so long as you live your life as a good person.

Pamakan physical and metaphysical concepts of life constituted a completely coherent system. The critical event in your life cycle happens just after you die. Your judgment day, a couple of days after you die, is an actual event in your neighborhood, and presided over by your relatives. Pamaka judgment involves no saints, no pearly gates, and no waiting for the by-and-by. Your judgment reckoning is the determination, at death, of whether you were a good person while alive and breathing. Getting into heaven for a Pamakan means that your yorka passed the test of your family, and you were found worthy to remain among them as an ancestor.

I learned from TiYan that your yorka remains near your dead body after death. That explained why your corpse, or a bundle of your hair and fingernails, will take your judgment day examinations. The test is pass-fail: were you a good person, or were you a witch? If you pass, you proceed to burial and transition to the realm of ancestors; if you are determined to be a witch, it is the end of the line. You die in ignominy.

CHAPTER TWENTY-ONE

JUDGMENT DAY

KutuKutu and I watched the examination of an old woman who had just died in Pikein Tabiki. The audience was the entire village, as well as the lineage ancestors brought to bear through copious libations of rum. The divination was conducted by lineage elders, with two bearers carrying a long, narrow plank about eight feet long. A small bundle of the deceased's hair and fingernails wrapped in a cloth was tied to the center of the plank. The bearers carried the divination board on their heads, one at either end. The procedure was similar to consultations with ancestors on major issues of life. The officiating elder posed a question and the oracle bearers would be moved by the oracle bundle. Guided by the oracle bundle, the bearers would lurch forward, backward, or side-to-side. The elder generally interpreted forward as being a "yes," backward was a "no," while side-to-side was, "ask another question."

Here, the first judgment procedure required the woman's yorka to lead the bearers over a secret (only to the bearers) line marked with rum. Elders poured a libation to the ancestors along the main path through the village, and poured rum in a line across the path. The libation at the path called on the ancestors to administer the test: if the person was a witch, do not allow her yorka to cross over this line. The bearers remained some distance away with the divination bundle and, supposedly, did not see where the rum line was.

The presiding elder called the bearers to bring her yorka to them, sitting on the path beyond the line of rum. As the bearers approached, the elder called out to the woman's yorka, 'Show that you are not a witch by guiding your bearers!"

The bearers proceeded slowly along the path. When they approached the line, they paused, and the crowd gasped. The bearers then moved forward again and, literally, crossed the line. The assembled village expressed relief and delight. Had the bearers stopped and not crossed over the libation line, the yorka would have been exposed as a witch. Today, the yorka was conditionally accepted by the ancestors as worthy of remembrance. This was high drama in the village; all were participating in judgment day of their recently departed relative. I was told that only two people in memory did not pass judgment of their kin and *really* died, yorka and all. Still there was suspense whether this yorka would be able to guide her bearers through the test. The judgment then proceeded to a second trial.

There was a festive air to the gathering, highlighted by a communal libation during the intermission. Ancestors were treated to healthy pours from two or three bottles of taffia rum, the rest of which was shared by everyone present taking a sip from a single glass carried through the crowd, and regularly replenished by the village basia. I was not concerned about sharing the glass with fifty or so people, since the taffia rum was almost pure alcohol.

For the second phase of judgment, elders directed three persons to go and conceal themselves in a house. Again, the bearers remained near the corpse, out of sight of the preparations. Once the three were hidden in the house, the woman's yorka was instructed to lead her bearers to the place where the people were hiding. The pole bearers began moving around the huts, being guided by the woman's yorka—a transcendental hide-and-seek with audience participation and humor.

After a few minutes, the bearers went directly to the hiding place. When the front bearer banged the oracle pole against the house door, the onlookers heckled playfully that the yorka is mistaken, it is the wrong house, no one is in there. The bearers persisted and kept knocking, and the crowd raucously insisted it's the wrong house. Finally, the designated hiders emerged to cheers for the yorka's demonstration of not having been a witch. Someone fired a shotgun in the air to mark the successful trial, and the start of the next phase of funerary transition.

While it was rare for a deceased to not pass this formal judgment of their family, it is one of the biggest events of a person's life (actually your *immediate* afterlife) and must serve as incentive to stay on good terms with your relatives during your life as a living neighbor. The ceremony depicts the bearers of the corpse as being guided by its yorka aura; of course, the active involvement of the family in the show clearly influences what the bearers do. Imagine the confusion of bearers if the family participants did not expect, or did not want the deceased to pass the judgment tests.

As I learned more about Pamaka concepts of distinct aspects of being, both in life and death, I realized that it was profound. They had crafted a logical and effective conceptual order of life on earth: you will enjoy several lifetimes in various configurations, so long as you live as a good person. A Pamakan knows that your lifetime as a living person is only the flesh and blood period of your being. At death—the most critical transition for each being—you must rely completely on your kin for ultimate judgment. It is your family (living and deceased members included) who sits in judgment of your life, and performs the necessary funerary rituals that mark the passage either into the rich afterlife of ancestors, or ultimate death and disappearance.

After judgment day proceedings in Pikien Tabiki, there were eight days of funerary preparations with the body wrapped in cloth lying in state under a thatch canopy. Oddly, I got used to the overwhelming feature that no one spoke about—the choking stench of a large rotting body laying on a table in tropic heat and humidity.

KutuKutu and four young guys were selected as the novices for gravedigger induction during the funeral phase, after the woman passed judgment. To my surprise, I was included in this class of inductees; essentially, an initiation to adult male status in Pamaka.

Becoming a gravedigger was a major transition ritual of a boy becoming a man. Being a gravedigger was one of the most important social roles a Pamakan man has. Few things are more important than the proper preparation and disposition of deceased kinsmen. Becoming a gravedigger ("*oloman*," literally "hole man") involved an elaborate series of rituals that symbolized the transition from boyhood to manhood.

At the gravesite clearing in the forest about fifteen minutes away by boat, we initiates were instructed to sit near the chief gravedigger and observe the work closely. Shoes and European-type shirts were not permitted in the burial area. Work began in the morning, marking out and digging the outline of a rectangular hole in the ground. The digging stopped at about midmorning for the gravediggers to have the first meal of the day. The initiates and the chief gravedigger began eating before the others. This was contrary to normal customs, where the young defer to elders in order of eating and such.

During food breaks, the men discussed issues of ancestors, death, differences among races of men, and so on. When the grave was about half completed, attention of the gravediggers turned to the initiates. One of the men began to paint large designs on the faces and chests of the initiates with wet clay from the grave. My full beard was a problem, so I got a forehead mark. I really wanted to see what I looked like but, of course, there were no mirrors, and no cameras.

I felt a little self-conscious with my chest design. All the other guys had super dark skin and perfect muscle structure. My practice was to avoid sunburn by wearing shirts, so I did not even have a tan, and my musculature was appropriate for someone who had spent the past two years in a classroom or library. While we were being painted, one of the gravediggers announced that he was going into the forest to find the special leaves to clean our eyes.

We novices, all painted up, were led to the muddy three-by-six-foot grave opening. It had been dug to about four feet deep by now, with the reddish clay dirt piled up on the long sides. The chief gravedigger performed a formal libation with rum at the foot of the grave. This libation required nearly a half bottle of rum, an indication of the high importance of the occasion. The libation speech addressed the lineage ancestors, and introduced each of the initiates to them. The speech went on to introduce the ancestors to the initiates. The elder concluded the libation with an admonition for the ancestors and the initiates to not fear each other, but to work together in a spirit of mutual responsibility and trust. Then each of the initiates had to climb into the grave and draw three shovels of dirt from the bottom. I was a lot taller than the other initiates, so I was able to climb, unassisted and unembarrassed, into and out of the deep, muddy grave.

Next came the cleaning of eyes. "Clean eyes" is a common euphemism for understanding something subtle or complex. In this instance, the clean eyes meant to understand gravediggers' responsibilities. They were going to symbolize this literally—we were going to get our eyes actually cleaned. We lined up, seated on a log and waited until one of the gravediggers emerged from the forest with a hand full of leaves that he then mashed into a moist pulp using a wooden mortar and pestle. His instruction to us was that the cleansing will be painful, but that this potion will cause our eyes to become clean so that we will be able to see clearly. I was in the middle of the log and caught a peek as the eye man approached the first initiate and held his head back, while holding the mashed-up leaves in his other hand. Uttering an incantation, he squeezed the mashed leaves to drop the liquid into the initiate's eyes.

I was not happy to be next in line for this eye treatment, but I toughed it out, wondering what new stuff I would be able to see. Well, *Ao!Ao!Ao! Jesus Christ!* I screamed silently. None of the initiates had made a sound so I was keeping in character. But it burned like hell, and I could not see anything for a good five minutes!

The grave digging was only one part of the important and symbolic passage from incarnate life to an ancestor existence. Becoming an ancestor is the culmination of a successful, good life, and means that you, as yorka, have passed the judgment day tests and are ready for the next phase of your being as an ancestor. Ancestors keep track of the daily lives of their matrilineal descendants. That is, your siblings (from the same mother), your mother and her siblings, your mother's sisters' children, your mother's mother and her siblings, then her mother and siblings, and so on ad infinitum.

CHAPTER TWENTY-TWO

CHURCH DEATH

The Pamaka concepts and cultural practices of death provided answers to the question of why the wake of the Gaaman's sister my first night in Langatabiki had turned into a scuffle between hymn singers and drummers. The most significant alterations of traditional ritual observances were found in the Moravian funeral. Traditional concepts relating to death were fundamental to the Pamakan funerary rituals. Every Pamakan knows that the day of death will be his or her day of judgment— by family members, not Saint Peter or a second coming of Jesus. If the deceased was judged worthy, the lineage ritually celebrated his transition to an ancestor state. The funeral celebration of several days marked this passage, while incorporating and reintegrating the extensive fabric of lineage social relations through corpse divination and associated rituals.

The Moravian church teaching was starkly manifest when it came to death. Church teaching denigrates the traditional judgment day practice and the concept of ancestor status for those found worthy. Instead, the church view was that a person is laid to rest at death in an ambivalent suspension of being until Jesus returns for the Judgment of Salvation—an incomplete redefinition of one's status in life or death. The Moravian funerals were, thus, relatively perfunctory and solemn affairs as compared with the extensive funeral rituals of the traditionalists.

One of the first innovations of the Moravian mission in Langatabiki was to establish a cemetery on the island adjacent to the village. This new cemetery provided an alternative to the traditional burial grounds in the Pamaka Creek. No longer would church people need to return to the bush to confront the *Sweli* and a sacred past. This Moravian cemetery established a clear description of the Christian concept of absolute and spiritually inert death. The mission cemetery was simply the repository of the dead bodies of people who are "sleeping" until the day of resurrection.

When a church person dies, the body is prepared for burial immediately. There is no consideration of yorkas or whether the deceased was a good person in life. In church, everyone receives the same burial. Moreover, there is no divination as to the cause of death. The obvious and preceding circumstance is sufficient explanation. The explanation of death caused by disease, getting hit by a falling tree, drowning, and so on, is sufficient. No inquiry with ancestors as to the real cause of death is permitted.

The two Pamaka head gravediggers perform the function of washing the corpse in both Catholic and Protestant communities. In the latter, the pastor is directly involved in the funeral preparations and ceremonies. The lineage of the deceased, as in the traditional community, bears most of the actual costs of the funeral, but lessens their expenses by direct house-to-house collections throughout the village. The Moravian lineage neighborhoods have neither ancestor shrines nor flags. The body is prepared in state in the deceased's own house.

In the Moravian funeral, there is a felt imperative to bury the body as quickly as possible. Men are chosen to make the coffin and dig the grave at once; both gravesite and coffin are prepared simultaneously. However, even in the Protestant community the coffin makers exercise traditional prerogatives to catch and cook village chickens, and treat their work with ritual caution. The gravedigger's role, on the other hand, loses much of its significance in the Moravian context. There is no initiation procedure for young men, and young women do not prepare a gravediggers' feast. The sense of pollution of the village by dirt imported from the church burial grounds is not important, and no ritual cleansing is required of returning gravediggers.

The evening of the day of death is an occasion for silent grieving. In contrast to the *touca* play of the traditionalists, the Moravians gather and sing Church hymns from the songbook. The mood of the event is somber, and there is no drumming or dancing at all. Eight days after the burial, there is a gathering again at the house of the deceased, for an all-night wake. Rum, beer, soft drinks and hot chocolate are served throughout the night. The session begins with hymns sung by everyone in unison, in a church-like atmosphere. After hours of singing, the congregation may take up Anansi tales and sing the traditional *mato* songs. There is no drumming permitted and often no dancing. Rhythm is provided by soft hand-clapping. Typically, people must be continually reminded of the solemnity of the affair, and the necessity for proper decorum—no joking, loud talking, and absolutely no drums! The traditionalists (the Catholics) had brought their drums to the evening service for the Gaaman's sister.

• • •

Following a spouse's death, there is a six-month period of church mourning which requires the surviving spouse to exhibit some outward sign of mourning (typically a black beret), show extreme deference and formal respect toward the lineage of the deceased, and avoid any thought of courtship·or marriage during this time. The end of the mourning period is an occasion for celebration. For both church and traditional Pamakans, the removal of mourning, and the return of the widow or widower into the social mainstream is one of the largest and most festive events for a family. Typically, the deceased's lineage prepares a feast to be distributed throughout the village in individual portions.

There had been a buzz of talk for a few days that there would be a *puu baaka* ("pulling mourning") ceremony for TiMoyo, whose wife had died about a year earlier. One Friday, TiGazzan arrived in the village from his camp upriver to preside at the ceremony. I liked him immediately; he was a fantastic fellow, maybe forty years of age. He was poised and dramatic in a brilliantly white t-shirt, with cotton-white hair and coal black skin. He could have stepped out of a *Vogue* ad, carrying a black zippered brief folio, and a snuff kit like D'Ayambe's Vicks jar, except Gazzan's was silver. He was jungle Gucci.

The setting for the ceremony was an open-walled communal house traditionally constructed with thatch roof and earthen floor. Six to eight men were seated casually around an impressive mound of liquor, food, beer, and soft drinks in the open front half of the house, an area about twelve-by-twelve-feet square. There were eight bottles of rum, two cases of soft drinks, a case of beer, assorted cans of beef, ham, a pan of freshly caught fish, and three large paper bags of rice. I was surprised that the pile of offerings included two birdcages, each with a terrified songbird. One of the cages was carefully labeled with a magic marker: "Wilson Pickett."

The ceremony got under way when Bashia Gazzan entered the room and poured out the first round of rum libation. There was only one glass in the house; later someone produced a calabash to drink out of. The bereaved TiMoyo entered later and took a seat at the corner of the house. He looked unhappy and sat gloomily as the speeches commenced. A man approached TiMoyo and with scissors cut a lock of hair, then combed his hair, dry-shaved his face with a bare razor, and combed his hair again.

Gifts of colorful pangi cloths were then laid out in front of TiMoyo. The gifts included a bright green, flowered shirt. A woman draped a pangi over TiMoyo's head while a prayer was offered. Food was being prepared by women in the neighboring thatch enclosure, and soon heaping pans of rice and steaming bowls of stewed fish were brought in. More libations were made with copious pours of rum. I, meantime, became indispensable to the proceedings because I was the only one there with a bottle opener—my Swiss Army knife.

CHAPTER TWENTY-THREE

OBIA

KutuKutu and I became regular participants in story-telling sessions and family counsels that formally aired issues such as illness, liaisons, and suspected infidelities. These counsels, *kuutu*, could involve a small or large lineage unit, depending on the nature of the issue and what type of disagreement needed resolution. When I had gained a fair measure of trust among the villagers, KutuKutu and I were generally welcome anywhere along the river. We spent many hours listening to stories of how ancestors and the various forces of the spirit world intercede in daily affairs, generally to avoid danger and maximize positive effects, whether in hunting, fighting, or love. The dreaded obia the Guyanese house matron warned me of turned out to be a conceptual system of the cause-and-effect relationship between the reality that we see, hear, and feel, and the unseen world of ancestors and other various energies.

An obia can refer to a deity or a specific supernatural element, such as the serpent spirit, that maintains direct, if occasional contact with humans. The term "obia" also refers to the *process* of contact between humans and the supernatural elements. Unusual events can be explained as the result of one "doing obia." When bad things happen to people, there is a baleful suspicion that someone has directed obia forces against that person. While further investigation through divination with ancestors may reveal an understandable and resolvable causation of individual problems, this witchcraft notion of obia persists.

Pamakans credit their supernatural connection with Africa as the obia that enabled their survival and continued existence as a people. The common feature of these various aspects of obia is the element of contact between the living and the world beyond our direct perception. The verbal sense of the term is clear: *an obia is what an obia does.* The workings of obia always involve communication between man and the spirit realm. To work divination, whether through a medium or the preparation of oracle devices, is to do obia; to prepare and administer a talisman or a medicine is to do obia.

Obia, I also learned, is the key feature in an understanding of a universe where there are no accidents. People do not *just* get sick or die. Everything, good and bad, happens for a reason. We mortals just have to pay attention to the spiritual realm to understand the real cause of perceived effects. Pamakans use obia generally for good purposes, and credit their very survival on the spiritual intercession of the Sweli obia that enabled them to prepare medicines, find food, and find their way deep in the forest. The dark side of obia stems from the suspicion that people will, or have used spiritual means to influence or create an ill effect. I began to realize that KutuKutu was taking no chances when he threw away his new shoes that seemed to move on their own.

To Pamakans, there is invariably a behavioral disorder behind bad things that happen. KukuKutu and I were visiting the upriver village of LokaLoka when we came upon a group of people attending to a man about my age with a seriously infected finger. The man had a cut that became infected to the point that he was in great pain; his hand was swollen, and he could not move his fingers at all. I was alarmed because I could see the infection was not responding to the local herbal treatments, and could quickly become gangrenous if not cleaned and repaired quickly. The man's family agreed with me that he needed to be taken to the French hospital in St. Laurent, about a four-hour trip down river. I did not understand initially why his family was not taking him right away. They said they had to conduct a kuutu to consult the ancestors about the matter.

We watched as an elder summoned the lineage ancestors with a formal libation of rum. He slipped into a trance state to consult the ancestors via divination. Like the judgment day test, the presiding elder tied a small cloth bundle of sacred objects to the center of a stick about six feet long. Two men carried the bundle, with one at each end of the stick, holding it with both hands on the top of their heads. The process took a while, but the elder was able to determine the cause of the injury by questioning the oracle through its bearers. What was determined was that the ancestors allowed the injury as retribution for a violent quarrel the guy had a few weeks previous with his sister over the use of his canoe. This type of social dissonance within a family is offensive to the ancestors, who indicate their disapproval by enabling problems such as infections.

The man's sister was called forward and the elder orchestrated a formal resolution of the sibling ill will in front of the assembled kin; and importantly, before the ancestors. A final libation closing the ceremony included a spraying of rum into the air, in addition to pours at the base of the lineage flags. I was happy to see the guy finally get hauled off to the hospital after a delay of two or three hours. I learned later that the wound responded rapidly to treatment in St Laurent. It was clear to his family, however, that it was vitally important to determine the cause of the infection, and to resolve the discord with the ancestors before treating the infection. The officiating elder explained to me that people get cuts all the time, but when one does not heal normally, there is a reason. The reason the cut turned into an infection had to be cleared up with the ancestors before the wound would respond to any treatment, however good the French doctors were.

• • •

I was fascinated by the *Kumanti* obia that virtually every male Pamakan participated in to one degree or another. The Kumanti obia likely derived from early quasi-ethnic grouping of captive Africans who were imprisoned and shipped to Suriname from the infamous Coromantyne slave ports in Ghana. Kumanti, among Pamakans, remains a man's preserve of semi-secret and sacred African knowledge. Kumanti knowledge and practices include a ritual language, a body of glyphic symbols, songs, dances, and ritual preparations for extraordinary activities and spirit possession. A man who adopts Kumanti powers takes on additional proscriptions, such as the requirement to observe a strict separation from the supposed polluting effects of menstruating women. A Kumanti man, for instance, must not sleep in the same house, or eat food prepared by a menstruating woman.

Pamakans point out that Kumanti spirit possession is entirely vocational. Unlike other spirit possessions, which appear to descend on people whether they want it or not, a man can train to become a Kumanti medium. A Kumanti novice must learn the Kumanti language and symbols, and the medicine and ritual preparations for possession. Kumanti possession enables the medium to divine causations of illness, hardship, and to drive out harmful foreign spirits.

The Kumanti power is like an insurance policy against death and injury. Through the Kumanti obia, men make themselves immune to bullets, knife wounds, thorns, wasps, and fire. Some men will demonstrate their Kumanti powers by dramatic displays of invincibility, such as walking on broken bottles or fire pits, picking up red-hot axe heads, or hacking at their bodies with machetes. Very few men aspire to become fire-walking Kumanti specialists—neither KutuKutu nor I had any interest in this career path. The various *man-nenge* obia devices, however, are pervasive. Nearly every Pamaka male over twenty will have some type of man-nenge obia. These are prepared by the *Kumanti* ritual specialists on request, and usually for a price. Most common of these obias are the special immunities to gunshot and knives, and special powers in fighting. These powers are transmitted with instructions on their proper use and commensurate personal prohibitions.

The Kumanti preparations can adjust to new circumstances and environments, as when Pamakan men travel outside of their villages for work. One popular preparation for upward mobility in the city was the ritual herbal wash, to assure successful completion of the driver's license test. For about ten dollars, a Kumanti specialist in license preparations will give an aspirant a bottle of consecrated "medicine" to wash three times with, and a driver's training manual to study weeks before the exam. It is made clear to the client that neither the medicine wash nor the study of the training manual alone could be effective in getting the applicant through the test.

The most popular man-nenge obia among young men, however, is the *bui*. The bui is an upper arm bracelet fashioned from heavy wire to fit tightly just above the bicep. The Kumanti specialist will prepare a drink, a wash, an amulet, or a combination of these for the client. The bui is typically prepared for immunity to knife and gun attacks when outside of Pamaka territory. I heard several stories in testament to the efficacy of the bui, especially in the city of Paramaribo.

One day, everyone was talking about BaMoini who went to the city to look for work. The story told was that one night he was attacked by a street gang. One of the assailants reportedly swung a machete at BaMoini with a force that would have decapitated a normal person. But when the machete hit BaMoini, it fell out of the thug's hand. There was no scratch on BaMoini, who then tore off his shirt. When the thugs saw BaMoini's bui on his arm, and no injury from the machete chop, they fled in fear.

The Kumanti specialists make it clear that the bui's power resides as much in deterrence as it does in actual immunity. This is especially true in its protection against gunshots. It was explained to me that an assailant who asserts that he will shoot, but ultimately does not, is actually deterred by the effect of the bui. The first line of the bui's defense is affecting a change of heart in the attacker, a misfire of the gun, or a miss in the aim. But I was assured repeatedly that even if the gun were fired properly and the bullets found their mark, the shot would either bounce off your skin or simply turn to water on contact—if the bui was in good order.

When a bui proves itself to be powerful, as in the example of BaMoini, it can be relied upon in personal divination. A man can suspend the bui on a string and pose a question: should I do such and such. He will observe the bui carefully and if it moves forward and backward, the response is positive; a side-to-side motion is negative.

Special purpose bui include wrestling and fist-fighting obias. One such bui is prepared with hair from the back of a cat, another is made with a concoction containing, among other things, a locked padlock and a fish noted for its death-gripping fins. These bui will, respectively, enable a wrestler to be confident his back will never touch the ground, and his armlock will debilitate his opponent.

In addition to their primary purpose, most bui will have side benefits depending on the Kumanti specialist's abilities. He can, for instance, prepare the bui to forewarn the wearer of danger. The story told by TiPali illustrated this power of the bui. When TiPali returned to Pikien Tabbiki after a trip to Paramaribo, he told the story of how his bui saved him from either witchcraft or pollution. He had ordered a meal in one of the many street corner Chinese restaurants, and when the waitress was bringing the plate to his table, she stumbled and dropped the food on the floor. This was obvious to TiPali that his bui caused the tray spill to prevent him from eating food that had either been poisoned, or prepared by a menstruating woman. TiPali said he left the restaurant immediately without saying a word, and probably without paying.

I, of course, wanted to have a bui, even though I did not need a combat bui—I was not expecting to get into any fights. I would borrow a single-shot twelve-guage shotgun to go hunting—the manliest thing a Pamakan man can do. A bui to enhance my hunting abilities would be a good thing, I thought. Hunting typically involves finding an animal trail so you don't have to make noise hacking away at vines and brush with your machete. The point is to trek quietly through the forest until you hear or see something to shoot—a peccary, monkey, armadillo, or any of the wild turkey-type birds that scamper through the brush at about sixty miles per hour. You have only one shot, one shell of buckshot, or a lead slug. These shotguns are not very accurate, so you have to get as close as possible to your target. Anything over fifty feet away, particularly if it is running, flying, or slithering, is likely to keep on going. And once you fire the big shotgun, the forest shudders and the birds become quiet. The shot can be heard far away, and you are pretty much done for the day. Plus, any people within a mile or so will hear the shot and ask loudly back at the village, "What did you get?" There is no good explanation for going back empty-handed after firing a shot.

Hunting in the forest was exciting and dangerous. My neighbor, Kapiten Niko of Langatabiki, walked slowly with a bad limp from snakebites, and setting off gun-traps while hunting. I was not very successful at hunting because I would focus more on making sure I knew my way back to the boat, and avoiding snakes, than on listening for the telltale sounds of game.

One afternoon, I went out to see if I could get something other than fish for dinner. I went slowly along the riverbank on the French side until I found a small opening in the green wall. There was a discernable path into to forest, so I tied the boat to a tree limb, clutched the shotgun and machete and stepped deliberately, slowly and quietly along the trail. The birds high in the forest canopy were unconcerned with me and kept up their distinctive *wheeee-wheeooo* whistles.

About a hundred yards into the forest, I saw a small clearing ahead, ideal to surprise some unsuspecting animal. I readied my shotgun and stalked, cat-like up to the open area. The clearing was the size of small living room, large enough to let a beam of sunlight through the canopy to the forest floor. I surveyed from the edge of the clearing—no dinner here. Happy to take a few normal steps, I started to cross the clearing and froze. In the center of my little space was a tarantula the size of a catcher's mit. I was on the lookout for snakes, but I was not prepared to confront a huge, hairy spider—-that can jump! Tarantula and I stared at each other (at least I thought it was looking at me) for the longest ten seconds I can recall. It was not moving, and I was not going to provoke it. I thought about just shooting it, but how could I explain the gunshot? I would never live down shooting a spider. I told the tarantula in a low, calm voice, "Know what, you can have the space, we're cool;" and did reverse stalk steps back to the path. I decided to let the spider have the whole damn forest and headed for the boat. Back at the village, I complained that the hunting these days is bad, that the game has retreated far into the bush. That evening I told KutuKutu and his father that I had seen a large hairy spider in the forest. I did not elaborate that it freaked me out, and that I abandoned my hunt venture; but they assuaged my embarrassment with horror stories of the *kikitappi*. I knew tarantulas could jump long distances, but KutuKutu's father explained that they are ill-tempered and prey on snakes and other small animals. He said the only thing that kills a *kikitappi* was a *mulala*, a centipede. The one forest centipede I ever saw was a fearsome creature about a foot long.

• • •

On one of my hunting explorations, I stopped in Badatabiki, two villages up from Langatabiki, to visit D'Adennie. D'Adennie was a thin, craggy old man living alone in a small thatch, dirt-floor hut. I had heard that he was a respected Kumanti obia man, but when I met him, he appeared eccentric and frail. He knew of me and welcomed my visit. We sat on the small, low stools in front of his hut and discussed the river (too high or too low?), the difficulty in finding *pingos* (peccary) to hunt, and village affairs in general.

I quickly turned the conversation to my interest in the obia powers for men—man-nenge obia. He was forthcoming and knowledgeable about the subject, and related stories of how a bui can provide protection and power. D'Adenni seemed to appreciate my attention. He leaned toward me to counsel that a bui is essential for a man, especially one who travels outside of Pamaka. He then offered to prepare a special bui for me at no fee. He said it would make me invisible when I needed to be. This had potential, I thought, and agreed to work with him to develop the arm bracelet that would enable me to disappear. Being able to become invisible would really help my hunting, but I wondered why all the men did not have this power. D'Adenni studied me carefully for several minutes and told me to come back when I could bring him some Bay Rum. He would work on my bui.

In a few weeks I procured a bottle of Bay Rum liniment from one of the Chinese stores in Albina and delivered it, along with a bottle of taffia clear rum, to D'Adenni in his dark little hut in Badatabbiki. We went through a very formal greeting before we sat down on the stools. He tried to maintain a serious air as an obia man, but was clearly delighted to have the bottles of rum. We motioned for me to go inside. We took our stools and sat face-to-face on the dirt floor in the dark as he started work on the bui. My eyes adjusted and I watched as he selected leaf and powder materials from a corner of his hut and mixed them in a calabash. He added the bay rum to make a slurry in the gourd bowl; the taffia rum was used in libation to D'Adenni's special Kumanti source. He dug out from his medicine corner a ten-inch length of wire with a gauge slightly larger than a dry cleaner hanger. As he worked to bend it into a loop, I wondered if this thing would work in Manhattan (maybe if I added additional ingredients for the preparation, like a nice Chardonnay)?

D'Adenni spoke to the calabash softly in, apparently, Kumanti, and solemnly put the looped wire into the gourd and covered it with a piece of pangi cloth. While the wire was being infused with the medicine, D'Adenni began the instructions on how the bui will work. First, I must keep myself worthy of its power by avoiding women during their menstruation period. This meant not only no intimacy, but no touching or eating food prepared by such a polluting woman. Whenever a bui fails to perform, it is typically ascribed to such pollution. To engage the invisibility feature, I would have to adopt a particular pose while leaning against a tree. He led me outside to demonstrate just how to place my left foot and the palms of both hands flat against the tree. Still thinking of using this power in New York, I asked, "What if there are no trees around?" D'Adenni thought for a moment and said a wall would suffice. I didn't tell him I wanted to try it out for hunting, too. He said that the bui had an added protective feature for me, and instructed that I wear it when venturing into an unfamiliar place; and if I feel the bui squeeze my arm, *Turn back!* Do *not* do whatever it was I was going to do, or go where I was going to go.

Back inside the hut I pulled up the stool and paused to let my eyes adjust to the dark. The strange old man gingerly removed the wire arm bracelet from the calabash, shook the liquid off, and handed it to me with both hands. I held it on my lap since he told me to take off my shirt. D'Adenni then stood over me and poured the leafy mixture from the calabash over the back of my neck and shoulders while chanting a Kumanti benediction. With that, it was now my bui. I stood up—wet and smelling like marinated bay leaves. D'Adenni said to put my bui on later and poured another libation with some of the drinking rum. With formal farewell greetings, and effusive thanks, I headed for my canoe. I could not wait to get back to Langatabiki to try my invisibility power on KutuKutu.

KutuKutu knew that I had been visiting D'Aenni; I did not tell him about the bui, however. That evening before dark back at Langatabiki, I put my bui on my left arm, and went to the rear of the house. I planted myself against the back wall of the house with palms and left foot flat on the wall as directed. KutuKutu was inside cooking a pot of rice on the propane stove. I called for him to come to the back of the house and closed my eyes while he bounded around the corner.

"What?" he asked.

I kept quiet; eyes closed. *He is wondering where I am*, I thought.

It didn't take long for him to ask, "BaMambo, what are you doing?"

I opened my eyes and saw that he was looking right at me. "You can see me?"

KutuKutu seemed incredulous: "Yeah, I see you."

"Shit!"

KutuKutu later consoled that at least I did not pay D'Adenni a lot of money for the bui. I swore KutuKutu to secrecy about my bui and the to-be-developed invisibility power. I felt a little silly expecting to become invisible; then again, it could be that the bui just needed time to adapt to me and Langatabiki. And maybe there was a woman to blame. I would try it again later; just not with snakes, tarantulas, or other things that get in the way of a hunt.

CHAPTER TWENTY-FOUR

BELIEF ENVY

The Pamaka system of concepts concerning life, death, and social order was extraordinary. An amazing feat, considering it was created in a short period of time by disparate Africans isolated as fugitives in a hostile forest on another continent. The more I became conversant with the way Pamakans integrated the physical and spiritual world, I began to appreciate the logical coherence of the conceptual system they had constructed from cultural shards salvaged from Africa. I also began to envy their unequivocal embrace of it. Pamakans knew what they knew, and what they knew was confirmed daily by observed life events: bad things happen to people who disrupt good social order. There were no accidents; every effect had a cause. Occasionally, it would take consultation with ancestors to determine a cause, but everything had its explanation.

In my first experience with spirit possession, when the young woman hosted a snake as her persona for about fifteen minutes, I analyzed endlessly what was going on. Was she having an epileptic seizure? Was there hypnosis involved? Was this an elaborate charade? In LokaLoka, where the young man with a badly infected cut underwent a lengthy ritual to consult ancestors to find *why* the cut got infected, was there a psychosomatic health explanation here? These events, and the many rituals I attended, made it clear to me that the Pamakans *knew* what was going on. It was not a matter of accepting a system of beliefs as a matter of faith, choosing one dogma over another, choosing to believe something that could never happen in the world we experience. How liberating it must be, I thought, to just *know* what is going on and why.

When I was asked by one of the Gaaman's sons, a churchman, if I had been baptized, I was honest in explaining that I did not remember ever being baptized. My family was nominally Protestant Christian, sort of. As a young teenager, I was encouraged to go to church, even though I never once saw my parents or grandparents in a church. They told me to try the Baptist Church, or the Methodist, to see what I liked. I even went to an Episcopal Church for a short while during college. To be a Christian, I thought, would require selecting a doctrine from a buffet of church menus, with each mandating a total commitment of faith. I could not suspend the critical thinking part of my brain to accept unquestioningly any of the competing versions of the Christ-as-Savior mythology.

The more I got to know and understand the Pamakans, I began to despair that perhaps I was missing out on an important aspect of life by not being able to *truly believe* in anything. This was the anthropologist's curse. To study the countless origin myths constructed by peoples to explain existential phenomena, you cannot know that one, indeed one's own included, is the true one while the others are interesting, but just-so stories.

I began to feel profoundly alone—a strange stranger on a river island thousands of miles from home. My last New York City connection, Daisy, died not long after Katie left. Daisy quickly learned that there was no canned cat food anywhere around. There was, however, an ample supply of small varmints scurrying around at night, so she became a resourceful hunter. One morning, however, she came in terribly sick, and died within a few hours. It seemed to me she came down with some jungle distemper, since she had no shots or likely natural immunity to the tough tropical environment. It was clear to KutuKutu, however, that she had been poisoned. I protested. "Who would poison BaMambo's cat? And why?" We agreed, finally, that she may have eaten a poison someone set out for rats, or the nuisance dogs that run freely in the village.

Around this time, I got sick with a jaundice condition such that my fingertips would show yellow when I pressed my nails. KutuKutu said my eyes were yellow around the pupils; I could not tell without a mirror of any sort. The worst of it, however, was that I could not get out of my hammock. I had no energy at all. I likely had hepatitis—not surprising with the riverbank being the source of drinking water, and everything else you use water for.

KutuKutu's mother came by one morning, assessed my condition and said, for certain, that I had "yellow sickness." This apparently was not an uncommon ailment there, and she had a cure. KutuKutu's father came over that same afternoon with what looked like a large caper bush he had just dug out of the ground. (I later learned that it was *scoparia dulcis*, or sweet broom.) He brushed the dirt from it and set a large pot of water on the fire. I was instructed to drink the brackish broth hot from the pot, straining the leaves with my teeth. When I drank as much as I could, they insisted I drink a little more. When I thought I would burst from the forced drinking, KutuKutu and his father pulled me out of my hammock and poured what was left of the warm concoction over my head, using the cooked stems and leaves as a sponge to wash me all over. After a few days of this treatment, I started to get strength back, and the yellow pallor of my fingernails resided. I was back on my feet.

I had a good supply of aspirin and was regularly called upon for a couple of tablets to back up a bush remedy. One day a neighbor came by with a bad cold and asked if I could help him out with some of my pills.

I told him to come back that evening, and I could do him better. I put together a concoction of rum, bay leaves, cloves, cinnamon, and honey, mixed in hot tea—a bush hot toddy. When he came over, I heated the potion up and instructed him to drink it down and get into his hammock. The next morning, he was effusive about how good that medicine was, and asked me to show him the secret. I shared the recipe since he was my neighbor, and told him that the special feature was to use seven cloves to add spiritual significance to the medicine. I did not want to become a purveyor of hot toddies to the whole village, so I asked my patient to keep this miracle cure quiet.

After about one year in Pamaka, I woke up one morning with a revelation—I had been dreaming in Pamakan! That day I noticed that I was also making thought commentaries to myself (mundane and snarky stuff) in the language. Still, the closer I got to becoming Pamakan in talking, thinking, and doing, the more I realized how different I was from them. I was getting along well in the language, but missed being able to kick back and talk about the Yankees, even the Mets; or just talk shit in comfortable English. I worried that an entire section of my brain would atrophy. I missed Manhattan, where more people lived in a single apartment complex than in all the Pamakan villages.

Despite the scale disparity, I recalled enjoying a greater sense of control over my space, and a comfortable degree of predictability with the people and events in the City than here. I had been immersed in graduate studies and adjunct teaching the two years before, and missed the rich discussions of theory and competing schools of thought of structural anthropology versus the Margaret Mead traditional analysis, and whether radical Marxist anthropology was legitimate. Here, there were no words for basic concepts like gravity. I was profoundly lonely; alone with my once familiar references that orient academic thought and conversation. Of course, Katie leaving me abruptly was a gut punch that left a lingering pain.

The constant daily mandatory ritualized greetings everywhere I went in the village began to get on my nerves. In New York, I would see hundreds of people each day, on the street and in the subway that I would never see again in life. Even eye contact with passers-by in New York was rare, and would prompt a 'what-was-that-about' thought. Here, I see the same few dozen people every day, and rarely anyone else. Every morning, every evening, every encounter along a path, one must pause and go through the formal greeting sequence.

The villagers told me often of a strange man who lives alone in a forest camp somewhere on the French Guiana side of the river. He speaks English, they would tell me. He was not a Pamakan. They described him as showing up and hiding out many years ago, a probable prison escapee. The legendary Devil's Island penal colony, which closed 20 years earlier, was located at the mouth of the river. (The villagers were not aware of *Papillon,* the book and film about the most famous escape up their river.)

Everyone said that I had to meet Papa Plai because he speaks English. No one suggested I go visit him. He was a recluse, and no one was sure where exactly he lived, nor did anyone really want to find out. One day some kids came running to find me, "Papa Plai is coming, Papa Plai!" More people gathered as the kids led me to the landing where a small canoe, paddled slowly by a lone man, was making its way to the island from the French side. A tall, lanky man in well-worn pants, a long-sleeve shirt, and fedora climbed out of the canoe and tied up. He made his way up the landing, and the crowd became excited at this epic meeting of Papa Plai and BaMambo. Plai had skin the color of very old green olives, and thin, curly, greying hair. He was an older man, probably in his mid-sixties, tall and erect at about six feet, but weighed maybe only 160 pounds.

As he reached the top of the landing, I extended my right hand with a hearty, "Welcome!" He seemed unsure who I was or what was going on, but smiled slightly and replied awkwardly, "Hallo. Thanks well."

"I understand you speak English. I'm pleased to meet you," I say in great anticipation. Even if he's a Mets fan, it will be fun to talk, I think.

"Hallo. Thanks well," was his response.

I was starting to lose what ephemeral eye contact we had. "Yeah, well they call me BaMambo and I'm an anthropologist working here for a while. You live on the French side?"

"Hallo. Thanks well." Plai then started fidgeting with a small bag he carried. He was ready to move on.

The crowd was disappointed and started to disperse. KutuKutu asked me what just happened. I said, hey, you speak more English than Plai. KutuKutu was incredulous, "He no speak Pamaka, no French, no

English!" We looked at each other, and without saying anything knew what we were thinking, "What *does* he speak?"

I could not help but extrapolate the question to an anthropological matter: is it possible for a human to exist today with no language at all? Plai may be the experiment of one getting by with a smattering of words from this and that language. It probably only works if you live alone and subsist on fish you catch, and nuts and berries you can forage from the forest.

My anticipation and utter disappointment in finding a linguistic soulmate in Papa Plai sunk me further into my funk. I started to feel more alone and adrift. My thoughts would swirl—in my own Okie-English—around my possibly missing a major feature of human sentient life by my inability to just *know* answers to fundamental questions of life like Pamakans do.

I could not escape inherent questions about everything I saw and was told. For me, the Pamaka belief system itself was fascinating and a significant subject for analysis, not unconditional acceptance. I was different here. Then there was the nagging issue for me of personal space—a little privacy, please. The crowds of children had stopped following me around, but in the village I was constantly among people I knew and who knew me. And there were dogs and chickens always under foot—roosters that do not crow just in the early mornings, but incessantly.

The plank and thatch houses were all bunched close together, so your business was the neighborhood's business. At one point, I confided with one of the Gaaman's sons who was about my age, and with whom I had become friends, "Do you think Gaaman would grant me a space just outside of the village where I could put up a house?" B'Amapata looked at me sternly and reached to hold my arm. He shook his head, and with great seriousness, said, "Only witches live alone, away from other people."

So much for my plan for a little peace and quiet in the suburbs.

CHAPTER TWENTY-FIVE

RESET

I shared my fieldwork angst in short, pre-stamped airmail letters to Professor Diamond back at the New School. They must have sounded dire since he wrote back that the Anthropology Club had taken donations to fund a mental health round trip to New York. I really did need a break, so I gladly accepted. A few days later I caught a boat to Albina, leaving KutuKutu in charge of the house. Back in Paramaribo, I got caught up on the joys of cold beer and found that PanAm had just started a once-a-week direct flight between Paramaribo and JFK. I got a one-week, up-and-back ticket.

It was February and freezing cold, with piles of dirty snow along the sidewalks in New York. Colleagues who met me at the airport thoughtfully brought a jacket and scarf. I still had shoes, but no socks. I was cold, but felt I was in my cognitive homeland. I could not stop talking and listening. The conversations were elixir to my brain and heart. I was hearing and speaking easy anthro stuff and colloquial small talk, infused with common conceptual references and shared assumptions. It was liberating to not have to think about what was being said to me, and how to respond appropriately.

I was warmed and moved by the genuine welcome of friends and colleagues. The couch accommodations in a friend's tiny apartment in Greenwich Village seemed luxurious. I settled in for my short stay; but quickly felt alone in a familiar city. This was less loneliness than a sense of loss. I was back home, but without Katie and Daisy. Katie did not want to see me at all; she had moved on to a new phase of her life as a film editor. I went for a long walk that first night along cold, anonymous sidewalks in Greenwich Village and had a good cry—something BaMambo could not, would not do in the forest village.

Next day, with my emotions settled, I plunged into meetings and discussions with colleagues and friends. At the New School, I looked for the Guyanese mailroom guy to hug him and thank him for the brilliant Tolsie Persaud gambit he gave me, and to ask, "Who *is* this guy?" Unfortunately, my mailroom connection had moved on and was no longer at the New School.

Manhattan was different to me; the air irritated my nose and throat. It was not just that it was cold; the air was dry and seemed second-hand. The people I talked with expressed interest in my field experiences, and remarked about how fulfilling it must be to be doing something rewarding and challenging. The throngs of men and women I saw on the streets every day seemed to be semi-conscious and busy, on their way to or from somewhere. There was no eye contact whatsoever with anyone encountered on the streets, much less a minute-long greeting. Everyone was a stranger, and each looked very different from each other. And it was so odd to be passing closely by hundreds of people daily who I would never see again in life; whereas, in Langatabiki I could see and talk with the same few dozen people every day for the rest of my life.

I started seeing New York City as BaMambo would. I was surrounded by massive, fast, man-made things: buildings, cars, subway trains. Back in Pamaka, all the "man-made" things were actually made by you, or men and women that you knew, or knew of. In the City, there was nothing I could see or touch that I felt I could have made—not even the styrofoam cup holding my coffee, much less a Volvo. As BaMambo back in Manhattan, I was astonished at the apparent disconnect between people and their environment.

The trip was short, but essential to begin recovery from the emotional car wreck of my marriage. It also confirmed that I had the beginnings of a dual identity and perspective as an anthropologist and as a Pamakan—I was becoming BaMambo.

I felt good climbing aboard PanAm Flight 227 direct to Paramaribo, with a suitcase full of books. I had an aisle seat and was surrounded by a family of fundamentalist Christian missionaries on their way to set up shop in Suriname for the first time. They were not wearing church nametags, but they were obvious in their missionary zeal. I politely asked the father of the family if he was a businessman. He replied loudly and with the enthusiasm of one on a mission from God, "Why, you might say I am a businessman. I'm a missionary, and that covers a lot of business— BIG business. Got a very exacting boss too, kind of always around looking over your shoulder... ." This called for a quick escape into a book for the rest of the flight.

When we landed at Paramaribo, I climbed eagerly down the stair ramp to the tarmac and was delighted that the local PanAm ground crew and one of the customs officials recognized me from the outbound trip and smiled "Welcome back." I could feel the outlines of my body diffusing into the moist, warm air. *I know this air, and it remembers me too*, I thought. I lost awareness of the sharp distinction of my body and the organic vapor that is the tropic air. I blended into the air, and no longer felt the inside of my nose. Instead, my skin wanted to wash in the air, to commune and laugh in it.

I felt like I was home.

CHAPTER TWENTY-SIX

THE PASSWORD

When I got back to Langatabiki, B'Aleke had returned from his sojourn and had taken up with a woman. I had to find another place to stay. The Gaaman said I could use an empty place in his lineage neighborhood, near his official residence. The new place was a large thatch house elevated on poles. It was a luxury to be off the dirt. I was now in a different neighborhood, home to a different lineage. Any mapping was long out of the question, so I made good mental notes.

In the following months, I plunged into all things Pamakan. KutuKutu was happy to see me back, half suspecting, I think, that I had left for good. My new household was complemented by a series of animal sojourners. Egelo the Capuccine monkey, Pawa the green parrot, and TuTu the toucan were not pets. They came to me as orphaned infant animals picked up by hunters. I fed them and talked to them in Pamakan. They had the run of the house—no cages or leashes. Pawa, when he was able, would fly out for a day and return to the house before dark. TuTu was just zany, and took off when he got it together to fly. Egelo seemed comfortable hanging around, but he was not going to wear a costume or hold a cup for tips. He was cool just being a monkey, not too far from where he came from.

KutuKutu became an increasingly valuable resource for access and knowledge, as well as a welcome companion. A little older now, I started to appreciate how smart and serious he was. He was comfortable with himself and, unlike Petrus, seemed to have few ambitions beyond Langatabiki. I liked that KutuKutu had little interest in looking or acting American, or anything other than himself. TiBaya, his father who protected me in the dust-up over the map, and washed me out of yellow sickness, became a true mentor in matters Pamakan, and life generally.

He once told me that if a man does not work and sweat, the sweat remains in his body and dilutes his blood, making him weak. That piece of wisdom has guided me ever since: persevere, work hard, sweat, and stay strong.

Through their history as an isolated fugitive people, Pamakans came to place great stock in group integrity and the careful screening of imports of people and things into their midst. It took nearly a year living among the Pamakans for me to earn a significant measure of trust and acceptance. The American airplanes had not come to bomb; I had gotten a sort of early clearance from the snake-possessed woman; KutuKutu had become a regular presence with me with no clear ill effect to him; and I gained a measure of fluency in communicating.

I noted an expression of acceptance when TiKambesu, one of the most respected elders, called me over for a story. He related the difficult time during which Pamakans had to fear all outsiders; Ndjuka, Amerindians, Dutch soldiers, and mercenaries could collect large bounties from plantation owners for capturing "unauthorized" free settlers. Pamakans had small and very isolated hideout villages along the small tributaries of the Marowijne. Pamakan scouts would keep a lookout for people entering their territory; and they developed a password protocol to determine the bona fides of anyone approaching.

I had not heard of the forest password test and was fascinated. He then gave me the password! A scout seeing an approaching boat or someone along a path, would remain hidden and call out, "*Wa Da?*" This was not a translatable word or phrase and made no sense unless you knew the protocol. The response must be, "*Fie Man!*" Without the proper response, the incoming person or persons were presumed to be enemies. This was a "Wow" Moment for me—from that point on, I considered myself an honorary Pamakan. I learned later that *Wa Da* is similar to the German *Werda*, the sentry's warning: "Declare yourself... who is there?"

· · ·

While ancestors are the most pervasive and important ethereal presences Pamakans contend with, the common boa constrictor snake is an odd combination of a spiritual presence within a physical menace. The actual boa constrictor snake is often encountered in cultivated fields and in the thatch huts. Stored rice attracts rats, which attract boa constrictors. Pamakans, for the most part, are not concerned about the origins of deities; most will say that the boa constrictor snake is not an ordinary snake, but a "thing of god" or a "kind of god." The boa constrictor is called *Foadu* or, sometimes *Papa Gaddu*. The Gaaman's version reflected a Moravian church-Old Testament influence when he explained to me that once in the early days, the snake was a human who fell in disfavor with God and was condemned to the form of a snake forever.

A different story told dismissively in Paramaribo was that the Bush Negroes' special regard for the boa constrictor stemmed from the plantation era when the field workers misunderstood the planters' tolerance for the snake. In this account, the Europeans valued the boas as a control of vermin, and occasionally enticed them to remain near their households by placing chicken eggs outside for the snakes. In this account, Africans saw this as a spiritual offering, and consequently adopted an attitude of special reverence toward the snake.

In any event, when a Pamakan encounters the snake, they avoid its gaze—eye contact with a boa constrictor is dangerous. In the villages and cultivated areas, people take measures to entice a boa constrictor away without causing it any discomfort. If the snake does not leave, a field or house will be abandoned until it moves on. To molest or to kill the snake is to risk spiritual retribution from it. This is where I figured into the boa constrictor story.

One day a woman, one of my new neighbors, came running up to my house in a high state of anxiety. She told me there was a *foadu* in the rafter of her house, and could I please, please come take it out. I was never fond of snakes. Growing up I encountered a lot of snakes up in Oklahoma—no boa constrictors, however. My Okie experience with snakes was to keep far away and kill them if you can. Capturing a large snake in a dark hut was not something I wanted to do, but it was not like being asked to apply lye to straighten hair—this seemed like a real emergency. I reached for my machete.

"No, No! You can't hurt it!" she cried. She explained that I must get it out of the house and take it somewhere and let it go, with minimal bother to the snake.

"Wait, where's TiLekie (her husband), and where are your brothers?" I asked, thinking *why is this my job?*

She explained to me, like telling a child something so obvious, "You're the only one in the village who can do it. The snake cannot go into your body."

So, that was it. BaMambo is not a Pamakan, so he is immune to the eye contact and spiritual infection by the boa constrictor spirit! I was stuck having to do something that just thinking about made my skin crawl.

A small crowd watched from a safe distance as I got a long canoe pole and a burlap bag and surveyed the dark interior of her small house from the doorway. There he was—a goddam snake about five feet long and five inches thick, ensconced along the top poles where the thatch panels were tied. This would be so easy with a shotgun, I thought, as I tried to devise a way to get the thing from the rafters and into the bag.

I got a canoe paddle at the ready, and poked the boa constrictor with the pole until it fell to the dirt floor. It headed for the pile of boxes and furniture in the back of the hut, but I pinned it down behind the head with the pole flat to the ground. No one dared to come in to help me with this now very strong and angry snake that was trying to wrap itself around anything it could reach. I had to keep my weight on the pole to keep it pinned down, but the paddle fell just out of reach. I used every tool skill

I could muster to reach the paddle, finally grabbing a nearby stool to pull the paddle closer. With the paddle, I dragged the burlap bag over, and started the awful, awful job of stuffing this snake into the bag without getting myself wrapped with it. Holding the bag open with one hand, I used the paddle to pull and push the snake into the bag, while keeping its head pinned to the ground by holding it with the pole. Thankfully, I thought, no one was watching this spectacle of me and this snake wrestling on the ground, with me using a pole and paddle to avoid touching (or being touched by) it.

I got the snake into the bag—not happy, but not injured. I was exhausted and sweaty as I emerged from the hut with the heavy bag of boa constrictor. The crowd gave me a wide passage as I took the bagged snake to my canoe. I took it to the downriver end of island, shook it out of the bag and watched it swim away with the current. I wondered if it would head for the Dutch or French side of the river. I came back a hero; everyone was relieved and grateful. The problem was that I then became the go-to guy for boa constrictor extractions. No matter that I knew the password and was fairly proficient by now in communicating and lore, it was very convenient to have someone around who was considered immune from the Foadu.

CHAPTER TWENTY-SEVEN

NONGOS AND MACHETES

My communication skills had reached the point where I could carry on normal conversations with adults. Learning the grammar structure and syntax, however, was only part of it. It seemed that there were only a few thousand words in the language, but communication was rich and varied through the nuance of pause and inflection in the word spoken, or the sound following the word. "*Lebie*," for example, is the word for the color red. If you want to describe something that is a distinct dark red, or perhaps red all over, you would say "*lebie ngaaang*." The more you stretch the "*ngaaang*," the redder the thing you are describing.

Complex sentiments are expressed in a rich lexicon of aphorisms called *nongos*. Nongos are a key part of the curriculum of tradition and meaning that older people pass along to their children, nephews, and nieces. These short allegories and their meaning are also valuable currency sought by children from elders in exchange for errands. An example is the phrase literally translated as "Monkey's mouth kills monkey." This nongo teaches that it is important not to brag of your valuables or accomplishments, as such braggadocio can incite others to envy and possible revenge.

Another nongo: "When you curse the buzzard it hurts turkey," expresses the caution to not speak ill of others since someone hearing you may be family to the one you are disparaging. Similar meaning is conveyed in the nongo, "Monkey's body is monkey's tail." Here the explanation is that if you take action against one person, you will likely have to answer to that person's relatives, as the monkey's tail is an integral part of its body.

"When turtle's belly hurts, he lies on his back," carries the warning to be careful of what you do to solve an immediate problem, as your solution may result in bigger problems. Along the same line, one of my favorites, "Alligator runs from the rain to jump in the river," suggests that you should think carefully about and prepare for actions that you take, lest you end up in a worse predicament.

Speeches and pronouncements of high importance are typically summarized by a nongo that captures the essence of message. Great speakers are adept at introducing remarks or demolishing an opposing sentiment with a nongo. Major events such a proposed marriage, or any serious disagreements, must be settled by lineage elders formally, and involve a lineage council hearing of the case. The council will be led by the senior lineage elder, and the proceedings are structured so that the council listens to both sides of the issue and recommends to the presiding elder a decision for resolution.

These council sessions, *kuutu* or sometimes called *mitie mofu* ("meeting of mouths"), were fascinating for their ritualized and choreographed discourse. First, no one speaks directly to another. There is a *piki man* (literally, "answer man") to whom each speaker addresses his or her talk.

Second, each speaker utters phrases to which the *piki man* responds, with a formal, "That's so," or "That's right," and so on. You can sometimes get by with a sentence, but never a full paragraph of a speech before the piki man must interject a "That's so." When the presiding elder makes a significant point, all participants do a quiet, slow, synchronized clap.

Speaking Pamakan well was a high art form—fun to learn and practice, and delightful to hear when performed by the good speakers. The people who were very good with the delivery were the most popular storytellers in evening sessions around a fire. Men would recount a hunt, whether of that very day or years before, with marvelous inflections and pantomimes of jaguars, wild boars, monkeys, or tapirs. The high point was always when the teller describes the shot (their only guns were single shot twelve-guage shotguns): "BAOOMMMMMMMM!" Quiet pause as the audience gasps.

The theatre for spoken art was the telling of Anansi stories. These were nighttime performances recounting the exploits of the spider trickster, "Anansi," a tradition that can be traced to West Africa. Anansi stories are usually associated with funerary ceremonies and provide a forum for singing and dancing throughout the night. During the formal telling of the Anansi tale, called *mato*, listeners will interject a song or side story by calling out "I was there." Someone will ask, "What'd you see?" and the I-was-there person would launch into a song. Everyone knows the songs, but individuals will often add lyrics for a pun. All join in joyful chorus, especially if the lyric is novel, or spot on to a current issue.

It was like going to see Hamlet; you know the story, but you go to enjoy the performance. The *matos* were a means of conveying life stories to children, who delighted in these performances. One story about how a lie hurts more than a sore— which I transcribe here, highly truncated— took all night to tell:

Turtle told monkey one day that a lie hurts more than a sore. Monkey said that that was impossible. Monkey thought nothing could hurt like a sore, and to prove it to turtle, he took a big tree branch and dropped it on turtle's back. Monkey then went away and left turtle underneath the branch.

Turtle was fastened under the branch for so long that the wood began to grow mold. Turtle ate the mold all up, got his strength back, and was able to crawl out from under the wood. He then went to an old mother and asked her to bake him some cookies. He wanted cookies such that you smell them far away, like from here to Loka-Loka.

Turtle took his cookies and soon jaguar caught the smell and came running. Jaguar asked turtle where he had gotten such sweet-smelling cookies. Turtle said that these cookies were really monkey's shit, monkey had shit them for him.

Jaguar went right away to find monkey. In those days, monkey lived on the ground like the other animals. When jaguar saw monkey, he caught him and demanded that he shit some of those sweet cookies for him, like the ones he had shit for turtle.

Monkey didn't know what to do, so he began to shit. Jaguar took the shit, but couldn't stand the smell at all. It didn't smell like the sweet cookies that turtle had; it smelled just like monkey shit. Jaguar thought that monkey was trying to fool him.

He knew that monkey could really shit sweet-smelling cookies, because turtle had told him that was where he had gotten his. This is the lie that turtle told to jaguar.

Jaguar grabbed monkey and told him that he would hold him until he shit some of those sweet cookies for him. Every time monkey would shit his bad smelling shit, jaguar would get mad and hold him tighter.

But one day, the paramount chief of the animals, agouti, called everyone to a big council meeting. Jaguar came, still holding onto monkey. Chief agouti told a story in the council, and everyone had to clap their hands. When jaguar went to clap, he let go of monkey. Monkey ran away and climbed up a tree and has stayed there over since. That is why he is a tree animal now.

The End.

For a Pamakan, childhood through teens is an apprenticeship to their lineage elders in the ways of adulthood. Young Pamakans are available to their elders for errands and assistance on an on-call basis. Through these arrangements, young people acquire language nuances and nongos, along with basic technical skills he or she will need as a self-sufficient adult. For boys, the basics involve boat and house building, hunting, and preparing fields in the forest for cultivation. For girls, basic skills include cleaning animals and fish for cooking, preparing juices from berries and palm nuts, and the complex process of turning cassava roots into flat bread or dried, coarse cereal.

Beyond survival basics, young people need to learn the sacred knowledge of medicinal preparations, the exploits and ways of the ancestors, the power and danger of the water and forest essences, and the history of the lineage and the Pamakans. One can be old without being respected as an elder. Prestige and status in age depends on an understanding and detailed knowledge of the ancestors—a knowledge which can only be acquired through deference and service as a youth. Menial errands, such as delivering messages and fetching water for elders establish the relationship whereby an elder will, on occasion, "pay" a youth by giving him a story of the elders, an explanation of a nongo, or a recipe for an herbal medicine. Knowledge of history and how things work in the forest are the currency of prestige.

KutuKutu and I learned one important triage procedure, almost at the expense of my left foot. We were helping TiAndoli clear a field for a plot for planting cassava, peanuts, and rice. He had chosen a spot pretty far into the forest; six of us in the work party took a canoe a couple of miles upriver from Langatabiki and trekked about a half-hour into the forest. Our job was to chop down all the trees, and clear away the vines and bushes. TiAndoli would let them dry for a few weeks and return with another crew of relatives to burn the brush, exposing the soil for his woman and her own work party to plant.

I was constantly amazed at how adept Pamakans were at wielding machetes and axes: the basic tools men, women, and children use every day. I could type better than any Pamakan; but chopping down a tree was another matter. I practiced, and got better, but could never hit the precise cut point with every swing of the axe like the others, even KutuKutu. I often wondered how good these guys would be at golf or pool with such exceptional hand/eye coordination.

By afternoon, I was exhausted and itching all over with mosquito and whatnot bites, as well as wood chips sticking to accumulated sweat. Determined to finish off a modest-sized tree I had been working on for a while, I took a wide, downward swing expecting a triumphant finale. Instead, my axe ricocheted and hit the ground with a trajectory that took it into my left leg just above my ankle.

The cut did not particularly hurt, but it was scary to see blood pouring out of my leg and a big flap of skin hanging quite out of place. I wiggled my toes and was relieved that my foot was still attached. One inch further left would have been a complete amputation of my foot. I reflexively touched my beads and silently uttered thanks for the near miss.

Then it occurred to me that being this far in the forest, I could get a major infection, if my blood did not all drain out first. I was mostly mortified that I had botched this most basic of men's work—chopping down a tree. I uttered a controlled "ouch," and put on the most stoic demeanor I could muster. When the men came over and appeared alarmed, I protested, "It's just a scratch," while wondering what it will be like with only one foot.

TiAndoli took a close look at my wound and told me to sit down. He'd be right back. He walked around the trees that were still standing, selected one and cut off a large piece of the outer bark to expose the pulpy sub layer of bark. Holding his machete with both hands on the ends he scraped this inner layer of the tree trunk and pulled out a hand full of moist, stringy pulp that looked like sauerkraut.

He pressed the hanging flap of skin back into place and covered the bleeding mess with the ball of pulp. He held it tight against my leg for about a minute until the bleeding stopped. One of the guys ripped a piece from one of our sweaty t-shirts and wrapped my leg, holding the sauerkraut tightly in place. They cut a walking stick for me and we all headed back to the canoe. I left the bush bandage on for a couple of days, not knowing what I could do better. My wound healed with no infection. I ended up with a distinctive scar and an enhanced reputation when the story went around the village that I handled a bad cut with aplomb, albeit fake.

CHAPTER TWENTY-EIGHT

TI MAMBO

I did not tell Gaaman or any of the church people about my bui. They probably all had their own, but did not speak of such things. A few weeks later, Gaaman hosted the annual clearing of the Moravian burial ground, about a ten-minute walk down a seldom-used path at the downriver part of Langatabiki. The men of the village, including me, headed off one morning to the burial ground—a cemetery without any headstones or markings of actual grave sites. It was essentially an acre or so carved out of the forest that gets quickly overgrown with the fast-growing tropical vines and bushes. Clearing and cleaning is hot, sweaty, arduous work whacking down waist-high plants and vines, vines, and more vines with machetes. Once you chop down the vines, bushes, and small trees, you have to pile up the large gaggle of brush and haul it to a corner of the clearing. As this was a church affair, there were no libations or body painting, and certainly no drumming or dancing.

After about four hours the work party returned to the village where the Gaaman and a group of about fifty people welcomed us with soft drinks. Gaaman Forster addressed the gathering and thanked the men who were all sweaty and covered with leaf shards as if camouflaged. I was completely exhausted and could not wait to jump in the river to wash up. Before I could leave without notice Gaaman Forster called out my name for special recognition. And he called me, *"Ti* Mambo!"

He told the crowd that TiMambo had helped out not only today in this project, but in all aspects of life there, so he is one of us. People looked at me appreciatively as I tried to shrink. But he did not let it go at that. I was really surprised when Gaaman went on to announce that, "as everyone knows, TiMambo does not have a woman. And we all know," he preached, "that it not good for a man to not have a woman." He closed the program by inviting the audience to help TiMambo find a woman.

It was graduation day of a sort! By that announcement, I not only achieved *Ti* status and became one of the men; I was cleared for the dating scene as well. It was a delicious idea to enjoy intimate female companionship, and there were beautiful women around. But this was tricky. Almost all the fights, large and small, that I had seen or heard of involved *that's-my*-woman or *that's-my*-man issues.

One of the older men in Langatabiki had a distinctive white patch of hair above his left eye. It was a perfect one-inch square of white in his full head of otherwise black hair. I learned that as a young man he had patch braids for his longish hair; during a fight over a woman someone grabbed a strand of his braids and yanked it completely out of his head. His bare patch grew back with snow-white hair and stayed that way.

I would have to take this slow and be very discrete. There was a well-practiced art form to hooking up in a village of bunched-up thatch huts, with no private space, let alone restaurants or clubs. I knew it was done, but I had not been part of this scene.

Shortly after my elevation to "Ti," I joined a couple of guys who were going to make a day trip to Albina for gasoline and other supplies. They had a fast boat so by leaving early we could make it back upriver by nightfall. I had not been out of the interior for a few months, plus, a cold juggo and some bami would be good therapy so I went along. We docked in Albina about noon and I headed straight for the bami joint which was right at the waterfront. First stop after a four-hour trip, of course, was the men's room. The restaurant itself was a bare concrete floor, tile wall, and a space with tables and chairs arranged in no particular order. Fluorescent lights made everything stark. I opened the bathroom door and froze! *Holy Shit!* I was seeing myself in the mirror for the first time in a long time. *I'm white!*

I had no mirror in the village, and the river water was in constant motion, so there was never a reflection. I peered at myself in strange amazement for half a minute. I had forgotten about my blue eyes and sharp nose, and had come to see myself as just like everyone around me. It was a moment of reintroducing myself to me. It was a revelation of sorts to realize just what my neighbors see when they look at me. No one had ever joked or made comments to me about my features, so different from theirs. I finished up and washed my hands, enjoying the fresh water flowing from a faucet. (I would have swooned if there had been hot water from a tap.) With one last look in the mirror, I headed for a table thinking, *Damn, I need a haircut.*

Back in the village that evening, I was again alone in my house of dried leaves, poles, and planks. The new place was high off the ground and comfortable. My hammock was tied to pole rafters close to the thatch. The *thockthockthockthockthockthock* sound of rain on thatch was wonderfully calming; nevertheless, I was emotionally sore, and quite alone.

My own general preventive medicine was to take a spoonful of local honey before folding into the hammock. The honey was so good, and obviously organic and unfiltered, I enjoyed it regardless of any medicinal benefit. On my quick trip to the riverhead town, Albina, I scored some weed from one of the young South Asian guys working the bus terminal. Marijuana was not a feature upriver at that time. No Pamakan that I knew discussed it or used it. There was no Pamakan term for marijuana then, so I kept this little vice to myself.

It had been a long and eventful day—a six or seven-hour boat trip, and confronting the reality that I looked so different from everyone around me. I decided I needed a "night out" in a sense. KutuKutu was at his parents' place, so I rolled a healthy joint of the Albina Gold (or whatever it was), tucked into my hammock, and gave it a big push off the pole. The weed was delightful, not life-threatening like the Guyanese stuff.

As I was swinging, I realized I had not taken my spoonful of honey for the night. I rolled out of the hammock and got the honey jar. Back in the hammock fold, swinging in complete rapture, a spoon of honey would not do. I held the honey jar high over my head like I had seen a *venenciadora* in Portugal pour sherry, and rather expertly held a long pour of honey right into my wide-open mouth. Impressive! I thought, right on target and no spills. In a moment, my sublime bliss turned to terror—I couldn't breathe! I had a full mouthful of thick honey, swinging on my back in a hammock. I tried to breathe through my nose—no good. *I'm drowning!*

In that instant, I accepted that death was inevitable and maybe this was my moment; *but wait!* My death cannot be so ignominious: drowning in honey, stoned in a hammock! My brain screamed: *I'M NOT GOING TO DIE LIKE THIS!* I rolled violently out of the hammock, face down onto the floor, clawing the honey out of my mouth, coughing and spitting for dear life—literally. Again, a spectacle I'm grateful no one witnessed. This was another experience I did not share with KutuKutu or anyone else. I added this to my personal do's and don'ts: don't do weed and honey together in a hammock.

CHAPTER TWENTY-NINE

THE UPRIVER ADVENTURE

After a few months in Pamaka, I became better at asking more comprehensive questions and understanding the answers. One area I found fascinating was Pamakan cosmography. To a Pamakan, the earth is oriented to the river and its flow; upstream (*opo se*) and downstream (*bilo se*) are the cardinal referents. It was difficult for me to adjust to upriver being south and downriver north. Directions in the villages or in the forest are still related in terms of the river. In hunting, for instance, terms such as "back", "far", and "deep" refer to east-west distance from the river, and even though one may be several miles away from the river, one always walks "upstream" or "downstream." These bearings apply equally to either side of the river, the *doishi se* (Dutch side) and the *fransi se* (French side).

The first waterfall was conceptually important to Pamakans and other free settlers in that "upriver from the falls" was considered that territory subject to the exclusive domain of the respective free settlement and Amerindian tribal authorities. Above the falls is where the Gaaman is more important than the (district) commissioner. The waterfalls establish an actual inaccessibility of the free settlements to the coastal government.

Upstream waters and territories often take on a frontier ethos in conversations. Since the first free settlements, plantations, colonial government, and slavery have been downstream dangers; escape and freedom have always been gained by moving upstream. Wherever one may be along the river, game and fish are invariably considered to be more plentiful upstream. Upstream water was considered "sweeter and cooler." It is not surprising that social distinctions among Marowijne people are often set in a geopolitical context of upstream and downstream.

All groups above the first falls speak of the "tide water people" with subtle condescension. People say navigating below the falls requires no special skills or knowledge of the river. It is pointed out that even Europeans and Chinese travel this part of the river in a variety of boats. The inland forest Ndjuka, in turn, consider the Pamakans a downstream people with relatively easy river passage among their villages. The contempt implicit in this assumption is most obvious when Pamaka boatmen wish to travel through dangerous rapids in Ndjuka territory. Often the Ndjuka paramount chief will insist that Ndjuka boatmen accompany the Pamakans, who, it is assumed, could not possibly be able to navigate the upstream waters without such assistance.

Once I achieved Ti-level standing and began feeling more confident in my Pamakan-ness, I began to question—and needle—KutuKutu and his friends about why they had never explored the big river upstream to its source. I really wanted to do this trip with these guys, an adventure within my adventure. It would be challenging; none of them had gone more than a day or so up the river from Langatabiki. The upriver Ndjuka were an officious lot with Pamakans, and it would cost a lot of money for a canoe, a big outboard motor, and the gasoline to get us up and back. By this time, I was no longer just an anthropologist standing by, observing, and reporting what these people do. Now I was an instigator, but doing so as TiMambo, not Mr. John the anthropologist.

One of the older guys, Afunki, had a sturdy, 24-foot canoe with a big Evenrude outboard motor. I put out a challenge one day: I would spring for the gas and give Afunki some money for his boat to go as far up the river as we can go.

"Who's in?" I asked. Afunki said he was game, and KutuKutu was all in. This would be a ten-day trip, up serious rapids on an unknown river. What everyone knew but did not talk about was that coming back *down* the rapids was far more dangerous than going up against the flow. We would need several guys with river experience.

Days later, I was sitting on my hammock enjoying a morning black coffee when KutuKutu came bounding up the ladder stair. "We have four people!" He had lined up two other guys in addition to Afunki and himself: Alaman and Shiliki.

"Hey, what about me?" I asked, trying a Brooklyn accent and gestures in Pamakan. The accent effect was lost on KutuKutu; "Ok, ok, you too." Afunki, Alaman and Shiliki were all a little older than KutuKutu, and had boat experience. None of us, of course, had been very far up the river we were going to explore.

I had saved up some cash from the small research stipend the New School sent and gave Afunki money to buy almost a barrel of gasoline on his next downriver trip to Albina. We started packing dried cassava bread and lots of *kwaka*. We would take some dried fish and canned sardines, but would mostly hunt and fish along the way for protein. I had no map; our plan was to follow the river upstream as far as we could go, taking the left fork up the Lawa to avoid going into Ndjuka territory and right by their Gaaman's village of Dritabiki.

There was still a morning fog over the river when Afunki brought his canoe around to the landing near my house. We all packed lightly, knowing we would have to offload and reload the canoe several times going through rapids upriver. Everyone brought a hammock and machete; one of the guys brought a shotgun. Afunki had loaded on an extra gas tank and a hose to siphon fuel from the barrel. He also brought a sturdy *kola tiki*—a long wooden pole for the bowman to measure depth and feel out rocks just below the water that would snap off propeller blades. (Also good for poking boa constrictors out of rafters.)

There was no big sendoff; a few women washing clothes waved from the bank as Afunki made a dramatic turn off the mud landing and roared off upriver!

Once out of sight of Langatabiki, we settled down for a few hours of familiar river. We waved to people in camps and villages and made a couple of stops. We overnighted at Sikintabiki, the last Pamaka village upriver. This was Asaiti country, but everyone seemed to have a relative of some sort in every village. We tied hammocks in an open thatch shed, and had a great meal brought to us, compliments of one of KutuKutu's relatives.

Day two, we moved beyond our comfort zone. We were in Ndjuka territory, so we stopped at Stoelman's Island, a Surinamese government outpost that had a small airstrip and a shop. This is where we took the left fork. The Marowijne River splits into the Lawa and Tapanahoni Rivers. The Lawa would avoid any hassles from the Ndjuka along the Tapanahoni; and as we traveled upstream, we would continue along the river border between Suriname on the right, and French Guiana on the left. We were motoring against a strong current, so we spent the night at Stoelman's Island to get an early start up the Lawa.

None of the guys had been up the Lawa, so we were all on lookout for rocks and rapids. The trick for getting through rapids (up or down) is to study the river before selecting your route. Generally, you aim for the largest channel, but often the current is too strong for the canoe to make it through. That's when we would have to select a shallow opening, unload the canoe and walk it through. Between rapids we passed a few camps and villages of the Boni people. Pamakans, I learned, enjoy a much better relationship with the Boni than with the Ndjuka. I had also read and heard of Arawak Amerindian villages upriver beyond Boni territory. The crew knew generally we were going into Indian Country ("*Ingi Kondey*") somewhere far up the Lawa.

By afternoon, and hours of constant motoring (Afunki did his version of in-flight refueling with his siphon hose), we saw a clearing in the forest wall and a few canoes docked on the French side. I motioned for us to stop and check it out. We pulled in beside well-made and maintained canoes with big motors. I hopped out and walked a few steps up the path. At the top of a rise was a magnificently appointed thatch compound—a jungle Shangri-La!

It was a large house set off the ground on high posts with a diesel generator and plumbing. No air-conditioning, but big European ceiling fans rotated slowly, gently wafting floor-length white chiffon curtains— an elegant way to keep mosquitoes away. Four or five Boni men and women were there as staff. We went through the formal greeting in hybrid Ndjuka and Pamakan, they offered us clear, clean drinking water as we chatted amicably. They explained that the house belonged to a Frenchman who was not there. That was about all they were going to divulge about their patron. My imagination ran wild; this was an idyllic jungle existence that required a full-time staff to maintain. When you clear a patch of forest to plant a field or construct a hut, you can almost see the vines, brush, and palm trees begin moving in to reclaim the void. The sad exception is gold mining, where belching diesel clearing machines scrape away the shallow nutrient soil to expose the hard, reddish gravel, which is then sifted for gold flakes or tiny nuggets. These clearings do not return to green and become permanent scars in the forest.

We did not stay long at the enchanting French villa. The staff was friendly, but it was clear we were not welcome as overnight guests. As we continued upriver, the rapids slowed us down. I could feel we were traveling uphill, and the current against us got faster. There were no camps or villages along the banks on this stretch of the Lawa. By late afternoon, we were getting hungry, and tired of the monotonous, noisy motoring. Afunki pulled close to the bank and killed the motor; we paddled quietly close to the bank for the next mile or so.

It was a pleasant relief from the smell and sound of the outboard, and we could hear the sounds of the forest. Shiliki was standing on the bow helping push us along with the *kola tiki* when he stopped and excitedly pointed to a treetop in front of us. Everyone was quiet and looking into the trees. I didn't see or hear anything; then, BOOOM! The trees above us come alive as a troop of monkeys made a frantic escape into the forest. Alaman said he shot one, and we heard a faint thud in the brush a few yards from the riverbank. Alaman and Shiliki took their machetes to cut a path to where we heard the fall. They drug back a limp, lanky black howler monkey that stretched out to about 3 feet—this would be dinner. Afunki fired up the Evinrude and we went further until we found a spot where we could tie the boat and step off. The riverbank was mostly dense brush and vines. We had to look hard for a spot with a clearing.

The machetes were sharp, and we quickly trimmed spaces to tie hammocks on trees; KutuKutu built a fire while Alaman prepared the monkey for dinner. He removed the long tail, burned the hair off, and splayed the carcass flat. We threw the guts and the tail in the river so they would not attract varmints to our campsite during the night. Nobody felt like cooking, so we just skewered the monkey over the wood fire, cut it up and ate it with kwaka that was softened in river water. I was never fond of monkey meat, but when I got the right shoulder, with a fully articulated arm, elbow, wrist with a right hand and fingers, I had to pass. I noticed Alaman give KutuKutu a "what's-with-this-guy" look; KutuKutu replied with a shrug. Everyone was enjoying their arms and legs of the monkey; I opened a can of sardines.

That night, I rolled up in my hammock sheet like some larva in a cocoon, making sure nothing of me was exposed. It was a little scary being so isolated on a strange river, hanging under trees in a dense forest that was not accustomed to humans. We kept the fire going. The next morning, we loaded up with only perfunctory morning greetings; the lack of banter suggested that the guys were also ill at ease in these unknown waters (or perhaps the quickly cooked monkey did not sit well with them and they would not admit it).

We left our makeshift camp right at sunrise and traveled steadily, but slowly from rapids to rapids for most of the day. There was neither boat traffic nor human sightings all day. It was like being far offshore in the ocean, but in a green canyon with treacherous surprise boulders or rocky shoals just below the surface. By late afternoon the river got wider and shallower. The current still flowed against us but with less roiling anger. The banks became higher, with red clay hills jutting up from the water, and the river started to give up large spaces of reddish sand and large, smooth rocks.

Afunki slowed down as we took in the changed environment. We rounded a slow turn and saw a few boats pulled up on sand at the bottom of a steep hill. These were dugouts, but not with the curved banana design or workmanship of our canoes. If this were a village, it was strange that no one was around. Typically, women and children would be all over a dock space in the afternoon washing clothes, preparing dinner, or bathing kids.

Afunki slowly nosed the canoe onto the sandy mud, and we started to move around in the boat, not exactly sure where we were, or what we would do here. Suddenly, our ever-vigilant bowman Shiliki gave a quiet, but urgent cry, "Look!" and gestured toward the hilltop. At the very top of the hill, about 100 steep feet from us stood a man looking down at us. He was a stocky young man, with reddish brown skin and long straight, black hair. He was wearing a bright red, eight-inch square cloth on a string around his waist that barely covered his penis. A long string from the top of his head, down his back to his ankles held a single feather that brushed the ground between his feet. What grabbed our attention most, however, was the long bow he held next to him. The bow was taller that he was, and he had a fist full of arrows. We sat silently, giving "oh, shit!" looks to each other.

After a moment of silent dread, I stood up from my spot in the middle of our canoe and gave him a smile and a wave. I called out a greeting in Sranan, the lingua franca of urban Suriname. He just looked without moving. Smiling broadly, I asked loudly if he understood Sranan—no response, and no movement. I then gestured that I wanted to walk up the hill and talk with him. He motioned for me to come up, so I stepped gingerly out of the boat, holding my arms out so he could see I was not armed. I was wearing shorts, apparently over-dressed for this place.

I climbed up the path of the steep hill, being super careful not to slip and ruin the moment. I got to a few feet of him, but still not at the top of the hill, allowing him the height advantage (I saw quickly that I was taller than he was.) With a mix of English, Sranan, and Pamakan, I explained that we were visiting from down river, and just passing through. He studied me closely and seemed to understand what I was trying to say, but said nothing.

I was racking my brain trying to think how to get to this guy, then the Marcel Mauss inspiration that worked so well getting me food my first night in Langatabiki—a gift! I reached for the Swiss Army knife that Katie gave me when I left New York and had carried ever since. I pulled it out of my pocket and presented it to him with both hands, palms up. "It's for you," I said with gestures that made it an unmistakable gift. It was a classic red, Swiss Army combination of cutting, twisting, and pinching tools. He looked at it and betrayed a slight smile as he took it in his hands and examined it. I reached in making slight contact and took it back to start showing him the various blades, saws, scissors that could be unfolded from it. Immediately we were two guys marveling at what the Swiss could do with a pocketknife. He relaxed and, with the red pocketknife in one hand and bow and arrows in the other, said in reasonably good Sranan that we were welcome to stay in his village, which, he motioned, was over his shoulder behind him. I waved for KutuKutu and the others to come up and bring the hammocks.

Our host greeted the others stiffly from a distance—no handshakes. He said his long name, which we reduced to "Sam." We followed Sam down a short path into a village that appeared to be twenty to thirty thatch huts and open shelters arranged in no apparent order. There were no painted or carved doors that are so remarkable in the African villages. Sam showed us to an open-sided thatch shed where he indicated we could tie hammocks. There were a few people around the huts who looked at us silently. None ran, either away from us, or towards us. KutuKutu and the team were clearly uncomfortable; we tied our hammocks, barely speaking.

Sam was about our age, compact, medium height, with amazingly smooth skin on full display. Being the stick figure guy of Pamaka, I took note that Sam had none of the body-builder muscle definition that virtually all the African guys seemed to have. In a nearby open-sided thatch shelter, three older women were sitting around a carved-out tree trunk shaped like a small, shallow bathtub. A few minutes later, Sam came back to check on us. He was not carrying his bow and arrows, and he was smiling and pleasant as he spoke to us in Sranan. He said something to the effect of "let's have a drink," and led us over to the shelter where the women were tending to the wooden bathtub perched up on a bench about a foot off the ground. The women were squatting on kindergarten-sized stools around a pile of over-ripe bananas. They looked up at us, but didn't smile or stop chewing the bananas. Trying not to stare, I watched as each woman would discharge her mouthful of banana into the tub! The tub was about two-thirds full of a watery liquid that seemed to be actively fermenting.

Sam took the large, wooden carved ladle hanging on side of the tub, gave it a big, slow stir, and savored the look and aroma like a brew master. He seemed pleased with the batch, and with a calabash bowl, skimmed back the foamy film on the surface and dipped out a healthy portion of the brew. He examined it, took a drink, and handed the calabash to me. I recalled the wonderful experiences with communal rice wine of the Montanards, so had no hesitation to go for it. Besides, the other part of gift giving is to accept graciously a return gift.

I took a drink and smiled as best I could. It tasted like fermenting banana saliva. I handed the calabash to KutuKutu, who gave me a "I'm-going-to-kill-you-in-your-sleep" look. He gamely took a sip and handed it off to Afunki. When all the guys had taken a turn, we handed the calabash back to Sam with formalized "thank-you-so-much," and out-sized "We're Good!" declinations of seconds.

I asked Sam if I could look around the village; he was happy to oblige. KutuKutu and the guys retreated to our hammock station, where they spent the rest of the day and evening. Every household Sam took me by had some type of wild animal as a pet. There were lots of parrots, Capuchin monkeys, and marmosets. One family had a young sloth. Word must have gotten around about the Swiss Army knife trade, every family we stopped at wanted to trade me an animal for something. I could have bartered for any number of these animals, but I was out of bargaining loot, plus the guys would want to eat any animal that I brought on the boat.

Sam brought over a large pot of stewed peccary, a pig-like mammal of the region, which we enjoyed over our *kwaka*. He sat and talked with me for a while and confided that there was an American family resident in the village. He was not forthcoming about where they were, and it seemed he wanted us to steer clear of them. They are church people, he said. He was circumspect, but it was obvious that they were tolerated like a pain in the butt. I wondered to myself if this was the family I encountered on the PanAm flight a few months earlier. I could not figure out how to translate "insufferable," so I responded with empathetic eye rolls and head shakes.

We turned in early, and during a comfortable sleep, I awoke to the most sensuous sound I had ever heard. I peeked out of my hammock; it was first light and a heavy mist hung over the village. The sound was coming from near the riverbank. It was music! Beguiling, soft music coming out of the mist, from the bank of a river in a rain forest—it was an "am-I-in-Heaven?" moment. I rolled back up and listened in rapture till the sun started to appear. Shortly the mist cleared, and the music stopped. I jumped out of my hammock and went toward the riverbank. There was a young man sitting on a large rock at the crest of the hill overlooking the river. He was holding a slightly curved tube about three feet long, fashioned from a bamboo branch. It was his musical instrument, but it only had a few holes bored in it. I asked him what it was, and he raised it and played a few notes. It was a nose flute! That's what made it such an enchanting sound in the early mist. He would blow on one end with one nostril and change the tone by manipulating three note holes with his right hand. The sound was haunting.

My expeditionary team was busy packing up when I got back to our camp. The guys were ready to move on, so we headed for our boat without any goodbyes or hot tea. The riverbed was rocky, and the water was getting increasingly shallow, with rapids all along. We would walk the boat through these areas; more annoyance than the terror of slogging against the dangerous cascades we would meet farther down river on the way back. We went the full day without seeing any other boat or signs of people. We camped at a pleasant clearing that evening. The landscape and feel of the place were different. We were at a higher elevation, and the sounds from the forest were different from our part of the river. I sensed a little are-we-there-yet unease among the guys, but no one complained.

We pulled into a pleasant clearing for the evening and Alaman jumped out of the boat to scout the area for a campsite. I saw him jump to swing his machete at a high tree branch. I thought this was odd because the branch was not blocking anything. Then I watched as he jumped back from something that had fallen from the branch. We ran over as Alaman was giving the thing on the ground more whacks with his machete—it as a good-sized snake that had been lounging in the tree. It was green, probably an anaconda; thank god it was not the foadu boa constrictor, I thought. KutuKutu chopped part of the snake into chunks and set out with a line to catch some fish. He tossed a few chunks into the water, then snapped off a tree branch and slapped it on the water and started shaking it violently in the water. Sure enough, piranha were suddenly all around, attracted to troubled water. It didn't take long for KutuKutu to land several flat, round, red-eyed piranha, each about the size of a hamburger bun. It was odd, I thought at the time, that I would associate these evil little fish with hamburgers—something I had not seen and enjoyed in a very long time! The trick to catching piranha is to jerk them out of the water immediately, before they bite through the hook or the line. They continue a violent chomping with their razor teeth until you dispatch them with a machete. Most piranha bites to Pamakans happened in boats or on land when people try to unhook them. KutuKutu was careful, and the piranha stew over kwaka that night was delicious.

The next day, after about two hours pushing upstream, we rounded an island to see a distinct, high hill straight ahead. The river started to diffuse, so we all concluded that this was it; we had made it to the end! Afunki pulled up to a clearing at the base of the hill, and we headed for the top. The hill seemed strangely nude; the dense forest covering gave way to shrubs. It was unusual to not have to clear a path through vines and tree limbs with machetes to walk—we could see the sky and the ground in sunlight. We reached the top after about a fifteen-minute climb and the view at the top was extraordinary, not so much as what we saw, but that we *could* see for miles all around! The Pamakan explorers were rapt as they studied the panorama. When you grow up in a rain forest environment, you have limited fields of vision. It was a memorable experience to have a 360-degree view of the horizon. The highlight of the view was that we could see Brazil to the south. We did not know where the border was, but we were certain we could see Brazil.

We lingered on the hill for a while and took in the unusual foliage. I found a wild pineapple, which tasted like a not-quite-ripe wild pineapple. Back at the boat, Afunki set course for downriver. The guys were tired and done with the adventure. They unanimously did not want to stop at the Indian village on the way back, and quickly vetoed my suggestion to stop again at the French guy's jungle palace. Going downriver with the current, and downhill through the rapids was fast and dicey, despite our elevated confidence as explorers. The trip back to Langatabiki took us two long days, and the team came back to Langatabiki with serious river creds for having made the voyage to the headwaters of the Lawa. And the adventure was everything I wanted; the only downside was that I had traded away my most trusted and valuable possession—my red Swiss Army knife.

CHAPTER THIRTY

SA TCHNGTCHNG

A Pamakan man, traditionally, is expected to provide for his woman—or women. A man can have as many women he can adequately support. A man must be proficient in hunting and fishing in order to provide protein for his family. In addition to a house and a paddle boat, a man must prepare fields by clearing areas of forest for each of his women to plant rice, cassava, and peanuts. The ornately painted and intricately carved doors of the houses and boat paddles demonstrate the prowess of the man who built it, as well as his affection for his woman.

Motorized dugout boats were introduced in Pamaka about fifteen years before my arrival. Men could earn enough money to buy an outboard motor by long and arduous treks in the forest climbing balata trees to collect natural latex. Later, they found paying work operating their large canoes along the river, and other work involving the forest or the river.

The fundamental importance of a man's self-sufficiency in the matters of men was made awkwardly clear to me on a trip KutuKutu and I made upriver with a couple of the most stalwart men of Langatabiki, TiAmoten and TiBampata. Bampata was the oldest son of Gaaman. TiAmoten, however, was something of an anomaly. He was not known as a churchman, yet he was highly successful in traditional categories. He had several boats with motors, and four wives. For each of his wives he had constructed a nice house and prepared forest fields. He was good looking, well spoken, and obviously resourceful and smart. We were going upriver to visit an area where TiAmoten wanted to put cattle. The government had a program to provide seed cattle for people of the interior. The program was halted when an Amerindian village far upriver reportedly took the cattle and let them loose in the forest to hunt them down later and kill them as game.

The trip was an early opportunity for me to experience other Pamakan villages up the Marowijne River. I learned a traveling protocol on this trip that I have incorporated in all my travels since. Before we would arrive at a village for a visit, TiAmoten would pull the boat over to tie up at a tree a mile or so away from our destination. We would take the time to relieve ourselves and to eat. TiAmoten explained that it was important as guests to never arrive at your destination hungry or having to pee.

TiAmoten was well known throughout Pamaka. When we arrived at LokaLoka, we made a walking tour of the village of about thirty houses/huts. At one of the houses, there was a young man trundling a makeshift wheelchair. We went over and with truncated greetings sat with him for a few minutes. TiAmoten commiserated about his inability to stand or walk; his right leg was shriveled. TiAmoten then offered the chair-ridden teenager the following advice: "Since you can never be a man, it is important for you to get an education. Be sure and go to school."

"What the hell does that say about me?" I thought as we offered farewell greetings to the kid. Here I was pursuing a doctorate after years in bachelors and masters programs. Was I in full retreat from manhood? This was an unsettling notion, which I kept to myself.

The traditional Pamakan man operates within a material environment where he is the one who makes everything that is "manmade." The house his woman and children live in, his boat, paddles, and furniture are products he, or someone he knows, made from wood, gourds, and leaves. Iron implements and shotguns are the exception. While there are obvious differences recognizable in individual men's abilities and talent, every Pamakan man learns how to make all the things that are made, and participates in making them throughout his life. This is one of the touchstones of manhood.

"How do you make an 'Evinlude?'" was a question put to me more than once. The logic behind the question was that if a white guy in America can make an outboard motor, they *all* can do it—with individual variation, of course.

Despite my inability to sit down and build an outboard motor from scratch, my self-sufficiency was growing. I was moving along with my communication skills and understanding better the ways living Pamakans interact with the spirit realm. I learned how to braid a gill net, and enjoyed paddling out just before dark to set the nets in tributaries along the river. The real fun was going back at dawn to see what was flapping around in the net. Often there would be large holes where piranha would have helped themselves to my catch, and a good part of my net.

Even with the competition of piranha and caiman, and the occasional scare of electric eels and snakes, the fishing was good, and I generally had fish to share with neighbors. My reciprocity network had grown to where I would provide fish and other goods to neighbors in exchange for cooked meals with green vegetables, rice, cassava, peanuts, and corn. When I got my larger canoe with the outboard motor, I became an even more significant participant in the barter economy.

During my time in Langatabiki, I witnessed the growing influence of money and city-oriented economic forces. Ordinarily, a large catch of fish or game was divided and distributed among kin. Under "city life," meat and fish were given a cash value (about twenty-five cents per pound) which remained constant regardless of variations of supply and demand. Only rarely, however, did supply exceed demand. Under the new money economy, the major advantage that a hunter's relatives realized was advance notice that game was available for purchase. When word passed through the village that someone was selling meat or fish, there was usually a rush to buy. Women also began selling chickens and any surplus in garden produce, such as bananas, okra, and peanuts.

I enjoyed a mix of the two food distribution systems, buying items only when there was nothing in the neighborhood sharing pool. For me the advantage of sharing meant was that I had a wide sampling of available food. Staples included mangoes, plantains, finger bananas, juices prepared from various palm nuts, and of course, coconuts. The hunts would bring in peccaries, tapir, armadillos, and various birds and rodents, large and small. One delicacy I had to pass on was monkey. I never got over the smell and image of the monkey's perfectly complete right shoulder, arm, elbow, wrist, and hand with fingernails intact served from the spit on the Lawa expedition. That remains today an image I would like to get out of my brain.

One morning I came back with my nets to find great excitement, with people running throughout the village with long sticks fashioned like nets and switches. The occasion turned out to be the periodic molting of a large cicada-like insect, flying slow and low to the ground as small clouds of fat larvae with wings. People were collecting as many of these bugs as they could whack down or catch in a net to spread them out to bake on large metal plates over the fire pits. The bugs tasted like raw peanuts inside big brown popcorn. I loved them.

• • •

I began thinking a lot about the girlfriend thing, and quietly checked out the unattached women in the village. The girls were pretty in their colorful cotton *pangi* skirts and brassieres. Women whose breasts did not require a device to hold them up, often did not wear them. And the braided hair designs were intricate works of art. The young men certainly appreciated the beauty all around them, but I never heard a whistle or comment concerning a woman's endowment or appearance. Even in private conversation, guys did not talk about breasts or butts, or muse about how so-and-so would be in a hammock. This was a stark contrast to my middle school and high school experience, where we guys obsessed about such things.

So, while I could appreciate, quietly, the beauty of the village maidens, they were mostly teenagers. By the time a woman is twenty, she will have had a couple of children already. The regular pairing process was simply not an option for me. I was not going to get involved with a fifteen or sixteen-year-old, no matter how pretty she was.

KutuKutu was staying over at my place less frequently, and I developed a regular food exchange relationship with a woman who lived nearby, SaTchngTchng. She was in her early twenties and, no surprise, had two children—a six-year-old daughter who had been sent to a French-run boarding school in St. Laurent, and an infant son. I never saw, nor heard of the father of her two children. SaTchngTchng's father was the lineage chief and the Gaaman's brother. Her parents lived just steps away from her house, and there were several brothers and uncles living nearby so she was well provided for.

I was impressed at how resourceful SaTchngTchng was. She could handle a canoe as well as any man, was precise and confident with a machete, and was exceptional at forest gardening. Her house was about twenty yards from mine, so she became a regular in my subsistence barter arrangement—and she was a great cook. I began spending less time with KutuKutu and more time with her. I would return dinner dishes in the evenings and I made sure she got the best fish of my morning net haul.

She was shy and formal with me (she called me TiMambo), but we gradually started to have conversations about matters other than how high or low the river seemed that day. She was very smart but had to leave the Moravian school after only a couple of years because of her first pregnancy. Our conversations were in Pamakan; she spoke no English.

SaTchngTchng and I became closer as we got to know each other better. I found her attractive and enjoyed our talks, even though—or perhaps because—we brought completely different life experiences that remained largely unexplored. There was not a single book, movie, sports team, hero, or villan of my life which could serve as a shared reference or context of conversation. Our friendship and conversations were oriented to the immediate and the very recent. People and events beyond the river were unknowns, and historical reference was limited to things that happened in the village in the past year. I began to orient my thoughts accordingly as we spent more time in conversations. My occasional terrors about missing a core aspect of life as a perennial outsider analyzing belief systems, and being the odd stranger in this tightly-bound family of Pamaka began to fade.

One evening we had a short, unresolved discussion about a friend of hers who was suffering severe headaches because a boa constrictor had entered her head. I assumed she meant a headache, so I broke out a couple of aspirin. She was annoyed and surprised that I did not understand that the snake was in her head and needed specialist treatment. Maybe that's why I was the only guy around who could pull boa constrictors out of houses without them getting into my head.

One evening SaTchngTchng brought over dinner and sat on a stool in my kitchen area while I organized my table. I, sort of, accidentally touched her bare foot as I reached for something on the floor. She did not flinch, and I was struck by how perfect her foot was, and how beautifully proportioned her ankles and legs were. We shared a look that changed everything.

I held her foot until she stirred to get up and leave. I jumped up and held her hands for the first time, ostensibly to help her up from the stool. She let me hold her arm as she started to climb down the ladder. "This is real," I thought. I didn't eat much of the dinner she had prepared that night. I now had a mission that required thought and planning.

Having only held hands the night before, there was a clear read when we looked at each other the next day. There was no mistake—this was going to happen. The two of us were connected; we just had to work out how to make it happen. There were strict protocols in courtship; and neighbors, including her parents, lived in the immediate vicinity—all of them in thatch houses. She brought dinner over the next few nights, and I let her know that I was fond of her. She did not object to my expressions of interest, and we would hold hands. This courtship seemed stilted and middle-school awkward, but at the same time completely natural and normal. After a few more dinner deliveries, I asked her one evening if I could visit her at her place later that night. She nodded lightly and cautioned that I must be careful and quiet so no one sees me.

It was late and dark when I slipped down my ladder stair. I made like I was going to the river to take a leak. No one was around when I made the right to her front door. I nudged it slightly; it was unlocked. My heart was pounding. I had not been inside her house before, but pushed the door halfway open and angled myself inside. She called in a quiet voice from behind a partition, "In here."

She was in a bed under a sheet. Having a bed itself was huge— contorting in a hammock takes practice. Her infant son was asleep in a crib right next to her bed. She folded a corner of the sheet down as welcome, and I quickly shed my clothes and joined her. Without a word, we held each other as if we had been lovers forever. We went from holding hands to a nose-to-toe embrace. She was different from any woman I had known—in feel, smell, sound, and taste. To me, there was something unexplainable going on, and there was a wonderful mutuality in loving the bond of our bodies.

I wanted to make the late visits regularly, and made discrete inquiries through trusted friends how to get a relationship recognized so we could be openly together. Their counsel was that it would be exceedingly difficult, and not worth pursuing. Sa TchngTchng's response was that if she became pregnant with my child, the elders would have no choice but to recognize the relationship. That was a lightning strike to my soul—I would impregnate her!

My purpose in life, and my understanding of the true meaning of life became clear. As a man, a male animal, there was nothing more important than making your woman pregnant and providing for her. I was no longer lonely, and I could not care less about not believing in belief systems. I had my animal mission—get SaTchngTchng pregnant, or as a Pamaka buddy told me, "load her boat."

I did not think about New York, or that I had a two-year visa, or the fact that I was still legally married to Katie. During the day, I would work like a maniac clearing my agricultural field, setting my nets, and all the things a man does to provide for his woman. At night, I was of one mind: make Sa TchngTchng my woman by impregnating her. This was sex I had never known. I was in my late twenties and had been married to Katie for four years. Sex was always fun, but cautioned by the potential consequence of pregnancy which we would take steps to prevent. Katie and I had never talked about starting a family. I think we were always too busy, or on some adventure to somewhere.

SaTchngTchng and I kept our affair quiet for a few weeks. Soon after, she told me that she thought she was pregnant, so we decided to go public. By protocol I had to make a formal request to her family through an intermediary. I engaged one of Gaaman's sons to be my emissary, and he made the initial overture with her mother, father, and one of her mother's brothers. The response was mixed. Her father, a lineage elder, neighborhood mayor and Gaaman's brother was okay with it, saying that the Gaaman himself set this thing in motion, so how could he oppose it. Her mother and uncle pushed back. The whole thing was too weird for them. This was a problem since, even though her father had clout, it was a woman's matrilineal, not patrilineal kin who were responsible for these types of life decisions. The word back was that the deal was a no-go.

We countered with the nuclear option: this had to happen because Sa TchngTchng was going to have TiMambos's baby. This news spread quickly. SaTchngTchng's lineage members, who lived in more traditional upriver villages, were outraged. People in Langatabiki were surprised, but generally okay with the baby and marriage idea. We made plans to go forward with the wedding ceremony, but the continuing objections made the proposed event contentious. Some members of her family threatened to physically block it and remove SaTchngTchng from Langatabiki, as was their right as her lineage elders.

There were several days of intense negotiations, and it was not going well. At one point, a counsel of young men led by the two sons of the Gaaman stepped in and invoked the authority of Gaaman as the paramount chief. This was an extraordinary and gutsy move by my representatives, who became my putative lineage elders. By tradition, the father and his lineage that included Gaaman had no authority or rights over SaTchngTchng—but this was not an ordinary marriage. Her kinsmen and her mother were not pleased, but finally acquiesced. I had to produce many bottles of taffia, and feed the entire neighborhood and visiting entourage of family the next day when everyone gathered for the formal sit-down.

The marriage ceremony itself was not an elaborate celebration at all. SaTchngTchng's lineage people sat stiffly on stools on one side, my

Langatabiki stand-in lineage family sat on my side. Her lineage ancestors were brought into the affair through copious libations. Gaaman himself showed up to make sure things were going allright, and to officially consecrate the union. The vows, as such, involved her lineage elder making a formal, ritual address in which their lineage "gave" Sa TchngTchng to me (ordinarily it would be my lineage through an elder that would take official possession.) Her lineage elder also formally required me to acknowledge that if she needed a beating, that I would bring her back and they would take care of it. I assured her elder, very formally, that I was okay with not beating her myself. (I did not add that I could not imagine SaTchngTchng being beaten for anything, by anyone.)

That was it; she was my woman, I was her man, and we, indeed, had a child on the way. One of the first public responsibilities of a man in marriage is to build a house for his woman. SaTchngTchng already had a nice place so I decided to build a structure that would serve as meeting space, work area and crash pad for visitors. There was space between my house and hers, so I marked out a floor plan in the dirt. I went to get a load of building material from Albina, and over the next few weeks, neighborhood guys and I put up a nice structure with a smooth cement floor and a corrugated tin roof. I was TiMambo, accomplished, and doing with my woman the most fundamental thing humans are on earth to do.

CHAPTER THIRTY-ONE

THE NEW YORK COMMUTE

Life was good as TiMambo. SaTchngTchng began showing her pregnancy and I provided well for her. I had not forgotten my commitment to Minister Goosen to reciprocate with language lessons in English, and started holding open sessions once a week in basic English in the open area under Gaaman's raised porch. My Pamakan students, it turned out, were more interested in learning about Africa than the English language. One day I found an old sixteen-millimeter film projector in a box stored under Gaaman's house. No one knew where it came from; no one had ever seen it used. That evening when the generator started its fitful tour,

I plugged it in and the light came on, it worked! I wrote to the International Film Institute in New York and they sent me a box of films about Africa. These film sessions, which I narrated in Pamakan, throwing in English here and there, were a big hit.

Perhaps it was the stand-up teaching gig at Gaaman's that energized the part of my brain that started reminding TiMambo: you are a doctoral candidate in anthropology. I had to tell myself in English that I was in Langatabiki on a visa expiring in a few months, with limited scholarships and stipends to do research for a dissertation. I had discovered meaning and purpose in life and was having a good time as a Pamakan, sure. But could I just walk away from the years of preparation and study for a PhD? Or was the TiMambo thing a cop-out to avoid the daunting job of writing a dissertation?

I had the field notes and a brain full of knowledge about the Pamakans for an ethnography, and there had been no prior study or research published about them. The difficulty was that I had gone too far in the participant observer relationship—I had "gone native." Getting too close to your subjects was usually a career-ending pitfall for field anthropologists.

I decided to meet the challenge and return to New York to write a dissertation focusing on the ethnography and the differences between the Moravian-aligned Pamakans and the traditionalists. I would analyze why one group only sang hymns at a funeral ritual, while others wanted to drum and dance. I need not include anything about me as a Pamakan, or my Pamaka family.

When I announced that I would be going back, SaTchngTchng's upriver lineage people preened with "we-told-you" condemnation, which added to the anxiety of my decision to leave Langatabiki for New York. It was an excruciating matter to leave before the birth of our child, but Sa TchngTchng had fulsome family support close at hand, and I would be able to send money to help with supplies. And if I were to wait, I knew it would be even more wrenching to leave with a baby in the picture. I promised to return as soon as I could, likely in a couple of months. SaTchingTching was stoic about it; she was not ready to defy her family by going with me, and she understood the challenges of living without family in a strange city with a new baby. In addition, she had two other young children to raise in Langatabiki.

Arriving at JFK in December was jarring. It was bitter cold, and again, I had no winter clothing. This confirmed my decision not to bring a pregnant wife into weather she could never imagine, and into a crush of people so foreign and unwelcoming. I breezed through U.S. Customs with my small bag, and walked out into the cold to catch a van to Manhattan. I had packed my bui and wore my beads. The beads I knew would help me get through this next chapter of life; they had worked well so far, and I never took them off. I was still not so sure about the bui, so it stayed in its sack. The van driver was a dark-skinned Black guy, so I reflexively greeted him warmly. I assumed this was Ti somebody driving the bus, and thought it was good to see a brother driving. He turned and gave me a cold "who-the-hell-are-you?" look. It took me a moment to process the shock and realize I was back in New York City and I was not TiMambo here. As I made my way through the City, I could not get any good vibe from the Black Americans I encountered on the subway, the street, or in the store buying a coat. I was not sure whether there was more tension that had grown over the time I was gone, or if it was the same as when I left but I was oblivious to it then.

My New School anthropology colleagues helped me find a small rent-controlled apartment in Greenwich Village where I settled in to write the dissertation. The apartment was tiny, and in a grimy four-floor walk up building across from a noisy 24-hour truck loading dock. It was painful leaving my family, but I was going to focus on organizing field notes and writing the dissertation. I drove a taxicab and did adjunct teaching gigs to pay rent and eat. When Katie learned that I was back in the City, I heard from her through a lawyer. She filed for divorce, a stark reality that TiMambo had been able to ignore while in Langatabiki. I was not sure whether she knew of my Pamakan wife and child on the way; we did not discuss details of either of our lives after she left.

By June I had completed and successfully defended my dissertation, and landed a full-time faculty position at a CUNY college in Manhattan starting in September. So, I achieved the goal of becoming a PhD anthropologist, perhaps more transcendental anthropology than Marxist. I had learned Pamakan by sitting on the ground with children playing, "What do you call this?" and pestering KutuKutu with endless questions about concepts of wind, light, dark, future and past tenses; sitting with old men snuffing a slurry of tobacco and ashes up my nose; and meeting with spirits inhabiting the bodies of neighbors. Through this second shot at growing up, this time as a Pamakan, I got a better perspective on what it means to be an adult, and a human being.

• • •

Our daughter, Afiamba, was born on Valentine's Day and I was desperate to get back to Langatabiki. On the trip back, I was packed to the limit with baby clothes and gifts. Seeing my daughter was the most exciting and fulfilling experience I'd had so far. I could not have been more thrilled. I checked in with the American Embassy and started the process for a birth certificate and citizenship status. I had only the summer to spend in Suriname.

The big question now was what to do with my family in Langatabiki and my work in New York. Moving SaTchngTchng and our daughter to my small apartment in the City was not a viable option. In addition, her family remained adamantly against her leaving and taking our child. They were the subjects of the lineage, after all, and there would be serious consequences were we to disregard their prohibition to leave. In addition, I did not think SaTchngTchng and our daughter would do well in the City. I had no family in the City, and I was not aware of any Surinamese community, so there would no support for her whatsoever. SaTchingTching's extraordinary capabilities were specific to the rain forest and maneuvering a tight-knit traditional village on a river island. She had never used a telephone and spoke not a word of English.

We worked out a solution. I bought her a house in Paramaribo in a comfortable, supportive community, so she would be able to visit back and forth between the city and Langatabiki where she had two houses. For me, I would be able to travel between Manhattan and Paramaribo.

We could take family trips to Langatabiki when necessary. At the end of that summer, I headed back to JFK to begin my dual life as TiMambo and college professor. This dual identity arrangement worked for a few years, and during that time SaTchngTchng and I had two other children, another daughter, Jeanette, and a son, Shelby.

AFTERWORD

The day I was dropped off at the Pamakan doorstep I entered a new phase of life, learning how to communicate and survive as the new and radically different kid in school. Pamakans welcomed me conditionally, vetted me through a serpent obia, watched me as I worked and played, and became alarmed when I asked too many questions. They ultimately extended me their trust, washed me at the Sweli sacred grotto, and shared the password they used as fugitives. Over the next three years, I learned from Pamaka so much more than their language, history, and cultural understanding of being. In the end, I discovered a dimension of human communication through which I came to know Pamakans, and they began to accept me as a functioning member of their community.

The Pamaka, by their very survival demonstrated the remarkable resilience and creativity of a people in extreme hardship. As people stolen from disparate areas of Africa, having escaped from different slave plantations and hiding as fugitives in a harsh Amazonian rain forest, Pamakans created a system of knowledge about the nature of life and death that was beautifully logical. And more, their worldview was based on the critical importance of individual and group integrity. Their capacity for social humanity was luminous. They embraced me despite the horrific experience of slavery by white people, my early missteps at drawing up bomb maps, and ultimately taking one of their women.

The admonitions of my Marxist professor to conduct field research, ever mindful of the dynamic of our presence among the people we were studying, never once left my mind. But after two years, I began to turn the issue around. What about the effect on *me?* By choosing to live among the Pamakans, I lost my American wife and first love. Learning their cultural constructs of life and being, I confronted a deeply disturbing tear in my own cultural foundation. My life plan and my sense of self in the universe were upended. But I solved the riddle of hymns versus drums as an anthropologist, and grew up a second time learning the language and ways of my hosts, to the point of acceptance as one of them (although I was still the one to pull the big snakes out of rafters.)

An unintended and lifelong benefit of the adventure of getting to Langatabiki from Manhattan was an appreciation of the value of listening to others. Had I not heard the mailroom guy's tip about Tolsie Persaud, I would have been out at first base. Had I not listened to Miss Mae's baleful answer that "that way" leads to the strange people of Suriname, I would have not taken the hummingbird's directions. The old Hindu man telling me that I looked like a holy man was oddly reassuring that I was on the right path and should keep going. The boy, Ronnie, taking me to meet his sister and mother got me an improbable audience with the Surinamese Minister of Public Works who directed me to Pamaka. This was a dimension of communication that could easily have been ignored. As a Pamakan, I came to know these messages were not accidents.

SaTchingTching's family remained adamant that the children stay in Suriname, so I continued the commute for years and maintained communication by sending children's books and reading to them via cassette tape recorder. I made sure they got U.S. citizenship and passports on the expectation that one day they would be able to leave Suriname. Our son was the first to come to New York with me when he was eight years old. The girls came a few years later. The three now live happily in the U.S. along with SaTchingTching. KutuKutu visits from Holland where he works for the Dutch postal service. I decided to pursue a career in law and began a new career as a public prosecutor.

KutuKutu left Langatabiki about the same time I did. He moved to Paramaribo where he got a job with the government forest service and ended up back in the rainforest surveying hydrographic sites. In 1983, a violent revolt against the government by a group called "Jungle Commandos" brought uncomfortable focus on Pamakans. KutuKutu, as Phil Ceder, had secured a Dutch passport after Surinamese independence in 1975 and was able to quickly move to the Netherlands. There he started working as a postman, and later became a long-distance truck driver for the postal service. He and I have maintained contact over the years as we have collaborated in producing this memoir.

The Pamaka landscape KutuKutu and I have described here reflects their life and times of the early 1970s. Much has changed since. There is now a road to Langatabiki from the coast; meaning today, a car is as important as an outboard motor was to us. I recently got a call from the new Pamacan Gaaman while I was standing in line at a coffee shop in Manhattan. He was calling from *his* cell phone from Langatabiki! KutuKutu had given him my number and he wanted to discuss the government's latest efforts to confiscate Pamakan land and sell timber and gold concessions to foreign companies. When I lived there, there were always stories of guys finding little gold nuggets along the river tributaries. It now turns out the Pamakans are sitting on a significant gold deposit that became the interest of a global mining company and the Surinamese national government. The massive hardwood trees that became canoes and houses are now reserved by the government for export. Pamakans have continued to be subjected to Christian proselytizing. The Moravians and Roman Catholic missions have been joined by various evangelical groups who compete to supplant traditional cultural concepts and practices.

I am not optimistic about the long-term survival of a recognizable Pamaka people and culture. The Sweli may not be able to protect them against concerted pressures to forswear not only their concepts of life and death, but their now highly valuable land as well. I do know that no matter what the future Pamaka will be, I will forever remain comfortable as TiMambo wherever I am. Whether I am in a boat on the river setting nets, or in a classroom, or a court of law, I am confident my akaa is intact and that my nenseki will pass muster with family, neighbors, and colleagues on my judgment day. And I know that my day of judgment will be wherever and whenever I die, and if all goes well, that I will be around for generations as a well-remembered, if ersatz, ancestor worthy of a libation now and then.

ACKNOWLEDGMENTS

I am forever grateful to the true statesman, Gaaman Cornelius Forster, who took me in provisionally as a guest and ultimately as part of the family. TiBaya, TiYan, and so many of the Pamaka elders who shared insight and life stories are now part of my adopted ancestors whom I acknowledge daily. They guided me with patience and compassion through some awkward periods of my learning to be a Pamakan.

This story became a book through reviews of first drafts and the encouragement of many friends and colleagues, the likes of Maurice Tamman and Thomas Litwack. Ann Shortt was instrumental in sanity checks of later drafts, while Janice Shay did the heavy lifting of wrangling it all together so that the pictures and words come together into a readable order. Most of the photographs, including the cover, are the work of Raymond Galbraith who passed through Pamaka in 1971 on a photographic expedition.

I sadly lost track of the New School mailroom guy whose Tolsie Persaud tip was key to getting the adventure started, and Petrus Domini, my first teacher and friend in Suriname. Of course, my invaluable resource from my first day in Pamaka was KutuKutu. He now lives in Holland as Phil Ceder, but we have remained friends for fifty years. Our latest adventure has been collaborating to produce this story of his people.

ABOUT THE AUTHORS

J.D. Lenoir earned a Ph.D. and taught Anthropology for six years at John Jay College in New York City. He went to law school and became a career criminal prosecutor with the Manhattan DA's Office and later the U.S. Department of Justice. Currently in private practice, he specializes in civil rights cases.

KutuKutu (Phil Ceder) was born in Langatabiki in 1956. He left Suriname in 1983 and drives a long-distance truck for the Dutch postal service.

NOTE FROM THE AUTHOR

Word-of-mouth is crucial for any author to succeed. If you enjoyed *Brother Mambo*, please leave a review online—anywhere you are able. Even if it's just a sentence or two. It would make all the difference and would be very much appreciated.

Thanks!
J.D. Lenoir

We hope you enjoyed reading this title from:

BLACK ROSE
writing™

www.blackrosewriting.com

Subscribe to our mailing list – *The Rosevine* – and receive
FREE books, daily deals, and stay current with news about
upcoming releases and our hottest authors.
Scan the QR code below to sign up.

Already a subscriber? Please accept a sincere thank you for
being a fan of Black Rose Writing authors.

View other Black Rose Writing titles at
www.blackrosewriting.com/books and use promo code
PRINT to receive a **20% discount** when purchasing.

CPSIA information can be obtained
at www.ICGtesting.com
Printed in the USA
LVHW081647140622
721263LV00012B/286

9 781684 338771